INNOVATIVE LIBRARY WORKPLACES

Transformative Human Resource Strategies

edited by
Lisa Kallman Hopkins
and Bridgit McCafferty

Association of College and Research Libraries
A division of the American Library Association
Chicago, Illinois 2025

The paper used in this publication meets the minimum requirements of American National Standard for Information Sciences–Permanence of Paper for Printed Library Materials, ANSI Z39.48-1992. ∞

Library of Congress Control Number: 2024951012

Copyright ©2025 by Association of College and Research Libraries

All rights reserved except those which may be granted by Sections 107 and 108 of the Copyright Revision Act of 1976.

Printed in the United States of America.

29 28 27 26 25   5 4 3 2 1

Contents

VII INTRODUCTION

PART 1. HUMAN RESOURCES IN LIBRARIES

3 Recruiting and Hiring

5 **CHAPTER 1**
HR as Strategic Partner: Practical Approaches for Building HR Capacity in an Academic Library Setting
Cinthya Ippoliti

21 **CHAPTER 2**
Subvert the Dominant Paradigm: Reimagining Academic Library Hiring Processes
Xan Arch and Isaac Gilman

35 **CHAPTER 3**
Toward a Growth-Based Paradigm: Centering Candidate Experiences in the Hiring and Onboarding Processes
Annie Bélanger, Sheila Garcia-Mazari, and Bruna Ngassa

53 **CHAPTER 4**
Moving toward More Inclusive Hiring
Lea J. Briggs and Rodney Lippard

67 Onboarding and Training

69 **CHAPTER 5**
Paving the Way for Professional Success with an Onboarding Road Map
Joyce Garczynski

81   **CHAPTER 6**
     Beyond Onboarding: Developing a Library Tenure Success Program
     Kim Clarke

95   **CHAPTER 7**
     Continuous Professional Development for Academic Library Employees
     Lisa Kallman Hopkins

111 **CHAPTER 8**
     Succession Planning from the Middle
     Brynne Norton and Jennifer E. M. Cotton

123 **Salary Studies and Unions**

125 **CHAPTER 9**
     Assessing Salary Equitably: A Review and Case Study of UVA Library's Salary Review and Adjustment Initiative
     Mira Waller, Carla Lee, Donna Tolson, and Gail White

143 **CHAPTER 10**
     A Salary Study Model for Academic Libraries: Leveraging Strategic Salary Studies to Generate Library Employee Goodwill
     Bridgit McCafferty and Shawna Kennedy-Witthar

163 **CHAPTER 11**
     Employee Unions in Academic Libraries: Something Old and Something New
     Bridgit McCafferty

PART II. WORK CULTURE AND ORGANIZATION

177 **Employee Morale**

179 **CHAPTER 12**
     Wellness Initiatives in Academic Libraries
     Dawn M. Harris, Bridgit McCafferty, Sandra Yvette Desjardins, and Johnnie Porter

199   CHAPTER 13
Offering More Than Just a Desk and Chair: Combatting Librarian Burnout
Jennifer Batson, Kelly Williams, Margaret Dawson, and Sandra Yvette Desjardins

219   CHAPTER 14
Damp, Dark, and Dull: Addressing the Impact of Library Workspace Woes on Health, Productivity, and Morale
Melinda H. Berg, Janet Chan, Janet Schalk, and Ann Coppola

239   Flexible Work Arrangements

241   CHAPTER 15
The New Normal: An Empirical Examination of Remote Work in Academic Libraries
Lisa Kallman Hopkins, Andria F. Schwegler, Rebecca L. Hopkins, and Bridgit McCafferty

271   CHAPTER 16
Flexible Work Empowers: An Inclusive Strategy for Recruitment and Retention of Academic Librarians
Dana Reijerkerk and Kristen J. Nyitray

283   Strategic Planning and Reorganizing

285   CHAPTER 17
Empowering Employees through Strategic Initiatives
Jessica J. Boyer

295   CHAPTER 18
Breaking Down Structures to Build Up Staff: Organizational Change in an Academic Library
Isaac Gilman

307   CHAPTER 19
Envision, Revision, and Balance: A Case Study of a Participation-Based, Employee-Focused Academic Library Unit Restructuring
Vickie Albrecht, Kristy McKeown, Coralee Leroux, and Geoff Sinclair

325 **CHAPTER 20**
Rebuilding the Structure at a Medium-Sized Research Library: A Case Study
Kimberly Burke Sweetman

345 **CHAPTER 21**
Rightsizing Technical Services: Practical Adaptations for Rapidly Evolving Libraries
Kathaleen McCormick, Kristy White, and Tracie Ballock

361 **CHAPTER 22**
Calming the Chaos of Library Technology
Todd R. Digby and Laurie N. Taylor

373 **ABOUT THE EDITORS AND AUTHORS**

Introduction

There is a chapter herein called "The New Normal," and that is a good jumping-off point to understand more broadly the context of the works collected here. The idea for *Innovative Library Workplaces* took root during the COVID-19 pandemic. The ongoing health crisis and the resultant quick shift to remote work combined to impact the way our society views labor, as well as the value placed on balancing between our jobs and the rest of our lives. After all, when faced with mortality, people's values shift, and they want more meaning from both their profession and their home life. Though this book took root during the pandemic, it is not of the pandemic. Our contention with this collection is that the shift is permanent—we are now in a new normal for the library workplace. The chapters we have included propose a way forward after this monumental change, recognizing that neither the pandemic nor the work culture prior to it is a good model for what comes next.

Central to this thesis—curled like a cat, resting just beyond the edges of these chapters—lies this question: What makes a good workplace? Marcus Buckingham wrote in the *Harvard Business Review*

> A good job is one where you feel seen for being the best version of yourself; you sense that your colleagues have your back; you don't feel discriminated against based on your gender, race, or sexual orientation; you feel your position is secure; and you have confidence that you'll get help navigating constant changes in the working world.[1]

Throughout the chapters that follow, we hope to provide you with the tools you need to make your workplace a good one for your employees based on this vision. This means that your employees will make enough money to live and support their families, they will feel seen for who they are, and they will be supported by their managers and coworkers. It also means that your workplace will operate so that employees receive the resources, mentoring, and training they need to be successful, no matter who they are, and that workspaces will be safe and conducive to productivity. Equity, fairness, transparency, and opportunity are values that will underpin the work of your administrators, who will help their employees navigate the changing world in which we live. Incidentally, administrators will also change with the times—these changes include reorganization and shifting of duties as the task of running a library becomes something new. Good workplaces are dynamic, even when they retain the core professional values on which librarianship was built. In short, good workplaces are inclusive—they see their employees and support them. They meet their employees where they are. This theme of inclusiveness underpins our vision of a better library.

Most of the authors included in this collection are managers, and for good reason. Though pay and benefits are the key elements that contribute to employee satisfaction, they are not enough. Data from Gallup's *State of the American Manager* survey shows that compensation cannot make up for a bad boss.[2] Supervisors at all levels of the organization directly contribute to the quality of the workplace. Though learning to manage employees can take years, few librarians receive more than a single class on this topic in their graduate programs, hardly enough time to define what good management means. We believe that libraries need to begin to grow the literature about library management to help the next generation of librarians face the changing work landscape.

Repeated throughout these chapters are two themes that are particularly important to excellent management: autonomy and collaboration. Though they may seem contradictory at first glance, in the best workplaces they combine to create satisfied, productive employees. Here, autonomy means giving employees a sense of ownership over how they work and where they work. Collaboration means encouraging employees to coordinate in pursuit of common goals. Good workplaces require both.

Through this collection, you will read about autonomy in many different contexts—for instance, in the way that libraries design wellness programs, which should allow employees to set their own wellness targets and use benefits as they see fit. Similarly, when employees participate in flexible work arrangements, administrators should provide the ability for them to design their own schedules; the lack of autonomy was a major flaw, which can now be remedied, in the remote work arrangements during the pandemic. Autonomy also comes up in the way a library is reorganized by allowing employees to provide feedback about where their work best fits in the larger scheme of the library. For salary studies, employees should be involved in the process of redesigning job descriptions and classifications because they are in the best place to know what they do every day. Employees will be motivated to stay abreast of new skills and technologies through professional development only when empowered to do so through choice and when they see their initiative rewarded by promotion and enhanced responsibility. Autonomy can help avoid burnout, allowing library employees to feel better supported and valued. Even in the hiring and onboarding processes, our new and future employees must have the autonomy to shape the experience so that it meets their needs, not just the needs of the employer. Here autonomy is not only an issue of making our employees more comfortable or giving their work more meaning, though it does both of these things. It is also a matter of equity, allowing our employees to do good quality work while also adapting their work to fit with the other facets of their lives.

Collaboration also recurs as a theme throughout this book. Almost every chapter proposes a collaborative approach to a variety of processes, including salary studies, reorganizations, workplace learning, and onboarding. For hiring, collaboration between the candidate and the hiring committee is proposed in many ways, each of which makes the process more meaningful and comfortable for those involved. Many chapters discuss the role of cross-training in academic libraries and how it can help in situations where employees grow ill or leave the library suddenly. Even in chapters that study employee wellness and trust, collaboration is at the foreground. This is especially true in relation to employee trust within work-from-home arrangements, where collaboration and communication are keys to success.

Many of these chapters discuss employee autonomy and collaboration together, as complementary aspects of the same process. This is to say that one overarching takeaway from this book is that libraries that are good places to work give their employees autonomy and ownership over their professional output, while also involving them in the collaborative process of administering the library. Library employees want to have the flexibility to determine how they work, where they work, when they work, and why they work, but they also value the teamwork that produces the best results in most libraries. They like the option to work remotely when they want, and they also like a good potluck every now and again. They want to participate in wellness programs through their employer, even competitive ones, but they do not want their employer to define what wellness should mean to them. They want to be able to join with other library workers in unions, should one be available. They want more freedom but miss the camaraderie of the old days.

How we provide autonomy and collaboration for our employees in the post-COVID-19 work environment is a big question that libraries have yet to answer. This book only begins that process. The first step is recognizing that the answers are different now than they were prior to or during the pandemic. Many of the old practices and those that we adopted to deal with the global crisis were not ideal for the changed workplace. The outdated idea of a nine-to-five job with everyone on campus every day does not exist anymore. If we are honest, it probably has not existed for a long while. Can you remember the last time you went a whole evening without answering an e-mail? We cannot.

Obviously, ensuring we have both autonomy and collaboration in our workplaces is a difficult balancing act. There is now an oasis in the distance calling administrators and executives of all stripes, saying you can get back to collaboration if only you give up autonomy; it is called return-to-office, and it is a mirage. This is the easy answer, the simple answer—the one that does not actually solve the myriad of problems revealed to us during the pandemic, least of which is the fact that we deserve to have balance in our work lives: If we answer e-mails at 9 p.m., we should be able to work in our recliner wearing slippers one day a week. The problem of autonomy will not go away now that employees know they can expect it. Self-direction is not subordinate to collaboration, but in concert with it. The only path forward is the one where we find a happy balance between the two. The difficult road is often also the best way.

We hope you learn as much from reading this volume as we did editing it. We believe deeply in library workplaces that work for library employees, and if we allow ourselves one wish for this text, it is the creation of a better world for librarians. In *Fostering Wellness in the Workplace*, Bobbi Newman bemoans the fact that there is a great deal of research about library wellness programs for patrons, but almost nothing about wellness in libraries for employees.[3] While we fully believe in libraries that serve their patrons well, we agree with her sentiment. This must be the first thing to change—it is time to make our libraries as supportive of our employees as they are of our communities.

Notes

1. Marcus Buckingham, "What Is a Good Job?" *Harvard Business Review*, September 19, 2022, https://hbr.org/2022/09/what-is-a-good-job.
2. Tom Nolan, "The No. 1 Employee Benefit That No One's Talking About," Gallup, accessed November 9, 2023, https://www.gallup.com/workplace/232955/no-employee-benefit-no-one-talking.aspx.
3. Bobbi Newman, *Fostering Wellness in the Workplace* (Chicago: ALA Editions, 2022), 9.

Bibliography

Buckingham, Marcus. "What Is a Good Job?" *Harvard Business Review*, September 19, 2022. https://hbr.org/2022/09/what-is-a-good-job.

Newman, Bobbi. *Fostering Wellness in the Workplace: A Handbook for Libraries*. Chicago: ALA Editions, 2022.

Nolan, Tom. "The No. 1 Employee Benefit That No One's Talking About." Gallup. Accessed November 9, 2023. https://www.gallup.com/workplace/232955/no-employee-benefit-no-one-talking.aspx.

Part 1
Human Resources in Libraries

Recruiting and Hiring

CHAPTER 1

HR as Strategic Partner
Practical Approaches for Building HR Capacity in an Academic Library Setting

Cinthya Ippoliti

Introduction and Problem Definition

Human resources is a topic that is growing in popularity in all types of libraries. Interestingly, however, the library literature is scarcer when discussing the human resource (HR) infrastructures, practices, and staffing that are needed to successfully develop an HR strategy that is holistic, person-centered, and dedicated to supporting library employees. There is a similar lack of literature examining the way in which HR functions are created and implemented across libraries, especially as a strategic partner.[1] This chapter will attempt to fill that gap by providing guidance for developing a flexible and forward-looking library HR strategy that can adapt over time by answering questions such as these: What are the scope and purpose of HR functions within a library? How is HR situated within the overall organizational structure? What campus HR structures exist, and how does the library fit within those? Are there specific groups that those with HR roles will need to meet and interact with on a regular basis? This chapter will outline a road map for transforming HR functions into a strategic framework that libraries can tailor to their own organizational context, including activities involved in the creation of an HR strategy, mission, vision, and goals, as well information about the development of a partnership framework and HR workforce plan. Finally, the road map includes resources and tools for further exploration and tips for getting started.

HR Overview in Libraries

This literature review begins with a historical perspective that outlines the evolution of HR in libraries as far back as fifty-two years ago with the American Library Association's "Guidelines to the Development of Human Resources in Libraries,"[2] indicating that libraries have long thought about the need to define and organize HR functions and pointing to similar issues being raised even in the early stages of HR work set within a library context. Both theoretical and practical applications of HR management are discussed, where library policies and operational practices affect employee growth and development because they underscore how the library chooses to implement its managerial philosophy. This is one of the first instances of HR endeavors being explicitly discussed within a library context, and it sets up the notion that HR is more than just a series of transactional tasks but rather a broader framework through which leadership can better support employees. The study described in Rooks's "The Technicolor Coat of the Academic Personnel Officer" remains relevant thirty-four years later, in that it analyzed how HR functions evolved to execute more complex operations and discussed the many roles HR staff have inhabited in order to effectuate a transition from the transactional to the strategic: development officer, recruiter, counselor, advocate, forecaster, paralegal, labor relations officer, and manager.[3] This is important because it points to the idea that HR work is multifaceted and requires a variety of skills and knowledge that encompass broad and often disparate responsibilities.

In addition to examining HR as a stand-alone function, there are several authors who highlight the ways in which HR shapes organizational development and capacity. Chan addresses the core competencies required for managing human resources, from communication to planning and affecting practices around hiring, training, and performance management, the range of which indicates the wide-reaching impact HR has across an organization.[4] Similarly, Hawthorne reviews the integration of HR management into all aspects of organizational development, stating that "the reinvention requires HR practitioners to continue to manage administrative and operational activities while adding new responsibilities for developing and managing strategic initiatives that enhance the performance and capacity of the organization and its workforce."[5] This role expansion is crucial in understanding the types of organizational functions where HR can truly act as a partner in employee growth and development. Hawthorne outlines four strategies for undertaking these efforts:[6]

- job analysis of all library positions, skills, and responsibilities as a way to develop a workforce plan;
- work redesign, examining functions across the entire library;

- creation of cross-functional teams to supplement committees and task forces; and
- change management that is present in activities such as strategic planning and reorganizations.

Looking at how HR is situated within the library, Mierke states that HR should be viewed as a strategic partner and "must have a seat at the senior leadership table to effectively contribute to strategy and decision-making" in order to achieve the library's goals and directions.[7] Mierke further stresses the importance of organizational culture and learning and effective leadership, which serve to align evolving workforce needs with the "library's vision of the future."[8] Evans and Chun state that "creating strategic planning objectives that are human resource-based to provide leadership in a discipline that is usually seen as support-based" helps lend shape to the notion that HR should be a strategic partner in furthering library vision and mission, not simply a service provider.[9] Furthermore, when looking at campus HR structures, Dennis Defa notices that "a trend in HR management in higher education is to push out many of the day-to-day functions to the appropriate administrative office," which necessitates having some type of library counterpart, however informal.[10] Defa further makes a case for a dedicated HR office within the library in order to understand specific library needs and provide support for day-to-day operations that may not be present otherwise.[11] While having a library HR office or positions may not be viable for all libraries, the road map can assist in the conceptualization of a model that provides strategic support to further organizational objectives and enable a holistic approach to workforce development.

In summary, HR operations in libraries have progressed over time from transaction-based functions to strategic operations. This shift can be seen in both HR structures that have themselves grown to include increasingly complex roles and responsibilities and in the type and level of guidance that is provided around functions ranging from training to organizational development and legal issues. The literature examined serves as background to highlight the work that libraries can emphasize in order to develop a comprehensive approach to their operations. These efforts require intentionally building out from the core functions expected as part of HR work to encompass an HR vision and mission, an overall strategy, a partnership model, and workforce plan that serves as a guiding framework both internal—to the library, as well as external—to the campus.

HR Development Road Map

The road map in figure 1.1 will help libraries outline the scope of HR activities they could undertake in order to situate HR as a set of functions that reinforces strategic library goals and operations and helps to propel library strategy to the next level by ensuring that employees are supported across all areas. The road map begins with an exploration of creating a holistic HR strategy that includes alignment with organizational strategic goals and conducting a needs assessment to identify priorities. Next is a focus on developing an HR philosophy and vision to help guide activities around person-centered practices. The road map will also explore strategies for developing HR partnerships with campus offices, ending with an analysis of how to structure HR staffing needs, including hiring and interviewing for HR.

Figure 1.1. Human resources road map

Developing a Holistic HR Strategy

Roger Martin, featured YouTuber for *Harvard Business Review*, defines strategy as a coherent set of choices within a particular setting or context that orients the organization for success.[12] The library therefore needs to define what that setting is—the context in which this work is occurring and why that context matters, as well as how it shapes the scope and type of HR functions offered. Because a strategy can be made up of several interconnected choices, those choices have to be outlined so it is clear to everyone why those particular choices are being made and how they will affect planning. For example, if being people-centered is a desired strategy, the library is therefore making a choice that it will consider the impact of services and policies on people before anything else, which means other aspects such as consistent implementation may be affected.

Looking more closely at HR, Berry Clemens, who has over twenty-five years of experience with talent and workforce management in IT and business, defines HR strategy as being "all about creating alignment around an organization's people, processes, and operating philosophies. It is a way to anchor strategic human resources management as the catalyst for amplifying broader organizational goals."[13] In order to effectuate this alignment, Clemens recommends taking a holistic approach that combines both strategic and operational elements around organizational culture and structure; employee engagement and development; and recruitment, training, and compensation.[14]

Success must also be defined—what does success mean and how does the library know when it has been achieved? Due to the fluid nature of HR work, success could mean different things at different times, and the analysis may be more meaningful broken down into segments as opposed to trying to answer that question for HR as a whole. Looking at the workforce development categories mentioned above, it may make more sense to examine each separately rather than trying to find some measures that apply to all of them, as that could be challenging and dilute the strength of each approach. For instance, measuring organizational climate is subjective and requires qualitative data and analysis gathered through employee feedback. If the overall institution is experiencing challenges that affect compensation, for example, it may also be useful to look at climate at different points in time to capture themes and gaps. In contrast, employee recruitment may correspond more closely with statistics regarding candidate demographics quantity, which are measured differently than actual recruitment experiences. Having a multimodal and multipronged approach to assessment will provide the most complete picture of areas that are inherently complex, tend to change quickly, and contain both strategic and operational components that can vary drastically in how they are measured and evaluated.

Identifying Areas of Priority
GAP ANALYSIS

Another way to identify areas of priority for an HR strategy is to begin with a gap analysis that outlines the current state, imagines the future, and defines what is needed to work toward achieving that future for HR. Lucidchart provides a good road map for how to conduct this type of assessment.[15] Work should be done collaboratively to ensure buy-in and transparency across the library and to define the possible limitations; for instance, compensation policies may be determined at a campus or system level and need to be factored into any planning that happens.

The core functions mentioned by Clemens—organizational culture and structure, employee engagement and development, recruitment, training, and compensation—are good places to start identifying areas for further exploration through a gap analysis. Conducting a brief survey or utilizing focus groups might provide library administration with an idea of which priorities might need to be addressed immediately. Another way to identify these priorities might be to examine known pain points, bottlenecks, and areas where anecdotal evidence indicates further attention is needed.

The Association for Talent Development describes the steps an organization can take that can assist with creating a list of priorities.[16] In some instances, it may make sense to employ a facilitator, especially if the organizational environment is such that there are issues with trust around the desire and ability of library administration to effectuate changes. Once project coordination and oversight have been identified, establishing a formal team might be beneficial, depending on the scope of the project. Ensuring that a wide variety of perspectives are included will be key, as will having a diverse team representative of all employee groups within the library. A project management plan will also be needed to establish deadlines, a communication plan, and project deliverables.[17] Start with a fact-finding phase and develop a data-gathering process between stakeholders and project coordinators where relevant information about the problem is gathered, analyzed, and reviewed.

SWOT AND PEST

A SWOT (strengths, weaknesses, opportunities, threats) analysis is helpful when thinking about the factors that might influence a particular solution to identified gaps and needs (figure 1.2). SWOT analysis can refer to both internal and external factors and can be applied to describing either the present situation or a presumed future where some of these

---

Interested in finding out more about Gap Analysis and SWOT?

Getting Started: Both methods are great tools to not only develop actionable solutions to addressing issues, but also as team-building opportunities that create spaces for inclusion and diverse voices and perspectives. Be deliberate about who is included in these conversations, how to structure feedback collection, sharing out of themes, and closing the loop with next steps so that it is clear to all involved how decisions will be made and communicated throughout each process.

Tips and Techniques: Weed out the things you cannot control. Think about what external engagement with stakeholders might be beneficial to help generate some solutions/responses to the areas you want to investigate further. Use this work as a way to identify and advocate for needed resources to help achieve that desired future state or build on strengths and opportunities.

Additional Resources:

- Gap Analysis: https://asana.com/resources/gap-analysis
- SWOT Analysis: https://asana.com/resources/swot-analysis

Figure 1.2. Gap Analysis and SWOT

issues may evolve differently. Similarly, PEST (political, economic, social, technology) analysis provides different lenses to view the situation but is usually applied to external factors, whereas the SWOT model can be used either internally or externally.[18]

FUTURES THINKING

Once the current landscape and potential gaps have been identified, futures thinking can deepen understanding of the driving forces shaping the future, identify gaps in knowledge and skill sets across an organization, and create a framework for adapting to unknown conditions (figure 1.3). "The Futures Toolkit" provides details about different types of activities that can help foster futures thinking, and there are three aspects that might be applicable here.[19] Backcasting, on the other hand, works backward from a desired outcome and examines what would have to happen in order to achieve that outcome. Scenarios provide details about various ways the environment might change and encourage an organization to think about how to respond; this approach is particularly useful when thinking about strategy and defining the setting within which those choices are being made. Visioning is the process whereby the scope and goals of an initiative are articulated and includes what the future will look like if that initiative is successful.

Interested in finding our more about Futures Thinking?

Getting Started: Encourage creative ideas and broad thinking before starting to prioritize and narrow solutions. As with Gap Analysis and SWOT, this is also an opportunity to bring together different stakeholders both internal and external.

Tips and Techniques: Futures thinking is not about predicting the future, it's about using the data you have to create a potential picture of the future where the organization moves forward in a way that is aspirational yet realistic.

Additional Resources:

- Five Principles: https://er.educause.edu/articles/2019/3/five-principles-for-thinking-like-a-futurist
- Getting Your Team to Think Differently about the Future: https://hbr.org/2015/01/an-exercise-to-get-your-team-thinking-differently-about-the-future

---

Figure 1.3. Futures thinking

SUCCESS INDICATORS AND EVALUATION

An action plan should then be created to include possible solutions and success indicators for how the gap is going to be addressed based on appropriate resources, capacity, limitations, themes identified, goals, and so on. This is also an opportunity to collectively refine proposed solutions and identify which action items will be implemented first by examining library and institutional strategic goals or known challenges that need to be addressed based on the conversations during the entry phase. Once solutions have been finalized, a new project management cycle begins for each solution and, depending on the scope, deliverables, and timelines, new project teams might be created along with a communication and implementation plan. Evaluation includes the continuous process of collecting data to determine whether the solutions are meeting the intended goals and achieving defined success indicators. One way to do this might include creating check-in points throughout each project that can be reported out as part of an evaluation report or a communication strategy that not only discusses project activities, but also offers continuous improvement depending on how a particular initiative is progressing.

Developing a Library HR Vision and Mission

Once an HR strategy has been identified, it is time to drill down to more specific elements that define the action items, making the strategy a reality. Developing a strong HR plan starts with defining HR vision and values, which must also align with those of the library. Without these elements, it is difficult to characterize what the organization as a whole cares about and how that focus manifests itself through policies, practices, and processes. When pursuing a shift toward viewing HR as a strategic partner, having a strong foundation upon which all operational functions are built is essential. Building an HR vision is much like crafting an organizational vision: it is usually forward-looking and aspirational—not so impossible that it can never be achieved, but just out of reach enough to inspire new directions and possibilities.

LIBRARY HR VISION

Developing the actual vision statement starts with articulating how HR might enhance employees' success and why that matters. In other words, this is the "why" of the library's HR and should focus on the core idea (think strategy!) the library wants to communicate—it can be a unique element, a theme, or a concept, or it can simply state what the library wants to work toward. It is important not only internally, so employees understand the philosophy that guides the actions of HR operations, but also externally, to establish which types of relationships and collaboration can strengthen this vision. A good vision statement begins with an action verb, includes the desired accomplishment, and is brief yet compelling, such as this: Strive to develop a person-centered organization through a culture of collective care and equity-centered practices. This statement makes it clear that people are at the center of the HR vision and that policies and practice are going to put people first.

LIBRARY HR MISSION

In addition to having an HR vision, a mission statement might be useful for articulating how the library plans to accomplish its vision. If the vision is the why, the mission is the how. While a vision is more abstract, a mission statement defines what work is going to be accomplished and is usually focused on the present, signaling to employees what types of values the library wants to emphasize. Symonds defines an HR mission statement as "a specific motto, goal, or philosophy followed by a company's HR department."[20] For the mission statement, create a brief sentence written in the present tense that addresses actions HR already does or would like to do, their desired impact, and how the work will be achieved. Remember to keep this fairly broad, as it is not meant to be an implementation plan, but rather a guiding direction from which goals and actions can emerge. For example: Support employees through equity-centered recruitment and retention practices to grow a diverse workforce.

VISION AND MISSION PLANNING ACTIVITIES

In order to develop these statements, HR may wish to involve the entire library in an activity that brings employees together to brainstorm what is important to the organization and how those areas are reflected in the work of HR. This can be done in many different ways, but a simple yet effective method is to provide question prompts ahead of a library-wide meeting; the prompts can be then used in small groups to generate ideas. Once the notes from each small group are collected, themes can be identified that can then serve as the main points to be included in a statement. Draft statements can then be circulated library-wide, and employees can either vote on their favorite or provide further edits to help develop a final version that everyone can champion. In addition to developing these statements, one of the most useful activities is to bring both the mission and the vision to life as a precursor to developing the goals and action items that support them. Brené Brown provides a relatively simple activity that involves starting with a list of values and asking participants to generate themes that can be turned into a core set of behaviors and actions under each value.[21]

Brown provides guidance on how to develop a focused list from that initial brainstorming: Are there current behaviors that create low morale and toxicity yet are continually being reinforced? If so, how can these be eliminated or minimized? What types of behaviors might stay with the organization for the long term? For what behaviors would you hold employees accountable during goal setting, feedback conversations or check-ins, and performance evaluations? Values can also extend to things like hiring—for example, if equity is a core value for the library, how can candidate pools be as diverse as possible and how might the interview process be altered to make candidates feel welcome? One way to address these questions might be to recruit diverse candidates directly. Intentional framing of the job position and including compensation information might present another opportunity to demonstrate to candidates how the library values diversity. Finally, making the interview process less daunting and setting up everyone for success represents another way in which equity can be operationalized. This is accomplished by providing interview questions ahead of time, offering flexibility, and having a consistent schedule so that each candidate has a similar experience, yet one that can be individualized to accommodate different needs as appropriate.

DEVELOPING HR GOALS

Taking a final pause here to answer a question related to goals and activities—Does HR need to create a strategic plan that brings all of these elements together? The answer is, it depends. Although the chapter is dedicated to highlighting HR as a strategic partner, the reality is that much of HR work is operational, and strategy ultimately informs action. If there are goals the library wants to focus on each year, it makes sense to add them to ongoing planning that occurs more broadly (figure 1.4). Goals would be developed just as other strategic objectives are, with high-level directions telescoping down to concrete action items that can be measured and tracked via project management mechanisms. If there is no need to focus on a particular initiative, however, keeping the strategy current and flexible to shift as library directions change will provide enough forward momentum. As an example, a strategy around compensation will always be necessary to maintain a competitive salary structure and opportunities for growth, but perhaps each year there is a desire to focus on something more detailed, such as creating a merit plan that might require additional attention in the form of a time-bound goal and activities that further its completion.

Interested in finding out more about developing HR goals?

Getting Started: Goals should be specific, measurable, achievable, relevant, and time-bound. You can still have aspirational goals, but they have to also be realistic and connected to available resources and capacity.

Tips and Techniques: A robust human resources strategy should align with both organizational priorities and operational activities. Think about how trends could affect how, when, and where work is done; understand the relevance and implication of defining the future of work for the library and how that might affect areas such as employee recruitment and retention as well as policies and processes.

Additional Resources:

- HR SMART Goals: https://www.aihr.com/blog/hr-smart-goals/
- What Is HR Strategy: https://www.gartner.com/en/human-resources/topics/what-is-hr-strategy

---

Figure 1.4. Human resources goals

Collaborating with Campus HR Offices

Whether a library has its own HR department or it relies on external assistance, it will likely have to interact with external units that set broader policies and processes. Those units are the ones that usually have a final say in whether or not specific workflows can be set to comply with state and federal regulations. Having a strong partnership with campus HR can also mean having access to additional expertise that the library may lack, such as knowing when exceptions can be made or suggesting other ways to work through a challenging situation. Libraries can think of it as a liaison model, where there is consistent and ongoing communication focusing on both day-to-day duties—such as training, changes in policies and procedures, and personnel actions—or bigger initiatives, such as compensation studies. Strong collaboration can also enable better communication and advocacy between the two areas.

This collaboration allows library HR employees to know who to reach out to on campus and also who to enlist when there may be a difference of opinion. If there is already a good working relationship between library and campus HR, it may be easier to push back if a particular policy does not make sense or may apply differently for the library. For example, if an institution has clearly outlined job codes and pay structures, might the library want to create a separate one that outlines job categories not found elsewhere? Campus HR has access to the university legal department, which can interpret the law and provide valuable perspectives and insights, especially salient in employment issues. In some instances, it might even make sense to consult with multiple offices or individuals at the same time in order to avoid receiving conflicting information.

DEVELOPING A COLLABORATION FRAMEWORK

Partnership building starts with setting up regular meetings and establishing clear lines of communication. Meetings may involve specific people on a regular basis as well as entailing broader group updates that the library can be a part of. In addition, training also falls under this category to ensure that library HR employees stay current. Ideally clarity around who can answer what types of questions helps create that network of support in case of confusion or when further advice might be needed. Sometimes mistakes happen because of a lack of communication or clarity around a process or because the library simply does not know about something. In this situation, action is usually taken retroactively and, for the most part, the majority of mistakes can be corrected in the form of changes in the system, an alternate approach, or simply overriding an action. But how can we know what we do not know? There is not an easy answer to that question, and unfortunately it takes learning by experience for the most part; putting in place some of the strategies discussed can help, as can knowing where there might be some gaps in expertise that can be filled with collaboration, and finally asking lots of questions and documenting the action so that the same mistake is not repeated.

CREATING AN OUTREACH PLAN

In addition, it might be useful to develop an actual outreach plan to help track who the stakeholders are, how often to communicate, and what type of information might be helpful to exchange (figure 1.5). This list can then be transformed into more formal documentation that can be kept as part of HR files and can also be updated as personnel and policies change over time. Here are some questions to ask to identify next steps:

- Who are the major stakeholders, and who needs to be part of regular meetings?
- How often should these meetings occur?
- Is there an established campus networking group that the library can join?
- What types of training opportunities does the campus provide?
- How can the library be included in broad initiatives such as compensation studies, changes to policies, evaluation planning, and training programs?
- How much leeway is there to create library-specific actions or workflows? What might that process entail?
- What happens if there is a disagreement about the application of a policy or process, and are there channels for these types of requests? If not, can they be created?
- How does legal work with HR, and when do you consult with each?
- How are mistakes corrected or dealt with?

Interested in finding out more about HR engagement strategies?

Getting Started: Make a list of all the individuals and offices on campus with whom you might need to interact, then determine what level of involvement they have with library HR operations and if that level is sufficient or needs to be altered and what an ideal collaboration looks like.

Tips and Techniques: Develop a stakeholder engagement and communication framework to determine who needs to be included, at what level, and how often you might need to meet and communicate with that particular stakeholder. In addition, noting where there are areas of support or resistance might also provide some guidance on where additional focus might be necessary.

Additional Resources:

- Stakeholder Engagement Framework: https://vetoviolence.cdc.gov/apps/evaluaction/assets/pdf/Engaging-Stakeholders-Throughout-Evaluation.pdf
- Stakeholder Engagement Plan: https://asana.com/resources/stakeholder-engagement-plan-template

---

Figure 1.5. Human resources engagement strategies

Creating a Library HR Workforce and Hiring Plan

HR workforce planning should consider the type and scope of HR responsibilities within a library. There are pros and cons to each model—if the library does not have its own department and is relying on campus HR support, the focus will be on ensuring strong relationships and collaboration as described in the previous section. If there is a library HR department, however, staffing is critical to ensuring the correct type and level of positions to provide adequate coverage for workflows. If only one person is doing the work, what are the core functions that need to be performed versus things that might be nice to accomplish, but not critical? Collaboration with campus HR entities is still important, but the focus with this model is about what can be accomplished in house and supplemented externally, as opposed to being completely reliant on that outside entity.

LIBRARY HR WORKFORCE PLANNING

Creating an HR workforce plan identifies the starting point and crystallizes what is crucial versus what might be preferred. As mentioned previously, it is also largely dependent on whether the library has or wants its own HR department and the extent to which hiring is feasible given fiscal limitations. The library should begin by identifying the current situation and taking inventory of the number and types of existing positions, the current level of each, turnover rates, and compensation outlook, and Defa describes several additional considerations when creating HR positions.[22] The HR position may be a librarian, but there is the risk that the focus might be on the librarianship aspect first, and HR second. In addition, how the role is perceived and evaluated may also suffer, as there might not be a strong understanding of HR duties within the library, making it more difficult to define success. Alternatively, the position may be staff, with an individual who has a business or HR-specific degree and experience. Concerns here might include employee perceptions that the individual is part of the administration first, and it might be difficult to have them coordinate faculty-related processes around evaluation and promotion if they are staff. The individual would have to establish clear boundaries around responsibilities and strike a balance between acknowledging employee needs and concerns while completing administrative goals.

The staffing model will also largely depend on the scope of HR functions as outlined by the following questions:
- Is the library seeking expertise in areas such as employee retention and engagement in addition to the basics such as payroll and hiring? If the work is transactional, a coordinator who can process payroll and conduct basic hiring tasks might suffice. If on the other hand a more strategic direction is desired, that usually means hiring individuals with additional education and experience in areas such as employee relations and equity-centered hiring practices.

- Does the position require significant experience, or does the library have the capacity to provide training if necessary? If there is no one in the library who can offer training, bringing someone in with more experience would be advisable.
- Would an additional position be needed to handle transactional activities if the focus is on strategic activities? One person might not be able to accomplish both transactional and strategic duties, and there will need to be clear expectations in place about what can realistically be accomplished while balancing operational tasks with strategic program development. Establishing a scope of service document might be useful in outlining what the priorities are, levels and types of actions such as payroll and hiring that are considered core, turn-around times and process expectations, as well what additional initiatives and services can be added once these baseline functions are in place.
- How does the role interface with other areas, such as finance and administration: Are they part of the library's administrative team? Having the position reporting directly to the dean or director may result in assumptions being made that HR is there only to support library administration as opposed to the entire organization. If HR reports to a different division or unit within the library, does it make sense for that area to manage HR, or is it seen as an afterthought and will actually limit what can be accomplished?

HIRING LIBRARY HR

This section describes some of the aspects to take into consideration when hiring for HR positions. It is important to get a sense of candidate expertise around relationship building, project management, and communication. As mentioned above, the role will likely need to balance a wide variety of tasks, expectations, and competing priorities. Interview questions would mirror this set of expectations and may revolve around candidate capacity to look at broad issues as well as delve into details, to be a strong collaborator, and to communicate effectively in different formats. In addition, questions may also establish how Equity, Diversity, Inclusion, and Accessibility fits into all aspects of the role and provide an overall vision for HR strategy and processes within the library. Depending on whether or not they are the only HR position in the library, questions that prompt discussion about how the candidate handles multiple projects at once, manages time, and addresses challenges in a proactive fashion might also be appropriate. If the individual will be a supervisor, questions about the candidate's management skills and experiences are important—just because someone is an HR professional does not automatically mean they are good managers! Finally, the ability to act as a liaison between the library and campus might also be an important element of consideration, as different policies and practices surrounding hiring, retention, and compensation will need to be translated from a general level to a more specialized environment.

Conclusion

HR tasks within libraries have evolved as employee needs change and as institutional policies and practices progress. As a result, work needs to be organized and structured to advance strategic goals and directions. While there are seemingly endless permutations of how this can be accomplished, certain elements persist regardless of organizational size, structure, and context. First, HR work needs to be positioned to underscore both strategic and operational aspects. Having a clear direction for HR functions helps to set a strong foundation for the type of work a library wants to undertake and articulate how HR supports strategic goals. Second, strong collaborations with outside offices can be developed to bolster this work. This means developing clear lines of communication and establishing strong relationships with colleagues outside of the library who are likely both able to help and be able to assist in implementing local and federal laws and guidelines. Finally, the type and scope of HR positions can themselves be considered an asset in meeting current needs and planning for future growth and development. Developing a model for how HR is structured can be both challenging and exciting, presenting an opportunity to redefine how libraries support employees throughout their entire journey.

Notes

1. Dennis Defa, "Human Resource Administration in the Academic Library," *Library Leadership and Management* 22, no. 3 (2008): 138, https://digitalcommons.cwu.edu/libraryfac/128/.
2. American Library Association, "Guidelines to the Development of Human Resources in Libraries: Rationale, Policies, Programs and Recommendations," *Library Trends* 20, no. 1 (Summer 1971): 103, https://www.ideals.illinois.edu/items/6551.
3. Dana Rooks, "The Technicolor Coat of the Academic Library Personnel Officer: The Evolution from Paper-Pusher to Policy Maker," *Journal of Library Administration* 10, no. 4 (1989), 101–11.
4. Donna C. Chan, "The Future Is Competencies: Competency-Based Human Resource Management in Public Libraries," in *The Future Is Now: Responses to the 8Rs Canadian Library Human Resources Study*, ed. Kathleen De Long and Allison Sivak (Ottawa: Canadian Library Association, 2011), http://www.ls.ualberta.ca/8rs/8rs-future-is%20now.pdf.
5. Pat Hawthorne, "Redesigning Library Human Resources: Integrating Human Resources Management and Organizational Development," *Library Trends* 53, no. 1 (Summer 2004): 173, https://core.ac.uk/download/pdf/4811437.pdf.
6. Hawthorne, "Redesigning Library Human Resources," 175.
7. Jill Mierke, "Defining Success for Library Human Resources," *International Information and Library Review* 48, no. 3 (2016): 218, https://doi.org/10.1080/10572317.2016.1205424.
8. Mierke, "Defining Success," 219.
9. Alvin Evans and Edna Chun, "Human Resources as Strategic Partner," in *Strategic Human Resource Planning for Academic Libraries: Information, Technology and Organization*, by Michael A. Crumpton (Waltham, MA: Chandos, 2015), 27.
10. Defa, "Human Resource Administration," 139.
11. Defa, "Human Resource Administration," 140.
12. Roger Martin, "A Plan Is Not a Strategy," *Harvard Business Review*, June 29, 2022, YouTube video, 9:31, https://www.youtube.com/watch?v=iuYlGRnC7J8.
13. Berry Clemens, "5 Steps for Developing and Implementing an Effective HR Strategy in 2021," LinkedIn, accessed December 21, 2022, https://www.linkedin.com/pulse/5-steps-developing-implementing-effective-hr-strategy-berry-clemens.
14. Clemens, "5 Steps for Developing."
15. *LucidChart* (blog), "What Is Gap Analysis: 4 Steps and Examples to Use," accessed December 21, 2022, https://www.lucidchart.com/blog/what-is-gap-analysis.

16. Association for Talent Development, "What Is Organization Development: The 5 Phases of OD," accessed December 21, 2022, https://www.td.org/talent-development-glossary-terms/what-is-organization-development.
17. Brianna Marshall, Dani Cook, and Cinthya Ippoliti, *Fostering Change* (Chicago: Association of College and Research Libraries, 2019), 67–72, https://www.ala.org/acrl/sites/ala.org.acrl/files/content/publications/booksanddigitalresources/digital/FosteringChange.pdf.
18. *LucidChart* (blog), "SWOT Analysis vs. PEST Analysis: Which Should You Use?" accessed December 21, 2022, https://www.lucidchart.com/blog/swot-analysis-vs-pest-analysis.
19. Government Office for Science, "The Futures Toolkit," accessed December 21, 2022, https://assets.publishing.service.gov.uk/government/uploads/system/uploads/attachment_data/file/674209/futures-toolkit-edition-1.pdf.
20. Cat Symonds, "How to Write a Truly Inspiring Mission Statement (with Examples)," *Factorial* (blog), July 5, 2022, https://factorialhr.com/blog/hr-mission-statement/.
21. Brené Brown, "Dare to Lead: Operationalizing Your Values: A Step-by-Step Process for Groups and Teams," accessed December 21, 2022, https://brenebrown.com/resources/operationalizing-your-values-a-step-by-step-process-for-groups-and-teams/.
22. Defa, "Human Resource Administration," 141.

Bibliography

American Library Association. "Guidelines to the Development of Human Resources in Libraries: Rationale, Policies, Programs and Recommendations." *Library Trends* 20, no.1 (Summer 1971): 97–117. https://www.ideals.illinois.edu/items/6551.

Association for Talent Development. "What Is Organization Development: The 5 Phases of OD." Accessed December 21, 2022. https://www.td.org/talent-development-glossary-terms/what-is-organization-development.

Brown, Brené. "Dare to Lead: Operationalizing Your Values: A Step-by-Step Process for Groups and Teams." Accessed December 21, 2022. https://brenebrown.com/resources/operationalizing-your-values-a-step-by-step-process-for-groups-and-teams/.

Chan, Donna C. "The Future Is Competencies: Competency-Based Human Resource Management in Public Libraries." In *The Future Is Now: Responses to the 8Rs Canadian Library Human Resources Study*, edited by Kathleen De Long and Allison Sivak, 40–51. Ottawa: Canadian Library Association, 2011. http://www.ls.ualberta.ca/8rs/8rs-future-is%20now.pdf.

Clemens, Berry. "5 Steps for Developing and Implementing an Effective HR Strategy in 2021." LinkedIn. Accessed December 21, 2022. https://www.linkedin.com/pulse/5-steps-developing-implementing-effective-hr-strategy-berry-clemens.

Defa, Dennis. "Human Resource Administration in the Academic Library." *Library Leadership and Management* 22, no. 3 (2008): 138–41. https://digitalcommons.cwu.edu/libraryfac/128/.

Evans, Alvin, and Edna Chun. "Human Resources as Strategic Partner." In *Strategic Human Resource Planning for Academic Libraries: Information, Technology and Organization*, by Michael A. Crumpton, 27. Waltham, MA: Chandos, 2015.

Government Office for Science. "The Futures Toolkit." Accessed December 21, 2022. https://assets.publishing.service.gov.uk/government/uploads/system/uploads/attachment_data/file/674209/futures-toolkit-edition-1.pdf.

Hawthorne, Pat. "Redesigning Library Human Resources: Integrating Human Resources Management and Organizational Development." *Library Trends* 53, no. 1 (Summer 2004): 172–86. https://core.ac.uk/download/pdf/4811437.pdf.

———. "SWOT Analysis vs. PEST Analysis: Which Should You Use?" Accessed December 21, 2022. https://www.lucidchart.com/blog/swot-analysis-vs-pest-analysis.

———. "What Is Gap Analysis? 4 Steps and Examples to Use." Accessed December 21, 2022. https://www.lucidchart.com/blog/what-is-gap-analysis.

Marshall, Brianna, Dani Cook, and Cinthya Ippoliti. *Fostering Change: A Team-Based Guide*. Chicago: Association of College and Research Libraries, 2019. https://www.ala.org/acrl/sites/ala.org.acrl/files/content/publications/booksanddigitalresources/digital/FosteringChange.pdf.

Martin, Roger. "A Plan Is Not a Strategy." *Harvard Business Review*, June 29, 2022. YouTube video, 9:31. https://www.youtube.com/watch?v=iuYlGRnC7J8

Mierke, Jill. "Defining Success for Library Human Resources." *International Information and Library Review* 48, no. 3 (2016): 217–23. https://doi.org/10.1080/10572317.2016.1205424.

Rooks, Dana. "The Technicolor Coat of the Academic Library Personnel Officer: The Evolution from Paper-Pusher to Policy Maker." *Journal of Library Administration* 10, no. 4 (1989): 99–113.

Symonds, Cat. "How to Write a Truly Inspiring Mission Statement (with Examples)." *Factorial* (blog), July 5, 2022. https://factorialhr.com/blog/hr-mission-statement/.

CHAPTER 2

Subvert the Dominant Paradigm
Reimagining Academic Library Hiring Processes

Xan Arch and Isaac Gilman

As academic libraries seek to remove systemic barriers to entering the library profession for librarians with minoritized racial and social identities, as well as to cultivate more diverse teams to better serve increasingly diverse student populations, library hiring practices have become an important focus. Over the past decade, library literature has increasingly acknowledged the ways in which our largely homogenous professional population has continued to replicate itself through hiring practices that discourage and exclude candidates who do not 'fit' existing library cultures.[1] This, along with similar concerns around faculty hiring within libraries' larger academic institutions,[2] has led to an emerging body of work dedicated to new, more inclusive hiring processes.[3]

Problem Definition

Whether within libraries, or within academic hiring in general, the proposed approaches for creating more inclusive processes often stop at the individual level, focusing on increasing the diversity of individuals in the candidate pool or educating hiring committee members about unconscious bias.[4] While these strategies can help create a process that outwardly appears more inclusive, institutions too often rely on these visible and easy-to-implement fixes rather than examining the core assumptions and structures of their hiring processes, which ultimately shape individuals'—both candidates and committee members—interactions, decisions, and outcomes. In order to create truly equitable and candidate-friendly hiring practices, libraries must identify and address noninclusive core assumptions and structures throughout their search processes.

Even for libraries without an explicit goal of creating more equitable hiring processes, transforming traditional hiring structures and implementing more inclusive practices can also contribute to libraries successfully hiring their top candidates. As library workers understandably advocate for more supportive work environments, inclusive and transparent hiring processes are an important way for libraries to signal the value they place on supporting employee agency and wellness. This value must, of course, be carried beyond the hiring process and through employees' onboarding and ongoing work experience; but for libraries that truly embody an ethic of care for their employees, the structure of the library's search and hiring process is the best way to implicitly communicate this value to prospective colleagues.

Review of Literature and Current Practice

As recently as fifteen years ago, a dominant discourse within academic hiring literature centered on the need for job candidates to discern, and successfully navigate, a hiring process full of unspoken expectations surrounding how candidates would 'fit' into library workplaces' existing cultures and norms. Researchers described the library hiring process as a "mystery,"[5] and prospective candidates were advised to take care in how they spoke, dressed, and sat—and even to ensure they were "friendly and pleasant, but not overbearing."[6] While there was limited research into what library search committee members actually looked for in a candidate, existing research at the time did bear out this advice: in a national survey of librarians (predominantly academic) who had served on hiring committees, 72 percent (260 out of 361) rated personality/attitude as very important, 71 percent (251 out of 362) rated fit at the institution as very important, and personal appearance was rated as either moderately important (37 percent) or important (32 percent) by most respondents.[7]

The source of these often-unspoken evaluative criteria has increasingly been recognized as not simply individual committee members' and hiring managers' preferences, but as a manifestation of the white cultural norms that dominate academia and librarianship. Sensoy and DiAngelo describe how the content of position descriptions, the composition of search committees, and the interview process can all be implicitly structured to privilege white-identifying candidates and white ways of being.[8] Within libraries, Galvan describes a similar issue: "Librarianship is paralyzed by whiteness. This will continue unabated without interrogating structures that benefit white librarians, including the performative nature of recruitment and hiring."[9]

Even with recognition in library literature that structural bias is present within our hiring processes, libraries are often focused more on helping individuals involved in the search process identify and control for their personal biases than on interrogating the structures that force candidates to be evaluated against norms that privilege whiteness. One common way that personal bias is approached is by libraries providing resources or training for committee members about the forms and ways that individual implicit biases manifest in search processes.[10] However, given the nature of hiring processes in general, which rely on limited information for decision-making and often operate under time pressures to fill a position,[11] implicit bias training alone is not enough to ensure an inclusive process. General literature on both interviewing and hiring processes points to the need to also identify and eliminate unstructured elements of selection processes that allow for irrelevant information about candidates (e.g., related to their identities and personal lives) to be introduced into deliberations and bias participants' perceptions of candidates' potential performance.[12] Transforming hiring processes in this way relies less on individual bias mitigation, and instead structurally limits opportunities for participants to shape the process and decision-making around their interests.[13]

Encouragingly, recent library literature and practice recommendations do extend beyond a focus on individual bias and responsibility to include strategies for incorporating structures into search processes to force better consideration and systemic mitigation of the ways invisible norms can intrude into hiring deliberations and decisions. Cunningham, Guss, and Stout and, more recently, Cole and Mross offer comprehensive recommendations for library hiring processes, including inclusive framing of job requirements; considerations for search committee compositions; structured candidate evaluation using a formal rubric; and approaches for committee interviews.[14] Other literature focuses on specific aspects of the hiring process. Brewer, Cheshire, and Bradshaw, for example, discuss how to meaningfully include candidate diversity statements in the application process,[15] while Arch and Gilman question the need for traditional social elements like meals, as well as providing recommendations for how to structure and evaluate (or not evaluate) these elements if they are used.[16] Individual institutions and library professional associations have also developed best practice recommendations for inclusive hiring. Prominent examples include guidelines created by Duke University Libraries, UNLV University Libraries, and the American Library Association's Core division.[17] However, while ample recommendations (and even substantive assessments of current practices[18]) have been developed, there are limited published examples of how these recommendations are practically applied within academic libraries in order to transform current hiring practices. The following cases describe parallel processes of transformation within two academic libraries and highlight specific areas of structural change within each organization's hiring practices.

Positionality

As white, cisheterosexual library administrators and hiring managers, we have both benefited from and employed hiring practices that prioritize majoritized identities and 'fit' with existing institutional culture. The process of reimagining our own libraries' hiring practices has greatly improved our understanding of the structural biases inherent in traditional processes; however, we continue to learn and make changes to create more inclusive and equitable libraries. The work presented here is not intended to portray a destination, but where we and our organizations currently are in our respective journeys. Finally, this work is not ours alone—our colleagues within the libraries have been important partners in developing and implementing these changes; they have served as search committee chairs and committee members and have done the work to make these transformations real and meaningful for our candidates and our libraries.

Discussion

To move our two academic libraries toward more inclusive hiring practices, we each led internal processes to holistically revise our hiring procedures and accompanying documentation. The case studies below discuss the processes, challenges, and specific core issues addressed through this work at our respective institutions, and the resulting principles and practices that we believe will result in a more equitable, transparent, and candidate-friendly process.

As we started to examine hiring practices, a core issue that emerged was the unexamined reliance on documents and institutional memory from past searches. Even as we began to incorporate new practices to increase diversity in our candidate pools and train search committees on the potential for unconscious bias, we had not considered reviewing the hiring processes themselves; but instead, with each new position, we scrambled for existing documents to use as a model so we could post the position as soon as possible. Time, as always, was the enemy of an inclusive, equitable process. A starting solution was to set aside the time for a complete revision of our hiring guidelines, but change required a catalyst. The spur to reconsider hiring practices was Oregon State University's (OSU) search advocate training.[19] The outcomes of this training were different at each of our institutions with regard to the role of the search advocate: at one, we have incorporated a search advocate position into our hiring committee structure because the institution supports this role in university hiring, while at the other, without the same institutional support, we adopted the principles and approaches behind the search advocate role but with an emphasis on collective responsibility for all hiring committee members. However, for both institutions, the training was inspirational in its emphasis on clear job requirements for advertised positions and the creation of a common understanding for both search committee members and external stakeholders of the ways in which a candidate can demonstrate their qualifications related to these requirements—core principles that we have both adapted into our new processes.

Pacific University

At the Pacific University Libraries (PUL), to structure our search processes we have historically relied on a combination of guidance from the university's human resources department and internal past practices carried forward across search committees. Prior to undertaking a comprehensive revision of our hiring practices, we had no established guidelines for the composition of search committees (with the exception of faculty searches, for which there was a minimally prescribed structure in the faculty handbook); a minimally structured process for evaluating how well candidates met required job qualifications; no requirements for what elements should or should not be included in finalists' interview schedule; and expansive opportunities for non-search committee members to provide feedback on candidates' fit for positions. Although we adhered to human resources guidance (e.g., regarding interview questions and reference checks) and made every effort to ensure each candidate received equitable consideration, we recognized that our processes were not as consistently structured as they should be—and that, often, elements of our process that were intended to be inclusive (especially providing an opportunity for all library employees to give feedback on candidates, even based solely on a social interaction) were potentially introducing bias into the search committee's deliberations.

To begin our comprehensive revision work, the library dean and two librarians attended the OSU search advocate training in 2020 and brought approaches and resources from the training back to PUL. The search guidelines revision was designated as an initiative under PUL's new Equity, Diversity, and Inclusion Plan, in support of our goal to "Create an organizational culture that reflects and advances equity, diversity, and inclusion." The project was assigned to the Library Steering Team, the dean's leadership advisory group with representation from across PUL. Due both to the relatively small size of PUL, and the fact that the university did not have structures in place to support external search advocates participating in PUL searches, we elected not to include an explicit search advocate role in our new process. Instead, we decided to have the committee chair, search committee, and dean collectively responsible for antibias practices—and to rely primarily on the structure of the process itself to help mitigate individual biases. The central focus of this process was ensuring that position requirements were appropriate for the job, but not overly prescriptive (e.g., allowing equivalencies for some requirements), and that there was a clear rubric for evaluating candidates against those requirements that could be consistently applied by all committee members across every phase of the search process—thus limiting opportunities for individual biases or judgements regarding sociocultural 'fit' in the workplace.

After completing an initial draft of new comprehensive search guidelines in spring 2021, the two librarians who had participated in the OSU training both had an opportunity to chair search committees for separate searches over the spring and summer of 2021 and, in doing so, use the new guidelines to identify areas that needed to be clarified or revisited based on their implementation. Both the committee chairs and committee members provided a range of feedback on these initial searches, with the most significant areas for improvement being the following:

- ensuring that the evaluative rubric the committee developed was clear; that all committee members had a shared understanding around the ways in which candidates could meet stated qualifications; and that the rubric was applied consistently throughout all stages of the search process;
- clarifying which elements of the search process, and particularly the on-site interview, were intended to be used to evaluate the candidates' qualifications—and, as part of that, who should be permitted to submit evaluative feedback to the search committee, and what form that feedback should take; and
- providing guidance, resources, and recourse for search committee members to help hold themselves and their fellow committee members accountable to antibias search principles, and to provide feedback to either the committee chair or dean if specific concerns arose about a search process.

Of these areas, the one requiring the most consideration, both during initial drafting and in subsequent revisions, was around defining which traditionally included elements of the on-site visit schedule should be included and which should be used to evaluate candidates; and, relatedly, determining who should be included in providing evaluative feedback and how that feedback should be structured.

Deliberation around the elements of on-site visit schedules focused primarily on two issues: first, how to ensure that the time commitment and preparation required of candidates was appropriate to the level of position for which they were applying; and second, how to balance opportunities for candidates and potential colleagues to interact with the need to prioritize visit elements that would support meaningful evaluation of candidates' qualifications. We determined that the length and intensity of on-site visits should be proportionate to the relative level of responsibility and compensation of the position in question—for example, interview visits for part-time positions should be less intensive and involve fewer stakeholders than for full-time staff or faculty positions. While there were initial concerns that treating positions differently in terms of visit schedule would signal a lesser value for some positions or would not provide as much opportunity for candidates and potential colleagues to interact, there was general agreement that limiting the time and financial burden on candidates was more important from an equity standpoint. For all position types, one of the most significant changes to the visit schedule was removing all purely social elements—specifically meals and casual meet-n-greets with snacks—from the schedule. Because these served no practical evaluative function related to the position requirements, and in the past had led largely to feedback about candidate 'fit,' which has been noted to disadvantage candidates who do not conform to existing norms within a workplace, they presented bias risks and no meaningful benefit for the search committee.[20]

Because removing the social elements of the visit schedule limited the number of people who would interact with candidates, we concurrently considered which individuals or departments *should* be added to a visit schedule and should be asked to provide evaluative feedback on the candidates in a more structured way. The team determined that additional stakeholder groups should be used to gather evaluative feedback on candidates based on the requirements of the position; for example, for positions in larger departments, members of the department not already on the search committee could be included as one stakeholder group. The process for coordinating between the search committee and stakeholder groups—that is, with regard to what questions the stakeholder group would ask and how the group would provide feedback to the search committee—was further developed during the second round of searches to use the new guidelines (in spring/summer 2022). The current process includes the search committee working with the stakeholder group to develop questions they will ask so that they complement the committee's interview questions and providing a feedback form to the group members through which they can submit candidate feedback, both individually and collectively, that is directly related to the committee's evaluative rubric and the position requirements.

In considering both which elements should be included in candidate visits and, more specifically, how meetings with stakeholder groups should be structured and evaluated, an overarching issue that became clear was the need for each visit element to have an intentional purpose and for that purpose to be understood by the committee, by any other stakeholder participants, and by the candidates. For the committee, it is important to understand how certain elements will be used in their evaluation of the candidate (e.g., which items on their evaluative rubric will be informed by a stakeholder group's feedback); for other visit participants, it is important to know whether their participation is intended to inform the search committee's deliberations or whether it is for the candidate's benefit (e.g., a meeting that is intended to let the candidate learn more about the library or university compared to a meeting that is intended to evaluate the candidate); and for candidates, it is important for their preparation (and stress levels) to know when they are being evaluated and who is providing evaluative feedback. To that end, each element on PUL's on-site visit schedule is now described as either "evaluative" or "nonevaluative." For example:

- *Staff in the department you will be leading have prepared questions relevant to the position requirements. This session is an interview element that will be evaluated; feedback will be provided to the search committee.*
- *This is an opportunity for you to ask questions about working at PUL and about the various roles and responsibilities as they interact with this position. The staff*

will not be interviewing or evaluating you but will be sharing their experiences and answering your questions. Search committee members will not attend.

Much in the same way that developing a candidate evaluative rubric requires reflecting on whether certain qualifications are necessary, are needlessly exclusive or privilege certain groups and identities, or are even possible to meaningfully evaluate, the process of developing these new search guidelines has led to significant reflection within PUL on what elements are necessary in an interview process, as well as which elements may create inequitable advantages or disadvantages for certain groups (e.g., internal and external candidates or neurodivergent candidates).

The result is a process that directs search committees—and all search participants—to focus on the ways that candidates' experience, knowledge, and skills fit with the needs of our positions, without regard for the ways in which a candidate 'fits' (or does not) into our existing culture or approach. We have a high degree of confidence that the general principles we have put in place have made the process more inclusive, more transparent for candidates, and ultimately well-constructed to give all candidates equitable consideration for our positions. However, we also realize that there are opportunities for continual improvement in the process and, in support of that, the dean requests feedback from search committee members after each search about areas for clarification or improvement based on their most recent experience.

University of Portland

At the University of Portland (UP), Clark Library, we started overhauling our hiring processes with the creation of the Hiring Practices Committee in 2019. We were fortunate to recruit a diverse group of library employees to the committee, providing a range of perspectives. Within the four-person committee, we initially had both faculty and staff, personnel from public and technical services functional areas, and both majoritized and minoritized identities.

This committee started by gathering existing literature on academic and library hiring, as well as historical practice documents found in library and university files. After outlining the steps of the hiring process, we methodically worked through the creation of guidelines for each step, from the formation of search committees and the construction of candidate interview schedules to the final search committee debriefing. By progressing linearly, we ensured that we were interrogating the entire process, looking both to standardize the structure of the hiring process and to bring in best practices to mitigate bias. Starting in 2019 also gave us the unsought opportunity to work through the challenges of the pandemic in 2020 and what each hiring practice would look like in an online format.

The committee solicited feedback from the library when the new guidelines significantly departed from previous practice. For example, one of the first finalized documents mandated the search committee composition. In the past, committees were primarily drawn from the hiring unit, but the composition varied because there were no formal guidelines. Our goal in creating guidelines was to require a committee structure that ensures a broader array of perspectives, thereby reducing the possibility of in-group thinking and overreliance on the idea of 'fit' with a work unit. Committees are now required to include a representative from a department outside the hiring unit and, for library faculty searches, a nonlibrary faculty member from elsewhere in the university.

For this and other process guidelines, the Hiring Practices Committee shared the document with the whole library team, gathered feedback, and then implemented immediately, without waiting for the completion of the entire manual. In this way, we were able to test new practices through actual searches and continue to refine over time.

Another significant change that the committee made in the hiring process is in the less structured aspects of the interview day. Because UP's librarian interview schedules were modeled after the faculty process used elsewhere in the university, we had always required a job talk from candidates. A job talk is a less structured element of an interview because it usually includes a broader group of attendees and the potential for a range of questions aimed at candidates. Interrogating the full hiring process allowed us to rethink this requirement. What did this job talk tell us about the potential for success in the position? In particular, if the position did not require public speaking or presenting as a main duty, was a job talk an appropriate evaluation measure? Past searches in our library had called the value of the job talk into question, as attendee feedback focused more on the candidate's speaking ability than their ideas. While some library positions do require the ability to teach or present to groups, many do not and requiring a presentation for every job means the evaluative measures may not fit the work of the position.

Public speaking styles may also be influenced by individual identity characteristics, including neurodiversity, which can make the presentation aspect of a hiring process significantly more challenging. Hand found that

> it may be the case that the "traditional" requirements of presenters and what are typically considered "good presentation skills" (e.g. eye contact with audience, confidence, well-paced fluent verbalizations; smooth and well-timed gestures) reflect unfair biases against neurodivergent individuals who may not be able to demonstrate these behaviors.[21]

Thus, if the position itself will not require regular presentations, a job talk may serve only to garner negative feedback from attendees who are asked to evaluate the candidate in this setting and disadvantage candidates whose presentation skills do not match an existing standard.

In rethinking the job talk, the Hiring Practices Committee decided to allow flexibility for hiring managers to choose the format that a candidate should use to discuss their ideas with a larger audience. Unlike committee composition, which, as a mandate, would ensure that future hiring managers take the time to find a diverse set of individuals to serve on the search committee, many of the new documents we created were constructed as nonmandatory guidelines that encourage hiring committees to think about alternatives. In this case, our new hiring guidelines state:

> When the role includes significant teaching or public speaking responsibilities, search committees should consider requesting a candidate presentation. If the role does not include teaching or public speaking, search committees should consider alternate ways to discern candidate knowledge of their field, including through interview questions or activities like a facilitated discussion.

Whether or not a hiring manager chose to require a job talk or another activity, the guidelines provide a prompt to consider the relevance of this element to success in the position.

These new guidelines for presentations were also effective immediately, as part of our rolling implementation of the new hiring practices, and in 2021, we had a search that allowed us to try them out. In hiring for a new head of public services, we asked candidates to facilitate a discussion with all library staff, rather than give a job talk, under the rationale that this position is a manager but will not teach or regularly present. Attendees were asked to evaluate candidates on their ability to focus the discussion and make sure all voices were heard.

The UP Library's Hiring Practices Committee released a full hiring manual in 2021, but committed to regular revisions because the literature about hiring continues to evolve.

Conclusions

To create an inclusive hiring process, institutions need to reimagine the entire hiring workflow, from position description to job offer. This innovative work must start by identifying and addressing firmly held assumptions and traditions about correct hiring practices and must then examine the purpose and potential bias risks for each element of the existing process. Though this work is time-consuming and can surface strong opinions from different stakeholders about the best ways to evaluate candidates, creating a comprehensive process that helps mitigate bias in hiring means a greater chance of an equitable evaluation of all candidates.

Best Practices

As libraries begin this work, we recommend the following practices:
- Set aside the time to review the entire hiring process in your library, with particular focus on how to structure the candidate experience and evaluative measures to match the requirements of the position.

- Identify, and clearly communicate to the library as whole, the assumptions and rationale behind significant changes in existing practices; this can help address concerns when elements like candidate presentations or social times are removed or substantially changed.
- While structural changes are critical, also ensure that individuals participating in hiring processes have the knowledge and tools needed to hold themselves and their colleagues accountable; this is especially important if there is no formal search advocate role on your hiring committees. This could include implicit bias training, as well as resources on calling in or calling out colleagues as appropriate if incidences of bias occur.
- Intentionally develop potential search committee chairs to be prepared to lead a search using the new process (particularly to lead the development of the candidate evaluative rubric, interview questions, and visit schedules); this could include simply serving on a committee before becoming a committee chair or creating cochairs by pairing an experienced chair with someone who has not served as a chair before.
- Assume that this will be an iterative process; it is often difficult to fully anticipate the impact of a process change until it has been implemented, so gathering feedback from those involved in the search and conducting a debrief with the search committee chair following each search (for at least several searches after implementing new processes) is useful for determining whether changes are having the intended impact, both for search outcomes and for participants.

Notes

1. Sojourna Cunningham, Samantha Guss and Jennifer Stout, "Challenging the 'Good Fit' Narrative: Creating Inclusive Recruitment Practices in Academic Libraries," in *Recasting the Narrative: The Proceedings of the ACRL 2019 Conference*, ed. Dawn M. Mueller (Chicago: Association of College and Research Libraries, 2019), 12–21; Angela Galvan, "Soliciting Performance, Hiding Bias: Whiteness and Librarianship," *In the Library with the Lead Pipe*, June 3, 2015, http://www.inthelibrarywiththeleadpipe.org/2015/soliciting-performance-hiding-bias-whiteness-and-librarianship/; Jennifer Vinopal, "The Quest for Diversity in Library Staffing: From Awareness to Action," *In the Library with the Lead Pipe*, January 13, 2016, http://www.inthelibrarywiththeleadpipe.org/2016/quest-for-diversity/.
2. Özlem Sensoy and Robin DiAngelo, "'We Are All for Diversity, but…': How Faculty Hiring Committees Reproduce Whiteness and Practical Suggestions for How They Can Change," *Harvard Educational Review* 87, no. 4 (Winter 2017): 557–80, https://doi.org/10.17763/1943-5045-87.4.557; Damani K. White-Lewis, "The Facade of Fit in Faculty Search Processes," *Journal of Higher Education* 91, no. 6 (2020): 833–57, https://doi.org/10.1080/00221546.2020.1775058.
3. Xan Arch et al., *Core Best Practices for Academic Interviews* (Chicago: Core, American Library Association, 2021), https://alair.ala.org/items/9f239ae6-35ad-44ab-b055-a2e569b617bd; Kathryn Houk, Jordan Nielsen, and Jenny Wong-Welch, *Toward Inclusive Academic Librarian Hiring Practices* (ACRL, 2024).
4. For example, Elizabeth A. Burroughs, "Reducing Bias in Faculty Searches," *Notices of the American Mathematical Society* 64, no. 11 (2017): 1304–7, https://doi.org/10.1090/noti1600.
5. Zhonghong Wang and Charles Guarria, "Unlocking the Mystery: What Academic Library Search Committees Look for in Filling Faculty Positions," *Technical Services Quarterly* 27, no. 1 (2010): 66–86, https://doi.org/10.1080/07317130903253449.

6. Suann Alexander, Jackie Dowdy, and Sharon Parente, "Demystifying the Academic Search Process, or Getting That Academic Library Position," *Tennessee Libraries* 59, no. 2 (2009), https://www.tnla.org/page/299/TL-v59n2-Demystifying-the-Academic-Search-Process-or-Getting-that-Acad.htm.
7. Megan Hodge and Nicole Spoor, "Congratulations! You've Landed an Interview: What Do Hiring Committees Really Want?" *New Library World* 113, no. 3/4 (2012): 148, https://doi.org/10.1108/03074801211218534.
8. Sensoy and DiAngelo, "We Are All for Diversity, but…"
9. Galvan, "Soliciting Performance."
10. As described, for example, in Cunningham, Guss and Stout, "Challenging the 'Good Fit' Narrative"; Ashley R. Brewer, Kelsey Cheshire, and Agnes K. Bradshaw, "Don't CTRL+F for Diversity: Articulating EDI Qualifications in Faculty Recruitment," in *Ascending into an Open Future: The Proceedings of the ACRL 2021 Virtual Conference*, ed. Dawn M. Mueller (Chicago: Association of College and Research Libraries, 2021).
11. Marc Bendick Jr. and Ana P. Nunes, "Developing the Research Basis for Controlling Bias in Hiring," *Journal of Social Issues* 68, no. 2 (2012): 238–62, https://doi.org/10.1111/j.1540-4560.2012.01747.x.
12. Jason Dana, Robyn Dawes, and Nathanial Peterson, "Belief in the Unstructured Interview: The Persistence of an Illusion," *Judgment and Decision Making* 8, no. 5 (2013): 512–20, https://doi.org/10.1017/S1930297500003612.
13. Michael G. Aamodt et al., "Do Structured Interviews Eliminate Bias? A Meta-analytic Comparison of Structured and Unstructured Interviews" (poster presented at the annual meeting of the Society for Industrial-Organizational Psychology, Dallas, TX, May 2006), https://www.researchgate.net/profile/Michael_Aamodt/publication/308753199_Do_structured_interviews_eliminate_bias_A_meta-analytic_comparison_of_structured_and_unstructured_interviews/links/57ee70d808ae8da3ce499e32.pdf.
14. Cunningham, Guss and Stout, "Challenging the 'Good Fit' Narrative"; Carmen Cole and Emily Mross, "Ensuring More Inclusive Hiring Processes," *portal: Libraries and the Academy* 22, no. 3 (July 2022): 507–15.
15. Brewer, Cheshire, and Bradshaw, "Don't CTRL+F for Diversity."
16. Xan Arch and Isaac Gilman, "One of Us: Social Performance in Academic Library Hiring," In *Ascending into an Open Future: The Proceedings of the ACRL 2021 Virtual Conference*, ed. Dawn M. Mueller (Chicago: Association of College and Research Libraries, 2021).
17. Katie Henningsen et al., *Task Force for Diversity in Recruitment Report* (Durham, NC: Duke University, 2018), https://hdl.handle.net/10161/22451; Avery Boddie et al., *Inclusion and Equity Committee Recommendations for Diverse Recruitment Report* (Las Vegas: University of Nevada, Las Vegas, February 2020), https://digitalscholarship.unlv.edu/lib_iec_reports/4; Arch et al., *Core Best Practices*.
18. See, for example, the Anti-racism Talent Management Audit project: Trevor A. Dawes et al., "Launching an Anti-racism Talent Management Audit: Translating Values into Action," *Ithaka S+R* (blog), February 2, 2021, https://sr.ithaka.org/blog/launching-an-anti-racism-talent-management-audit/.
19. Oregon State University, *Search Advocate Handbook*, March 2019 revision.
20. Arch and Gilman, "One of Us."
21. Christopher James Hand, "Neurodiverse Undergraduate Psychology Students' Experiences of Presentations in Education and Employment," *Journal of Applied Research in Higher Education* 15, no. 5 (2023): 1600–17, https://doi.org/10.1108/JARHE-03-2022-0106.

Bibliography

Aamodt, Michael G., Ellyn G. Brecher, Eugene J. Kutcher, and Jennifer D. Bragger. "Do Structured Interviews Eliminate Bias? A Meta-analytic Comparison of Structured and Unstructured Interviews," Poster presented at the annual meeting of the Society for Industrial-Organizational Psychology, Dallas, TX, May 2006. https://www.researchgate.net/profile/Michael_Aamodt/publication/308753199_Do_structured_interviews_eliminate_bias_A_meta-analytic_comparison_of_structured_and_unstructured_interviews/links/57ee70d808ae8da3ce499e32.pdf.
Alexander, Suann, Jackie Dowdy, and Sharon Parente. "Demystifying the Academic Search Process, or Getting That Academic Library Position." *Tennessee Libraries* 59, no. 2 (2009). https://www.tnla.org/page/299/TL-v59n2-Demystifying-the-Academic-Search-Process-or-Getting-that-Acad.htm.
Arch, Xan, Lori Birrell, Kristin E. Martin, and Renna Redd. *Core Best Practices for Academic Interviews*. Chicago: Core, American Library Association, 2021. https://alair.ala.org/items/9f239ae6-35ad-44ab-b055-a2e569b617bd.
Arch, Xan, and Isaac Gilman. "One of Us: Social Performance in Academic Library Hiring." In *Ascending into an Open Future: The Proceedings of the ACRL 2021 Virtual Conference*, edited by Dawn M. Mueller, 125–36. Chicago: Association of College and Research Libraries, 2021.
Bendick, Marc, Jr., and Ana P. Nunes. "Developing the Research Basis for Controlling Bias in Hiring." *Journal of Social Issues* 68, no. 2 (2012): 238–62. https://doi.org/10.1111/j.1540-4560.2012.01747.x.

Boddie, Avery, Brittany Paloma Fiedler, Michaelyn Haslam, Eva Luna, Edi Martinez-Flores, Thomas Padilla, Susan B. Wainscott, et al. *Inclusion and Equity Committee Recommendations for Diverse Recruitment Report*. Las Vegas: University of Nevada, Las Vegas, February 2020. https://digitalscholarship.unlv.edu/lib_iec_reports/4.

Brewer, Ashley R., Kelsey Cheshire, and Agnes K. Bradshaw. "Don't CTRL+F for Diversity: Articulating EDI Qualifications in Faculty Recruitment." In *Ascending into an Open Future: The Proceedings of the ACRL 2021 Virtual Conference*, edited by Dawn M. Mueller, 92–97. Chicago: Association of College and Research Libraries, 2021.

Burroughs, Elizabeth A. "Reducing Bias in Faculty Searches." *Notices of the American Mathematical Society* 64, no. 11 (2017): 1304–7. https://doi.org/10.1090/noti1600.

Cole, Carmen, and Emily Mross. "Ensuring More Inclusive Hiring Processes." *portal: Libraries and the Academy* 22, no. 3 (July 2022): 507–15.

Cunningham, Sojourna, Samantha Guss, and Jennifer Stout. "Challenging the 'Good Fit' Narrative: Creating Inclusive Recruitment Practices in Academic Libraries." In *Recasting the Narrative: The Proceedings of the ACRL 2019 Conference*, edited by Dawn M. Mueller, 12–21. Chicago: Association of College and Research Libraries, 2019.

Dana, Jason, Robyn Dawes, and Nathanial Peterson. "Belief in the Unstructured Interview: The Persistence of an Illusion." *Judgment and Decision Making* 8, no. 5 (2013): 512–20. https://doi.org/10.1017/S1930297500003612.

Dawes, Trevor A., Jennifer K. Frederick, Curtis Kendrick, and Christine Wolff-Eisenberg. "Launching an Anti-racism Talent Management Audit: Translating Values into Action." *Ithaka S+R* (blog), February 2, 2021. https://sr.ithaka.org/blog/launching-an-anti-racism-talent-management-audit/.

Galvan, Angela. "Soliciting Performance, Hiding Bias: Whiteness and Librarianship." *In the Library with the Lead Pipe*, June 3, 2015. http://www.inthelibrarywiththeleadpipe.org/2015/soliciting-performance-hiding-bias-whiteness-and-librarianship/.

Hand, Christopher James. "Neurodiverse Undergraduate Psychology Students' Experiences of Presentations in Education and Employment." *Journal of Applied Research in Higher Education* 15, no. 5 (2023): 1600–17. https://doi.org/10.1108/JARHE-03-2022-0106.

Henningsen, Katie, Winston Atkins, Fouzia El Gargouri, Jack Hill, Heather Martin, Sierra Moore, and Teresa Tillman. *Task Force for Diversity in Recruitment Report*. Durham, NC: Duke University Libraries, 2018. https://hdl.handle.net/10161/22451.

Hodge, Megan, and Nicole Spoor. "Congratulations! You've Landed an Interview: What Do Hiring Committees Really Want?" *New Library World* 113, no. 3/4 (2012): 139–61. https://doi.org/10.1108/03074801211218534.

Houk, Kathryn, Jordan Nielsen, and Jenny Wong-Welch, eds. *Toward Inclusive Academic Librarian Hiring Practices*. ACRL, 2024.

Oregon State University. *Search Advocate Handbook*. March 2019 revision.

Sensoy, Özlem, and Robin DiAngelo. "'We Are All for Diversity, but…': How Faculty Hiring Committees Reproduce Whiteness and Practical Suggestions for How They Can Change." *Harvard Educational Review* 87, no. 4 (Winter 2017): 557–80. https://doi.org/10.17763/1943-5045-87.4.557.

Vinopal, Jennifer. "The Quest for Diversity in Library Staffing: From Awareness to Action." *In the Library with the Lead Pipe*, January 13, 2016. http://www.inthelibrarywiththeleadpipe.org/2016/quest-for-diversity/.

Wang, Zhonghong, and Charles Guarria. "Unlocking the Mystery: What Academic Library Search Committees Look for in Filling Faculty Positions." *Technical Services Quarterly* 27, no. 1 (2010): 66–86. https://doi.org/10.1080/07317130903253449.

White-Lewis, Damani K. "The Facade of Fit in Faculty Search Processes." *Journal of Higher Education* 91, no. 6 (2020): 833–57. https://doi.org/10.1080/00221546.2020.1775058.

CHAPTER 3

Toward a Growth-Based Paradigm
Centering Candidate Experiences in the Hiring and Onboarding Processes

Annie Bélanger, Sheila Garcia-Mazari, and Bruna Ngassa

Organizations spend a lot of time recruiting the best candidate, yet often leave onboarding as an afterthought. Further, they may treat inclusion and equity as work that gets added on, rather than embedded in their efforts for diverse hiring. This disconnect is surprising considering that human resources is one of the largest expense categories in most libraries. Focusing in, hiring and onboarding are expensive endeavors that should allow both the organization and the candidate to make an informed decision about the path forward, foster belonging, and demonstrate the organizational culture of the hiring institution.

The Hiring to Onboarding life cycle model provided in figure 3.1 is used to articulate the major phases that an individual goes through in working with an organization from initial attraction to onboarding. These include: (1) attraction, (2) recruitment, (3) selection, (4) hiring, and (5) onboarding.

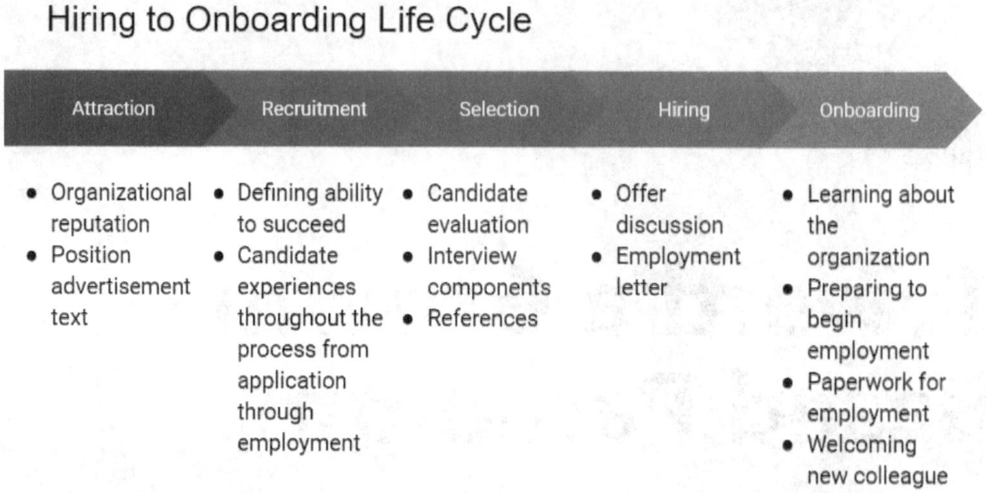

Hiring to Onboarding Life Cycle

Attraction	Recruitment	Selection	Hiring	Onboarding
• Organizational reputation • Position advertisement text	• Defining ability to succeed • Candidate experiences throughout the process from application through employment	• Candidate evaluation • Interview components • References	• Offer discussion • Employment letter	• Learning about the organization • Preparing to begin employment • Paperwork for employment • Welcoming new colleague

Figure 3.1. Hiring to onboarding life cycle[1]

This framework grounds an organization in viewing the hiring and onboarding processes as distinct components of a continuum, whereby organizations can engage actively in creating equitable and accessible approaches that center candidate experiences and promote inclusion. Additionally, organizations can use accountability, accessibility, and equity as ways to decenter whiteness and white-coded professionalism in each of these stages.

In this chapter, the authors will discuss their work critically examining existing hiring processes, designing an inclusive recruitment approach, and implementing a new growth-based hiring and onboarding structure. Through a case study of the practices implemented at Grand Valley State University (GVSU), a public liberal education university located in the Midwest, the authors will also illustrate how they centered an empathetic approach toward both applicants and new colleagues as they engaged in these processes. To conclude, the authors will provide practical tips, tools, and reflective prompts for readers to explore their local hiring and onboarding practices in order to center empathy as a way to advance inclusive and equitable processes.

Problem Definition

As it stands, hiring and onboarding processes in higher education institutions and academic libraries are employer-centered and serve as gatekeeping mechanisms, particularly for members of historically underrepresented groups. Many of the success indicators that search committees and hiring managers seek align with a culture of whiteness, further rooted in classism. These indicators include a focus on quantity of work over quality, which does not take into account the impact of the work and what it can communicate about the candidate's values; the need for a written record to validate completed work, which further erases the invisible that which often falls on women and Black, Indigenous, and people of color (BIPOC) in the academy,[2] and the belief that there is one right way to do things, which stifles a culture of growth and innovation. All of these are indicators of white supremacy culture.[3] Further, these indicators reinforce the hidden curriculum of unspoken norms, which prevent individuals who are not privy to these norms from flourishing in academic work environments.[4]

Whiteness is anchored in the reality that a "global history of colonization and imperialism of generally lighter peoples over darker, discrimination on the basis of skin color and other manifestations of prejudice have played a pivotal role in shaping the world."[5] Whiteness centers the customs, culture, and beliefs of white people as the standard operating approach, which is then used to judge all other groups.[6] As whiteness centers the superiority of white norms and behaviors, then whiteness can logically be equated with white supremacy culture. Tema Okun defines white supremacy as

> the ways in which the ruling class elite or the power elite in the colonies of what was to become the United States used the pseudo-scientific concept of race to create whiteness and a hierarchy of racialized value in order to disconnect and divide white people from Black, Indigenous, and People of Color (BIPOC).[7]

Libraries' patriarchal and classist roots are intertwined with and reinforced by white supremacy. To disrupt these traits, the majority of the profession, which benefits from white supremacy, will need to deliberately and intentionally recognize the entanglements in systems and practices.

As articulated above, whiteness favors responsibility over accountability. While employees are responsible for things, they are accountable to and for people. Accountability becomes critical in organizations that are seeking to decenter whiteness and anchor in equity. Shannon Perez-Darby shares the definition that "accountability is taking responsibility for your choices and the consequences of those choices."[8] Kaba quotes Connie Burk's definition which frames accountability as "an internal resource for recognizing and redressing harms we have caused to ourselves and others."[9] The authors of this chapter argue that within the context of organizations, accountability encompasses fulfilling job responsibilities as well as impact on the workplace culture.

In further considering accountability, particularly for white-bodied colleagues, there is a need to differentiate between discomfort, hurt, and harm. For the purpose of organizational change, we can define

- discomfort as being uncomfortable, which does not produce damage;
- hurt as being often unintentional, which produces repairable damage; and

- harm as being often intentional, which produces damage that is frequently permanent.

In all cases, accountability will mean owning impact and seeking to repair the relationship.

In order to create processes that center candidate growth, learning, and well-being, key stakeholders in the onboarding and hiring processes must critically evaluate and examine their approach toward reimagining progressively inclusive practices. This includes shifting from a culture where the candidate must prove their worth to one where employers also feel accountable to candidates, focusing on their needs as individuals and creating an environment where they can fully communicate their potential for success in a role. As candidates make the transition to employees, the onboarding process plays a key role in their retention; therefore, the onboarding process requires the same level of evaluation and adaptation to inclusion and equity principles.

Literature Review

To survey the ongoing conversation in library workplaces regarding candidate-centered experiences, hiring and onboarding practices were examined, focusing on the role of libraries in higher education and their understanding of workplace culture. In conducting the literature review, the authors first defined critical terms to support an understanding of the problem. The critical terms defined include *cohort hiring*—which is the process of hiring candidates in groups, rather than individually—in order to foster a collaborative experience and create a diverse pool of candidates.[10] *Onboarding* refers to the integration of employees into the workplace community with the goal of making them feel a sense of belonging and community.[11] These key terms contextualize current library practices in implementing growth-based structures and designing inclusive recruitment approaches.

From there, the authors interrogated the centering of whiteness in the workplace and the institutional practices stemming from a culture of whiteness. Tema Okun's definition of white supremacy connects to the problem of reconciling inherent power differences between hiring committees and candidates, which are amplified for BIPOC candidates. Though many higher institutions have diversity, equity, and inclusion statements on their home pages, many job interviews enforce listing relevant experiences to demonstrate candidates' commitment to diversity, equity, and inclusion, which instead borders on performative.[12] Many of these problems can be attributed to the idea of vocational awe, which is a set of values and beliefs libraries have about themselves being inherently good and above critique.[13] This notion is a clear problem as it prevents libraries from growing with the times and addressing the current issues relating to race and equity.

Lastly, the authors reviewed literature that addressed whiteness and power dynamics within librarianship. Librarianship is a profession dominated by whiteness, historically lacking diversity when it comes to librarians of color. This power structure exists to categorize individuals as either being close to whiteness, and therefore acceptable, or being different and therefore being excluded.[14] Many of the systems in place in libraries are designed to benefit white employees, casting aside minorities or making things harder for them. Examples of this white normativity can be seen when a librarian of color is mistaken for a library assistant by a white colleague or when nonbinary librarians are made to choose between binary gender groupings.[15] Many organizations will have job postings that enforce hiring power dynamics, such as asking for five years of experience for an entry-level position.[16] These instances of white normativity contribute to the low retention rate for BIPOC candidates and discourage them from applying to these jobs. Many workplace environments give the impression that they are benevolent institutions but oftentimes mistreat their employees due to unconscious bias, leading to self-doubt and insecurity within individuals.[17]

The literature demonstrates the reasons why it is important to implement new strategies in library hiring and onboarding practices. These new practices should be ones that offer support to candidates, financially and otherwise, as well as create safe, open spaces for BIPOC colleagues. Yet a survey published in 2021 about Carnegie Research Libraries' onboarding initiatives showed that "library-based diversity and inclusion training is less widespread than hoped."[18] Additionally, Kung, Fraser, and Winn's systematic review found most efforts focused on recruitment of early career librarians and "located few publications about efforts to retain diverse librarians once they enter the profession or about career advancement initiatives to recruit them into leadership positions." [19] These findings showcase that this is an ongoing issue in libraries, one that requires strategies that integrate recruitment within a whole person approach to support the professional success of a candidate.

Discussion

There are many leading practices that can help organizations develop more inclusive and equity-based processes throughout the employee life cycle, with a focus on recruitment to onboarding. At GVSU, a predominantly white, large, regional public institution located on Anishinaabe land within what is currently called West Michigan, the University Libraries worked closely with the Division of Inclusion and Equity to reframe our hiring process to center on the candidate experience, their ability to succeed in the interview and the role, and to align and advance the libraries' organizational values. As a result, the hiring process was reframed through the lens of equity, care, and integrity (where possible), and with a learner-centered mentality, ensuring that candidates were reviewed through a growth lens, instead of focusing solely on prior experience. Additionally, the University Libraries examined the organizational readiness for inclusive hiring as well as manager preparation.

Preparing for Change

To center candidate experience through the earliest stages of the employee life cycle, the first step was to question the local practices to articulate a clear purpose between each search component and the collective ability to make a decision to hire or join the organization. In parallel, we invited colleagues to reflect on when they had great experiences, as well as negative ones, within organizations. The key concerns that surfaced were the lack of communications, hiring as a black box, awkward interactions with future colleagues, and a feeling that only the worthy survive the process.

To address these concerns, the University Libraries started working on our organizational culture to ensure our lived values were woven throughout our work, to create accountability for interactions with colleagues, and to focus on inclusion and equity before diversity. Campus partners offered training to library colleagues on why inclusive hiring was important, what role they played, and how they could actively mitigate their bias as they engaged with candidates. The training also covered best practices for interacting with candidates using high empathy, kindness, and active communications. Lastly, the training covered what not to do in terms of questions to candidates, scheduling pace, and so on.

The University Libraries also did process mapping* to identify hiring pain points and how to engage colleagues appropriately in a process that focused on what candidates need to make an informed decision. Pain points included items within the libraries' control and some within the campus's control. Here are the key pain points, who had ownership, and how we worked to resolve them:

- *Lack of centralized support.* Owned by the libraries. Dean's office centralized coordination, and over time, the assistant to the dean became involved in all visiting and permanent role searches.
- *Long and delayed search processes.* Owned by the libraries and campus. The libraries altered their procedures to ensure that all interview materials and associated calendar holds are in place before the ad closes. This enables the libraries to move to phone interviews promptly and share the time line for the second round of interviews with candidates early in the process. In parallel, campus implemented several design-thinking efforts to reduce duplication of efforts and bottlenecks. Current librarian searches now take three to four months on average from opening to offer, whereas past searches lasted six to nine months.
- *Inconsistent materials used with candidates.* Owned by the libraries. The appropriate associate deans are involved in reviewing materials to ensure qualifications are covered, values in actions surfaced, and equity exists in the questions.
- *Lack of transparency for candidates.* Owned by the campus. Libraries created a public hiring FAQ to surface difficult-to-find information as well as to share information that is critical to candidates and is not to be added to ads per campus procedures. The libraries advocated for changes to campus procedures, leading to changes such having the ability to share salary ranges in ads.

---

* The tool is discussed later in the chapter.

- *Onboarding inconsistencies.* Owned by the libraries and campus. Libraries have iterated on the onboarding process with the help of newer colleagues as well as created a supervisor's guide to onboarding to ensure shared understanding. Additionally, the dean's office coordinates the early onboarding to ensure that procedural steps, such as tax paperwork, are completed promptly. Next, the libraries will build an onboarding approach for new managers. In parallel, the libraries advocated to campus to make improvements to shared campus-wide onboarding processes.

Ultimately, the process mapping had one overarching theme—all of the hiring and onboarding processes need to center the experience of the individuals engaging in them. To this end, the libraries decided to leverage empathy and care to create a human-centered approach to these processes.

Engaging with Candidates

The University Libraries developed a high-empathy approach[†] to engaging with candidates from the time of application to extending an offer.[‡] A high-empathy approach allows for an individual to move beyond what they may consider to be a logical or reasonable reaction or response to an issue and force themselves to think about alternate approaches rooted in understanding the emotional aspects of that decision.[20] By using a high-empathy approach, the libraries can center the experience and needs of the candidate to foster their ability to success, build trust with them, and ensure an accessible process.

The high-empathy approach translates to a higher number of detailed communications with the candidates throughout the hiring process as outlined in figure 3.2. In each communication, the libraries provide a lot of information about where they are in the process, what is next, how to get support, and who to reach out to. Ahead of interviews, the libraries will share what criteria are used for the evaluation; who will be present and why; what components will occur and why; and tips for a successful interview. The libraries share their organizational values and provide links to information a candidate might need, rather than having the candidate expend energy to learn about the libraries by digging across organizational websites. Additionally, as part of the interview invitation e-mails, the assistant to the dean or the search chair also offers the ability for candidates to ask questions and asks that they share dietary needs and preferences and ask for accommodations—sharing details of accessibility features already in place. At the conclusion of the process, the search chair offers to provide the candidate with feedback about strengths noted and ways to be more competitive in future searches—in the e-mail communication

---

[†] High empathy, also commonly referred to as radical empathy, includes both cognitive empathy, whereby "you understand another person's situation on an intellectual level," and emotional empathy, whereby "you go beyond imagining what a person must feel, and actually experience those same emotions yourself." (Jacqui Paterson, "Radical Empathy: What Is It and What Are the Benefits?" Happiness.com, accessed July 10, 2023, https://www.happiness.com/magazine/relationships/radical-empathy-extreme-what-is-it.)

[‡] Eventually, the University Libraries broadened that to include pre-boarding, onboarding, and a one-year check-in.

for first-round (screening) interviews and in a phone call for second-round interviews—as well as solicits feedback the candidate would like to give us.

What To Expect: Timely Communications

Phone Interview Prep	In Person Interview Prep	Pre-Visit	Selection	Non-Selection
• Express excitement for candidacy • Search Committee members information • Process & time line overview • How to request accommodations • Other things to know about us	• Build upon your last message • Agenda with focus statements, who will be there, and evaluation criteria • Process & time line overview • State financial coverage • How to request accommodations	• Ensure candidates food needs are shared • Pickups - give license plate and description of the vehicle for safety • Share questions for search committee component • Share presentation topic two weeks ahead	*Get permission to do reference check* Offer call • Express excitement • Articulate how salary is set (and if negotiations can occur) • Outline benefits • Provide clear time line for response • Answer questions	Schedule a call to let them know they were not chosen • Thank them for investing in the search • Offer to share feedback: 1) What particular strengths and 2) What areas of growth to be more competitive in future

Bélanger, Annie and Gorecki, Preethi. "ACRL Diversity Alliance Webinar - Kindly Hire Me: The Process and Impact of Inclusive Hiring" (2022). *Presentations.* https://scholarworks.gvsu.edu/library_presentations/102

Figure 3.2. Inclusive and timely communications with candidate

Creating Clear Accountability

To ensure that the high-empathy approach occurred, the libraries defined clear roles and accountabilities for hiring managers and search chairs, as well as redefined what is considered a successful search.* The search committee is responsible for identifying, recruiting, and selecting applicants who will be able to succeed in the role based on the required and preferred qualifications. The search committee needs to be charged with the responsibility to provide a fair, equitable, and inclusive search without unlawful discrimination. In this effort, the organization must foster active allies and provide appropriate training; otherwise, it will fall short of its goal by continuing to adopt processes centered around gatekeeping. Therefore, it is important that, at a minimum, search chairs are trained in identifying and calling in bias, as well as meeting the need for a positive, accessible candidate experience. Additionally, search committees must be trained on the steps expected in the search process, the decisions made at each step, and their accountability for a positive candidate experience.

---

* We redefined a successful search as one where the candidate has the ability to succeed, rather than having a proven track record or simply being the most qualified on paper. In parallel, a failed search is one where we fail to hire for success, not one where we fail to hire. Our reasoning was that privilege compounds itself.

Search committees are accountable for leveraging leading practices in preparing and enacting the search process. The search committee should collaboratively develop and implement a recruitment plan; write the job ad; create interview questions for phone screenings and in-person visits; and finalize an agenda for the interview day ahead of starting to review any candidate materials. Another leading practice is to challenge interviewing habits by asking the search committee to articulate why each portion of the interview exists and how it will support the decision-making process of the search committee and the candidates. This articulation can be turned into focus statements for each component of the agenda to support candidates' understanding of expectations and associated evaluation criteria. Another leading practice is to ensure that questions focus on required and preferred qualifications by having the search committee indicate which qualifications are being addressed and develop success criteria[†] for a strong answer.

Outside of the search committee members, active allies[‡] are critical to advocate for and continue the organizational change needed to foster equity and active inclusion among colleagues and in institutional systems. Allies can be cultivated by demonstrating that the organization values equity and inclusion and by building these into lived values and expectations for workplace behaviors. Over time, as equity and inclusion are part of core hiring expectations, more individuals will come to share the commitment. Additionally, when an organization embeds expectations around equity and inclusion into performance reviews, it begins to align its incentive structure with expectations of the workplace, thereby creating a virtuous cycle. Organizations also need to provide continued development of knowledge and skills related to equity and accessibility as well as methods for calling in bias and holding colleagues accountable for their behavior. Lastly, organizations should consider how job descriptions support and make explicit their commitment to equity and inclusion.

Supporting Candidates

Supporting candidates begins with the job ad and associated materials. The language used throughout and in the materials is another critical component to both equitable and inclusive searches as well as high-empathy approaches. The feelings of belonging that can be elicited by a job ad are important in creating job appeal; language that appears to cater to one identity creates a barrier for applicants of other identities.[22] In developing written materials, consider who is positively or negatively affected by the language, how organizational values and mission are demonstrated in the writing, and if the qualifications are truly the minimum needed to succeed within the first year. Additionally, consider highlighting not only what the organization and the job needs, but also what the candidate

---
† Success criteria are the concepts that the committee agrees the question is seeking in a strong answer. To develop them, a search committee should consider the aptitudes to meet a qualification as well as the organizational values that could be applied—for example, time management, clear communication, understanding of impact on others, empathy.
‡ An ally is someone who uses their privilege and power to act in support of a structurally excluded group.

may gain from working in this position. It is also important to provide clarity around compensation and benefits. Throughout the process, the language used should demonstrate the lived values of the organization.

When organizations are seeking to hire colleagues who will be able to succeed in the role, they must acknowledge that interview skills do not always translate to job success. To shift their approach, search committees and colleagues should focus on supporting the candidates' comfort and needs so that candidates' knowledge and values can shine through. There are many simple practices that can support candidates: (1) simplifying questions; (2) sharing questions ahead; (3) developing question prompts to help reframe or dig deeper; (4) having a purpose statement for each search component;* 5) providing frequent breaks, water, and snacks; and 6) being flexible in the schedule. Flexibility, at minimum, should include providing at least one time slot for the candidate to select a component that would help in their decision-making, such as meetings with a benefits manager, disability support services, an affinity group leader, a campus tour guide, and so on. Flexibility can also include the ability to either wholesale reschedule or to be aware of the optional components that can be more easily rescheduled if something comes up for a candidate.

Using Tools to Center Equity and Inclusion in Processes

Many tools can help advance the work for organizational change to enable inclusive hiring and onboarding within the context of an equitable approach to the employee life cycle, especially when critically examining local practices. In addition to the approaches discussed above, the authors have identified several other tools that were most effective in shifting local practices at GVSU Libraries, an organization that was already committed to moving to an active practice of inclusion. The authors acknowledge that additional tools not mentioned here may support other local realities.

In considering the overarching processes and components, organizations can use an equity lens at the beginning, during, and after the interview, and through the onboarding processes. An equity lens is a set of questions that an organization asks itself about its work to center equity and ensure systems-level thinking—"it is explicit in drawing attention to the inclusion of marginalized populations, typically [Black communities,] communities of color [and Indigenous communities], and can be adapted to focus on other communities."[23] Excerpted from the "Building Inclusive Libraries: Kindness, Equity, and Candidate Experiences in Hiring and Onboarding Toolkit," the following equity lens questions focus on interview planning and associated components:

---

* For example: (1) Presentation: Why is there a presentation, what is the topic, who will be at the presentation, what does the organization want to learn about the candidate's skills, and how will it be evaluated? (2) Meeting with the dean: Why is there a meeting with the dean, what should the candidate expect in the meeting, and what should be prepared?

- Have we planned all of the interview components ahead of reviewing candidate materials?
- Do all of the interview components help us make our decisions?...
- Have we created an evaluation rubric that... [mitigates bias] and [is] reflective of our values?"
- Are our questions aligned with the job qualifications?...
- Are we creating an accessible and inclusive environment for the candidates?...
- Are we supporting the candidates' ability to make their decision whether to join us?[24]

While an equity lens will help organizations review equity and impacts to vulnerable stakeholders, at times, an overview of the whole process is needed to ensure that it is the right process with the proper steps. Process mapping, a visual representation of a process, can identify pain points in the interview process and areas to focus change efforts, as demonstrated above. Process mapping can be done alone or in groups as well as in low-tech and high-tech ways. There are six critical steps:

1. Identify the process to map
2. List all the activities involved—[Consider noting who is responsible]
3. Write out the sequences of the steps
4. Create a flowchart or [sequenced mapping of the steps]
5. Finalize and share out
6. Analyze for areas to improve[25]

Once you have a process map, it can increase understanding of the process, identify inefficiencies, and ultimately redefine the process steps. In redefining the process and components, organizations can leverage universal design principles† to ensure that candidates' experiences are centered and barriers are reduced.

Recognizing the mental models at play can be used to elevate where internal and external bias may be occurring. To identify and challenge mental models, individuals and groups can use the Ladder of Inference. This is a tool that allows for the discovery and challenge of mental models, assumptions, and reflexive beliefs.[26] This ladder breaks down the steps from data observation to conclusions. To use the ladder, one typically walks downward. This can be done by using a series of questions, such as the ones articulated by Mind Tools:

---

† "Universal Design is the design and composition of an environment so that it can be accessed, understood and used to the greatest extent possible by all people regardless of their age, size, ability or disability." Center for Excellence in Universal Design. "What Is Universal Design?" Accessed March 10, 2023. https://universaldesign.ie/what-is-universal-design/ (page discontinued).

Chapter 3

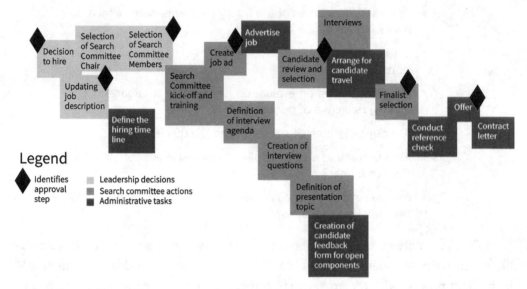

Figure 3.3. Hiring process sample process map

- Actions: Why do I believe this to be the right action? What are some alternative options?
- Beliefs: What beliefs do I hold about this? What conclusions are they based on?
- Conclusions: Why did I conclude this? What are my assumptions there?
- Assumptions: Are my assumptions valid? Why am I assuming this?
- Interpretations: Am I looking at this data objectively? What other meanings could they have?
- Selected data: What did I ignore or didn't pay attention to? Are there other sources of data I didn't consider?[27]

This might be useful, for example, if a candidate is late. The search chair has had an employee who was frequently late and had to be on a performance improvement plan as they were not meeting their job expectations. The search chair makes the split-second judgment that the candidate does not care about the job and proceeds to engage half-heartedly in the job interview, having made the decision they will not hire the candidate. Alternatively, if the search chair were to walk down the ladder, they might see the past connections, the judgment they made, and their automatic action response. Instead of shutting down, the search chair decides to check their understanding by asking the candidate if everything is OK and how they might help them refocus. The candidate shares that their pet was violently sick just before they were going to drive in and had to go to the emergency vet. The candidate apologizes profusely. The search chair shares concern, asks for help shifting the schedule for the day to ensure all components are covered, gets a cup of tea for the candidate to help them settle, and proceeds with a successful interview. The candidate is selected and becomes a strong team member.

Gaining Agency as a Candidate

> *"We can disagree and still love each other unless your disagreement is rooted in my oppression and denial of my humanity and right to exist."*
>
> ~James Baldwin

As a candidate, gaining agency can be one of the most difficult aspects of both the hiring and the onboarding processes. Through the lens of an employer-centered model, the candidate must prove their worth not only during the hiring process, but continuously throughout the onboarding process as well, as the performance of a new employee in the first few months after their hire has traditionally been used to gauge potential and the level of success in a role.[28] This holds true for library roles, which may have a probationary period of a few months to even a few years. Tenure-track library roles, in particular, can often be viewed as an extension of the onboarding and probationary processes, where a candidate's performance is scrutinized, and determinations of continuing employment are made. The hiring and onboarding processes, therefore, create a high level of stress for a candidate and can, from the outset, disempower them.

While inclusive hiring and onboarding practices can help mitigate the impact of processes that disempower candidates, the candidates themselves can use a variety of tools at their disposal to gain agency. For example, the Green Book for Libraries, a guide to working conditions in libraries across the United States and Canada, is a crowdfunded resource maintained by a community of volunteers.[29] The guide highlights the experiences of BIPOC, in particular, and is open only for use by individuals who identify as members of these communities. Users can provide a review for their workplace and engage in conversations with others in the space. The concept of the Green Book is to highlight safe working environments for BIPOC professionals and to provide a form of agency for individuals who are job searching. Through this resource, they are able to gather information about a workplace and determine whether or not it is a space where they can thrive.

Other such resources and networks within librarianship may not be as openly available. Candidates may often reach out to a friend of a friend who may provide in-depth information of their own experiences within an institution and any challenges that a new employee may face. Often characterized as employee whisper networks, such tools are powerful counteragents to the official secret model inherent within bureaucracies,[30] where decision-making is closely guarded and serves as "a way of gatekeeping, where information is used to dominate marginalized groups."[31] Whisper networks can also serve as a form of self-protection for current employees, who may face repercussions for speaking truthfully about their experiences in a hostile workplace.

In addition to information sharing among peers and personal networks, candidates can exercise agency by viewing their interviewing and onboarding experience through the lens of critically examining a future workplace. Most candidates are attuned to the actions and dialogue that may indicate a future employer is facing similar challenges as a current or former employer, and the candidate has the agency to decide whether or not they will pursue a position. Areas of potential concern will differ from individual to individual and may include a lack of accommodations built into the interview process, such as not providing questions ahead of time or not providing candidates sufficient breaks, or the inability of interviewers to clearly answer candidate questions about the status of an institution's equity and inclusion efforts. For early-career librarians, these red flags, so to speak, may not be as pronounced, and can be easily overlooked. Early-career librarians can consider building networks through social media, particularly if the privilege of time and financial capacity to join conferences or professional organizations to form these networks may not be at their disposal.

Making the decision to self-advocate becomes harder during the onboarding process. Therefore, it becomes important for the manager to consider addressing concerns early on in an employee's experience with an institution. This can begin during the interview process, whereby hiring managers can actively acknowledge the inherent power structure between themselves and the candidate and carve out space for a candidate to address any concerns that arise.* Having this difficult conversation early provides space for a candidate to also make an informed decision as to whether or not the institution will meet their needs. Once a candidate transitions to becoming a new colleague, supervisors can begin to build on this exchange and address further concerns they may have. While the employee can determine their individual boundaries as powerful tools to set guardrails for when it may be time to walk away, the manager can further support this development through their one-on-one meetings. The manager can be proactive in preparing for a discussion around accommodations to ensure individual success as this can be difficult for new employees who are concerned about losing a role. There is no prescriptive solution for a manager to support an employee beyond listening and providing feedback that is grounded in the well-being of the employee, and not necessarily in the well-being of the institution at large. It is vital for managers to be consistent and transparent when noting what they are trying to change institutionally in order to improve an employee's situation, while also acknowledging when they themselves may be facing barriers in attempting

---

* This can be done by having the hiring manager or senior administrator ask if there are any red flags or dissonance they can address during one-on-ones.

to lead healthy change. Consider the following questions to determine your needs and ensure follow-through:
- What limitations are you (the employee) experiencing?
- How do these limitations affect you? Your job performance?
- What responsibilities are easiest to accomplish?
- What responsibilities are the hardest?
- What is the environment or conditions when you are most productive?
- What is the environment or conditions when you are facing struggles?
- What portion of your job might need an alternate way of approaching it?
- What support might you need from your colleagues? What do they need to know? What training might they need?
- Once the accommodations are in place, how effective are they in supporting you?

Candidates and employers alike should ensure that they document all information exchanged during a conversation about accommodations. Having an open dialogue about what a candidate may need to succeed ultimately not only helps the individual but can also help the employer understand areas of opportunity to improve the overall employee experience.

Conclusions

A job interview and starting a new role are inherently stressful situations and can be harmful when handled poorly by the hiring organization. Ensuring intentionality when designing the interview and onboarding processes will lead libraries toward not only recruiting early-career librarians, but also retaining the talent within their institutions. Inclusive processes throughout the employee life cycle can spearhead a shift in cultural practice, away from the white-coded norm of a candidate proving their value, to an inclusive candidate-centered approach to foster success in the workplace.

As processes shift and individual institutions determine the best practices for their local needs, all stakeholders—from search committee members to hiring managers, to the candidates themselves—can use the learning loop questions provided below to embrace a growth-based paradigm and self-reflect on lessons learned in order to drive change:
- What did I try?
- Where did I succeed?
- Where did I struggle?
- What did I learn?
- What will I try next?

While no individual experience is indicative of the encounters of all candidates and employees that have interviewed using GVSU's growth-based paradigm for hiring and onboarding, there are key takeaways that can be shared from GVSU's approach. The first is that iteration is core to this work. Without continual improvement, a candidate-centered, equitable approach can become performative, as it indicates that an institution was not ready to fully commit to a growth-based paradigm. Additionally, inclusion and equity training is vital at all levels of the library and should be continually built on. A one-off training may prove ineffective, as individuals are provided with a wealth of information but are not guided through active application of these concepts and approaches. Further, single trainings do not aid employees in keeping abreast of evolving best practices. Finally, it is imperative to ensure not only that leadership is fully trained in this approach, but that they are fully committed to the principles of inclusion and equity. This requires leadership to continually interrogate the power dynamics and how their role may have upheld barriers to entry, particularly for librarians with identities that are historically marginalized in academia.

The work of creating a more inclusive workplace is dynamic, evolving alongside the organizational culture and employee needs. Therefore, it is incumbent on search committees to be aware of when their institutional culture may not be welcoming to candidates, particularly for BIPOC individuals. For these workers, the employee life cycle model may be a continual struggle in a noninclusive workplace. It is the hope of the authors that the practical tools provided in this chapter, such as equity lenses and process mapping, can help to jump-start institutional reviews of pain points within current hiring and onboarding processes in librarianship and by extension, serve to shift current practices toward embracing a growth-based paradigm throughout the employee life cycle. Centering the candidate in hiring and onboarding processes is, as of yet, an imperfect iterative model, but its flexibility and potential for change is what makes it one of the most inclusive tools to finally integrate long-overdue change.

Notes

1. Elizabeth Mull, "Using the Employee Lifecycle as Your Roadmap to Employee Engagement," Connected Trifecta, Last modified March 7, 2023, https://connectedtrifecta.com/2017/11/the-employee-lifecycle-is-your-roadmap-to-building-an-engaged-employee-experience/ (page discontinued).
2. Kimberly A. Truong, "Making the Invisible Visible," Inside Higher Ed, May 28, 2021, https://www.insidehighered.com/advice/2021/05/28/why-and-how-colleges-should-acknowledge-invisible-labor-faculty-color-opinion.
3. Tema Okun, "White Supremacy Culture," dRworks, 1999, https://socialwork.wayne.edu/events/4_-_okun_-_white_supremacy_culture_-_still_here.pdf.
4. Alexia Hudson-Ward, "Addressing Academia's Hidden Curriculum of Unspoken 'Norms,'" *TIE Blog*, Choice, April 6, 2021, https://www.choice360.org/tie-post/addressing-academias-hidden-curriculum-of-unspoken-norms/.
5. Anna Lindner, "Defining Whiteness: Perspectives on Privilege." *Gnovis* 18, no. 2 (Spring 2018): 44, https://repository.library.georgetown.edu/bitstream/handle/10822/1050459/Lindner-Defining-Whiteness-Perspective-on-Privilege-2.pdf.
6. National Museum of African American History and Culture, "Whiteness," accessed February 10, 2023, https://nmaahc.si.edu/learn/talking-about-race/topics/whiteness.
7. Okun, "White Supremacy Culture," 2.

8. Kiyomi Fujikawa, Shannon Perez-Darby, and Mariame Kaba, "Building Accountable Communities," recorded October 26, 2018, on Zoom by Barnard College, New York, NY, video, 1:35:24, https://bcrw.barnard.edu/event/building-accountable-communities/.
9. Fujikawa, Perez-Darby, and Kaba, "Building Accountable Communities."
10. Melissa Morse, "What Is Cluster Hiring?" *HR Daily Advisor*, February 6, 2020, https://hrdailyadvisor.blr.com/2020/02/06/what-is-cluster-hiring/.
11. Latesha Byrd, "How to Embed DEI into Your Employee Onboarding Process," LinkedIn, August 31, 2022, https://www.linkedin.com/pulse/how-embed-dei-your-employee-onboarding-process-latesha-byrd-/?trk=pulse-article_more-articles_related-content-card.
12. Mimosa Shah and Dustin Fife, "Obstacles and Barriers in Hiring: Rethinking the Process to Open Doors," *College and Research Libraries News* 84, no. 2, (February 2023): 55–58, https://doi.org/10.5860/crln.84.2.55.
13. Fobazi Ettarh, "Vocational Awe and Librarianship: The Lies We Tell Ourselves," *In the Library with the Lead Pipe*, January 10, 2018, https://www.inthelibrarywiththeleadpipe.org/2018/vocational-awe/.
14. April Hatchcock, "White Librarianship in Blackface: Diversity Initiatives in LIS," *In the Library with the Lead Pipe*, October 7, 2015, https://www.inthelibrarywiththeleadpipe.org/2015/lis-diversity/.
15. Hatchcock, "White Librarianship in Blackface."
16. Shah and Fife, "Obstacles and Barriers in Hiring."
17. Glenn Jeffers, "Want to Retain Your Diverse Workforce? Focus on Removing Bias," Vistage Research Center, September 2, 2020, https://www.vistage.com/research-center/talent-management/20200902-remove-unconscious-bias/.
18. Jenny Lynn Semenza, Tania Harden, and Regina Koury, "Survey on Onboarding Practices in Carnegie Research Institutions," *Library Management* 42, no. 1/2 (2021): 116, https://doi.org/10.1108/LM-10-2020-0148.
19. Janice Y. Kung, K-Lee Fraser, and Dee Winn, "Diversity Initiatives to Recruit and Retain Academic Librarians: A Systematic Review," *College and Research Libraries* 81, no. 1 (January 2020): 104, https://doi.org/10.5860/crl.81.1.96.
20. Jacqui Paterson, "Radical Empathy: What Is It and What Are the Benefits?" Happiness.com, accessed July 10, 2023, https://www.happiness.com/magazine/relationships/radical-empathy-extreme-what-is-it.
21 Annie Bélanger and Preethi Gorecki, "ACRL Diversity Alliance: Kindly Hire Me: The Process and Impact of Inclusive Hiring," Webinar. Recorded February 28, 2022, on Zoom, Grand Rapids, MI. Video, 1:01:46. https://www.youtube.com/watch?v=QKS5hhGQKnw (recorded presentation) and https://scholarworks.gvsu.edu/library_presentations/102, slide 6.
22. Danielle Gaucher, Justin Friesen, and Aaron C. Kay, "Evidence That Gendered Wording in Job Advertisements Exists and Sustains Gender Inequality," *Journal of Personality and Social Psychology* 101, no. 1 (July 2011): 109–28, https://doi.org/10.1037/a0022530.
23. Center for Nonprofit Advancement, "What Is an Equity Lens?" last modified 2020, https://www.nonprofitadvancement.org/files/2020/12/What-is-an-Equity-Lens.pdf.
24. Annie Bélanger et al., "Building Inclusive Libraries: Kindness, Equity, and Candidate Experiences in Hiring and Onboarding Toolkit," GVSU Library Reports and Communication, 2023, 17–18, https://scholarworks.gvsu.edu/library_reports/26.
25. Asana, "Guide to Process Mapping: Definition, How-to, and Tips," *Asana Blog*, November 21, 2022, https://asana.com/resources/process-mapping (page content changed).
26. Art of Leadership Consulting, "Mental Models—Ladder of Inference," March 2, 2017, https://artofleadershipconsulting.com/mental-models-ladder-of-inference/.
27. Mind Tools, "The Ladder of Inference," last modified 2022, https://www.mindtools.com/aipz4vt/the-ladder-of-inference.
28. Association of College and Research Libraries, *A Standard for the Appointment, Promotion and Tenure of Academic Librarians* (Chicago: Association of College and Research Libraries, 2020, upd. 2021), https://www.ala.org/acrl/standards/promotiontenure.
29. Green Book for Libraries, "About," accessed April 26, 2023, https://librarygreenbook.com/.
30. Kieran Allen, *Max Weber* (London: Pluto Press, 2004): 113, quoted in Lalitha Nataraj et al., "'Nice White Meetings': Unpacking Absurd Library Bureaucracy through a Critical Race Theory Lens," *Canadian Journal of Academic Librarianship* 6 (2020): 8.
31. Nataraj et al., "'Nice White Meetings,'" 8.

Bibliography

Art of Leadership Consulting. "Mental Models—Ladder of Inference." March 2, 2017. https://artofleadershipconsulting.com/mental-models-ladder-of-inference/.

Asana. "Guide to Process Mapping: Definition, How-to, and Tips." Asana Blog, November 21, 2022. https://asana.com/resources/process-mapping (page content changed).

Association of College and Research Libraries. *A Standard for the Appointment, Promotion and Tenure of Academic Librarians*. Chicago: Association of College and Research Libraries, 2010, upd. 2021. https://www.ala.org/acrl/standards/promotiontenure.

Bélanger, Annie, Sarah Beaubien, Kat Bell, Krista Benson, Lori Cawthorne, Sheila García Mazari, Takeelia Garrett, et al. "Building Inclusive Libraries: Kindness, Equity, and Candidate Experiences in Hiring and Onboarding Toolkit." GVSU Library Reports and Communication, 2023. https://scholarworks.gvsu.edu/library_reports/26.

Bélanger, Annie, and Preethi Gorecki. "ACRL Diversity Alliance: Kindly Hire Me: The Process and Impact of Inclusive Hiring." Webinar. Recorded February 28, 2022, on Zoom, Grand Rapids, MI. Video, 1:01:46. https://www.youtube.com/watch?v=QKS5hhGQKnw (recorded presentation) and https://scholarworks.gvsu.edu/library_presentations/102 (slides and notes).

Byrd, Latesha. "How to Embed DEI into Your Employee Onboarding Process." LinkedIn, August 31, 2022. https://www.linkedin.com/pulse/how-embed-dei-your-employee-onboarding-process-latesha-byrd-/?trk=pulse-article_more-articles_related-content-card.

Center for Excellence in Universal Design. "What Is Universal Design?" Accessed March 10, 2023. https://universaldesign.ie/what-is-universal-design/ (page discontinued).

Center for Nonprofit Advancement. "What Is an Equity Lens." Last modified 2020. https://www.nonprofitadvancement.org/files/2020/12/What-is-an-Equity-Lens.pdf.

Ettarh, Fobazi. "Vocational Awe and Librarianship: The Lies We Tell Ourselves," *In the Library with the Lead Pipe*, January 10, 2018. https://www.inthelibrarywiththeleadpipe.org/2018/vocational-awe/.

Fujikawa, Kiyomi, Shannon Perez-Darby, and Mariame Kaba. "Building Accountable Communities." Recorded October 26, 2018, on Zoom by Barnard College, New York, NY. Video, 1:35:24. https://bcrw.barnard.edu/event/building-accountable-communities/.

Gaucher, Danielle, Justin Friesen, and Aaron C. Kay. "Evidence That Gendered Wording in Job Advertisements Exists and Sustains Gender Inequality." *Journal of Personality and Social Psychology* 101, no. 1 (July 2011): 109–28. https://doi.org/10.1037/a0022530.

Green Book for Libraries. "About." Accessed April 26, 2023. https://librarygreenbook.com/.

Hatchcock, April. "White Librarianship in Blackface: Diversity Initiatives in LIS." *In the Library with the Lead Pipe*, October 7, 2015. https://www.inthelibrarywiththeleadpipe.org/2015/lis-diversity/.

Hudson-Ward, Alexia. "Addressing Academia's Hidden Curriculum of Unspoken 'Norms.'" *TIE Blog*, Choice, April 6, 2021. https://www.choice360.org/tie-post/addressing-academias-hidden-curriculum-of-unspoken-norms/

Jeffers, Glenn. "Want to Retain Your Diverse Workforce? Focus on Removing Bias." Vistage Research Center, September 2, 2020. https://www.vistage.com/research-center/talent-management/20200902-remove-unconscious-bias/.

Kung, Janice Y., K-Lee Fraser, and Dee Winn, "Diversity Initiatives to Recruit and Retain Academic Librarians: A Systematic Review." *College and Research Libraries* 81, no. 1 (January 2020): 96–108. https://doi.org/10.5860/crl.81.1.96.

Lindner, Anna. "Defining Whiteness: Perspectives on Privilege." *Gnovis* 18, no. 2 (Spring 2018): 43–58. https://repository.library.georgetown.edu/bitstream/handle/10822/1050459/Lindner-Defining-Whiteness-Perspective-on-Privilege-2.pdf.

Mind Tools. "The Ladder of Inference." Last modified 2022. https://www.mindtools.com/aipz4vt/the-ladder-of-inference.

Morse, Melissa. "What Is Cluster Hiring?" *HR Daily Advisor*, February 6, 2020. https://hrdailyadvisor.blr.com/2020/02/06/what-is-cluster-hiring/.

Mull, Elizabeth. "Using the Employee Lifecycle as Your Roadmap to Employee Engagement." Connected Trifecta. Last modified March 7, 2023. https://connectedtrifecta.com/2017/11/the-employee-lifecycle-is-your-roadmap-to-building-an-engaged-employee-experience/ (page discontinued).

Nataraj, Lalitha, Holly Hampton, Talitha R. Matlin, and Yvonne Nalani Meulemans. "'Nice White Meetings': Unpacking Absurd Library Bureaucracy through a Critical Race Theory Lens." *Canadian Journal of Academic Librarianship* 6 (December 2020): 1–15. https://doi.org/10.33137/cjal-rcbu.v6.34740.

National Museum of African American History and Culture. "Whiteness." Accessed February 10, 2023. https://nmaahc.si.edu/learn/talking-about-race/topics/whiteness.

Okun, Tema. "White Supremacy Culture." dRworks, 1999. https://www.whitesupremacyculture.info/uploads/4/3/5/7/43579015/okun_-_white_sup_culture.pdf.

Paterson, Jacqui. "Radical Empathy: What Is It and What Are the Benefits?" Happiness.com. Accessed July 10, 2023. https://www.happiness.com/magazine/relationships/radical-empathy-extreme-what-is-it.

Semenza, Jenny Lynn, Tania Harden, and Regina Koury. "Survey on Onboarding Practices in Carnegie Research Institutions." *Library Management* 42, no. 1/2 (2021): 109–18. https://doi.org/10.1108/LM-10-2020-0148.

Shah, Mimosa, and Dustin Fife. "Obstacles and Barriers in Hiring: Rethinking the Process to Open Doors." *College and Research Libraries News* 84, no. 2 (February 2023): 55–58. https://doi.org/10.5860/crln.84.2.55.

Truong, Kimberly A. "Making the Invisible Visible." Inside Higher Ed, May 28, 2021. https://www.insidehighered.com/advice/2021/05/28/why-and-how-colleges-should-acknowledge-invisible-labor-faculty-color-opinion.

CHAPTER 4

Moving toward More Inclusive Hiring

Lea J. Briggs and Rodney Lippard

For over twenty years, the library profession has been calling for more diversity in staffing and to have library employees that look more like the students they serve. The authors, both of whom have over fifteen years of experience in academic library administration, have tried to heed this call as best they can, knowing that it is the right thing to do. However, practical steps to achieve this goal have not been easy to come by. Over the years, there have been many conversations between the authors regarding the implementation of multiple diversity, belonging, inclusiveness, and equity (DBIE) initiatives in their respective institutions. One author is currently manager of administration and operations in the College of University Libraries and Learning Sciences at the University of New Mexico (UNM University Libraries) and has served as library director at two other colleges and universities. The other became the director of the Torreyson Library at the University of Central Arkansas (UCA) in the last year and has served in library director roles at other colleges and universities, most recently the University of South Carolina Aiken (USCA). Their administrative roles position them to influence and lead institutional change in this area.

Recognizing that this lack of diversity is a growing and ever-changing problem and that what works to address issues in one instance may not work the same way the next time, the authors have written this chapter to introduce ideas that improve hiring inclusivity. The chapter will give suggestions for the pre-search phase, the search process, and the post-hiring transition to help others with the journey toward more inclusivity in the hiring process.

Statement of Problem

Hiring practices in academic libraries have needed retooling for many years. Over their tenures in academic libraries, the authors have been involved with forming and serving on search committees, in addition to experiencing this process in the candidate role; therefore, they are well aware of what an exhausting process it can be for all parties involved. Additionally, hiring practices are perpetuating a certain demographic in academic libraries: the most recent American Library Association statistics note that the profession is overwhelmingly female (81 percent) and white (86.7 percent).[1] According to the National Center for Education Statistics for 2022, the student population at UNM identifies as 58.4 percent female and 29.5 percent white, and at UCA as 61 percent female and 66.2 percent white.[2] Granular demographic data is unavailable for the employees of the authors' libraries, but using the national means, the staff at their libraries are not representative of the student body. Through outdated processes at both institutions, great candidates that would more accurately represent the student body and community demographics are likely overlooked or lost.

The pandemic provided the opportunity to rethink approaches to the hiring process, in part because we were unable to bring candidates to campus for interviews.[3] Larger societal conversations on the topics of equity and justice were also occurring at the same time. This combination of forces provided the impetus to implement some DBIE practices that we had been discussing. The profession, as well as individual libraries, would do well to keep up the momentum with substantive changes to make the process more equitable in terms of gender and race as a starting point. Hiring and retention need to be a focus for the long term. Practices need to be more inclusive and accessible in order to bring forward the best candidate for the job and to keep them.

Literature Review

The literature related to hiring practices in academic libraries in North America is rather limited. Practical advice on techniques and activities during each phase of a search to increase DBIE was of particular interest, but little was found. However, as far back as 1997, John Lehner was calling for a critique of the job selection process.[4] He emphasized looking outside the higher education arena and to the body of human resources and psychology literature for hiring practices with greater validity. The authors found, as did Koury, Semenza, and Shropshire, that while there is a commitment to increasing DBIE in most academic libraries, there is a lack of "mechanisms that can assist with their implementation."[5] However, this is changing, most notably with the Association of College and Research Libraries publication *Implementing Excellence in Diversity, Equity, and Inclusion: A Handbook for Academic Libraries*.[6] Additionally, Harper covers a wide range of recruitment and retention strategies for diversity in the profession and the workplace.[7]

Recommendations from these sources include professional development on cultural intelligence; encouragement for employees at all levels of an organization to take personal responsibility and action; and organizational change strategies. This chapter will help fill the gap in the current literature.

There is further work on this topic at the level of higher education more broadly, but the publications are still surprisingly sparse. In her article "8 Ways for Search Committees to Be Inclusive" in *The Chronicle of Higher Education*, Crutchfield focuses on search committees, from creating and first meetings, where the committee builds "rapport and trust," to training, and through the interviews.[8] Emphasis on the hiring committee is supported in O'Meara, Culpepper, and Templeton's literature review on faculty hiring from 1985 to 2018, where they found empirical evidence regarding bias in four areas of faculty hiring: search committees and job advertisements; recruitment activities; the evaluation of candidate applications; and the campus visits and final decisions.[9] Bombaci and Pejchar investigate the efficacy of requiring faculty candidates, particularly those in the STEM (science, technology, engineering, and math) fields, to provide diversity statements with their application documents. Their survey of academic personnel with diversity responsibilities found that most support including diversity statements as a way to advance DBIE on campus; however, doing so is somewhat problematic. Firstly, it may seem inequitable for those candidates who may be equity-minded but have not had an opportunity or been encouraged to act on this in previous employment situations; secondly, search committees have not been adequately trained in evaluating diversity statements; and finally, requiring a diversity statement could set up a false expectation if the institution is not as committed to DBIE as the candidate might expect.[10] Until there is more literature on academic library workforce recruitment strategies for diversity, it will be important to turn to colleagues in other areas of the academy.

Discussion

As mentioned earlier, the authors have over thirty years of combined experience in academic library administration; over the years, there have been many conversations between the two regarding implementing DBIE initiatives in their respective institutions. Examples of ways to emphasize DBIE shared here have been gleaned from the authors' experiences at their current institutions, UNM and UCA, as well as their previous institutions, such as USCA.

UNM is a designated Hispanic-Serving Institution. As part of supporting diversity and inclusiveness efforts at the institutional level, UNM's Office of the Provost has begun to provide required training for faculty search committees, search chairs, and hiring officers that incorporates a lens of DBIE throughout the various phases of the faculty search process, from creation of the job ad, to reviewing candidates, to the on-campus interview, and through the hiring process. Two online training courses are required, one centering on an exploration of unconscious bias, particularly as it relates to evaluating candidates during recruitment, and the other on suggested practices for search committees.

The first training describes how unconscious bias influences recruitment, hiring, and advancement decisions. It identifies myths and stereotypes about people of color, women, people with disabilities, and people with minority sexual orientations and gender identities, and then presents strategies for challenging those biases. This training also recognizes that even people who are experienced and knowledgeable, who want very much not to discriminate against members of any identity group, can still cling unknowingly to stereotypes and myths, leading to decisions affected by unconscious bias. The focus is to name the issues, begin conversations, and provide support to move forward confronting biases.[11]

Recommendations for search committees from the second training include ensuring the membership is diverse, using posting language about the university as people-friendly in its policies, and being as general as possible with position qualification requirements to encourage a broader applicant pool. Each committee member is encouraged before the first committee meeting to consider the possibility that they or other committee members feel resistant to diversity initiatives and, accordingly, could be resistant to one of the committee's primary purposes. Addressing this issue is identified as one of the chair's responsibilities by, among other things, delineating the diversity initiative scope and goals, establishing an atmosphere free of shame, and separating process from personal character. Other recommended steps to counter diversity resistance in the hiring process include encouraging the committee members to speak up about observed bias, taking sufficient time for the search to be diversity-competent, setting ground rules, reaching a collective understanding of the term *diversity* and the goals of the search, connecting diversity to the institution's educational mission, and articulating and ranking the search criteria in order of priority to be able to complete the job before the search begins. Committees are advised to advertise broadly, including in diversity job boards and publications, to fill the pipeline by constantly keeping an eye out for promising candidates, and to build networks to access diverse talent. Practicing three interviewing skills for diversity-competent candidate interviews is supported: establishing rapport by searching for similarities, eliciting details about a candidate's experiences to reveal strengths that may not otherwise appear to the evaluators, and including tasks in the interview process that will give the search committee a more accurate, less biased picture of each candidate's skills and strengths.[12] The overall university goal is not to just meet minimum standards for diversity, but to exceed them as a nationwide role model of a majority-minority institution in a majority-minority state.

UCA also has a very strong DBIE program. UCA has a *Minority Recruitment and Retention Plan* that applies to students, faculty, and staff.[13] The Office of Institutional Diversity and Inclusion developed and delivered a series around inclusive hiring that included programs on "Crafting Inclusive Position Descriptions" and the "Inclusive Interview Process," as well as a program on "Retaining Historically Underrepresented

Colleagues." These were recorded and may be viewed at any time, such as whenever a search committee is formed.[14] This office also hosts affinity groups for faculty and staff. Additionally, the Torreyson Library has its own Diversity, Inclusion, and Accessibility Committee that is charged with reviewing all aspects of the library through this lens and fostering an inclusive environment.[15]

Diversity, belonging, inclusiveness, accessibility, and equity need to be the focus at every stage of the hiring process for a search to be most effective. The hiring process can be divided into three stages, pre-search, search, and post-hiring, with the first two stages offering the best opportunity to open the process and attract more diverse candidates. Setting the stage with the first two sections helps to cast a wide net and remove barriers in order to recruit a more diverse workforce; however, the post-hiring is essential to maintaining diversity in the organization. What follows is the culmination of conversations between the authors, the literature review, and practices initiated to improve various stages of the hiring process at each respective institution.

Pre-Search Phase

The pre-search stage of the process involves creating a job description, identifying search committee members, and creating questions to ask candidates. While Lehner was not focused on DBIE, his critique provides a useful jumping-off point beginning with the job analysis, through the search committee process, and ending with the interview and selection.[16] Every hiring process should begin with a thorough job analysis and the creation of a job description that accurately describes the duties, using inclusive language that is free of bias. The advertisement is the first important opportunity to clearly articulate the organization's culture and expectations about support for DBIE.

Application requirements should be deliberatively interrogated. Reconsider minimum and preferred qualifications with intention. The Commonwealth of Pennsylvania recently eliminated the four-year degree as a requirement for approximately 92 percent of state government jobs, instead focusing on skills and experience as the main qualifications during the hiring process.[17] Items such as cover letters and letters of recommendation have been found to increase barriers for some candidates and are now required less. Diversity statements could be useful but are not universally supported. If diversity statements are requested, ensure the committee has been instructed on how to evaluate such statements. As mentioned earlier, simply requiring diversity statements may misrepresent the level of commitment of the institution. At the writing of this chapter, some colleges and universities are dropping this requirement due to political backlash, and at least one court case is in the works.[18]

Positions should be advertised broadly. Venues where positions are posted should extend beyond traditional outlets to target publications, groups, and associations that reach a wider demographic, such as the job boards for Blacks in Higher Education, Hispanics in

Higher Education, or the American Library Association affiliates and caucuses. Identify appropriate recruitment channels and provide adequate budgetary support.

The following are examples of how the authors' institutions are implementing changes in their pre-search processes. At the most basic level of the hiring process, the librarians at USCA's Gregg-Graniteville Library began a recent search by examining the standard statement on equal employment required by the Equal Employment Opportunity Commission that the university's Human Resources Office added to all job advertisements. The concern was that it was not welcoming and inclusive enough, so the librarians edited it to be so. Also, the library worked with the then new director of diversity initiatives at the university to identify online job posting sites that would appeal to more diverse candidates. Additionally, the library stopped requiring letters of reference to accompany the application and require only the names and contact information for references. Similarly, at the UCA Torreyson library, administrators are experimenting with no longer requiring cover letters for staff applications; though it is doubtful this will ever be the case for faculty applications, the thought is that removing cover letters for staff leads to a more equitable experience for potential candidates.

In addition, the UNM University Libraries have added some other quick-to-implement changes to position postings to increase opportunities for candidates. They now deliberatively interrogate a position's required minimum qualifications, including degree. Significantly, for some positions, a terminal degree in a subject-related field can be substituted for the traditional MLS or MLIS. This move can be contentious with certain positions (e.g., associate dean) but is less controversial with others (e.g., open educational resources librarian) that are not seen as traditionally anchored in librarianship. The important thing is for the search committee to have the conversation every time a posting is created. Job postings at the UNM University Libraries also now include the minimum salary or a salary range, depending on the classification of the position. Postings are written with a focus on inclusiveness, supported by the library's new strategic plan. Also, librarians were leaders in the effort for campus to create the university's land acknowledgement statement, and the University Libraries were among the first units to include it in job postings.

Another component of the pre-search stage is formation of the search committee. Depending on the institution, the search committee may be formed prior to the advertisement being placed so they may be involved in constructing the job description and advertisement; such is the case at UNM. However, at other institutions the search committee may not be formed until after the posting is in place; for example, at UCA, the search committee does not convene until after a job is posted. Either way, the composition of the search committee itself should be carefully considered. If a lens of inclusiveness across a variety of dimensions is used in selecting the membership, the committee will have representation from marginalized, underrecognized, and disenfranchised populations, as well as from different employee categories—for example, tenured and non-tenure-eligible faculty, staff, and students. Once the search committee is formed, appropriate training can take place, including an initial meeting where they are given their charge and made aware of their responsibilities in carrying out a fair and inclusive search. Providing members with inclusiveness and unconscious bias training prior to the review of applicants is also essential.

In his meeting to charge the search committee, the dean of the UNM University Libraries reminds the search committee of the commitment to inclusiveness, including the intentionality of selecting minimum and preferred requirements, including degrees. USCA, at the institutional level, began requiring any employee, faculty or staff, who might be called upon to serve on a search committee to participate in unconscious bias training for search committee members. Additionally, while it is imperative that all search committee members carry out their duties with an eye toward diversity and inclusion, each search committee is required to designate one member as the diversity compliance member, who ensures that the process and review of candidates is equitable. At UCA, the director attends the initial meeting of the search committee to issue the charge; to remind the committee of the importance of equitable treatment of candidates and each other; and to suggest selected viewings from the university's inclusive hiring series, mentioned above.

Search Process

Once the committee has formed, the search process can begin. Having structure for this group is one major way to improve the hiring process. Creating a scoring system for evaluating résumés that is rooted in the job requirements is a great place to start. Using a rubric provides a clear and standardized way to evaluate candidates, making it easier to assess objectively and consistently, as well as increasing transparency and fairness in evaluation. Using the position description is the best method for creating the rubric (see figure 4.1). At the minimum, the rubric will be used to determine if the candidate has the required and preferred qualifications; from there, it can be more nuanced to determine the degree to which the candidate shows aptitude in the various aspects of the job requirements.

The search stage of the process includes the steps of reviewing application materials, identifying candidates to interview, the interview itself, and evaluating candidates. Consider conducting blind reviews of the candidates' application materials. Studies have shown bias can occur when candidate names are unfamiliar to search committee members, or when institutions where candidates received degrees are less well-known. Blind reviews are intended to focus on more objective information by redacting identifying details such as names and addresses of individuals, schools attended, or employing institutions. Neither author's home institution currently conducts blind reviews of materials. However, one author had a recent interview experience as a candidate where they were asked to keep their camera off during a Zoom interview and to remove pronouns from their displayed name so as to reduce potential bias in the committee. The questions for interviews, which are devised by the search committee and asked of candidates, should be consistent, avoid biased language, and focus on job-related experiences and skills.

Rubric for Library Faculty Candidate

CANDIDATE 1

Required Qualifications:
- Accredited Master's Degree in LIS   Yes   No   Other:
   - Other Example: Master's Degree or Doctorate in the relevant area,
- Proof of eligibility to work in the US   Yes   No   Other:

Preferred Qualifications (should match position description):

Qualification	0	1	2	3	Notes
Supervisory Experience	No evidence	Student assistant supervision only	1-2 Years of staff supervision	3+Years of staff supervision or faculty supervision	
Teaching Experience	No evidence	1-2 Years common classes (No prep)	3+ Years common classes or 1-2 years original classes	3+ Years common classes and 1-2 Years original classes	
Library Experience	No evidence	Worked as a student employee	1-2 Years as staff	3+ Years as staff or 1-2 years as faculty	
Additional Earned Degrees	No evidence	Some work toward, but not completed	Additional Bachelor's or Master's Degree	Doctorate	
Additional Funding	No evidence	Grants applied but not awarded	1-2 Grants received	3+ Grants received	
Scholarship	No evidence	1-2 Publications or presentations, not peer-reviewed	1-2 Peer-reviewed publications or presentations	3+ Peer-reviewed publications and presentations	
Totals					Total Score:

Figure 4.1. Sample rubric for library faculty candidate evaluation

When it comes to the logistics of the day, schedule interviews with a pace that takes into consideration the needs of candidates. Include plenty of breaks to allow candidates to maintain energy and personal comfort.

At the institutions where the authors serve or have served, a standardized list of interview questions is created for each advertised position. Additionally, at most of the institutions, a standardized rubric to score candidates in relation to the requirements and position description has been de rigueur. During initial online screening interviews at the UNM University Libraries, the questions are sent to candidates shortly before the interview, usually one hour ahead of time, so they can better prepare answers or have a copy to refer to during the meeting, offering another modality beyond hearing the question. During on-campus interviews, questions are sent to candidates a day ahead of time. Meetings are offered in different formats, including in-person, online, or hybrid, depending on the group involved, to allow participation by a larger number of library employees.

Post-Hiring Phase

Being inclusive does not stop once the offer has been made and accepted. Once the new employee starts, they must be adequately onboarded, which is considered the post-hiring phase. Graybill and colleagues recognize that orientation is not the same as onboarding. Onboarding is the process through which new employees are integrated into the organization, and it is essential to continue with inclusivity. New employees must be met with a welcoming attitude to enhance their sense of belonging.[19] Currently, the Torreyson Library at UCA has a task force in place to examine its onboarding experience with an eye toward belonging. The aim of this task force is to create a consistent approach to onboarding complete with policies and procedures that will not only orient new faculty and staff to the library but also will do so with an open and welcoming mindset. As the task force is still in process, the outcome is undetermined at this time. However, as stated before, the scrutinizing of procedures with a DBIE lens is necessary at every phase including the post-hire. The UNM University Libraries use a mentoring system as part of the onboarding process for new faculty. A mentor is selected by the new faculty member; that person's role is to help the new person learn about the institution and meet peers, and to support the faculty member through the tenure process.

Future Changes

While the steps already taken at each institution are moving in the right direction, there are other changes both authors would like to implement, particularly in the pre-search and search phases. Detailing information about the position and search, whether on a web page, by video, or in a live session, would help potential applicants better understand the library environment and the role and expectations of the position. Another step is to create a listing of potential advertising spaces that reach groups in broader demographics, including free or low-cost options such as social media and professional networks.

An additional area of potential positive impact is the on-campus interview. Current faculty interviews require an entire day of on-campus meetings. The authors feel strongly that it is important for candidates to visit in person to get a sense of the campus and library environment and to meet their potential colleagues. However, an entire day is grueling for all parties involved, candidate and search committee members alike. The authors are considering reworking the schedule to break the visit up into an afternoon of meetings followed by final meetings the next morning, allowing for an overnight break. This would potentially make for a longer stay for the candidate and increased expenses for the library. A longer stay may be a barrier for candidates, and added costs would impact the library budget. However, the interview experience stands to be significantly improved. The authors have also reviewed the specific meetings needed and are considering shifting those that are simply information sharing to e-mail or video call ahead of time; for example, an explanation of benefits, including various insurance options, retirement contributions, and so on. The candidate could then follow up at the in-person interview if there are questions.

No matter the progress made, there are still limitations to what can be done to make the search process successful. There are factors in place in hiring and retaining employees that cannot always be overcome, particularly for academics (e.g., location, salary, and the two-body/two-professional-careers problem). Until DBIE is the default mindset, attention will need to be deliberately called to the areas that need improvement.

Conclusion

The search process in academic libraries is ripe for improvements to enhance DBIE in faculty hiring. This listing of recommended practices is far from comprehensive but is a good place to start to make a difference:

- Set institutional expectations around valuing diversity and provide training to support all staff in recognizing and combating unconscious bias.
- Pre-search
    - Select search committee members with an eye toward diversity; provide diversity training; set ground rules.
    - Carefully review the job description; interrogate required minimum qualifications; use inclusive language.
    - Advertise broadly; purposefully target venues that reach diverse audiences; detail information about the position and search on a web page, by video, or in a live session to provide a better understanding of the library environment and the position.

- Provide an information session for potential candidates to learn more about the position, institution, and community.
- Search
  - Use a standard set of interview questions; create a rubric to evaluate responses; share interview questions ahead of time.
  - Consider blind review of applications and possibly blind screening interviews.
  - Practice interviewing skills: establish rapport, elicit details to reveal strengths, and include tasks that give a more accurate, less biased picture of candidate skills and strengths.
  - Plan the interviews with a reasonable pace; provide breaks.
- Post-hiring
  - Establish an onboarding process that effectively integrates new employees into the organization.

Final Takeaways

An ideal future would reveal that including DBIE efforts at the beginning of and throughout the hiring process could set the stage for meaningful change at the organization, improving diversity knowledge, understanding, and behaviors among all staff. These steps would also provide long-term help in hiring and retaining candidates of marginalized, underrecognized, and disenfranchised populations; ease the burden of searches on all participants; and most importantly, result in excellent candidates and hires that more accurately reflect student bodies and communities:

- Understand that every person is starting from a different point in their understanding of their own unconscious biases and support of DBIE principles.
- The roots run deep on this problem. Until LIS graduates are more diverse, it will be hard to get diverse candidate pools.
- Review processes and iterate for continuous improvement.

Notes

1. Kathy Rosa and Kelsey Henke, *2017 ALA Demographic Study* (Chicago: ALA Office of Research and Statistics, 2017), https://alair.ala.org/server/api/core/bitstreams/4d524ee4-a0ed-49d0-8162-741ca5a834b2/content.
2. National Center for Education Statistics home page, accessed June 2, 2023, https://nces.ed.gov/.
3. Brandon Q. Rogers et al., "COVID-19 and OD: Unplanned Disruption and the Opportunity for Planned Talent Development," *Organization Development Review* 53, no. 2 (Spring 2021): 61–67; Grady Blue Brazelton and Brianna K. Becker, "Hiring Student Services Professionals Virtually," *New Directions for Student Services* 2021, no. 176 (2021): 47–55, https://doi.org/10.1002/ss.20405.

4. John A. Lehner, "Reconsidering the Personnel Selection Practices of Academic Libraries," *Journal of Academic Librarianship* 23, no. 3 (May 1997): 199–204, https://doi.org/10.1016/S0099-1333(97)90099-9.
5. Regina Koury, Jenny Lynne Semenza, and Sandra Shropshire, "A Survey of Diversity and Inclusiveness Initiatives at Carnegie Doctoral Research Institutions Libraries," *Library Management* 40, no. 1/2 (2019): 30, https://doi.org/10.1108/LM-10-2017-0117.
6. Corliss Lee et al., *Implementing Excellence in Diversity, Equity, and Inclusion* (Chicago: Association of College and Research Libraries, 2022), EBSCOhost.
7. Lindsey M. Harper, "Recruitment and Retention Strategies of LIS Students and Professionals from Underrepresented Groups in the United States," *Library Management* 41, no. 2/3 (2020): 67–77, https://doi.org/10.1108/LM-07-2019-0044.
8. Amy Crutchfield, "8 Ways for Search Committees to Be Inclusive," *Chronicle of Higher Education*, March 28, 2022, https://www.chronicle.com/article/8-ways-for-search-committees-to-be-inclusive.
9. KerryAnn O'Meara, Dawn Culpepper, and Lindsey L. Templeton, "Nudging toward Diversity: Applying Behavioral Design to Faculty Hiring," *Review of Educational Research* 90, no. 3 (June 2020): 311–48, https://doi.org/10.3102/0034654320914742.
10. Sara P. Bombaci and Liba Pejchar, "Advancing Equity in Faculty Hiring with Diversity Statements," *BioScience* 72, no. 4 (April 2022): 365–71, https://doi.org/10.1093/biosci/biab136.
11. Vector Solutions, "The Influence of Unconscious Bias in Decision Making (Faculty Search Committees)," accessed June 2, 2023, https://unm-nm.safecolleges.com/training/home (requires login).
12. Vector Solutions, "Skills for Members of Search Committees (Faculty Search Committees)," accessed June 2, 2023, https://unm-nm.safecolleges.com/training/home (requires login).
13. University of Central Arkansas, *Minority Recruitment and Retention Plan: 2022-2026* (Conway: University of Central Arkansas, June 30, 2021), https://uca.edu/about/files/2021/06/uca_mrr_plan_2022-2026.pdf.
14. University of Central Arkansas, "Diversity—Inclusive Hiring Series," accessed June 1, 2023, https://uca.edu/diversity/inclusive-hiring-series/.
15. University of Central Arkansas, "Torreyson Library Bylaws," revised April 20, 2022, https://uca.edu/library/files/2022/05/Torreyson-Library-Bylaws-revised-4_20_2022.pdf.
16. Lehner, "Reconsidering the Personnel Selection Practices."
17. Marley Parish, "In His First Executive Order, Shapiro Removes Degree Requirement for Thousands of State Jobs," *Pennsylvania Capital-Star* (blog), January 18, 2023, https://www.penncapital-star.com/government-politics/in-his-first-executive-order-shapiro-removes-degree-requirement-for-thousands-of-state-jobs/.
18. Adrienne Lu, "Are Diversity Statements Illegal?" *Chronicle of Higher Education*, May 31, 2023, https://www.chronicle.com/article/are-diversity-statements-illegal.
19. Jolie O. Graybill et al., "Employee Onboarding: Identification of Best Practices in ACRL Libraries," *Library Management* 34, no. 3 (2013): 200–18, https://doi.org/10.1108/01435121311310897.

Bibliography

Bombaci, Sara P., and Liba Pejchar. "Advancing Equity in Faculty Hiring with Diversity Statements." *BioScience* 72, no. 4 (April 2022): 365–71. https://doi.org/10.1093/biosci/biab136.
Brazelton, Grady Blue, and Brianna K. Becker. "Hiring Student Services Professionals Virtually." *New Directions for Student Services* 2021, no. 176 (2021): 47–55. https://doi.org/10.1002/ss.20405.
Crutchfield, Amy. "8 Ways for Search Committees to Be Inclusive." *Chronicle of Higher Education*, March 28, 2022, https://www.chronicle.com/article/8-ways-for-search-committees-to-be-inclusive.
Graybill, Jolie O., Maria Taesil Hudson Carpenter, Jerome Offord, Mary Piorun, and Gary Shaffer. "Employee Onboarding: Identification of Best Practices in ACRL Libraries." *Library Management* 34, no. 3 (2013): 200–18. https://doi.org/10.1108/01435121311310897.
Harper, Lindsey M. "Recruitment and Retention Strategies of LIS Students and Professionals from Underrepresented Groups in the United States." *Library Management* 41, no. 2/3 (2020): 67–77. https://doi.org/10.1108/LM-07-2019-0044.
"Inclusive Hiring Series — Diversity." Accessed June 1, 2023. https://uca.edu/diversity/inclusive-hiring-series/.
Kathy Rosa and Kelsey Henke, *2017 ALA Demographic Study* (Chicago: ALA Office of Research and Statistics, 2017), https://alair.ala.org/server/api/core/bitstreams/4d524ee4-a0ed-49d0-8162-741ca5a834b2/content.
Koury, Regina, Jenny Lynne Semenza, and Sandra Shropshire. "A Survey of Diversity and Inclusiveness Initiatives at Carnegie Doctoral Research Institutions Libraries." *Library Management* 40, no. 1/2 (2019): 23–33. https://doi.org/10.1108/LM-10-2017-0117.

Lee, Corliss, Brian Lym, Tatiana Bryant, Jonathan Cain, and Kenneth Schlesinger. *Implementing Excellence in Diversity, Equity, and Inclusion: A Handbook for Academic Libraries.* Chicago: Association of College and Research Libraries, 2022. EBSCOhost.

Lehner, John A. "Reconsidering the Personnel Selection Practices of Academic Libraries." *Journal of Academic Librarianship* 23, no. 3 (May 1997): 199–204. https://doi.org/10.1016/S0099-1333(97)90099-9.

Lu, Adrienne. "Are Diversity Statements Illegal?" *Chronicle of Higher Education*, May 31, 2023. https://www.chronicle.com/article/are-diversity-statements-illegal.

National Center for Education Statistics home page. Accessed June 2, 2023. https://nces.ed.gov/.

O'Meara, KerryAnn, Dawn Culpepper, and Lindsey L. Templeton. "Nudging toward Diversity: Applying Behavioral Design to Faculty Hiring." *Review of Educational Research* 90, no. 3 (June 2020): 311–48. https://doi.org/10.3102/0034654320914742.

Parish, Marley. "In His First Executive Order, Shapiro Removes Degree Requirement for Thousands of State Jobs." *Pennsylvania Capital-Star* (blog), January 18, 2023. https://www.penncapital-star.com/government-politics/in-his-first-executive-order-shapiro-removes-degree-requirement-for-thousands-of-state-jobs/.

Rogers, Brandon Q., Kelly I. O'Brien, David L. Harkins, Thomas G. Mitchell, and Deborah A. O'Neil. "COVID-19 and OD: Unplanned Disruption and the Opportunity for Planned Talent Development." *Organization Development Review* 53, no. 2 (Spring 2021): 61–67.

University of Central Arkansas. "Diversity—Inclusive Hiring Series." Accessed June 1, 2023. https://uca.edu/diversity/inclusive-hiring-series/.

———. *Minority Recruitment and Retention Plan: 2022–2026.* Conway: University of Central Arkansas, June 30, 2021. https://uca.edu/about/files/2021/06/uca_mrr_plan_2022-2026.pdf.

———. "Torreyson Library Bylaws." Rev. April 4, 2022. https://uca.edu/library/files/2022/05/Torreyson-Library-Bylaws-revised-4_20_2022.pdf.

Vector Solutions. "The Influence of Unconscious Bias in Decision Making (Faculty Search Committees)." Accessed June 2, 2023. https://unm-nm.safecolleges.com/training/home (requires login).

———. "Skills for Members of Search Committees (Faculty Search Committees)." Accessed June 2, 2023. https://unm-nm.safecolleges.com/training/home (requires login).

Onboarding and Training

CHAPTER 5

Paving the Way for Professional Success with an Onboarding Road Map

Joyce Garczynski

One of the most critical pieces to retaining newly hired library workers is integrating them into our organizations. Many workplaces, including libraries, are struggling to successfully communicate what new employees need to do to succeed in their new roles. This is problematic, because when employees feel their onboarding is insufficient, they are more likely to leave the organization, which ultimately impacts workplace initiatives, culture, and morale, as well as diversity, equity, and inclusion.

As a new middle manager in a midsize academic library launching a number of new services to address institutional priorities, I was especially interested in retaining new hires. In order to take the guesswork out of onboarding new library employees, I developed a road map document for each new employee in my department. This document outlines where we are with the projects the new employee will take over (the starting point), where we hope to go with each project (the destination), the time it should take to complete each task (the travel time), and what tasks the employee will need to accomplish in order to complete the project (the directions). I then discuss the road map with the new employee, and they provide feedback, which is incorporated into the final document. All of the employees who have been onboarded using this road map have reported it has been very helpful because they have clarity about what they should be working on.

This chapter's journey through the road map will begin with a discussion about the onboarding literature in libraries and other industries. Then I will focus on how the road map addresses the onboarding challenges many libraries face. Finally, I will discuss how the road map is constructed, shared with new employees, and assessed. This section will address how I balance the need for structure while avoiding being overly prescriptive and how I carefully invite the employee's feedback into the document to increase their buy-in.

Problem Definition

Onboarding is "the process that helps new employees learn the knowledge, skills, and behaviors they need to succeed in their new organizations."[1] *Onboarding* and *orientation* are often used synonymously, but they are distinct concepts.[2] While orientation usually lasts less than a week, includes introductory activities like completing benefits paperwork, and focuses primarily on "introducing new hires to the workplace," onboarding is a larger, months-long process that focuses on assimilating employees to "their new environment by exploring the organization's culture, mission, vision, values, and strategies."[3] Therefore, effective onboarding is critical to employee success and organizational well-being. Researchers have found when an organization successfully onboards its employees, workers experience a plethora of positive outcomes: they are more likely to be satisfied with their job, engaged with their work, and clear on their role in their organizations; have greater senses of self-efficacy and social acceptance among their colleagues; perform their job duties at a higher level; are more committed to the organization; and desire to remain at the organization longer.[4] The organizations that systematically onboard also reap benefits, including as much as 50 percent greater employee retention and 62 percent greater productivity compared to those organizations without onboarding programs.[5]

Unfortunately, though onboarding has the potential to positively impact workplaces, researchers have found many employees believe the programs at their organizations have fallen short. While the shift to remote work brought on by the COVID-19 pandemic certainly made onboarding more difficult, organizations were struggling to implement effective onboarding practices well before 2020. A 2017 CareerBuilder study found more than a third of employers lack a comprehensive and well-organized onboarding program, and employees have been impacted by this deficit.[6] According to Gallup, only 29 percent of new hires say they feel fully prepared and supported to excel in their new role after experiencing onboarding at their organization.[7] Similarly, one-third of new academic librarians reported their onboarding experience would have been more successful if their organizational leadership paid more attention to their programs.[8] This dissatisfaction means numerous library supervisors are faced with the challenge of determining how to create or improve their new employee onboarding programs so their employees and organizations can experience the benefits of successful onboarding.

Literature Review

Research suggests onboarding programs can be successful if they instill new employees with a sense of belonging.[9] From a psychological perspective, onboarding creates belonging when employees feel integrated into the organizational culture, feel connected with others in the organization, and are able to use their skills to add value to their workplace.[10] From mentorship programs to new employee retreats, organizational leaders have constructed innovative ways to foster belonging among new hires. While researchers have examined the effectiveness of these social components to onboarding, they have also begun to look at how organizations can successfully onboard employees through more routine communications such as task assignment and goal development. A series of recommended practices has emerged from this literature focusing on the timing, content, and mode of new employee role communications. These include planning onboarding communications for the first six months or even longer,[11] differentiating onboarding strategies based on role seniority,[12] incorporating a discussion of both job responsibilities and organizational culture and politics in onboarding,[13] developing a written onboarding plan that includes an outline of the new employee's goals and responsibilities,[14] and creating a checklist so new employees can observe their onboarding progression.[15]

With so many best practices focused on communicating job responsibilities, goals, and tasks, researchers and practitioners recommend branching out beyond the standardized HR orientation to add manager and supervisor involvement in the onboarding process. In their examination of the role that welcoming plays in the onboarding process, Cesário and Chambel argue managers play a significant role in preparing new hires to be effective employees through the information they share.[16] This is especially the case when it comes to onboarding employees who are working remotely. After interviewing three new library employees, Martyniuk, Moffatt, and Oswald encourage managers to consider that onboarding teleworking employees will require them to adapt or even develop custom programs centered on connecting new employees with their colleagues in a meaningful way.[17] Ultimately, as Sibisi and Kappers contend in *Harvard Business Review*, managers are the driving force behind whether a new hire's onboarding will be successful: "As a manager, it's your job to ensure each new employee's experience in the workplace is a positive one."[18]

Discussion

In 2021, Towson University leadership announced their aspiration to achieve the R2 Doctoral University with High Research Activity Carnegie Classification.[19] In order to facilitate the increase in research activity required to meet this goal and to fill staffing vacancies created by the COVID-19 pandemic, Towson University's Albert S. Cook Library established the Communication, Outreach, and Digital Scholarship (CODS) Department in 2022. As the assistant university librarian for communication and digital scholarship, I was the natural choice to lead CODS. I would supervise our data science librarian, assessment and analytics librarian, publishing and open scholarship librarian, research impact librarian, and marketing and development coordinator. Over the course of 2022, I onboarded the entire five-person department, and each new employee came in with unique onboarding needs. Three of the employees were new to Towson University, and two transferred into CODS from other library departments. Only one new employee was filling an existing role, while four new CODS employees came into brand new or substantially revised positions. Because each of these new roles would be critical for the library's ability to support Towson University's transition to R2 status, retaining these new employees was my paramount concern. Knowing that successful onboarding can establish role clarity, which enhances belonging and retention, I developed a tailored road map document for each new employee I onboarded.

Components

The new employee road map is a document detailing the major projects and job-related tasks that a new employee will work on during the first six to twelve months in their new position. Each road map document is made up of three sections: the introduction, the project outline, and the task listing. A template for creating a road map document with these sections is contained in figure 5.1.

The introduction launches the road map, beginning with a statement of welcome for the new employee. Even though it is just one word with an exclamation point, I wanted to start the road map document, and their position, with a greeting that would encourage a feeling of belonging and hopefully offset the sometimes daunting length of the document. Next, I provide an overview of the road map and what to expect as they make their way through the document. I explain that the road map will outline where we are with their position's main responsibilities (the starting point), where we plan to go with the position's main responsibilities (the destination), and how the new employee can help get us to the destination (the route). Finally, the introduction closes with a statement about how the new employee should use the document. This is where I emphasize the road map may not be inclusive of every single part of the new employee's duties, because there may be bumps in the road and detours as priorities shift; but it will give them an overview of how to get started in their new position.

The second section of the road map, the project outline, is the heart of the document. It details the projects the new employee will undertake, containing segments for major project responsibilities that are listed in the employee's job description, as well as for those projects the dean of University Libraries specifies as priorities for the new employee. For example, the road map for our data science librarian contained a segment focused on research data management because not only is that duty specified in the position description, but also the dean indicated she wanted our data science librarian to work on

Road map for [EMPLOYEE NAME]

Welcome! This document is a road map for getting started in your position as our [POSITION NAME]. It will outline where we are with [JOB ROLE] in our library, what our destination is, and how you can help get us to that destination.

This document may not be inclusive of everything you need to work on and how. There will likely be new things you learn along the way, and you may be detoured as priorities shift, but it will give you a sense of how to get started on your journey at [LIBRARY NAME].

[FIRST JOB-RELATED PROJECT]
- **Destination**: [Description of the end results of the first project that the employee will undertake and how that project relates to the organization's goals and objectives]
- **Travel Time**: [Explanation of how the employee will move toward the destination and how long it should take the employee to reach the destination]
- **Starting Point**: [Factually focused description of where the project or responsibility stands as the employee assumes their new role]
- **Route**: [Bulleted list of tasks the employee needs to complete to start the journey toward the destination]
- **Passengers**: [A list of partners and stakeholders that the new employee should work with to help them reach the destination]

[SECOND JOB RESPONSIBILITY]
- **Destination**: [Description of the end results of the second job responsibility that the employee will focus on and how their work relates to the organization's goals and objectives]
- **Travel Time**: [Explanation of how the employee will move toward the destination and how long it should take the employee to reach the destination]

[PROJECT THAT FALLS UNDER THAT RESPONSIBILITY]
- **Starting Point:** [Factually focused description of where the project or responsibility stands as the employee assumes their new role]
- **Route**: [Bulleted list of tasks the employee needs to complete to start the journey toward the destination]
- **Passengers**: [A list of partners and stakeholders that the new employee should work with to help them reach the destination]

Task List
- [First task listed under a route that the new employee needs to address first]
- [Second task listed under a route that the new employee needs to address first]
- [Third task listed under a route that the new employee needs to address first]
- [Fourth task listed under a route that the new employee needs to address first]

Figure 5.1. Onboarding road map template

implementing a data management plan tool as one of his first projects. It is important to note that for librarian positions, I include segments discussing scholarship and committee service in all road maps because they are included in our job descriptions. In some cases, the road map document for an employee will have subsegments detailing multiple specific projects that make up the umbrella segment. This was the case in the road map document for our marketing and development coordinator. The road map document for onboarding this position included a library events segment, because that is a major responsibility of the position, and the subsegments included details about upcoming events this position would be administering. Road map segments are ordered chronologically, with the projects or responsibilities the employee will need to address first at the top.

Each road map segment or subsegment in the project outline contains a bulleted list describing a destination, travel time, starting point, route, and passengers for the project. I intentionally replicate the order of steps the individual will use when traveling to their destination in my detailed lists. In the destination, I detail projects and describe their role in the library's larger strategic plan. For example, the road map for the publishing and open scholarship librarian contained a segment discussing the implementation of Open Journal Systems, an open-source journal publishing platform. The destination item for that segment included a general description of the faculty interest in the system and how the implementation of Open Journal Systems fits into our library's larger scholarly publishing goals. The purpose of this enumeration is to provide role clarity and sense of belonging by enabling the new employee to have an immediate sense of what they will need to do fulfill the responsibilities of their position and how their role contributes to the larger organization.

The next segment component is the travel time, which describes when and how quickly the employee should get to the destination. While the segments are placed on the road map in the order they need to be addressed, some job tasks need to be addressed promptly by the new employee, but ultimate completion will take months. The travel-time bullets on a road map communicate our expectations to the employee for when they will arrive at their destination.

The starting point describes the status of a project or job responsibility when the new employee assumes it. In the example above, the starting point details the status of Library Information Technology's configuration of the product, the creation of support documentation, and two potential journal projects involving this publishing software. For projects or responsibilities that have not yet begun, the road map will describe any related projects that may have led to the genesis of this new project. Also, some new employee responsibilities are coordinated by staff outside of the department, such as information literacy instruction and committee work. In those cases, I provide less detail in the starting point and encourage conversation between the new employee and the appropriate coordinator, who will have additional information.

The next project outline component is the route, which describes the tasks the employee will undertake to get to the destination. I try to avoid providing exact turn-by-turn directions here, but rather describe key landmark tasks that the employee should complete to move forward on the journey. I recognize each person has a unique way of working, and I want to provide the new employee with some autonomy to shape the projects they will work on as they learn more about the organization. As a result, many of the tasks in these road map segments center around the employee beginning conversations with others in the organization who are stakeholders on their projects. I also provide some context for why this task is included in the list. For example, the route tasks listed under the data management segment of our data science librarian's road map included meeting with the assistant university librarian (AUL) for Special Collections and University Archives. In this list item I provided contact information for the AUL and articulated the AUL's connection to data management, suggesting they have a conversation about the library's digital preservation program and data archiving capabilities. The next action steps after these conversations are not enumerated in the road map but are collaboratively constructed during subsequent regularly scheduled one-on-one meetings.

The final piece of each project outline segment is the list of passengers who are along for the ride as the employee undertakes this project or job responsibility. This is a listing of the stakeholders whom the new employee would expect to interact with as they collaborate on this work. The role each passenger plays is described in the route's tasks, so this list serves as a quick reference point for the new employee to ensure they are involving all stakeholders as they develop a project or program.

Each road map concludes with a task list. This list is made up of shorter versions of the tasks enumerated in the project outline. These tasks are arranged in chronological order with the ones the new employee needs to complete first listed first. Aligned with onboarding best practices, this task list can serve as a checklist for new employees to organize their time the first six months to a year in their new position.

Implementation

The process of creating a road map for a new employee begins with a meeting between the dean of University Libraries and myself about two or three weeks before the new employee's start date. We discuss the tasks or position description components the dean wishes the employee to prioritize and focus on in the first six months. I incorporate that feedback in drafting a road map document for the employee. It is important to note I include different levels of specificity in the document itself, depending on the new employee's role and their familiarity with the department, the library, and the university. For employees who are new to the library, I draft the road map document in consultation with the dean. For employees who are more familiar with our organization, I will draft an outline of a road map and meet with them to fill in the document together. In either case, just before the employee starts in their new position, I will e-mail them the road map document and set up a meeting invitation to discuss the document one or two days after they start. The reason for this timing is that anyone new to the university will spend their first day in a university orientation and will likely need some additional time to get the materials and supplies they need before they can get started on job duties. At the initial road map meeting, we will go through the segments in the road map's project outline, and I ask if they have questions about any of the tasks. Because the literature suggests onboarding should include some discussion of workplace culture and politics to be effective, I also use this initial meeting to be candid and verbally tell the employee about any potential challenges or roadblocks they are likely to encounter. I will then work with the employee to craft strategies for navigating those challenging situations. After that initial meeting, I hold regularly scheduled one-on-one meetings with the employee so they can share their progress and talk through next steps.

Assessment

It has been my experience that road map documents simplify the goal-setting and mandatory review processes for the employees I supervise. Towson University mandates every new employee undergo an interim review after six months. During this six-month review, the employee reports on the goals that had been set for them during their first six months and sets goals for the second six months of their position. Employees onboarded with a road map have expressed appreciation for having a document that made it easier for them to define and report on their goals. In addition, the dean of University Libraries meets independently with every new employee three months into their position, and the dean has reported to me that at least one new employee praised their road map for eliminating confusion about what they needed to work on during those initial few months.

Conclusions

Management and library researchers have found that successful onboarding results in positive outcomes for both the new employee and the organization; however, many workplaces, including libraries, struggle with onboarding employees in a meaningful way. In an effort to operationalize onboarding best practices as I welcomed five new employees into a new academic library department over the course of a year, I developed the road map document discussed above. Each tailored road map set goals for a new employee by outlining what tasks they will need to perform and what relationships they will need to build in the first six months to a year of their position in order to fulfill their job responsibilities. The document, coupled with an initial meeting to offer political and cultural context, has resulted in successful onboardings for my organization. Both library management and employees have praised the road map for its ability to provide employees with role clarity and its ability to streamline the mandatory review process. My hope is that the road map document process will be more widely adopted throughout my organization and by other libraries in the future. I can envision the road map could be adapted to a variety of onboarding situations, such as the creation of a new committee or the beginning of a large library-wide project. Leaders can do this by framing the road map to focus on the knowledge that needs to be transferred to the newcomers and incorporating the pathways to gaining that knowledge into the document. For example, a road map for a new committee member would include the completion of a committee project as a destination, and the other components would focus on how the new member is expected to contribute to completing the project. Whenever a library is beginning something new, whether it is the tenure of a new employee or a new project, setting goals and clarifying roles helps develop a sense of belonging, which increases the likelihood of success and retention. Thus, the creation and implementation of the onboarding road map document, which resulted in positive outcomes for Towson University's CODS department, has the potential to create these same benefits for numerous libraries and their employees.

Takeaways

After using the road map approach to onboard my entire department, the need for its consistent application across our entire organization became apparent. When there is a disparity in onboarding between employees in similar roles across a library, those differences can result in detrimental outcomes for the new hires and the larger organization. This includes festering resentment and even microaggressions between employees who experienced differential levels of support when they entered the organization. Employing a consistent and well-structured road map onboarding approach across the organization will provide libraries with the best chances for new employee success and retention.

Notes

1. Talya N. Bauer and Berrin Erdogan, "Organizational Socialization: The Effective Onboarding of New Employees," in *APA Handbook of Industrial and Organizational Psychology, Vol 3*, ed. Sheldon Zedeck (Washington, DC: American Psychological Association, 2011), 51.
2. Remone Robinson, "Understanding the Difference between Orientation and Onboarding," *SHRMBlog*, Society for Human Resource Management, September 27, 2022, https://blog.shrm.org/blog/understanding-the-different-between-orientation-and-onboarding (page discontinued).
3. Robinson, "Orientation and Onboarding."
4. Gallup, "How to Improve the Employee Experience," accessed January 6, 2023, https://www.gallup.com/workplace/323573/employee-experience-and-workplace-culture.aspx; Zibin Song et al., "Impact of Organizational Socialization Tactics on Newcomer Job Satisfaction and Engagement: Core Self-Evaluations as Moderators," *International Journal of Hospitality Management* 46 (April 2015): 186, https://doi.org/10.1016/j.ijhm.2015.02.006; Talya N. Bauer et al., "Newcomer Adjustment during Organizational Socialization: A Meta-analytic Review of Antecedents, Outcomes, and Methods," *Journal of Applied Psychology* 92, no. 3 (May 2007): 712, https://doi.org/10.1037/0021-9010.92.3.707.
5. Ron Carucci, "To Retain New Hires, Spend More Time Onboarding Them," *Harvard Business Review*, December 3, 2018, https://hbr.org/2018/12/to-retain-new-hires-spend-more-time-onboarding-them.

6. Adam Uzialko, "What Does Poor Onboarding Really Do to Your Team?" *Business News Daily*, upd. June 29, 2022, https://www.businessnewsdaily.com/9936-consequences-poor-onboarding.html (page content changed).
7. Gallup, "Employee Experience," 8.
8. Bruce Keisling and Melissa Laning, "We Are Happy to Be Here: The Onboarding Experience in Academic Libraries," *Journal of Library Administration* 56, no. 4 (May 2016): 388, https://doi.org/10.1080/01930826.2015.1105078.
9. Christian Harpelund, Morten T. Højberg, and Kasper U. Nielsen, *Onboarding* (Bingley, UK: Emerald Publishing, 2019), 49.
10. Harpelund, Højberg, and Nielsen, *Onboarding*, 50–51.
11. Howard J. Klein and Beth Polin, "Are Organizations Onboard with Best Practices Onboarding?" in *The Oxford Handbook of Organizational Socialization*, ed. Connie Wanberg (Oxford, UK: Oxford University Press, 2012), 267–86.
12. An Ju et al., "A Case Study of Onboarding in Software Teams: Tasks and Strategies," *Proceedings of the 43rd International Conference on Software Engineering* (ACM Conferences, May 22, 2021), 621, https://doi.org/10.1109/ICSE43902.2021.00063.
13. Jolie O. Graybill et al., "Employee Onboarding; Identification of Best Practices in ACRL Libraries." *Library Management* 34, no. 3 (2013): 211, https://doi.org/10.1108/01435121311310897.
14. Klein and Polin, "Are Organizations Onboard," 276.
15. Klein and Polin, "Are Organizations Onboard," 276; Graybill et al., "Employee Onboarding," 212.
16. Francisco Cesário and Maria José Chambel, "On-boarding New Employees: A Three-Component Perspective of Welcoming," *International Journal of Organizational Analysis* 27, no. 5 (2019): 1472, https://doi.org/.10.1108/IJOA-08-2018-1517.
17. Julia Martyniuk, Christine Moffatt, and Kevin Oswald, "Into the Unknown: Onboarding Early Career Professionals in a Remote Work Environment," *Partnership: The Canadian Journal of Library and Information Practice and Research* 16, no. 1 (2021), https://journal.lib.uoguelph.ca/index.php/perj/article/view/6451/6383.
18. Sinazo Sibisi and Gys Kappers, "Onboarding Can Make or Break a New Hire's Experience," *Harvard Business Review*, April 5, 2022, https://hbr.org/2022/04/onboarding-can-make-or-break-a-new-hires-experience.
19. Kim Schatzel, "A Great Time to Be a Tiger," Presidential Communications, Towson University, May 12, 2021, https://www.towson.edu/about/administration/president/communications/2021/st-academic-year-recap-2021.html (page discontinued).

Bibliography

Bauer, Talya N., and Berrin Erdogan. "Organizational Socialization: The Effective Onboarding of New Employees." In *APA Handbook of Industrial and Organizational Psychology, Vol 3: Maintaining, Expanding, and Contracting the Organization.*, edited by Sheldon Zedeck, 51–64. Washington, DC: American Psychological Association, 2011.

Bauer, Talya N., Todd Bodner, Berrin Erdogan, Donald M. Truxillo, and Jennifer S. Tucker. "Newcomer Adjustment during Organizational Socialization: A Meta-analytic Review of Antecedents, Outcomes, and Methods." *Journal of Applied Psychology* 92, no. 3 (May 2007): 707–21. https://doi.org/10.1037/0021-9010.92.3.707.

Carucci, Ron. "To Retain New Hires, Spend More Time Onboarding Them." *Harvard Business Review*, December 3, 2018. https://hbr.org/2018/12/to-retain-new-hires-spend-more-time-onboarding-them.

Cesário, Francisco, and Maria José Chambel. "On-boarding New Employees: A Three-Component Perspective of Welcoming." *International Journal of Organizational Analysis* 27, no. 5 (2019): 1465–79. https://doi.org/.10.1108/IJOA-08-2018-1517.

Gallup. "How to Improve the Employee Experience." Accessed January 6, 2023. https://www.gallup.com/workplace/323573/employee-experience-and-workplace-culture.aspx

Graybill, Jolie O., Maria Taesil Hudson Carpenter, Jerome Offord Jr., Mary Piorun, and Gary Shaffer. "Employee Onboarding; Identification of Best Practices in ACRL Libraries." *Library Management* 34, no. 3 (2013): 200–218. https://doi.org/10.1108/01435121311310897.

Harpelund, Christian, Morten T. Højberg, and Kasper U. Nielsen. *Onboarding: Getting New Hires off to a Flying Start*. Bingley, UK: Emerald Publishing, 2019.

Ju, An, Hitesh Sajnani, Scot Kelly, and Kim Herzig. "A Case Study of Onboarding in Software Teams: Tasks and Strategies." *Proceedings of the 43rd International Conference on Software Engineering*, ACM Conferences, May 22, 2021, 613–23. https://doi.org/10.1109/ICSE43902.2021.00063.

Keisling, Bruce, and Melissa Laning. "We Are Happy to Be Here: The Onboarding Experience in Academic Libraries." *Journal of Library Administration* 56, no. 4 (May 2016): 381–94. https://doi.org/10.1080/01930826.2015.1105078.

Klein, Howard J., and Beth Polin. "Are Organizations Onboard with Best Practices Onboarding?" In *The Oxford Handbook of Organizational Socialization*, edited by Connie Wanberg, 267–286. Oxford, UK: Oxford University Press, 2012.

Martyniuk, Julia, Christine Moffatt, and Kevin Oswald. "Into the Unknown: Onboarding Early Career Professionals in a Remote Work Environment." *Partnership: The Canadian Journal of Library and Information Practice and Research* 16, no. 1 (2021). https://journal.lib.uoguelph.ca/index.php/perj/article/view/6451/6383.

Robinson, Remone. "Understanding the Difference between Orientation and Onboarding," *SHRMBlog*, Society for Human Resource Management, September 27, 2022. https://blog.shrm.org/blog/understanding-the-different-between-orientation-and-onboarding (page discontinued).

Schatzel, Kim. "A Great Time to Be a Tiger." Presidential Communications, Towson University, May 12, 2021. https://www.towson.edu/about/administration/president/communications/2021/st-academic-year-recap-2021.html (page discontinued).

Sibisi, Sinazo, and Gys Kappers. "Onboarding Can Make or Break a New Hire's Experience." *Harvard Business Review*, April 5, 2022. https://hbr.org/2022/04/onboarding-can-make-or-break-a-new-hires-experience.

Song, Zibin, Kaye Chon, Geng Ding, and Cao Gu. "Impact of Organizational Socialization Tactics on Newcomer Job Satisfaction and Engagement: Core Self-Evaluations as Moderators." *International Journal of Hospitality Management* 46 (April 2015): 180–89. https://doi.org/10.1016/j.ijhm.2015.02.006.

Uzialko, Adam. "What Does Poor Onboarding Really Do to Your Team?" *Business News Daily*. Updated June 29, 2022, https://www.businessnewsdaily.com/9936-consequences-poor-onboarding.html (page content changed).

CHAPTER 6

Beyond Onboarding
Developing a Library Tenure Success Program

Kim Clarke

After three years of intense recruitment to fill a mix of vacant and newly created positions, the library administrators at the University of Calgary amassed the largest cohort of untenured academics in their history. This presented an opportunity to devise a new program that would enhance the assimilation of new academics in the institution, support them on their path to tenure, and assist them in developing a satisfying and successful career, which would also have a positive impact on staff retention.

The program was designed to supplement the existing research-related supports and onboarding activities that assist new librarians in learning their responsibilities and integrating into the workplace. All librarians at the university are guaranteed release time to focus on research and scholarly activities and are provided with an annual sum, called the Professional Employee Reimbursement fund, to expend on research activities, including purchasing technology, covering travel, or supporting other professional development costs. Other tenure supports were formerly provided on an informal basis, either when a librarian sought assistance from their supervisor or a tenured colleague or when this aid was voluntarily offered. The casual nature of this support caused tenure-track librarians to receive varying types and degrees of assistance and resulted in gaps, or even inaccuracies, in the information provided, depending on the tenured librarian's knowledge and experience. This could impact the librarian's tenure application, resulting in weak or poorly written tenure packages.

The lack of systemic supports needlessly caused the librarians significant stress and anxiety and could adversely affect their view of, and engagement with, the institution. The new program, called the Academic Success Program, formalized tenure supports, ensuring all tenure-track academics received the same supports and consistent information about the tenure process and expectations and providing each with personalized guidance on fulfilling these requirements. The administrator drew activities and supports from focused tenure programs offered at other libraries—mentoring programs, research committees, and peer tenure support groups—to create a more comprehensive library tenure support program. This chapter features a case study of the Academic Success Program, including lessons learned and best practices.

Problem Definition

Academic libraries invest considerable staff time and money into recruiting librarians.[1] Recruitment can be especially difficult for tenure-track positions, as many recent graduates and new academic librarians do not want to work at organizations where librarians have faculty status, according to the ACRL's Ad Hoc Task Force on Recruitment and Retention Issues.[2] To maximize their return on investment and reduce the frequency of recruitment to replace departing librarians, libraries have implemented onboarding programs designed to assist new employees with integrating into the workplace and laying the foundation for a long, engaged, productive, and satisfying career for employees.[3] Onboarding programs do not, however, adequately provide the assistance librarians require on their multiyear path to tenure. Tenure-focused and longer-term support programs are needed to assist faculty librarians in this endeavour. Wolfe states that without support "many early-career librarians are not reappointed, denied tenure, or become dropouts in the last year."[4]

Most libraries offer discreet forms of tenure assistance like research release time and travel funding,[5] which are helpful but are not enough. Librarians crave assistance in interpreting tenure requirements and understanding the expectations placed on them. They are seeking an environment where they can ask questions and receive tips and advice. Addressing "the ambiguity of the tenure process along with balancing daily job responsibilities" alone is very stressful for tenure-track librarians, according to Cameron, Pierce, and Conroy.[6] Indeed, their study found that the lack of support from the employer caused the tenure-track librarians more stress than the job itself.[7]

Some libraries have implemented more fulsome and longer-term tenure support systems to provide additional forms of assistance, such as mentoring programs, research committees, and peer tenure support groups. Each of these programs offers valuable, but different forms of support; mentoring programs do not normally offer the supports provided by research committees, for example. The danger in implementing only one of these programs is that it limits the types of support available to librarians, forcing those wanting additional assistance to seek it from their supervisor or colleagues, if they feel comfortable doing so. Only 44 percent of the tenure-track librarians in Vilz and Poremski's study were satisfied or highly satisfied with the tenure support offered by their institution.[8]

A solution is to create a more holistic program, combining aspects of mentoring programs, research committees, and tenure support groups. Implementing and promoting the program will benefit both the employee and employer—positively impacting the recruitment of quality applicants for tenure-track positions, alleviating the stress librarians experience on their path to tenure, and reducing staff turnover rates due to increased levels of commitment to their employer.

Literature Review

The *Oxford English Dictionary* defines *onboarding* as "the action or process of integrating a new employee into an organization."[9] Onboarding is a coordinated socialization process through which the employee discovers the expectations of their role and learns about the people, values, culture, and policies of the workplace, which allows them to become, and feel like, an effective member of the organization. While the onboarding process is an opportunity for the employer to introduce the newcomer to their local priorities, policies, and culture, there is significant consistency in the activities undertaken by the employers.

Socialization actions implemented throughout the employee's first week of work can help make the newcomer feel welcome and ease them into the workplace. Graybill and colleagues' review of onboarding documentation solicited from members of ACRL's Personnel Administrators and Staff Development Officers Discussion Group generated a long list of welcome activities utilized by libraries, including greeting new hires at the door, providing a gift bag, ensuring their office equipment is set up, scheduling a lunch with senior staff, and holding a welcome event to introduce them to colleagues.[10]

Discussions surrounding the expectations of position and the assessment process further ease the newcomer's transition into the workplace. Every library in Graybill and colleagues' study and 77 percent of the employers in Semenza, Harden, and Koury's study of libraries at Carnegie doctoral-research intensive institutions included these discussions in their onboarding.[11] Practical advice and insight from colleagues who previously held the new librarian's position or who have similar positions in the unit allow them to confidently begin undertaking their responsibilities. Similarly, all the libraries in Graybill and colleagues' study and 82 percent in Semenza, Harden, and Koury's study reviewed relevant university and library policies and procedures with employees during onboarding on subjects such as leaves, attendance, nondiscrimination, and safety and security.[12] In addition to this formal discussion, conducted by the supervisor or a human resources staff member, newcomers often learn the unwritten polices, practices, and rules, essentially "how things work around here,"[13] in conversations with their colleagues.

Ascertaining the norms, culture, and politics of the workplace accelerates new employees' acclimatization; however, gaining this knowledge can be challenging.[14] Graybill and colleagues explain that few libraries formally incorporate these matters in the onboarding process, because either "they are difficult to discuss or [they] are perceived as painting a negative picture."[15] They suggest that these topics might be better addressed informally through discussions with an assigned onboarding buddy,[16] other colleagues, or their supervisor when the topic arises. In fact, a majority of libraries (57 percent) in Semenza, Harden, and Koury's 2020 study indicated new librarians were introduced to the employers' norms through informal means, with only 22 percent utilizing formal processes to do so.[17]

Employers also benefit from the implementation of an onboarding program. Effective onboarding programs reduce the time it takes newcomers to integrate into their work environment and to become productive in their position.[18] Oud, after surveying new librarians on their adjustment to the workplace, stated that "long-term retention is affected in part by the experiences of new employees during transition and adjustment to their new workplace."[19] Increased staff retention results in a significant financial savings for the employer. Hall-Ellis asserts that "the total cost of replacing an employee can be as high as 150 percent of the annual salary after calculating lost productivity, recruiting expenses, retraining and time-to-productivity."[20] Staff retention ensures no gap in the provision of services to library patrons, which may be of primary importance to employers. Finally, the implementation of onboarding activities that help new employees assimilate in the workplace and be successful in their position "contributes to the organization's positive culture,"[21] which could affect staff retention in general.

While studies show that libraries discuss the expectations of position with new hires during onboarding, the literature is less clear on whether they discuss tenure and promotion and to what extent. Semenza, Harden, and Koury, the only study to date that directly inquired whether tenure and promotion expectations were discussed during onboarding, found that 65 percent of the libraries did so.[22] Graybill and colleagues identified three libraries whose onboarding documentation stated "faculty information" was discussed during onboarding, but it is unclear if that encompasses tenure requirements, and one discussed "promotion" with new employees.[23]

Even if the expectations of promotion and tenure are discussed, onboarding's relatively short time frame means that meaningful tenure supports cannot be offered through that program. While most studies acknowledge that onboarding begins when a job offer is extended, there is no agreement over the appropriate length for the program. Graybill and colleagues found the length of the libraries' onboarding programs ranged from one day to one year, stating that "most respondents identified having fewer than 30 days to devote to onboarding activities."[24] Authors recommend different lengths of time in their work, without necessarily referencing sources for their opinion. Hall-Ellis says the onboarding process ends after three to six months,[25] and Oud refers to an adjustment period of "six to nine months or more."[26] Even Graybill and colleagues state that onboarding "covers an employee's first year,"[27] which is more definitive than suggested by the libraries' onboarding documentation.

As librarians typically apply for tenure after six years of employment, tenure supports must continue after onboarding concludes. Many libraries offer discreet forms of research support to tenure-track librarians. In a 2013 survey of tenure-track academic librarians from across North America, Vilz and Poremski found that 45 percent of the respondents received off-campus release time and 18 percent received on-campus release time to focus on their research activities.[28] Ninety-seven percent of the librarians received funding for tenure-related activities, including travel funding to attend conferences or to conduct scholarly research.[29] More expansive, longer-term supports, in the form of mentoring programs, research committees, and peer tenure support groups, have also been implemented by libraries.

Many libraries have mentoring programs, since mentoring assists newcomers with their "acclimatization and peer networking and builds a needed foundation for enhanced professional development."[30] Mentoring programs can be expanded to take the tenure process into account, allowing mentors to guide mentees on interpreting the guidelines and provide tailored advice on how to meet the expectations. Mentoring programs can either be formal, where senior librarians are assigned as mentors to junior librarians, or informal, where the onus is on the junior librarian to find a mentor from among their colleagues. Forty percent of the libraries in Vilz and Poremski's survey had a formal mentoring program, with an additional 30 percent of the respondents finding a mentor on their own.[31] Neville and Henry's 2003 survey of academic libraries in Florida showed that 100 percent of libraries at doctoral-research institutions had a mentoring program, with 18 percent having a formal program and 82 percent an informal program.[32]

Research committees are less common than mentoring programs, with only 24 percent of doctoral-research libraries and 10 percent of all academic libraries in Florida having one, according to Neville and Henry.[33] Research committees seek to encourage and support librarians with their research endeavours through a variety of services. Tamera P. Lee explains that the Library Research Advisory Committee at Auburn University serves in "advisory roles as it provides guidance and leadership in facilitating research" by counselling, advising on, and reviewing research proposals, providing editorial guidance, offering research-related seminars and symposia, communicating information about research and writing opportunities, and purchasing technology to support librarians' research.[34] Mississippi State University's library research committee also offers research-related programs and informal discussions and communicates information about research and writing opportunities to librarians.[35] In addition, it provides mentoring support and editorial review services to individuals.[36]

Peer tenure support groups are designed to provide mutual support and assistance to its participants. According to Wilkinson, they allow participants a safe environment to "seek emotional support, discuss tenure-related experiences and anxieties, and to share and receive tips and strategies."[37] Some programs are also designed to assist participants to find collaborators and obtain feedback on their writing.[38] As with mentoring programs, these groups can be formal or informal. The formal tenure support group at Texas A&M University is led by cochairs elected for one-year terms.[39] Miller and Benefiel explain that the cochairs create the annual schedule of meeting topics selected from member suggestions, identify and invite presenters, and follow up on questions asked during meeting.[40] Twenty-six percent of the respondents in Vilz and Poremski's study indicated they had a tenure peer support group at their institution.[41]

The promotion and tenure program for librarians, archivists, and curators at the University of Calgary combines aspects of all three of these forms of tenure support systems and supplements the onboarding programming offered to new librarians, as discussed in the case study below.

Case Study

The University of Calgary (UCalgary) is a doctoral-research institution, according to the Carnegie Classification of Institutions of Higher Education,[42] with more than 26,000 undergraduate students and more than 6,000 graduate students, located in Calgary, Alberta, Canada. Libraries and Cultural Resources (LCR) is the administrative unit containing the libraries, archives, special collections, art museums, and university press at UCalgary. LCR is a member of the Association of Research Libraries and the Canadian Association of Research Libraries.

Librarians, archivists, and curators are academics at UCalgary and are covered by the same collective agreement as the teaching faculty members. UCalgary has a three-tier academic ranking system: assistant, associate, and full. Academics can be hired in tenure-track (continuing) or contract (sessional, limited term, or contingent) positions. The vast majority of LCR academics are tenured or in tenure-track positions.

While the tenure process our academics face is the same as teaching faculty, the criteria are unit-specific, developed by LCR's Academic Council. LCR academics are evaluated on their professional practice, research and scholarship, and service for promotion and tenure purposes. They are assessed on the quantity, quality, and impact of their performance of their day-to-day responsibilities for professional practice and of their scholarly activities for research and scholarship. Their committee work is assessed for service, in terms of the committees they are members of (faculty, university, professional, related industry, etc.) and the roles they play on the committees. More credit is given for leadership, invited, or elected roles and for membership on national or international committees. Academics spend between 75 percent and 90 percent of their time on their professional practice activities and 5 percent to 20 percent of their time on each of the other two categories. The academic negotiates these percentages annually with their supervisor.

New tenure-track academics and faculty are hired in either four- or five-year renewable appointments, with the first step in the tenure process occurring in fall of the penultimate year of their appointment. At that time, academics can elect either to seek renewal of position or to apply for promotion and tenure. Renewal of position provides the academic with an additional two years to apply for tenure.

The Onboarding Program

New academics are presented with a multifaceted onboarding process at UCalgary. Human Resources (HR), which is a centralized unit, is responsible for the university-wide onboarding. HR created an onboarding portal with a checklist outlining some basic business requirements the newcomers must undertake either before or shortly after their arrival, such as creating an IT account, setting up payroll details, obtaining their ID card, and completing online mandatory health and safety courses. Their socialization with the institution also begins at this phase with the UBegin Program, a series of online courses containing information about the university.

The academics are not left to maneuver through university onboarding alone, as LCR's administration coordinator supports them through this process. She also meets with them on their first day of work to discuss outstanding matters on their checklist, provide an overview of their benefits, and discuss LCR onboarding topics, including information about e-mail discussion lists and communication and productivity systems.

The academic's supervisor is responsible for the unit- and position-specific onboarding. Much of the first few days are spent on socialization activities, including familiarizing them with their office, providing a tour of the library, introducing them to colleagues, and holding a welcome event. The supervisor discusses their responsibilities and the expectations of their position, but also has colleagues participate in the newcomer's training. The academic is provided with a list of individuals they meet over the next month to learn about computer products, processes, and systems that will impact their job. Tenure and promotion are rarely discussed during onboarding unless the academic raises the topic.

The Academic Success Program

With the arrival of a new vice-provost (LCR's university librarian–equivalent position) in 2018, the administration filled several vacant positions and created new academic positions to expand the volume and enhance the quality of LCR's services. In early 2021, LCR had the largest number of untenured academics at one time in its history to that date (seventeen; the number increased to twenty-two the following year). As the director of staff engagement, I was tasked with devising a program to assist the untenured academics in developing a successful career and, ultimately, obtaining tenure. The program was meant to supplement, not supplant, the tenure assistance provided by supervisors and would focus on their research and scholarship and service activities. It would also ensure all academics received the same level of assistance and type of supports on their tenure journey. I called the resulting program the Academic Success Program (ASP).

My initial focus was on advanced onboarding matters designed to assist the academics in their adjustment to the university and to deepen their understanding of the expectations they face. Through a series of group meetings, I supplemented HR's general introduction to the university by discussing key individuals, committees, and offices whose work impacts the academic side of the institution. Guest speakers, including a member of the Faculty Association's board and our representative to the General Faculties Council (GFC), were invited to discuss the role of these entities and how they impact librarians, archivists, and curators. Other group meetings were aimed at helping them understand the academic processes of renewal, promotion, tenure, and merit. These discussions revolved around the three documents that govern academic careers at UCalgary (our collective agreement, the GFC *Academic Staff Criteria and Processes Handbook*, and LCR's *Handbook for Academic Staff*). The role of each document and relationship between them was discussed before we analyzed the procedures, requirements, and timeline for each of the individual academic processes.

Socialization was another onboarding outcome that continued through the ASP. Simple actions, such as reviewing LCR's complicated nine-page organizational chart and arranging tours of our facilities, which are spread around the city, were undertaken at our first meeting to provide the academics with a more complete picture of the structure and how the units fit together. The participants of the program quickly formed a cohort, recognizing that they faced the same pressures, and providing encouragement and emotional support to one another. They also acted as scholarship sounding boards and found collaborators among the group.

I provided personalized career and tenure support and advice to each academic through regular one-on-one meetings. Our first meeting began with a review of the contents and format of their curriculum vitae (CV), with suggestions on how they could revise it to be more effective. Common themes in the CV review include new graduates using a résumé rather than a CV, failing to describe their responsibilities and accomplishments in previous roles, omitting service roles, and formatting matters to increase the document's impact. The renewal and tenure requirements were discussed and applied to their CV, focusing on their scholarship and service activities. We discussed the type of scholarly activities they could undertake, identified potential conferences and journals they could present at or publish in, brainstormed topics they could focus on, named potential collaborators, and determined professional associations and groups they could join for future service opportunities. The knowledge I gained through these meetings allowed me to forward scholarly calls for articles, book chapters, conference presentations, and service opportunities to them—sometimes to the entire group, but often to individuals based on their role or their expressed interests. Subsequent meetings, held every three or four months, allowed me to obtain a progress report from the new faculty member, with the remainder of the meeting spent discussing any issues or questions they had.

Recognizing that some ASP participants were hesitant to undertake, or maybe even fearful, of undertaking, research or scholarly projects, I created a research committee with the training and development librarian and a PhD librarian who is a very experienced researcher. Our series of research sessions, open to all LCR academics, covered topics from a list generated by soliciting our colleagues. The topics included generating research ideas, preparing a poster presentation, using voice projection techniques in your presentations, best practices for collaborating, and the peer review process from the perspective of the author, reviewer, and journal editor.

The final component of the ASP is the document review service. This service began at our first individual meeting with me advising them how to make their CV more impactful. The significant review work, however, is performed for the academics seeking renewal, promotion, and tenure. Librarians often volunteer to read their colleagues' tenure packages, but that review is usually fairly cursory, with them pointing out grammatical errors, typos, and lapsed trains of thought. The tenure package review conducted through the ASP is much more thorough, involving a combination of the work performed by a peer reviewer and an editor.

The ASP initially operates parallel to the regular onboarding program but continues long after onboarding ends. New academics join the ASP immediately upon arriving at LCR: the program is discussed during onboarding, and I send them a welcome e-mail when they arrive. They remain in the ASP until they obtain official notice that they were granted tenure.

Over the past two academic years, ten ASP members successfully sought renewal, promotion and/or tenure. Three academics had their contract renewed, six received tenure and promotion from the rank of assistant to associate, and an associate librarian obtained tenure. The ASP program continues to thrive, with nineteen members as of the time of writing.

Conclusions

Reflecting on the past two years of the ASP's operations revealed multiple lessons learned and best practices that may be useful to others considering a similar tenure support program.

Lessons Learned

- The ASP has, unexpectedly, become a recruitment tool. The program is discussed during academic interviews, either in response to the candidate's question about the tenure process or raised by the committee chair, often during the informal lunch discussion, to illustrate the type and level of support they will receive if they join LCR.
- While we anticipated the affirmative impact the ASP would have on the untenured academics and their perception of LCR, we had not considered the positive effect it would have on the tenured academics. The creation of the program generated goodwill with this group, as it demonstrated that the senior administrators are concerned about their academic staff members and are willing to

invest in their career development. Including tenured academics in some ASP activities, such as the research sessions, inviting them to hear our guest speakers, and offering to review their applications for promotion to full librarian enhanced their positive feelings.

- Our tenured academics welcome the chance to participate in the program, agreeing to be guest speakers, presenting at research sessions, and serving as mentors during my leave. Their participation in the program strengthens links and increases the sense of collegiality between the tenured and untenured academics.

- The eagerness the members of the program displayed in acting on the advice they received in our first meeting was somewhat of a surprise. At my first check-in meeting with each of them, approximately three months after our initial meeting, every untenured academic had acted on the development plan we discussed. They had submitted conference presentations, written a book review, joined professional associations, and sought service opportunities, among other actions. While I expected some of them to do this, I had not expected all of them to. This was one of the most rewarding experiences in my career.

- A separate plan for how to cover the materials discussed in the group sessions for academics hired after the initial round of group sessions was required. A new librarian arrived three months into the ASP, starting the week of our third group session. I considered three options when faced with this scenario: to review the group session presentations with each individual as they arrive, to wait until there were at least two new academics before meeting with them, or to convert the presentation into a video that they could watch on their own. I immediately disregarded the last option as it ran counter to my desire to create a relationship with the academics. I chose the second option as it allowed the academics to meet other members of the group, supporting their socialization into LCR. I kept the first option as backup to be used if there was a significant time lag without another academic being hired, which has not happened to date.

- There is no "one size fits all" approach to how to structure and administer the program. The ASP was wholly administered by one individual when it was initially created. A different structure was utilized during the administrator's leave, however, with multiple tenured academics assuming different roles in the program.

- The tenure package review process takes a significant amount of time, on both the reviewer's and applicant's parts. Developing and adhering to a mutually agreed-to work schedule is critical, especially if the time extends over the summer months when either or both parties will want to take vacation. Be realistic when determining the length of time each component of the package will take to draft, review, and edit. Start with the end date and work backward to identify the drop-dead date when the academic must begin writing their tenure package.

Best Practices

- Good communication between the ASP administrator and the supervisors is critical to the success of the program. To maintain good relations with the supervisors, ensure they understand the program is meant to supplement, not replace, the advice and support they provide their academics. Learn how they interpret the criteria they will be applying in their evaluation of the academics to allow for the provision of consistent information and advice. The administrator should speak to the supervisor in a timely manner if there are any concerns that an academic's lack of productivity may impact their ability to obtain renewal or tenure, rather than letting them be unpleasantly surprised later.
- If multiple people are administering the program, they should work as a team and discuss matters, asking for the others' opinions to ensure the provision of consistent and accurate information.
- Consider allowing contract librarians to participate in the program. Their inclusion may cause the librarian to feel more strongly supported by the administration, potentially resulting in them becoming more engaged and productive. Their participation will provide them with a deeper understanding of the requirements of a tenure-track position, which, along with the support received through the program, may increase their confidence in their ability to be successful in that type of role.
- Cast a wide net for topics for the group meetings. The sessions can address any topic of interest to the plurality of the group, or any topic that supervisors believe would benefit their development. Ask tenured colleagues to think back to what they would have liked to know at that stage of their career. Do not hesitate to cover some very practical issues, such as how to complete an expense reimbursement form or tips on using the performance annual review platform.

Onboarding lays a foundation upon which librarians can build a satisfying, meaningful, and successful career with their employer, which will only be strengthened through the provision of tenure supports. Libraries must establish supports beyond onboarding to provide systematic assistance to librarians on their path to tenure. Employers can gather aspects of mentoring, research committees, and peer tenure support groups to create a more comprehensive tenure support program that meets the various needs of their librarians. The multifaceted academic success program implemented at UCalgary is a model that can be adapted to fit other institutions' needs and operational structures, for the benefit of both employee and employer.

Notes

1. Jolie O. Graybill et al., "Employee Onboarding Identification of Best Practices in ACRL Libraries," *Library Management* 34, no. 3 (2013), 201, https://doi.org/10.1108/01435121311310897.
2. Association of College and Research Libraries, Ad Hoc Task Force on Recruitment and Retention Issues, *Recruitment, Retention, and Restructuring: Human Resources in Academic Libraries* (Chicago: American Library Association, 2002), 19.
3. Graybill et al., "Employee Onboarding Identification of Best Practices in ACRL Libraries," 211.
4. Judith Ann Wolfe, "Navigating the Gate Keepers: A Mixed Method Study of Early Career Librarians in the Tenure Process," (PhD diss., University of Nebraska, 2012), 3, https://digitalcommons.unl.edu/dissertations/AAI3504005/.
5. Amy J. Vilz and Molly Dahl Poremski, "Perceptions of Support Systems for Tenure-Track Librarians," College and Undergraduate Libraries 22, no. 1 (Jan-Mar 2015), 155–56, https://doi.org/10.1080/10691316.2014.924845.
6. Laura Cameron, Stephanie Pierce, and Julia Conroy, "Occupational Stress Measures of Tenure-Track Librarians," *Journal of Librarianship and Information Studies* 53, no 4 (2021), 552, https://doi.org/10.1177/0961000620967736.
7. Cameron, Pierce, and Conroy, 555.
8. Vilz and Poremski, "Perceptions of Support Systems for Tenure-Track Librarians," 159.
9. *Oxford English Dictionary Online*, s.v. "Onboarding," accessed May 8, 2023, https://www-oed-com.ezproxy.lib.ucalgary.ca/view/Entry/85201761?redirectedFrom=onboarding.
10. Graybill et al., "Employee Onboarding Identification of Best Practices in ACRL Libraries," 211 and 218.
11. Graybill et al., 207; Jenny Lynne Semenza, Tania Harden, and Regina Koury, "Survey on Onboarding Practices in Carnegie Research Institutions," *Library Management* 42, no. 1/2 (2021), 112, https://doi.org/10.1108/LM-10-2020-0148.
12. Graybill et al., 208; Semenza, Harden, and Koury, 112.
13. Joanne Oud, "Adjusting to the Workplace: Transitions Faced by New Academic Librarians," *College and Research Libraries* (May 2008), 264, https://doi.org/10.5860/crl.69.3.252.
14. Oud, 260 and 264.
15. Graybill et al., "Employee Onboarding Identification of Best Practices in ACRL Libraries," 211.
16. Graybill et al., 211.
17. Semenza, Harden, and Koury, "Survey on Onboarding Practices in Carnegie Research Institutions," 112.
18. Sylvia D. Hall-Ellis, "Onboarding to Improve Library Retention and Productivity," *The Bottom Line: Managing Library Finances* 27, no. 4 (2014), 139, https://doi.org/10.1108/BL-10-2014-0026.
19. Oud, "Adjusting to the Workplace," 252.
20. Hall-Ellis, "Onboarding to Improve Library Retention and Productivity," 139.
21. Hall-Ellis, 138.
22. Semenza, Harden, and Koury, "Survey on Onboarding Practices in Carnegie Research Institutions," 112.
23. Graybill et al., "Employee Onboarding Identification of Best Practices in ACRL Libraries," 210 and 218.
24. Graybill et al., 207 and 211.
25. Hall-Ellis, "Onboarding to Improve Library Retention and Productivity," 139.
26. Oud, "Adjusting to the Workplace," 265.
27. Graybill et al., "Employee Onboarding Identification of Best Practices in ACRL Libraries," 201.
28. Vilz and Poremski, "Perceptions of Support Systems for Tenure-Track Librarians," 155.
29. Vilz and Poremski, 156.
30. Nikhat Ghouse and Jennifer Church-Duran, "And Mentoring for All: The KU Libraries' Experience," *portal: Libraries and the Academy* 8, no. 4 (2008), 375, https://doi.org/10.1353/pla.0.0022.
31. Vilz and Poremski, "Perceptions of Support Systems for Tenure-Track Librarians," 157.
32. Tina M. Neville and Deborah B. Henry, "Support for Research and Service in Florida Academic Libraries," *Journal of Academic Librarianship* 33, no. 1 (January 2007), 84, https://doi.org/10.1016/j.acalib.2006.06.003.
33. Neville and Henry, 84.
34. Tamera P. Lee, "The Library Research Committee: It Has the Money and the Time." *Journal of Academic Librarianship* 21, no. 2 (March 1995), 112, https://doi.org/10.1016/0099-1333(95)90123-X.
35. Deborah Lee, "Mentoring the Untenured Librarian: The Research Committee." *College and Research Libraries News* 66, no. 10 (November 2005), 711, https://doi.org/10.5860/crln.66.10.7522.
36. Deborah Lee, 711.

37. Zara Wilkinson, "Rock Around the (Tenure) Clock: Research Strategies for New Academic Librarians," *New Library World* 114, no. 1/2 (2013), 61, https://doi.org/10.1108/03074801311291965.
38. Wilkinson, 61.
39. Jennifer P. Miller and Candace R. Benefiel, "Academic Librarians and the Pursuit of Tenure: The Support Group as a Strategy for Success," *College and Research Libraries* 59, no. 3 (May 1998), 262, https://doi.org/10.5860/crl.59.3.260.
40. Miller and Benefiel, 262.
41. Vilz and Poremski, "Perceptions of Support Systems for Tenure-Track Librarians," 157.
42. "Carnegie Classification of Institutions of Higher Education." Carnegie Classification of Institutions of Higher Education, accessed October 25, 2024, https://carnegieclassifications.acenet.edu/.

Bibliography

Association of College and Research Libraries, Ad Hoc Task Force on Recruitment and Retention Issues. *Recruitment, Retention, and Restructuring: Human Resources in Academic Libraries*. White paper. Chicago: American Library Association, 2002.
Cameron, Laura, Stephanie Pierce, and Julia Conroy. "Occupational Stress Measures of Tenure-Track Librarians." *Journal of Librarianship and Information Studies* 53, no 4 (2021): 551–58. https://doi.org/10.1177/0961000620967736.
Ghouse, Nikhat, and Jennifer Church-Duran. "And Mentoring for All: The KU Libraries' Experience." *portal: Libraries and the Academy* 8, no. 4 (2008): 373–86. https://doi.org/10.1353/pla.0.0022.
Graybill, Jolie O., Maria Taesil Hudson Carpenter, Jerome Offord Jr., Mary Piorun, and Gary Shaffer. "Employee Onboarding Identification of Best Practices in ACRL Libraries." *Library Management* 34, no. 3 (2013): 200–18. https://doi.org/10.1108/01435121311310897.
Hall-Ellis, Sylvia D. "Onboarding to Improve Library Retention and Productivity." *The Bottom Line: Managing Library Finances* 27, no. 4 (2014): 138–41. https://doi.org/10.1108/BL-10-2014-0026.
Lee, Deborah. "Mentoring the Untenured Librarian: The Research Committee." *College and Research Libraries News* 66, no. 10 (November 2005): 711–24. https://doi.org/10.5860/crln.66.10.7522.
Lee, Tamera P. "The Library Research Committee: It Has the Money and the Time." *Journal of Academic Librarianship* 21, no. 2 (March 1995): 111–15. https://doi.org/10.1016/0099-1333(95)90123-X.
Miller, Jennifer P., and Candace R. Benefiel. "Academic Librarians and the Pursuit of Tenure: The Support Group as a Strategy for Success." *College and Research Libraries* 59, no. 3 (May 1998): 260–65. https://doi.org/10.5860/crl.59.3.260.
Neville, Tina M., and Deborah B. Henry. "Support for Research and Service in Florida Academic Libraries." *Journal of Academic Librarianship* 33, no. 1 (January 2007): 76–93. https://doi.org/10.1016/j.acalib.2006.06.003.
Oud, Joanne. "Adjusting to the Workplace: Transitions Faced by New Academic Librarians." *College and Research Libraries* 69, no. 3 (May 2008): 252–66. https://doi.org/10.5860/crl.69.3.252.
Semenza, Jenny Lynne, and Tania Harden. "Survey on Onboarding Practices in Carnegie Research Institutions." *Library Management* 42, no. 1/2 (2021): 109–18. https://doi.org/10.1108/LM-10-2020-0148.
Vilz, Amy J., and Molly Dahl Poremski. "Perceptions of Support Systems for Tenure-Track Librarians." *College and Undergraduate Libraries* 22, no. 2, (Apr–Jun 2015): 149–66. https://doi.org/10.1080/10691316.2014.924845.
Wilkinson, Zara. "Rock Around the (Tenure) Clock: Research Strategies for New Academic Librarians." *New Library World* 114, no. 1/2 (2013): 54–66. https://doi.org/10.1108/03074801311291965.
Wolfe, Judith Ann. "Navigating the Gate Keepers: A Mixed Method Study of Early Career Librarians in the Tenure Process." PhD diss., University of Nebraska, 2012. https://digitalcommons.unl.edu/dissertations/AAI3504005/.

CHAPTER 7

Continuous Professional Development for Academic Library Employees

Lisa Kallman Hopkins

Creating an effective and stimulating culture of continuous professional development can be a powerful tool for recruiting and retaining academic library workers, while at the same time ensuring the library is providing relevant, cutting-edge services to library users. Professional development in libraries is by no means a new concept—even a glancing survey of the literature reveals thousands of articles, chapters, and dissertations, stretching back into the 1950s. The literature illustrates the ways that libraries have offered and promoted professional development strategies with a focus on meeting the needs of library users. Those educational opportunities continue to thrive, with evolving methodology, venues, and content available for professional growth for academic library employees.

Recently the literature has revealed increasing emphasis on the ways professional development opportunities impact the workplace itself, leading to changes in how an organization's administrative support for its learning culture is communicated and promoted to current and future employees. In her opening address for the Sixth World Conference on Continuing Professional Development and Workplace Learning nearly two decades ago, Ann Ritchie called out the need for heightened, continuous workplace learning, both formal programs and informal, along with everyday opportunities, in a profession that is "reinventing itself" to adapt to a quickly changing world.[1] The technology explosion since then, and the fundamental need for library employees to expand their knowledge and skills to stay current, demands "continuous learning in order to [renew] the expertise and skills needed to assist patrons in this information age."[2]

What Is Continuous Professional Development?

The *Cambridge Business English Dictionary* defines professional development as "training that is given to managers and people working in professions to increase their knowledge and skills."[3] Continuous professional education, likewise, is the "systematic method of learning that leads to growth and improvement in professional abilities"[4] and functions to "fill in the knowledge gaps between formal education and the needs of the professional practice."[5] In libraries, particularly academic libraries, it is imperative that all staff be given the intellectual tools they need to serve library users in myriad ways: hardware questions (e.g., how to operate scanners and web-based printers), software questions (e.g., learning management systems, Microsoft Word, and other student-facing programs), digital literacy, bibliographic instruction, data services, and online searching, to name a few. Library workers also crave personally enriching opportunities, such as training in diversity, equity, and inclusion;[6] coaching and mentoring; teamwork and morale building; interpersonal, written, and oral communication; time management and organization; decision-making and empowerment; and leadership guidance.[7]

Benefits of Continuous Professional Development

Library administrators that integrate professional development expectations into the job descriptions, responsibilities, and time allocations of professional staff guarantee the following: they address the inevitable ever-widening knowledge gaps that staff experience between skills learned during formal education and those required to stay abreast of current technology and trends;[8] and they succeed in creating a workplace in which engaged staff members experience job satisfaction and personal growth.[9] There have been many studies demonstrating that staff training and professional development boosts productivity and enhances job performance, positively influencing job satisfaction and job retention.[10] Majid advises that continuous professional development activities play a "crucial role in maintaining professional competence, which is necessary for the very survival of libraries."[11] This is echoed by Shonhe, who observed that without employees "engaged in continuous education, learning organizations such as libraries may not be able to meet the demands of the 21st century information seekers and may be rendered irrelevant."[12] Further, demonstrating that the library is staffed with informed, current, and competent professionals sends a message that the library is acting responsibly and can shepherd the university community expertly into the future.[13]

In addition to allowing library staff to keep up with the rapidly changing environments and compensating for the gaps in preprofessional education, professional development provides library employees the tools necessary for their work, which include "intellectual capacity, emotional engagement, and thought."[14] This requires adeptness in enhanced communication, conflict resolution, outreach, and collaboration—skills developed through the commitment of engaging in lifelong learning and continuous professional development, not simply in day-to-day experience or even one-off trainings.[15]

While the benefit for the academic library itself of having its staff participate in educational opportunities is clear, library administrators are responsible for "fostering an environment conducive to learning"[16] and should examine the extrinsic and intrinsic motivations that would compel staff members to engage in professional development. In their recent study, Rehman, Majeed, and Ganaie found that keeping up to date with changes in librarianship, meeting the demands of their current job, and attaining personal satisfaction were the top three motivational factors in librarians' pursuit of professional development. The study confirmed that librarians are more sensitive to intrinsic motivation—such as cultivating expertise, providing user service, cooperation, job satisfaction, job motivation, higher self-esteem, and the satisfaction that comes from mastering skills and knowledge—than extrinsic motivation, which consists of higher pay, improved employability, promotions, and role mobility.[17]

Despite the importance of intrinsic motivation, personal sense of accomplishment will go only so far if there is no recognition or further incentive. Managerial support must also include job performance feedback, opportunities to develop and strengthen new skills, and advocacy on behalf of employees in terms of career goals and compensation.[18] Administrators can help identify appropriate opportunities as a result of both understanding the library's needs and knowing their staffs' interests and strengths.[19] To combat financial obstacles and demonstrate the institution's commitment, Shahzad and colleagues observe that the existence of a separate allocation in the library budget for professional development encourages library employees to attend conferences and other learning opportunities.[20] It probably does not surprise anyone that lack of time is the most consistently articulated barrier to professional development participation, surpassing lack of managerial and financial support.[21] It is an unfortunate irony that with the increasing pressure to keep up with rocketing technology and do more with shrinking budgets, information professionals find themselves struggling to fulfill their assigned responsibilities with no time to accomplish the very training that would alleviate some of that pressure.

Clearly, library administrators must create a culture of and opportunities for continuous professional development for all library employees. Communication about expectations, opportunities, and support must be present at every level and throughout every stage of employment for the academic library to thrive and become a vibrant campus center. Although it may be daunting to contemplate, there are ample resources and guidelines available to support the establishment of such a professional development program.

Resources for Developing Continuous Professional Development Programs

International Federation of Library Associations and Institutions—IFLA Guidelines for Continuing Professional Development: Principles and Best Practices

One such resource is the *IFLA Guidelines for Continuing Professional Development: Principles and Best Practices*,[22] an invaluable publication for both individual library professionals and library administrators, which assigns appropriate responsibility and best practices to individuals and organizations. Namely, it is the individual's responsibility to pursue "ongoing learning" to address known knowledge gaps and prepare for potential future responsibilities in order to both "support the employing organization's goals for excellent service" and to "further one's own career development, and ultimately to contribute to profession-wide growth and improvement."[23] Likewise, the guidelines explicitly lay out the library employer's responsibility to demonstrate support and commitment to staff professional development. New assignments, compensation, or promotion should reward an employee's pursuit of professional learning. Employers should also provide "access to a broad range of learning opportunities, both formal and informal, which follow best practices for continuing education design and delivery."[24] Specifically, employers should earmark a minimum of 0.5 percent to 1.0 percent of institutional budget for professional development, and approximately 10 percent of work hours should be "provided to professionals for attendance at workshops, conferences, in-service training, and other educational activities, as well as for informal learning projects, including professional association and publishing work."[25]

The *IFLA Guidelines for Continuing Professional Development* is an indispensable resource for library administrators seeking to create or enhance a professional development program and for librarians either beginning their career path or pursuing professional growth. It dedicates a chapter of principles and best practices to each role, including the learner, the employer, and the educating organizations. For example, the chapter on the learner includes the principle, rationale, best practices, instructions for self-assessment, performance appraisal, examination of competency gaps, creating a personal learning plan, and current position preeminence (recognizing that the individual "seeks learning needed for present responsibilities before preparing for new position).[26] The chapter on the employer adds sections on serving as the overseer for staff development, employees' needs assessment, learning opportunities, staff progress documentation, identifying budget and work time provisions, and then evaluating the programs. The appendix provides a list of continuing education guidelines, the Competency Index for the Library Field published online by Web Junction, and examples of learning resources.

Professional Development Methodologies

The options for providing professional development are as varied as the content: formal and informal, free and paid, in-house and external, self-taught and instructor-led, individual and group learning, structured and self-directed, and so on (figure 7.1). Auster and Chan defined formal professional development activities as courses and workshops offered by in-house staff, educational institutions, or professional associations, and informal professional development activities as implicit processes that occur during participation in real-life contexts such as engaging in discussions with colleagues, participating in e-mail discussion lists, reading professional literature, and pursuing "self-directed projects."[27]

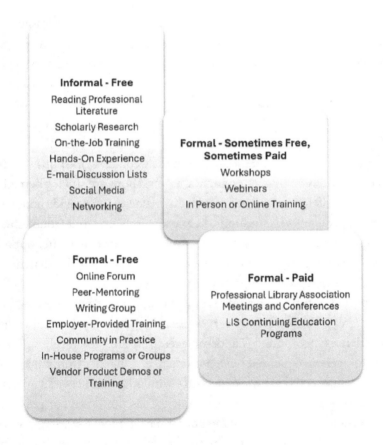

Figure 7.1. Professional Development Types

In practice, however, the lines between formal and informal activities blur. For example, while attending a conference, in person or virtually, individuals will attend numerous formal workshops and information sessions, but they will also engage in informal activities such as networking with colleagues from other institutions and vendors.

Fuhr examined librarian preference for data services training and noted the top means of training, from most important to least, were (1) learning by doing (trial and error); (2) self-directed learning; (3) attending workshops or bootcamps; (4) communities of practice; (5) mentorship with a library peer; (6) online courses; (7) attending conferences; (8) mentorship with research or other faculty (nonlibrary staff); and (9) attending webinars. It is interesting to note that the top two initiatives, on-the-job or hands-on learning and self-directed learning, cost no money but do involve a "considerable investment in time and need for support from supervisors."[28] In other words, all training costs—whether it is time, money, or managerial support. It is worthwhile to keep that in mind when analyzing the efficiency, effectiveness, and overall worth of professional development opportunities. Following is a look at some of the most common methods of professional development, starting with those Fuhr claims are the preferred means of learning.

Self-directed learning and learning by doing. Preparing a talk for a professional meeting or conference, scholarly writing for publication, or preparing and teaching a course are intense, self-directed, highly focused opportunities to expand one's knowledge about a particular topic. Reading literature to gain knowledge is a very common means of autodidactic training.[29] Similarly, spending time playing with a new library system, database, website, or program to gain hands-on experience with technology can keep librarians and library staff ahead of the curve—as long as their administration is forgiving of the occasional catastrophe. (It might be a good idea to explore sandbox options where one can try things in a protected environment.)

Workshops and courses. Differentiated from the webinar, workshops are often held in person and often last more than an hour. Many workshops are single-themed, offered in conjunction with conferences as preconference workshops and provide hands-on practice with experts who can answer questions, help problem-solve, and troubleshoot issues.[30] Workshops not only remedy gaps in knowledge, but they also often offer opportunities to build relationships and grow support systems.[31] Courses are formal instructional sessions that can be offered virtually or in person, either asynchronously or live, and often span a prescribed period of time. In a study examining a formal course designed to enhance information literacy, Namaganda observed that the most valuable and transformative learning experiences incorporate "hands-on exercises, substantial content, collaborative inquiry, peer-to-peer dialogue, and reflective practice."[32] In other words, taking full advantage of the opportunity to share the experience with other learners and an instructor.

Communities of practice and writing groups. The community of practice model is based on a conceptual framework that includes three interactive elements: domain (interest, expertise, or commitment shared by the group); practice (work or norms for that work, often tied to a profession); and community (network for sharing and discussing information where the group interacts, helps, and learns from each other.)[33] Unlike a mentorship program, which usually features a one-to-one pairing of the mentor and the mentee, the community of practice model allows for a more diverse group of individuals to come together with a common goal. Communities of practice may arise out of a desire to collaborate across departmental lines, incorporate support from senior faculty, create a space to "safely develop innovative ideas," and focus on the career goals of each member therein.[34] Henrich and Attebury created a community of practice in their library at the University of Idaho, and from that experience urge the following best practices: appoint a facilitator or secretary to ensure regular meetings, consistent note taking, and momentum; establish a sense of community; ensure there is always interest in a topic; and include a structured portion in every meeting.[35] Writing groups, reading groups, or discussion groups can function similarly to communities of practice by creating long-term, consistent, highly interactive groups of varying formality. These groups support research and scholarly output through encouraging discussion and scholarship review and by creating a forum for ideas; they create a microworld of intersection and knowledge exchange.[36]

Mentorships/mentoring programs. Mentorship and mentorship programs are common methods of workplace learning, as can be seen from their prominence in the literature. Harker and colleagues attest to the benefits for mentored protégés, including "professional skill development, scholarly productivity, networking, professional confidence, career advancement, improved job satisfaction, and reduced stress."[37] In a study among New England academic librarians, Freedman cites the top three self-reported benefits of a mentorship program: (1) the exchange of career-related advice and support (65.5 percent); (2) long-lasting professional relationships tied with role modeling (43.6 percent); and (3) providing resources and opportunities (41.8 percent).[38] Freedman cautions that for a mentorship program to be successful, the following must be in place: mentors must not be supervisors, members must have the ability to opt in without being forced into a mentorship, and there must be clearly articulated goals, guidelines, and assessments. With those guardrails in place, the mentoring program can provide support for navigating the tenure or promotion process, as well as scholarly publishing, to name a few critical pathways to success.[39]

The Colorado State University Libraries implemented a mentorship program as a strategy for retention in addition to supporting librarians going through the tenure process. Level and Mach state the formation of the program resulted in "improved communication among all faculty regarding the tenure process… [and] the formation of new cross-departmental partnerships."[40] Their advice:

- Gain administrative support and be flexible, allowing the group's structure to change as needed.
- Invite tenured faculty to be part of the learning process.

- Create open discussion time where junior faculty can talk among themselves freely.
- Make involvement voluntary.
- Use e-mail discussion lists to help everyone stay in touch between meetings.
- Create internal web pages to call attention to resources.
- Share and celebrate successes.[41]

Mentorship programs benefit the mentor as well as the educational institution, ensuring "greater success in retaining faculty and [creating] a reputation for developing talent."[42]

Free and paid webinars. The ubiquitous webinar, both free and for a wide range of costs, has become extremely popular. Live and recorded one-hour webinars are offered on nearly every e-mail discussion list, newsletter, vendor e-mail, and organization website on every imaginable topic. With their low- (or no-) cost price tag, their convenience, immediacy, and global accessibility, webinars feature heavily in the professional development routine of every library employee.[43]

Professional library association meetings and conferences. Professional association conferences have been cited as a meaningful way to keep librarians engaged, inspired, and informed.[44] Attending regional, national, or specialist conferences provides a variety of opportunities, including professional and social networking, workshops, roundtables, and professional meetings. There are opportunities for individuals and panels to share knowledge about new technologies, foundations, and disciplinary practices. Attending a conference exposes librarians to new ideas and new ways of doing things. It can also provide more objective perceptions about the library services, department practices, workflows, or individual's methodology by introducing librarians to alternative points of view.[45] Conferences can be extremely expensive when the conference registration, transportation, lodging, and meals are all added up, so it may not be feasible to send larger groups to the conference. One solution to distribute the information and broaden involvement is to invite the conference attendees to give a written or in-person presentation to their colleagues about what they learned.[46] In addition to attending conferences, individuals who serve on library association committees build relationships, creating a support system that they can draw upon as new knowledge gaps arise in the future.[47]

Employer-provided training and in-house academic librarian support networks. Most libraries provide in-house training on a semi-regular basis,[48] in which staff teach other staff in formats varying in formality. Some libraries create formal programs and networks. For example, the University of South Florida Libraries' in-house academic librarian support network features workshops to promote scholarly discourse between librarians; the workshops are presented by members of the research and publishing committee, writing and discussion groups, writing partnerships, and reading groups.[49] The Cambridge University Library created a Research Support Ambassador Programme, short and intensive, running once a year to provide research and training to subject librarians. The program combines formal education with practical elements and is "aimed at a self-selecting group of library staff... who wish to gain in-depth knowledge of research support and offers a chance to learn theory while putting that to practical use by creating a training resource."[50]

E-mail discussion lists and online forums. Professional organization e-mail discussion lists provide current, useful information and help subscribers remain knowledgeable on new trends and emerging issues.[51] Forums are also often housed on e-mail discussion lists and allow for a real-time written discussion and sharing of ideas.

Social media and Web 2.0. Luo and Hostetler describe the "global phenomenon" of pursuing professional development through social media (such as X—formerly Twitter, Facebook, and blogs). These platforms promote discussion; create a networked community; allow for resource sharing, patron outreach, and engagement; and enable "professionals in LIS of varying roles and positions, novel and seasoned, to develop an authentic relationship through dynamic interactions made possible by these tools."[52]

Finding Professional Development Opportunities

For library employees looking for specific skills or ongoing, continuous learning opportunities, there is a long list of venues, organizations, and types of professional development providers. This chapter cannot possibly list them all. However, below are examples of professional development opportunities one might find.*

- *Professional associations.* Some examples of professional associations are the American Library Association (ALA) and its divisions, the Association of Research Libraries (ARL), the Special Libraries Association (SLA), IFLA, and many state library associations. Each of these provides continuing education opportunities. Some of the state library associations have expanded their free offerings beyond their own state border, such as the Georgia Library Association's Carterette Series Webinars. IFLA chair Ritchie claims that these professional associations have a "leading role to play... because they are the bodies charged with the responsibility for maintaining standards for education, as well as professional practice."[53]

- *Consortia.* Libraries in a region or state often come together to create a cooperative group for purchasing and sharing resources. Oftentimes they also provide free or discounted training for consortia members (e.g., Amigos Library Services, TexShare, and Research Libraries Group).

- *Leadership institutes.* Many organizations have dedicated leadership institutes, and there are some entities that specialize in leadership alone. Library

---

* Several university libraries have created LibGuides that identify library-related organizations offering online learning, such as Maryland State Library Agency (https://marylandlibraries.libguides.com/staffdevelopment/libraryrelated) and Denison Libraries (https://libguides.denison.edu/ProfessionalDevelopment/OnlineLearning).

leadership opportunities include ALA Leadership Institute, Leadership Institute for Academic Librarians, Pacific Northwest Library Association Leadership Institute, North Exposure Leadership Institute, and so on.

- *Vendor user groups.* Many vendors have user groups that offer a platform for libraries to communicate directly with them to request technology enhancements, get system updates, and attend user conferences to receive training and news about upcoming changes in the platforms. Examples of vendor user groups are Ex Libris's ELUNA, EBSCO's EDS user group, Innovative User Group, and so on.
- Other nonprofit and for-profit organizations offering library skills training:
  - *Library Juice Academy.* A "range of online professional development courses for librarians, archivists, and other staff, focusing on practical topics to build new skills."[54]
  - *LYRASIS.* Works with knowledge professionals "to create, support and deliver innovative programs, services and technologies that allow for equitable access to the world's knowledge and cultural heritage."[55]
  - *PCI Webinars.* Offers "top of the line web-based learning to libraries, consortia, and state libraries."[56]
  - *Project ENABLE.* Offers tools for "creating a library that accommodates the needs of all patrons."[57]
  - *WebJunction.* "Builds the knowledge, skills, and confidence of library staff to power strong libraries that are the heart of vibrant communities. A program of OCLC Research, WebJunction is free and welcome to all libraries to use, regardless of size, type, or location."[58]

Conclusion

Graduate library schools provide a solid foundation for librarians entering the workforce, but as in any field that undergoes vast technological advances, it is imperative that information professionals participate in continuous professional development.[59] All library employees need opportunities and encouragement to increase their understanding and ability to respond to the questions they will receive while interacting with patrons at the circulation desk, reference desk, or elsewhere. In *Staff Development: A Practical Guide*, Giesecke and McNeil expanded and updated ALA's core competencies, identifying twelve core competencies for *all* library employees:

1) analytical skills, problem solving, and decision making; 2) communication skills; 3) creativity and innovation; 4) effective leadership; 5) expertise and technical knowledge; 6) flexibility and

adaptability; 7) interpersonal and group skills; 8) organizational understanding and systems thinking; 9) ownership and accountability; 10) planning and organizational skills; 11) user satisfaction; and 12) value management.[60]

No one course, training, or workshop can adequately address these skills, but viewing the core competencies as a target or road map serves as a basis for a continuous professional development program for all library staff. There is ample evidence that investment in professional development programs has a demonstrated, if not always direct, impact on the library user through more engaged and satisfied library employees and an influx of new ideas entering the organization.[61] Especially in the academic setting, a culture of continuous learning and development can be achieved through a variety of programs, allowing individuals to choose the strategies that work best for their learning styles and information needs. One of the most admirable qualities of the library community is a willingness to share information and resources, and continuous professional development opportunities harness this knowledge exchange, ultimately benefitting the wider community.

Notes

1. Ann Ritchie, "Conference Opening Address," in *Continuing Professional Development—Preparing for New Roles in Libraries: A Voyage of Discovery: Sixth World Conference on Continuing Professional Development and Workplace Learning for the Library and Information Professions*, ed. Paul Genoni, and Graham Walton, IFLA Publications (Munich: De Gruyter Saur, 2005), 12. EBSCOhost.
2. American Library Association, "Furthering Your Library Career…," accessed May 27, 2024, https://www.ala.org/educationcareers/archive/professionaldevelopment/ce/continuingeducation; Anushie Moonasar, "Continuing Professional Development and the Changing Landscape of Academic Libraries," *Library Management* 45, no. 3–4 (2024): 227, https://doi.org/10.1108/LM-09-2023-0100.
3. *Cambridge Business English Dictionary*, s.v. "Professional Development (n.)," accessed May 27, 2024, https://dictionary.cambridge.org/us/dictionary/english/professional-development.
4. Jennifer Campbell-Meier and Anne Goulding, "Evaluating Librarian Continuing Professional Development: Merging Guskey's Framework and Vygotsky Space to Explore Transfer of Learning," *Library and Information Science Research* 43, no. 4 (2021): article 101119, p. 2, https://doi.org/10.1016/j.lisr.2021.101119.
5. Shaheen Majid, "Continuing Professional Development (CPD) Activities Organized by Library and Information Study Programs in Southeast Asia," *Journal of Education for Library and Information Science* 45, no. 1 (2004): 59, https://doi.org/10.2307/40323921.
6. Keren Dali, Norda Bell, and Zachary Valdes, "Learning and Change through Diversity, Equity, and Inclusion Professional Development: Academic Librarians' Perspectives," *Journal of Academic Librarianship* 47, no. 6 (December 2021): article 102448, p. 9, https://doi.org/10.1016/j.acalib.2021.102448; Elvira Basibas Lapuz, "The Changing Roles of Librarians and Information Professionals: Recommendations for Continuing Professional Development and Workplace Learning in Academic Libraries," in *Continuing Professional Development—Preparing for New Roles in Libraries: A Voyage of Discovery: Sixth World Conference on Continuing Professional Development and Workplace Learning for the Library and Information Professions*, ed. Paul Genoni, and Graham Walton, IFLA Publications (Munich: De Gruyter Saur, 2005), 80. EBSCOhost.
7. Lapuz, "Changing Roles of Librarians," 80.
8. Ramirose Ilene Attebury, "Professional Development: A Qualitative Study of High Impact Characteristics Affecting Meaningful and Transformational Learning," *Journal of Academic Librarianship* 43, no. 3 (2017): 232, https://doi.org/10.1016/j.acalib.2017.02.015.
9. Ikhlaq ur Rehman, Uzma Majeed, and Shabir Ahmad Ganaie, "Continuous Professional Development of LIS Professionals in Academic Libraries: Channels, Challenges and Motivation," *Global Knowledge, Memory and Communication* (forthcoming), intro, https://doi.org/10.1108/GKMC-08-2023-0298.

10. Moonasar, "Continuing Professional Development," 229; Rehman, Majeed, and Ganaie, "Continuous Professional Development," intro and paragraph 2.1.
11. Majid, "CPD Activities," 70.
12. Liah Shonhe, "Continuous Professional Development (CPD) of Librarians: A Bibliometric Analysis of Research Productivity Viewed through WoS," *Journal of Academic Librarianship* 46, no. 2 (March 2020): article 849, p. 2, https://doi.org/10.3390/su15010849.
13. Mike Freeman, "A Sense of Direction: Librarianship and CPD," *Librarian Career Development* 2, no. 3 (1994): 26; Moonasar, "Continuing Professional Development," 229.
14. Christina Neigel, "Professional Development for Library Workers: Exposing the Complicated Problems of Equity and Access," *Partnership: The Canadian Journal of Library and Information Practice and Research* 11, no. 2 (2016): 3, https://doi.org/10.21083/partnership.v11i2.3795.
15. Neigel, "Professional Development for Library Workers," 3.
16. Rehman, Majeed, and Ganaie, "Continuous Professional Development," para. 4.4.
17. Rehman, Majeed, and Ganaie, "Continuous Professional Development," para. 4.3.
18. Donna Chan and Ethel Auster, "Understanding Librarians' Motivation to Participate in Professional Development Activities," in *Continuing Professional Development—Preparing for New Roles in Libraries: A Voyage of Discovery: Sixth World Conference on Continuing Professional Development and Workplace Learning for the Library and Information Professions*, ed. Paul Genoni and Graham Walton, IFLA Publications (Munich: De Gruyter Saur, 2005), 165, EBSCOhost.
19. Ramirose Atterbury, "The Role of Administrators in Professional Development: Considerations for Facilitating Learning among Academic Librarians," *Journal of Library Administration* 58, no. 5 (2018): 425, https://doi.org/10.1080/01930826.2018.1468190.
20. Khurram Shahzad et al., "E-Learning for Continuing Professional Development of University Librarians: A Systematic Review," *Sustainability* 15, no. 1 (2023): article 849, para. 3.14, https://doi.org/10.3390/su15010849.
21. Donna Chan and Ethel Auster, "Factors Contributing to the Professional Development of Reference Librarians," *Library and Information Science Research* 25, no. 3 (2003): 269, https://doi.org/10.1016/S0740-8188(03)00030-6; Maura Corcoran and Claire McGuinness, "Keeping Ahead of the Curve: Academic Librarians and Continuing Professional Development in Ireland," *Library Management* 35, no. 3 (2014): 191, https://doi.org/10.1108/LM-06-2013-0048; Moonasar, "Continuing Professional Development," 229; Rehman, Majeed, and Ganaie, "Continuing Professional Development," para. 4.4.
22. Jana Varlejs, *IFLA Guidelines for Continuing Professional Development*, 2nd ed. (The Hague, Netherlands: IFLA, 2016).
23. Varlejs, *IFLA Guidelines*, 9.
24. Varlejs, *IFLA Guidelines*, 10.
25. Varlejs, *IFLA Guidelines*, 10.
26. Varlejs, *IFLA Guidelines*, 23.
27. Ethel Auster and Donna C. Chan, "Reference Librarians and Keeping Up-to-Date: A Question of Priorities," *Reference and User Services Quarterly* 44, no. 1 (Fall 2004): 59, https://www.jstor.org/stable/20864288.
28. Justin Fuhr, "Developing Data Services Skills in Academic Libraries," *College and Research Libraries* 83, no. 3 (2022): 484, https://doi.org/10.5860/crl.83.3.474.
29. Deborah L. Lauseng, Carmen Howard, and Emily M. Johnson, "Professional Development in Evidence-Based Practice: Course Survey Results to Inform Administrative Decision Making," *Journal of the Medical Library Association* 107, no. 3 (2019): 397, https://doi.org/10.5195/jmla.2019.628.
30. Attebury, "Professional Development," 240.
31. Attebury, "Professional Development," 240.
32. Agnes Namaganda, "Continuing Professional Development as Transformational Learning: A Case Study," *Journal of Academic Librarianship* 46, no. 3 (2020): article 102152, p. 5, https://doi.org/10.1016/j.acalib.2020.102152.
33. Hope Kelly and Erica R. Brody, "A Digital Petting Zoo of Learning Objects: An Online Professional Development Program to Support a Community of Practice among Employees at an Academic Library," *Medical Reference Services Quarterly* 41, no. 2 (2002): 158, https://doi.org/10.1080/02763869.2022.2054182.
34. Kristen J. Henrich and Ramirose Attebury, "Communities of Practice at an Academic Library: A New Approach to Mentoring at the University of Idaho," *Journal of Academic Librarianship* 36, no. 2 (2010): 160, https://doi.org/10.1016/j.acalib.2010.01.007.
35. Henrich and Attebury, "Communities of Practice," 161.
36. Attebury, "Professional Development," 240; Karen R. Harker, Erin O'Toole, and Catherine Sassen, "Assessing an Academic Library Professional Development Program," *portal: Libraries and the Academy* 18, no. 1 (January 2018): 201, https://doi.org/10.1353/pla.2018.0010.
37. Karen Harker et al., "Mixed-Methods Assessment of a Mentoring Program," *Journal of Library Administration* 59, no. 8 (2019): 874, https://doi.org/10.1080/01930826.2019.1661745.
38. Shin Freedman, "Mentoring Experience of Academic Librarians: A Pilot Study of Mentorship in Academic Libraries," *Library Leadership and Management* 35, no. 2 (2021): 12, ProQuest.

39. Freedman, "Mentoring Experience," 15.
40. Allison V. Level and Michelle Mach, "Peer Mentoring: One Institution's Approach to Mentoring Academic Librarians," *Library Management* 26, no. 6/7 (2005): 308, https://doi.org/10.1108/01435120410609725.
41. Level and Mach, "Peer Mentoring," 308–9.
42. Harker et al., "Mixed-Methods Assessment," 874.
43. Attebury, "Professional Development," 240; Shahzad et al., "E-Learning for Continuing Professional Development," 14.
44. Betty Garrison and Steve M. Cramer, "What Librarians Say They Want from Their Professional Associations: A Survey of Business Librarians," *Journal of Business and Finance Librarianship* 26, no. 1–2 (2021): 89, https://doi.org/10.1080/08963568.2020.1819746.
45. Ruth Jenkins, "Professional Development through Attending Conferences: Reflections of a Health Librarian," *Health Information and Libraries Journal* 32, no. 2 (2015): 157, https://doi.org/10.1111/hir.12101.
46. Shu Guo, "Developing Effective Professional Development Programs: A Case Study," *New Library World* 115, no. 11/12 (2014): 545, https://doi.org/10.1108/NLW-05-2014-0048.
47. Attebury, "Professional Development," 240.
48. Majid, "CPD Activities," 58.
49. LeEtta Schmidt et al., "Increasing Scholarly Productivity: Developing an In-House Academic Librarian Support Network," *Journal of Academic Librarianship* 47, no. 5 (2021): article 102385, https://doi.org/10.1016/j.acalib.2021.102385.
50. Claire Sewell and Danny Kingsley, "Developing the 21st Century Academic Librarian: The Research Support Ambassador Programme," *New Review of Academic Librarianship* 23, no. 2–3 (2017): 151, 156, https://doi.org/10.1080/13614533.2017.1323766.
51. Garrison and Cramer, "What Librarians Say," 92.
52. Tian Luo and Kirsten Hostetler, "Making Professional Development More Social: A Systematic Review of Librarians' Professional Development through Social Media," *Journal of Academic Librarianship* 46, no. 5 (2020): article 102193, https://doi.org/10.1016/j.acalib.2020.102193.
53. Ritchie, "Conference Opening Address," 12.
54. Library Juice Academy website, accessed May 30, 2024, https://libraryjuiceacademy.com/.
55. Lyrasis, "What We Do," accessed May 30, 2024, https://www.lyrasis.org/Pages/Main.aspx.
56. PCI Webinars website, accessed May 30, 2024, https://pciwebinars.com/.
57. Project ENABLE, "General Inclusive & Accessible Library Training," accessed May 30, 2024, https://projectenable.syr.edu/.
58. WebJunction, "About Us—Overview," accessed May 30, 2024, https://www.webjunction.org/home.html.
59. Erin O'Toole et al., "Creating a Sustainable Professional Development Program," *Journal of Library Administration* 63, no. 1 (2023): 1, https://doi.org/10.1080/01930826.2022.2146438.
60. Joan Giesecke and Beth McNeil, "Core Competencies for Libraries and Library Staff," in *Staff Development: A Practical Guide*, 4th ed., ed. Andrea Stewart, Carol T. Zsulya, and Carlette Washington-Hoagland (Chicago: ALA Editions, 2014), 62–63.
61. Campbell-Meier and Goulding, "Evaluating Librarian Continuing Professional Development," 11.

Bibliography

American Library Association. "Furthering Your Library Career…" Accessed May 27, 2024. https://www.ala.org/educationcareers/archive/professionaldevelopment/ce/continuingeducation.

Attebury, Ramirose Ilene. "Professional Development: A Qualitative Study of High Impact Characteristics Affecting Meaningful and Transformational Learning." *Journal of Academic Librarianship* 43, no. 3 (2017): 232–41. https://doi.org/10.1016/j.acalib.2017.02.015.

———. "The Role of Administrators in Professional Development: Considerations for Facilitating Learning among Academic Librarians." *Journal of Library Administration* 58, no. 5 (2018): 417–33. https://doi.org/10.1080/01930826.2018.1468190.

Auster, Ethel, and Donna C. Chan. "Reference Librarians and Keeping Up-to-Date: A Question of Priorities." *Reference and User Services Quarterly* 44, no. 1 (Fall 2004): 57–66. https://www.jstor.org/stable/20864288.

Campbell-Meier, Jennifer, and Anne Goulding. "Evaluating Librarian Continuing Professional Development: Merging Guskey's Framework and Vygotsky Space to Explore Transfer of Learning." *Library and Information Science Research* 43, no. 4 (2021): article 101119. https://doi.org/10.1016/j.lisr.2021.101119.

Chan, Donna, and Ethel Auster. "Factors Contributing to the Professional Development of Reference Librarians." *Library and Information Science Research* 25, no. 3 (2003). https://doi.org/10.1016/S0740-8188(03)00030-6

Chan, Donna, and Ethel Auster. "Understanding Librarians' Motivation to Participate in Professional Development Activities." In *Continuing Professional Development—Preparing for New Roles in Libraries: A Voyage of Discovery: Sixth World Conference on Continuing Professional Development and Workplace Learning for the Library and Information Professions*, edited by Paul Genoni and Graham Walton, 157–69. IFLA Publications. Munich: De Gruyter Saur, 2005. EBSCOhost.

Corcoran, Maura, and Claire McGuinness. "Keeping Ahead of the Curve: Academic Librarians and Continuing Professional Development in Ireland." *Library Management* 35, no. 3 (2014): 175–98. https://doi.org/10.1108/LM-06-2013-0048.

Dali, Keren, Norda Bell, and Zachary Valdes. "Learning and Change through Diversity, Equity, and Inclusion Professional Development: Academic Librarians' Perspectives." *Journal of Academic Librarianship* 47, no. 6 (December 2021): article 102448. https://doi.org/10.1016/j.acalib.2021.102448.

Freedman, Shin. "Mentoring Experience of Academic Librarians: A Pilot Study of Mentorship in Academic Libraries." *Library Leadership and Management* 35, no. 2 (2021): 1–27. ProQuest.

Freeman, Mike. "A Sense of Direction: Librarianship and CPD." *Librarian Career Development* 2, no. 3 (1994): 26–28.

Fuhr, Justin. "Developing Data Services Skills in Academic Libraries." *College and Research Libraries* 83, no. 3 (2022): 474–502. https://doi.org/10.5860/crl.83.3.474.

Garrison, Betty, and Steve M. Cramer. "What Librarians Say They Want from Their Professional Associations: A Survey of Business Librarians." *Journal of Business and Finance Librarianship* 26, no. 1–2 (2021): 81–98. https://doi.org/10.1080/08963568.2020.1819746.

Giesecke, Joan, and Beth McNeil. "Core Competencies for Libraries and Library Staff." In *Staff Development: A Practical Guide*, 4th ed., edited by Andrea Stewart, Carol T. Zsulya, and Carlette Washington-Hoagland, 59–80. Chicago: ALA Editions, 2014.

Guo, Shu. "Developing Effective Professional Development Programs: A Case Study." *New Library World* 115, no. 11/12 (2014): 542–57. https://doi.org/10.1108/NLW-05-2014-0048.

Harker, Karen, Erin O'Toole, Setareh Keshmiripour, Marcia McIntosh, and Catherine Sassen. "Mixed-Methods Assessment of a Mentoring Program." *Journal of Library Administration* 59, no. 8 (2019): 873–902. https://doi.org/10.1080/01930826.2019.1661745.

Harker, Karen R., Erin O'Toole, and Catherine Sassen. "Assessing an Academic Library Professional Development Program." *portal : Libraries and the Academy* 18, no. 1 (January 2018): 199–223. https://doi.org/10.1353/pla.2018.0010.

Henrich, Kristen J., and Ramirose Attebury. "Communities of Practice at an Academic Library: A New Approach to Mentoring at the University of Idaho." *Journal of Academic Librarianship* 36, no. 2 (2010): 158–65. https://doi.org/10.1016/j.acalib.2010.01.007.

Jenkins, Ruth. "Professional Development through Attending Conferences: Reflections of a Health Librarian." *Health Information and Libraries Journal* 32, no. 2 (2015): 156–60. https://doi.org/10.1111/hir.12101.

Kelly, Hope, and Erica R. Brody. "A Digital Petting Zoo of Learning Objects: An Online Professional Development Program to Support a Community of Practice among Employees at an Academic Library." *Medical Reference Services Quarterly* 41, no. 2 (2002): 157–68. https://doi.org/10.1080/02763869.2022.2054182.

Lapuz, Elvira Basibas. "The Changing Roles of Librarians and Information Professionals: Recommendations for Continuing Professional Development and Workplace Learning in Academic Libraries." In *Continuing Professional Development—Preparing for New Roles in Libraries: A Voyage of Discovery: Sixth World Conference on Continuing Professional Development and Workplace Learning for the Library and Information Professions*, edited by Paul Genoni and Graham Walton, 75–82. IFLA Publications. Munich: De Gruyter Saur, 2005. EBSCOhost.

Lauseng, Deborah L., Carmen Howard, and Emily M. Johnson. "Professional Development in Evidence-Based Practice: Course Survey Results to Inform Administrative Decision Making." *Journal of the Medical Library Association* 107, no. 3 (2019): 394–402. https://doi.org/10.5195/jmla.2019.628.

Level, Allison V., and Michelle Mach. "Peer Mentoring: One Institution's Approach to Mentoring Academic Librarians." *Library Management* 26, no. 6/7 (2005): 301–10. https://doi.org/10.1108/01435120410609725.

Library Juice Academy website. Accessed May 30, 2024. https://libraryjuiceacademy.com/.

Luo, Tian, and Kirsten Hostetler. "Making Professional Development More Social: A Systematic Review of Librarians' Professional Development through Social Media." *Journal of Academic Librarianship* 46, no. 5 (2020): article 102193. https://doi.org/10.1016/j.acalib.2020.102193.

Lyrasis. "What We Do." Accessed May 30, 2024. https://www.lyrasis.org/Pages/Main.aspx.

Majid, Shaheen. "Continuing Professional Development (CPD) Activities Organized by Library and Information Study Programs in Southeast Asia." *Journal of Education for Library and Information Science* 45, no. 1 (2004): 58–70. https://doi.org/10.2307/40323921.

Moonasar, Anushie. "Continuing Professional Development and the Changing Landscape of Academic Libraries." *Library Management* 45, no. 3/4 (2024): 226–42. https://doi.org/10.1108/LM-09-2023-0100.

Namaganda, Agnes. "Continuing Professional Development as Transformational Learning: A Case Study." *Journal of Academic Librarianship* 46, no. 3 (2020): article 102152. https://doi.org/10.1016/j.acalib.2020.102152.

Neigel, Christina. "Professional Development for Library Workers: Exposing the Complicated Problems of Equity and Access." *Partnership: The Canadian Journal of Library and Information Practice and Research* 11, no. 2 (2016): 1–7. https://doi.org/10.21083/partnership.v11i2.3795.

O'Toole, Erin, Catherine Sassen, Shannon Willis, Steven Guerrero, and Jermey Berg. "Creating a Sustainable Professional Development Program." *Journal of Library Administration* 63, no. 1 (2023): 1–26. https://doi.org/10.1080/01930826.2022.2146438.

PCI Webinars website. Accessed May 30, 2024. https://pciwebinars.com/.

Project ENABLE. "General Inclusive & Accessible Library Training." Accessed May 30, 2024. https://projectenable.syr.edu/.

Rehman, Ikhlaq ur, Uzma Majeed, and Shabir Ahmad Ganaie. "Continuous Professional Development of LIS Professionals in Academic Libraries: Channels, Challenges and Motivation." *Global Knowledge, Memory and Communication*. Forthcoming. https://doi.org/10.1108/GKMC-08-2023-0298.

Ritchie, Ann. "Conference Opening Address." In *Continuing Professional Development—Preparing for New Roles in Libraries: A Voyage of Discovery: Sixth World Conference on Continuing Professional Development and Workplace Learning for the Library and Information Professions*, edited by Paul Genoni and Graham Walton, 11–13. IFLA Publications. Munich: De Gruyter Saur, 2005. EBSCOhost.

Schmidt, LeEtta, Jason Boczar, Barbara Lewis, and Tomaro Taylor. "Increasing Scholarly Productivity: Developing an In-House Academic Librarian Support Network." *Journal of Academic Librarianship* 47, no. 5 (2021): article 102385. https://doi.org/10.1016/j.acalib.2021.102385.

Sewell, Claire, and Danny Kingsley. "Developing the 21st Century Academic Librarian: The Research Support Ambassador Programme." *New Review of Academic Librarianship* 23, no. 2–3 (2017): 148–58. https://doi.org/10.1080/13614533.2017.1323766.

Shahzad, Khurram, Shakeel Ahmad Khan, Yasir Javed, and Abid Iqbal. "E-Learning for Continuing Professional Development of University Librarians: A Systematic Review." *Sustainability* 15, no. 1 (2023): article 849. https://doi.org/10.3390/su15010849.

Shonhe, Liah. "Continuous Professional Development (CPD) of Librarians: A Bibliometric Analysis of Research Productivity Viewed through WoS." *Journal of Academic Librarianship* 46, no. 2 (March 2020): article 102106. https://doi.org/10.1016/j.acalib.2019.102106.

Varlejs, Jana. *IFLA Guidelines for Continuing Professional Development: Principles and Best Practices*, 2nd ed. The Hague, Netherlands: IFLA, 2016.

WebJunction. "About Us—Overview." Accessed May 30, 2024. https://www.webjunction.org/home.html.

CHAPTER 8

Succession Planning from the Middle

Brynne Norton and Jennifer E. M. Cotton

Introduction

Succession planning is typically approached as a top-down process, but if you are a middle manager, what can you do to develop your own succession plan in both directions? This question is an important one that is not addressed in scholarly literature about academic institutions more generally, or in the library literature specifically. This chapter will focus on academic libraries, but many of the challenges and solutions apply equally to public, special, and school libraries, and it is the authors' hope that this will prove useful to a variety of readers.

While there is a considerable body of literature addressing succession planning from a business perspective, libraries have attributes and priorities that are inconsistent with those found in businesses with profit-driven approaches. Additionally, academic libraries situated within higher education change at a much slower pace than most businesses. Though leadership structures are present in libraries, the types of positions and levels of management also make it challenging to map concepts directly from the business literature, leaving middle managers in libraries with limited resources when working on succession planning.

Further complicating matters, different types of succession planning are discussed in business literature under a variety of names, including administrative succession planning, technical succession planning, replacement planning, and talent management, among others. All these topics fall under the broad umbrella of succession planning, though they have very different processes and outcomes. The two types of succession planning discussed in this chapter are administrative, which focuses on people, and technical, which focuses on information, with Rothwell and Poduch's definitions used to anchor this conversation within the broader context of succession planning.[1] (A fuller discussion of these definitions is in the literature review section of this chapter.)

This distinction between types of planning does not mean that one approach should be employed while any other is ignored. Middle managers have a unique viewpoint in this matter, since both types of succession planning discussed here may potentially impact them personally, for their own career advancement; institutionally, when working with upper leadership; and managerially, as they work to ensure continuity of services. However, the perspective of middle managers is frequently overlooked both within the literature and in the implementation of succession plans by administration, which results in confusion for those managers around what role they should have in the process. This chapter will discuss succession planning in libraries from a middle manager's perspective through a literature review and a real-life case study, while offering suggestions for getting started and best practices for middle managers who are ready to jump into succession planning in order to positively impact the future directions of their own careers and those of their supervisees, as well as their institutions.

Problem Definition

The impact of the Great Resignation has yet to be studied in libraries, but it is notable that librarianship has long been a graying profession. Since 2002, American Library Association has been sounding the alarm about librarian shortages, predicting that one in four librarians would be retiring before 2019.[2] The Bureau of Labor statistics reports that there are 55,000 librarians and media collections specialists as of 2022 aged 55 and older,[3] which means that almost 33 percent of librarians are at or nearing retirement age. This is exacerbated by the fact that baby boomers will be reaching retirement as a generation by 2030. The US Census is referring to these upcoming retirements as a "gray tsunami."[4] These predictions point to the fact that succession planning is vital to the future of libraries and needs to be better understood and implemented.

Administrative succession planning typically employs a top-down approach by focusing on key leadership positions. This type of succession planning is important to middle managers because it directly impacts the leadership roles in a library and could also impact a middle manager's career advancement if they are interested in positions of increasing authority and responsibility. Middle managers have limited power in what they can do in terms of succession planning moving up the organization chart due to their limited authority, but they can work on administrative succession planning from the middle down. Helping employees explore potential career paths by understanding what those paths are and identifying skills that can be developed by offering them career coaching and professional development opportunities are aspects of succession planning that middle managers can utilize with employees that they supervise. Managers can help guide career path exploration and development through discussions of their own experiences, as well as potential internal or external promotion opportunities within the library job market. In this way, middle managers have a direct impact on succession planning, even if it is limited to the middle down of the organizational structure.

Instead of focusing on people, technical succession planning focuses on information. The daily operations of a team are vitally important to a middle manager as they think about continuity of services when employees depart or unexpected circumstances arise. These disruptions are intensified by a lack of documentation around vital guidelines and procedures. Middle managers have a vested interest in technical succession planning to ensure that proper documentation and institutional knowledge are captured and passed along. This type of work can be challenging to approach with those employees who take ownership over their work and feel threatened by creating documentation or cross-training others. However, middle managers can help create a culture of documentation so that it becomes part of daily operations, instead of an enormous task that begins only when a person decides to resign or retire. By ensuring that technical succession is part of the daily work of every employee, some fears can be assuaged. Starting with the reasoning behind technical succession planning helps employees understand the end goal and benefits.

While middle managers have a unique perspective on succession planning in libraries, they frequently do not realize the importance of this work or the possibilities of their role in the process. The case study in this chapter will show how the authors dealt with a real-life succession planning failure and what they implemented to prevent disruptions of services and gaps in leadership moving forward.

Literature Review

Literature about succession planning is varied and is found in all types of industries; however, library literature on this topic is sparse according to both Bridgland and Nixon.[5] Literature written explicitly from the middle management perspective is also absent from the conversation. For the purposes of this chapter, only succession planning literature about libraries will be reviewed, with one exception: *Effective Succession Planning: Ensuring Leadership Continuity and Building Talent from Within*, by Rothwell.[6] This comprehensive book, now in its fifth edition, is widely accepted as an important starting point for succession planning, regardless of industry or topic.

Rothwell provides an overview of succession planning as a whole, with key context and definitions for the process, as well as how it can be used. For the purposes of the middle manager, there are two important types of succession planning: administrative and technical. Rothwell and Poduch define administrative, or managerial, succession planning as "finding and developing the 'right people' to place in the 'right positions' and in the 'right locations' at the 'right times' to achieve the 'right (because strategically-important) objectives.' The emphasis is really on who."[7] Conversely, technical succession planning is "isolating, distilling and transmitting 'right information' to people at the 'right times' to ensure the continuity of operations and provide a foundation for future improvements. The emphasis is really on what—exclusively the implicit and explicit experiences of running a process and/or operation."[8] In these definitions there is a clear distinction between a people-focused and an information-focused approach to succession planning, both of which are vital to middle managers and are widely applicable to succession planning regardless of the field. The combination of these types of planning provides a framework for understanding the unique position of the middle manager in ensuring continuity of leadership and services simultaneously.

Existing library literature misses the middle manager's perspective and focuses on either administrative or technical succession planning without providing targeted guidance for middle managers. Galbraith, Smith and Walker surveyed thirty-four ARL libraries, but asked only questions about deans, assistant or associate university librarians, and heads or chairs, with a focus on the top-down approach to hiring and leadership.[9] While middle management positions were included in this survey, the focus was on how they were promoted within libraries and not about their role in the process. Goldman conducted a thematic analysis of interviews with six library deans in organizations with flat structures, also highlighting the top-down approach.[10] Chute wrote an overview of six case studies where Institute of Museum and Libraries grants were used to specifically address succession planning through case studies,[11] and Murray wrote about the Cambridge University Library as a case study.[12] Both of these case studies offer practical examples but maintain a focus on administrative succession planning from the top down. Nixon writes about succession planning specifically for business librarians, including attributes of these positions that are unique to this specific subject knowledge.[13] While some aspects of succession planning are universal, focusing on subject knowledge limits the scope of applicability. These articles identify benefits and challenges in succession planning, but address middle managers only in passing or tangentially rather than centering their role in the process.

While leadership may understand succession planning is important, the actual planning is often not implemented, or not implemented well, according to Galbraith, Smith and Walker's survey.[14] These challenges stem from a variety of sources. One challenge is the increase of flat structures described in Goldman's interviews about California State University Libraries, and in Murray's work.[15] Flat structures limit the ability to implement administrative succession planning because they reduce or eliminate middle managers, meaning that those who could be promoted never get a chance to develop the needed skills. The lack of mid-career librarians in the pipeline exacerbates challenges as well according to both Nixon and Murray, as there are not enough people to fill the coming vacancies.[16] The lack of leadership competencies to steer development of employees is specifically noted by Chute as a challenge to implementing succession planning, because managers may not know what their employees need to learn in order to be successful in future leadership roles.[17] All of these challenges make it increasingly difficult to successfully implement administrative succession plans.

Weare takes a different approach from other articles written about succession planning in libraries by arguing against the process and its value as a whole, as opposed to identifying challenges that need to be met.[18] Weare examines articles that review changes in position announcements to ground his argument. He includes four recommendations based on this analysis: focusing on mentorship, assessing the climate of the library, evaluating the organizational structure with each vacancy rather than perpetuating an outdated system, and hiring for leadership outside of the organization in order to bring in new perspectives. Weare focuses on the fact that there is scarce literature that is critical of succession planning, but there is also not evidence that it is effective when implemented. While Weare does make some concessions in limited circumstances—notably that technical succession planning can have value—he also argues that this type of planning is not a vital aspect of continuity of services because "there is some possibility that time, energy, and money would be invested in assuring transfer of knowledge in an area where that knowledge may no longer be needed in the future."[19] These criticisms are valid, but discount the view of the middle manager who is charged with keeping services running when employees depart with little to no documentation or knowledge transfer. Middle managers need a more practical approach with regard to continuity of services because they must think about services that need to work tomorrow while also thinking about high-level changes in the future.

Hiring is an important aspect of succession planning, as well as management more generally, and hiring an internal candidate can be a challenge for a variety of reasons beyond the stagnant structural concerns identified by Weare. Concerns about hiring internally include the capabilities and qualifications of external talent according to Murray.[20] In addition, Galbraith, Smith and Walker identified, using direct quotes from survey respondents, that in many cases internal hires simply do not apply for leadership positions.[21] They pointed out the positive aspects that internal hires have, including starting out with institutional knowledge and a reduced need for onboarding when internal candidates do choose to apply. In the end Galbraith, Smith, and Walker and Bridgland recommend a mixture of both internal and external hires in order to build the best possible institution with a mix of institutional knowledge and outside perspective.[22]

Challenges to technical succession planning are in the literature, but since there is not as much literature on this type of planning, the topic has not been explored extensively. Siewert and Louderback investigated the impact of knowledge transfer, tacit knowledge, and institutional knowledge as characteristics of technical succession planning.[23] They conducted a survey on the state of succession planning in libraries, which showed that libraries have a significant portion of long-term employees who are nearing retirement. This article also identifies the differences between explicit and tacit knowledge, two aspects of technical succession planning in terms of documentation and institutional knowledge, noting that only "18% of respondents feel that their institution provides 'enough' written procedures to do their work."[24] They outlined the challenges involved in capturing tacit knowledge. This article is a great first step in justifying the need for succession planning, but the issues involved with implementation and best practices are listed only as future directions for research.

The scholars cited in this chapter identify similar sequences to begin implementing succession plans. These generally include assessing the state of succession planning; identifying key individuals or positions; and offering mentorship, professional development, and interim chances to build skills with an eye toward competencies established for future leadership roles. These steps are largely built around the administrative leadership model but can be applied to technical succession planning if the development of people is replaced with the development of documentation and information. Middle managers can take the existing literature as a jumping-off point as they balance the needs of leadership with the need for continuity of services.

Discussion

The authors' experience with the streaming media reserves service at the University of Maryland Libraries provides a useful case study in what can happen if succession planning is ignored. In this instance, the transfer of streaming media reserves staff from a separate unit at a different library branch is examined to identify what happened and what should have happened. This transfer of services and collections occurred rapidly and was made more challenging as long-term employees departed.

The University of Maryland, College Park, (UMD) is the state's flagship university, with over 40,000 students in 100 undergraduate and master's programs, as well as eighty doctoral programs. The UMD Libraries have eight branches that provide course reserves to an average of 300 courses per semester through hard-copy and textbook reserves, electronic (text-based) reserves, and streaming media reserves. The course reserve service is located in the Resource Sharing and Reserves (RSR) unit, housed in the McKeldin Library, the main library on campus. RSR has ten FTE staff members, 4.5 of whom are primarily dedicated to course reserves.

In the summer of 2019, the UMD media collection was moved from another branch to McKeldin, and the Library Media Services (LMS) unit was disbanded. The media librarian who had run the unit retired and was not replaced, and the staff were distributed across other units. The streaming media reserves service, which had previously been run separately from the rest of course reserves, and the staff members (1.5 FTE) who had worked on it, were moved into RSR. With these changes, the largely undocumented institutional knowledge about media was dispersed across the UMD Libraries or lost to the institution entirely.

By the end of 2019, the long-term staff member who ran the streaming media reserves service departed the UMD Libraries, and it quickly became clear that technical succession planning had not been a priority for this unit in its previous incarnation. Minimal documentation and limited institutional knowledge were captured. In addition, LMS utilized a single-expert staffing model, where in many cases only one person answered questions or handled problems for a service, and there was no plan for continuity during absences or emergencies. Limited documentation exacerbated these issues because there was nothing available to refer to without the presence of the single expert. In the definition above, technical succession planning consists of ensuring continuity of services through a focus on information, but this type of planning had not occurred. Since no documentation was captured prior to the employee who ran the streaming media reserves service announcing a resignation, what ensued was a frantic notice period whereas much information was captured as possible. During this time, two weeks of training for remaining RSR staff occurred, which was not enough to effectively cross-train on a complex process. Working with the long-term employee, who was departing as sweeping changes were made to the procedures, was also challenging. The employee was deeply invested in the service, but the way in which it had functioned would not be sustainable for RSR in the future. As a result, the entire request process and workflow changed. The documentation that was captured was enough to maintain the service, albeit with frequent disruptions. The experience was challenging for the remaining RSR employees, who were unsure what they were doing, and instructors, who were used to a different model of service.

In contrast with streaming media, and as a long-standing best practice, RSR has routinely engaged in technical succession planning. Each employee has an area of expertise and specialization, but all employees share general knowledge (used during RSR on-call hours) and are cross-trained to provide support to each other during particularly busy times and as coverage for absences. This cross-training happens over time and allows for many opportunities to practice. Extensive and frequently updated documentation for all procedures is kept on a wiki. Due to the complicated nature of the work in the RSR unit, the wiki is a living tool that is constantly referred to and updated in order to maintain consistency of services. In addition, this practice addresses both prongs of succession planning—while focusing on information sharing and cross-training ensures the continuity of services, the practice also facilitates administrative succession planning by giving employees interested in career advancement a broader knowledge base. The transfer of streaming media reserves into RSR made it clear that LMS had not engaged in similar practices.

Further, with the arrival of the COVID-19 pandemic in early 2020, the UMD Libraries shifted suddenly to an entirely remote model, followed by an extended period of mostly remote operations, where only a few staff members were working in person, generally at staggered times. This also meant reshuffling job duties to accommodate which employees were on-site and which were remote, a task that was particularly onerous for streaming media reserves due to the lack of prior cross-training. The university as a whole remained remote during this time, which increased the demand for streaming media reserves. This demand was challenging to meet, as limited staff were on-site, and those on-site had no previous experience with streaming media reserves. The onset of the pandemic also prompted university budget cuts and a hiring freeze, meaning that hiring a new single expert for streaming media reserves was impossible, even if doing so would be desirable.

Despite these difficulties, the RSR team remained committed to providing the best services possible under the circumstances. In the absence of existing documentation for the streaming media reserves procedures, new documentation was created and added to the RSR wiki, starting with the information captured during the previous employee's notice period. As workflows and policies were updated to accommodate the new circumstances, those updates were also recorded in the interest of avoiding a similar situation in the future. This content remains a part of the wiki and is periodically reviewed. Creating and updating documentation is a key aspect of technical succession planning as it is the capture of the explicit information needed to maintain continuity of services when an employee departs suddenly.

During the remote period, some of the other services RSR normally offers were suspended or decreased in volume (particularly those related to hard-copy materials), and so a general reshuffling of duties and additional training allowed for the streaming media service to be maintained. When the hiring freeze was eventually lifted, a new employee was hired for a position specializing in streaming media, but with cross-training across RSR. This employee has worked to keep the wiki current with any changes. While there is once again an employee focused specifically on streaming media reserves, the position and the person holding it are now integrated with the rest of RSR. Cross-training continues to ensure that a baseline of knowledge is available to all members of the unit. This cross-training helps assist with continuity of services, but also with the capture of tacit knowledge that can be obtained only through experience. Employees who are cross-trained have an opportunity to learn a service, including its procedures and workflows, in order to better understand the overall process in case support is needed.

Supervisors in the RSR unit also work on administrative succession planning from their positions as middle managers. In order to do this, supervisors focus on ensuring that employees have opportunities and support for professional development. These come in the form of cross-training to expand individuals' skill sets, assistance in obtaining funding for professional development when needed, and ensuring that employees have time to participate in these opportunities. The three supervisors in the unit also coach employees on career path options by sharing information about their own path and potential alternate tracks.

As part of the streaming media reserves integration, RSR was structurally reorganized. At the beginning of the reorganization, reserves consisted of the streaming coordinator, a reserves supervisor, and two specialists. When the streaming coordinator departed, the reserves supervisor was promoted to coordinator and a streaming specialist was added. This restructuring allowed for better overall integration of the service into course reserves, but also added a professional step, creating a career path that could, theoretically, lead from specialist to coordinator to head of the unit, with skills that could be scaffolded across these positions. Education could be obtained along the way.

Conclusions

In terms of administrative succession planning, there are some advantages, some challenges, and some specific actions that can be taken by middle managers. Supporting employees and helping them develop for future career advancement can be an advantage in multiple ways, especially when there are opportunities for internal promotions. For one thing, this support and development can help boost morale as it shows that a manager and an institution are invested in employees' success. Internal promotions, like the promotion of the reserves supervisor to the reserves coordinator in RSR, allow for institutional knowledge to be leveraged, meaning that employees who are promoted internally start in a new position with a firm basis of knowledge about the institution, library, and patron population.

In the case of streaming media reserves at the UMD Libraries, the departure of the long-term streaming media employee from the university caused a loss of institutional knowledge that was extremely disruptive to instructors who expected services to operate as they did previously. If that employee had been retained (even in a new capacity), or had someone else been prepared to take over streaming media reserves, this disruption would have been significantly diminished. A major argument against succession planning is that the employees who have benefitted from this kind of support may choose to depart; however, there is an overall benefit to the profession as individuals are mentored, developed, and supported. After all, the entry-level staff of today are often the library leaders of tomorrow.

The main challenge of a middle manager when it comes to administrative succession planning is the limited control they have over hiring and budget processes. While they can face these challenges by advocating for employees, they are not typically the final decision-makers. A best practice for administrative succession planning is to determine areas where middle managers can provide impact through identifying development opportunities, as well as advocating for funding and release time for employees.

From the middle manager perspective, a best practice is to talk with employees about their career aspirations in order to identify competencies that can be developed. From there, individualized plans can be created in partnership with the employee, to include things like the aforementioned professional development, but also cross-training and opportunities for employees to participate in cross-functional teams so that they can grow their knowledge base and get chances to build skills in ways that they might not be able to in the day-to-day functions of their job. In the case of RSR, these practices have led to an engaged and enthusiastic team, with employees who understand their work in the larger context and feel empowered to suggest new ideas and improvements. These types of opportunities for employees to grow their knowledge base and build skills should always be voluntary, with decisions based on the employee's goals.

While middle managers must find ways to approach administrative succession planning indirectly due to their limited power and influence, technical succession planning can be directly employed in order to maintain continuity of services. Technical succession planning is crucial for middle managers in order to ensure that, as employees leave, services can continue, which is evident in the case study presented. One of the ways to engage with technical succession planning is through documentation. Each middle manager, depending on the area they are responsible for, should determine what type of documentation is needed for their team, how to capture it, and how to maintain it. This could be anything from text to screenshots to video tutorials. Wikis are generally a best practice for documentation as they can be easily updated by a variety of people and help the documentation remain current. Almost as important as creating the documentation in the first place is the need to establish a culture of ongoing documentation maintenance, where employees are actively engaged in keeping it updated and consistent. If documentation is not updated frequently, it can quickly become useless.

One of the advantages of having a culture of documentation is that it helps get employee buy-in, which can be a challenging part of this process. Some employees find writing down how they do their jobs stressful. They may be concerned that managers want to force them out or replace them. Employees may feel ownership over their tasks, and the idea of training someone else, or cross-training someone else, can cause anxiety. By focusing on creating a culture of documentation through making it a part of every employee's job duties, some of these fears can be assuaged.

Initially approaching employees with the reasoning behind the documentation is important: ensuring continuity of services before someone moves on with little to no notice is essential to capture their wealth of knowledge. While this is a primary motivation for ensuring documentation is up to date and employees are cross-trained, another big benefit of technical succession planning is that employees can take leave without their job duties going undone (or being done poorly). When they return from leave, they will not return to an unreasonable backlog of work. Cross-training also ensures that there are others around to help during periods of high volume or during times when individuals are engaging in professional development.

Change is an inevitable part of life and libraries, whether that comes from departures, retirements, vacations, or pandemics. However, that does not mean that the disruptions and stress that change causes cannot be minimized. By keeping the broader picture at the forefront and being mindful about both administrative and technical succession planning, middle managers can help ensure that their units are well equipped to handle whatever comes their way.

Notes

1. William J. Rothwell and Stan Poduch, "Introducing Technical (Not Managerial) Succession Planning," *Public Personnel Management* 33, no. 4 (2004): 405–19. https://doi.org/10.1177/009102600403300405.
2. American Library Association, "Need for Librarians on the Rise," news release, last modified January 1, 2002, https://www.ala.org/ala/pio/piopresskits/recruitpresskit/Needforlibrarians.htm (page discontinued).
3. US Bureau of Labor Statistics, "Labor Force Statistics from the Current Population Survey," last modified January 25, 2023, https://www.bls.gov/cps/cpsaat11b.htm (page content changed).
4. America Counts Staff, "By 2030, All Baby Boomers Will be Age 65 or Older," US Census Bureau, December 10, 2019, https://www.census.gov/library/stories/2019/12/by-2030-all-baby-boomers-will-be-age-65-or-older.html.
5. Angela Bridgland, "To Fill, or How to Fill—That Is the Question: Succession Planning and Leadership Development in Academic Libraries," *Australian Academic and Research Libraries* 30, no. 1 (1999): 20–29, https://doi.org/10.1080/00048623.1999.10755074; Judith M. Nixon, "Growing Your Own Leaders: Succession Planning in Libraries," *Journal of Business and Finance Librarianship* 13, no. 3 (2008): 249–60, https://doi.org/10.1080/08963560802183229.
6. William J. Rothwell, *Effective Succession Planning*, 5th ed. (New York: American Management Association, 2016), EBSCO eBook
7. Rothwell and Poduch, "Introducing Technical," 408.
8. Rothwell and Poduch, "Introducing Technical," 409.
9. Quinn Galbraith, Sara D. Smith, and Ben Walker, "A Case for Succession Planning: How Academic Libraries Are Responding to the Need to Prepare Future Leaders," *Library Management* 33, no. 4 (2012): 221–40, https://doi.org/10.1108/01435121211242272.
10. Crystal Goldman, "Structure, Culture, and Agency: Examining Succession Planning in California State University (CSU) Libraries," *Journal of Library Administration* 60, no. 1 (2020): 1–21, https://doi.org/10.1080/01930826.2019.1671035.
11. Mary Chute, "Efforts in Leadership and Succession Planning, Large and Small," in *Continuing Professional Development: Pathways to Leadership in the Library and Information World*, ed. by Ann Ritchie and Clare Walker (Munich: K. G. Saur, 2007), 85–99.
12. Anne Murray, "Growing Your Own: Developing Leaders through Succession Planning," *Liber Quarterly* 17, no. 3/4 (2007), https://doi.org/10.18352/lq.7886.
13. Nixon, "Growing Your Own Leaders."
14. Galbraith, Smith, and Walker, "Case for Succession Planning."
15. Goldman, "Structure, Culture, and Agency"; Murray, "Growing Your Own."
16. Nixon, "Growing Your Own Leaders"; Murray, "Growing Your Own."
17. Chute, "Efforts in Leadership."
18. William H. Weare, "Succession Planning in Academic Libraries: A Reconsideration," in *Library Staffing for the Future* (Advances in Library Administration and Organization, Vol. 34), ed. Samantha Schmehl Hines and Marcy Simons (Bingley, UK: Emerald Group Publishing, 2015), 313–61, https://doi.org/10.1108/S0732-067120150000034013.
19. Weare, "Succession Planning," 339.
20. Murray, "Growing Your Own."
21. Galbraith, Smith, and Walker, "Case for Succession Planning."
22. Galbraith, Smith, and Walker, "Case for Succession Planning"; Bridgland, "To Fill."
23. Karl G. Siewert and Pamela Louderback, "The 'Bus Proof' Library: Technical Succession Planning, Knowledge Transfer, and Institutional Memory," *Journal of Library Administration* 59, no. 4 (2019): 455–74, https://doi.org/10.1080/01930826.2019.1593716.
24. Siewert and Louderback, "'Bus Proof' Library," 463.

Bibliography

America Counts Staff. "By 2030, All Baby Boomers Will be Age 65 or Older." US Census Bureau, December 10, 2019. https://www.census.gov/library/stories/2019/12/by-2030-all-baby-boomers-will-be-age-65-or-older.html.

American Library Association. "Need for Librarians on the Rise." News release. Last modified January 1, 2002. https://www.ala.org/ala/pio/piopresskits/recruitpresskit/Needforlibrarians.htm (page discontinued).

Bridgland, Angela. "To Fill, or How to Fill—That Is the Question: Succession Planning and Leadership Development in Academic Libraries." *Australian Academic and Research Libraries* 30, no. 1 (1999): 20–29. https://doi.org/10.1080/00048623.1999.10755074.

Chute, Mary. "Efforts in Leadership and Succession Planning, Large and Small." In *Continuing Professional Development: Pathways to Leadership in the Library and Information World*, edited by Ann Ritchie and Clare Walker, 85–99. Munich: K. G. Saur, 2007.

Galbraith, Quinn, Sara D. Smith, and Ben Walker. "A Case for Succession Planning: How Academic Libraries Are Responding to the Need to Prepare Future Leaders." *Library Management* 33, no. 4 (2012): 221–40. https://doi.org/10.1108/01435121211242272.

Goldman, Crystal. "Structure, Culture, and Agency: Examining Succession Planning in California State University (CSU) Libraries." *Journal of Library Administration* 60, no. 1 (2020): 1–21. https://doi.org/10.1080/01930826.2019.1671035.

Murray, Anne. "Growing Your Own: Developing Leaders through Succession Planning." *Liber Quarterly* 17, no. 3/4 (2007). https://doi.org/10.18352/lq.7886.

Nixon, Judith M. "Growing Your Own Leaders: Succession Planning in Libraries." *Journal of Business and Finance Librarianship* 13, no. 3 (2008): 249–60. https://doi.org/10.1080/08963560802183229.

Rothwell, William J. *Effective Succession Planning: Ensuring Leadership Continuity and Building Talent from Within*, 5th ed. New York: American Management Association, 2016. EBSCO eBook.

Rothwell, William J., and Stan Poduch. "Introducing Technical (Not Managerial) Succession Planning." *Public Personnel Management* 33, no. 4 (2004): 405–19. https://doi.org/10.1177/009102600403300405.

Siewert, Karl G., and Pamela Louderback. "The 'Bus Proof' Library: Technical Succession Planning, Knowledge Transfer, and Institutional Memory." *Journal of Library Administration* 59, no. 4 (2019): 455–74. https://doi.org/10.1080/01930826.2019.1593716.

US Bureau of Labor Statistics. "Labor Force Statistics from the Current Population Survey." Last modified January 25, 2023. https://www.bls.gov/cps/cpsaat11b.htm (page content changed).

Weare, William H. "Succession Planning in Academic Libraries: A Reconsideration." In *Library Staffing for the Future* (Advances in Library Administration and Organization, Vol. 34), edited by Samantha Schmehl Hines and Marcy Simons, 313–361. Bingley, UK: Emerald Group Publishing, 2015. https://doi.org/10.1108/S0732-067120150000034013.

Salary Studies and Unions

CHAPTER 9

Assessing Salary Equitably

A Review and Case Study of UVA Library's Salary Review and Adjustment Initiative

Mira Waller, Carla Lee, Donna Tolson, and Gail White

Salary plays a significant role in retention and recruitment, but it can be challenging to establish an appropriate and equitable baseline for pay. In 2018, the University of Virginia (UVA) Library collaborated with UVA Human Resources (UVA HR) to create a compensation review process that would establish salary equity both internally and with respect to peers in academic libraries. This work required a new focus on job responsibilities and position descriptions across all job types and the development of a career ladder for nonfaculty librarians. The review considered salary market ranges for similar work at other academic libraries and institutions, as well as the relevant experience and education of each employee. Due to the size of the library staff, the many different types of job profiles, and the need for the library to self-resource this initiative, the process was designed to take four years, with approximately a quarter of the staff reviewed each year. The library has just completed the data collection phase for the fourth year of this process and dedicated a recurring commitment of approximately $720,000 to this initiative to date.

In each year of the review, the library has learned valuable lessons that have helped to refine and improve the process. This chapter will include a brief overview of the literature about compensation, relevant to academic libraries, and then focus on lessons learned while developing and implementing a large-scale, multiyear salary review and adjustment process. We will also share how those lessons are applicable to others looking for practical guidance on designing and managing this type of pay equity initiative. Through sharing our process, the challenges we encountered, and the lessons we learned, we hope to contribute to best practices in the literature and reinvigorate research about pay equity across all jobs in academic libraries.

Problem Definition

Although there is general literature supporting the importance of compensation reviews, pay equity, and salary adjustments,[1] less scholarship exists specific to academic libraries. Even less is current and comprehensive across all job classifications and positions. The COVID-19 pandemic accelerated retirements and resignations and exacerbated challenges around recruitment and retention of high-performing staff in many areas, including academic libraries.[2] Therefore, it will be critical to investigate, study, and implement strategies to reduce staff turnover and retain and recruit talent. This is an enormous topic that touches on so many areas. This chapter will focus on one approach to addressing compensation equity through a case study of the UVA Library's iterative development and implementation of a multiyear salary equity review.

Literature Review

A 2021 pay equity research report, conducted by the Society for Human Resource Management, concludes that pay equity best practices, including pay equity reviews, provide a competitive advantage and are good for both employees and the organization.[3] Pay equity can "increase efficiency, creativity, and productivity by helping to attract the best employees, reduce turnover, and increase commitment to the organization."[4] Salary equity, pay audits, compensation reviews, and the importance of pay as one of the factors relevant to employee churn and recruitment have been key topics of study in several industries.[5] This general literature even includes models and examples of how to do a salary equity study and implement a salary equity adjustment plan for faculty in higher education.[6] While library literature in this area exists, recent research is sparse given the heightened importance of recruitment and retention as COVID-19 spurred the Great Resignation.[7] The literature that exists is focused on librarians, sometimes even more narrowly defined as librarians who also have faculty status, rather than all library staff.[8]

Little attention has been paid in library literature to all the positions that are not librarians, even though the largest percentage of staff in most libraries are not librarians.[9] Surprisingly, there is minimal discussion of salary and benefits negotiation by individuals in library scholarship, as well as a gap in the literature regarding surveys of librarians' experiences with compensation negotiation prior to a study by Farrell and Geraci in

2017.[10] Furthermore, literature that includes a comprehensive review of salaries across an academic library, regardless of position type or employee classification, is almost nonexistent. The North Carolina Library Association's pay equity project, which was completed in 2009, is the most recent resource examining the salaries of all positions across libraries, from librarian to bookmobile driver to systems administrator.[11] While the few sources that give detailed library salaries do include the salaries of paraprofessional positions, librarian salaries are still much better documented. For example, the salary survey by the American Library Association and the Allied and Professional Association (ALA-APA) includes librarian salary information for 2006–2011, 2014, 2016, and 2019, while it includes only 2006–2007 salary information for positions that do not need an MLS.[12] Given that fewer MLS graduates identify as librarians working in a library, while more describe themselves as "nonlibrarians" that work in a library,[13] it is likely that any library pay review or salary equity study will need to include more than librarians to be considered effective and equitable.

Case Study

Background

UVA is a doctoral university at the "very high research activity level" per the Carnegie Classification system.[14] The main campus in Charlottesville, Virginia, consists of twelve schools, including a medical school, law school, and business school. The university works on a distributed governance model and a responsibility-centered financial model (RCM), with each school operating largely independently. While there are university policies and some central services, such as the library, many functions are decentralized, with each school making its own decisions and devising independent procedures.

However, in 2018, the university shifted to a more centralized model for providing HR support. In this model, units no longer employ HR personnel but work with a UVA HR business partner, assigned and supervised by UVA HR, which provides customized support for the unit, while working with specialized central teams who serve the whole university. One advantage of this new structure is deep subject expertise in areas such as recruitment, employee relations, and compensation. Through UVA HR business partners, core HR services are strategically linked with individual school and unit needs. This model of HR support was key in the project outlined below, as it tapped into both an HR professional familiar with the library functions and staff, and a pool of professionals specializing in compensation review.

When John Unsworth, dean of libraries and university librarian, joined UVA in 2016, he held one-on-one meetings with all the staff. One of the themes that emerged from these interviews was a sense that compensation was low and not equitable. He asked that we develop a plan for a compensation review that would include staff of all categories, looking particularly to address these issues:

- *Inequity by employment classification.* UVA permits employees to remain in their original employment classification even when a classification is retired. At the time we began the review, library employees belonged to three different classifications: Administrative and Professional (A&P) Faculty, University Staff, or Classified Staff. A&P Faculty and University Staff policies are governed by the university, while Classified Staff policy is governed by the state. Multiple employment classifications resulted in different annual increases. University Staff and A&P Faculty classifications had reliable increases based on merit, but Classified Staff, whose increases were granted by the state legislature, had some years with no increase, nor are they eligible for merit pay. Instead, they receive across-the-board increases if the state budget includes increases for state workers.
- *Pay stagnation.* Staff who had been in the same role over many years had minimal increases. A&P Faculty had access to a promotion process, unlike University Staff or Classified Staff.
- *Inclusion and comprehensiveness.* Although the university occasionally conducted equity studies for a specific role or sector (e.g., information technology), we had never conducted a review that included everyone in the organization. Also, some staff had the perception that performance evaluations were inflated by a subset of managers, resulting in possible uneven application of merit pay increases.
- *Market competitiveness.* Failed recruitment and loss of personnel in some roles, sometimes to other units at the university, raised concerns that we were not offering competitive salaries. We needed to have a better understanding of how our salaries compared to similar roles both within UVA and at other academic institutions.

In summary, our goal was to develop a rigorous and repeatable process that included both equity and market factors across all positions in the library.

Development of the Process

Our first step was to engage with compensation experts based in UVA HR, through the library's UVA HR business partner. From the compensation experts we learned about job profiles and their importance in compensation. More general than a position description but more complete than a job classification, each profile identifies a set of responsibilities, job requirements, and a salary range. The compensation experts explained that they would first conduct external market reviews for job profiles in the library. UVA HR's compensation team routinely used market data from Educomp and the College and University Professional Association. We provided data from the Association of Research Libraries (ARL) as well, although, as noted in the literature review, this source does not include salary data for lower-paid, nonprofessional job titles. If the salary range for a UVA job profile was substantially lower than the salary range for comparable profiles at other employers, then UVA would adjust the salary range attached to the job profile. Once the salary range for a profile was confirmed or adjusted, the compensation team would perform an equity review of the individual salaries for all employees within the profile at the library, based on years of experience and, if appropriate, significant differences in responsibility. For profiles with only one or two employees in the library, the team would look at salaries of employees in the same profile in other units of the university.

Once we understood the compensation review process, we needed to determine the parameters we would apply to each year's review. After identifying a rough annual budget for recommended increases (we allocated $200,000 in the first year, including fringe benefits), we made an educated guess on the number of employees in our 225-person organization that could be reviewed each year. We arrived at a four-year plan, reviewing between fifty and sixty employees each year, which should allow us to make salary adjustments for about half the number included in the review. We would start with the lowest paid employee profiles, where we also had the highest proportion of Classified Staff who had experienced the most pay stagnation over the last decade. One additional parameter important to us was timing: we wanted the recommendations and resulting adjustments to be completed before the annual merit increases. This seemed a logical extension of the equity principle—to ensure that an employee's annual increase would be based on the newly adjusted, equitable salary. Our final procedural requirement was to gain approval of the plan from the office of the provost, to whom the dean reports. The concept of the review was approved, and UVA HR was given authority to approve any salary adjustments we implemented based on their recommendations for staff positions. When we included faculty in the reviews, which would not happen until year three, we would need the provost's approval for any faculty salary adjustments.

Year One: July 2018–April 2019

We began by establishing our data-gathering protocol. We needed to provide the compensation team with a list of job profiles (figure 9.1), with employee names, education, and years of experience. We selected the profiles based on average salary and number of employees in the profile. We then asked managers for the employees included in the review to compare each employee's specific duties to those in their more general job profile. In most cases, the current job profile was confirmed, but in a few cases, an employee's duties had changed substantially enough to warrant a new job profile assignment. For example, one employee who had moved from a circulation role to a data analysis role with the assessment team was changed from a library coordinator profile to a data analyst profile. These types of changes were made in close consultation with the UVA HR business partner.

Because the compensation team used market data that matched University Staff profiles, we had to identify the best University Staff profile match for Classified Staff.

This was generally a straightforward process, especially when we had University Staff employees with similar roles. It also gave us the ability to focus on job responsibilities, irrespective of different employee classifications. Once the job profile was confirmed or selected, managers collected information on the highest degree held by the employee and years of experience. In the first year, we gathered both total years of experience at UVA (which was already in the HR system), and total years of experience relative to the current role (which was not). After the first year, we amended this practice to provide only years of experience relative to the current role. For instance, an employee who had four years of experience as a director, but twenty years at UVA, would be compared to other employees who had similar years of experience in the director role, regardless of service length at UVA. This also allowed us to include relevant experience earned outside UVA.

In our initial year, we learned a great deal about how the market and equity review processes worked. Salary ranges for four UVA library roles were reviewed (library assistant, coordinator, specialist, and supervisor), using the job profile description of duties and qualifications to ensure that UVA job profiles were compared to equivalent roles in the Educomp and College and University Professional Association data. All the library roles were found to have salary ranges in line with comparable roles at other Association of American Universities institutions. As a result, the salary range parameters for these roles were not changed.

Year 1 Job Profiles

Library roles:	Library Assistant
	Library Coordinator
	Library Specialist I
	Library Supervisor
Other roles:	Administrative and Office Specialist I, II
	Data Analyst
	Facility Coordinator
	Intermediate Administrative Assistant
	Inventory Technician
	Public Relations and Marketing Specialist III
	Store and Warehouse Specialist III
	Technical Support I

Figure 9.1. Year 1 job profiles

Equity reviews looked at an individual employee's placement within the salary range of their job profile. Expected placement depended entirely on experience in the role, since substantial differences in responsibility or expertise should have resulted in different job profiles. Differences in education were relevant only if an employee's education was lower than required for the job profile—in that case, the required education level could be met by a certain number of years of experience (e.g., four years of experience could replace a bachelor's degree requirement for an employee who had only a high school diploma). Education above the job profile's educational requirement and certifications did not affect placement in the salary range. Additionally, no differences were factored in for performance, employment classification, or other elements that may have resulted in differential pay over the years. Since we award merit-based raises, we did not want to erase merit-based differences entirely, but we also wanted to address inequities based on nonperformance criteria. We determined reviews should focus on equity within the pay scale based on years of experience but decided not to reduce current salaries that were higher than expected by the equity review.

After completing the market and equity reviews, the compensation team provided us with multiple scenarios for recommended adjustments. Examples included scenarios that used years of experience at the library versus years of experience in a current role; scenarios that recommended increases based on placement in the range versus placement against all other UVA employees in the profile; and scenarios that capped increases at 10 percent (the allowable increase at UVA for a noncompetitive job change) versus non-capped increases. After considering the options, we chose to use years of experience in the current role for placement in the salary range, as well as to cap salary adjustments at 10 percent per year. Even with these decisions, the total recommended salary adjustments ended up being $227,770 (figure 9.2), and we elected to increase the annual amount we would commit.

EQUITY REVIEW FROM 2019
UVA HR RECOMMENDATION: PAY INCREASES FOR 40 EMPLOYEES

	Aggregate data for 60 employees in 14 profiles
Years of experience of 60 employees	1066
Current, Base Pay Annually	$2,667,273
$, Change	$163,393
%, Change	6.1%
Future, Base Pay Annually	$2,830,666
Fringe Cost (39.4%)	$64,377
Total Annual Cost of Recommendations	$227,770

Figure 9.2. UVA HR recommendation: pay increases for 40 employees

In the first year, we learned a great deal about how the process would be viewed by employees. For instance, years of experience in the role was a better index for salary level than total years of experience at the library, but since we had collected both, it was confusing for staff who had the same length of service, but different years of experience in their role. For example, an employee who was a library specialist for twenty years should have a salary in the upper third of the range for the library specialist profile, but an employee who had started as a library specialist and moved up to a supervisory role within the last five years would be in the lower third of the library supervisor profile (which has a higher salary range). Even when we explained this difference in experience, some staff members were frustrated since we had collected both total years of experience and years of experience in the role. To address this confusion and frustration moving forward, we developed better communication workflows, collected only years of experience relevant to the current role, and provided concrete examples of what counted as experience relevant to the current role.

We also learned that matching employees in Classified Staff profiles to the most appropriate University Staff profile could be difficult. In general, Classified Staff profiles are broader in scope than University Staff profiles, which meant that employees in the same Classified Staff profile might be matched to different University Staff profiles depending on the level of their skill set or responsibilities. Our UVA HR business partner was crucial in helping managers make the most accurate match and in explaining how the match was selected to Classified Staff employees. The UVA HR compensation team worked very collaboratively with us, asking us for details about positions when they were not certain how to compare data. We also met several times after receiving their recommendations to talk through the recommended options.

Lastly, we learned the importance of communication. The associate dean for administration shared the plan with the entire organization at a town hall and explained which job profiles would be included in the first round via e-mail to the entire staff. Letters were sent to every employee included in the review, indicating what profile they were in or had been matched to, whether an increase was recommended, what the increase would be, and when it would appear in their paycheck. Even so, many employees consulted their managers with questions, and the managers were unprepared to explain the process and outcomes to each employee. While the associate dean for administration and UVA HR business partner met with every employee who had questions, we resolved to include managers more fully in the notification process so they were better prepared. The associate dean for administration also prepared a deep dive presentation explaining the process in detail in an open meeting for staff.

Year Two: July 2019–April 2021

In the second year of the review, we included finance and administrative support roles and tackled the librarian job profile (figure 9.3). In the University Staff system, there was only one profile for librarian, accounting for thirty-eight of our employees ranging from subject librarians to preservation specialists to catalogers. Even though we had other profiles for library managers and directors, a single profile was inadequate to cover the diversity of expertise and levels of professional responsibility represented by these librarians. Additionally, as we had learned while matching Classified Staff to University Staff profiles, we would need more specific profiles to accurately match our A&P Faculty librarians to University Staff profiles for their inclusion in the review in year three.

To understand this, it may be helpful to explain how UVA has changed the way professional librarians are classified in the last thirty-five years. Before 1989, professional librarians were hired as professors. Most librarians moved to the non-tenure-track A&P Faculty classification, when it was established, which includes self-governance, with promotion available and three-year appointment cycles.[15] In 2008, the University Staff classification was established, and most A&P Faculty at the university, but not all librarians, transferred into the University Staff system. In 2014, after UVA signaled that it would retire the A&P Faculty classification and develop a new non-tenure-track faculty policy, the dean decided to stop hiring A&P Faculty. Beginning in 2015, all staff, including librarians, were hired into the University Staff classification. This classification is not faculty and therefore does not offer tenure and has no cycle of renewal.[16]

When our current dean joined the library in 2016, he lobbied the university administration to include librarians in a newly designed non-tenure-track faculty classification, Academic General Faculty (AGF). Over time the policy for AGF was edited to include a librarian track, which, much like the A&P Faculty policy, allows opportunities for promotion, self-governance, and three-year appointment cycles.[17] We are just now in the process of implementing the AGF librarian track and posting our first AGF positions. Librarian positions are eligible for AGF if the role's primary responsibilities include "the production of original scholarship for publication, teaching, or innovation in research methods."[18] Currently library manager and director positions are not eligible for the AGF classification. When implementation is complete, UVA librarians may be in one of three classifications (AGF, A&P Faculty, or University Staff), all non-tenure-track but allowing for the possibility of promotion.

All of this activity around the establishment of the AGF librarian track highlighted a known inequity between professional librarians in the faculty and University Staff classifications: University Staff librarians had no opportunity for promotion as individual contributors, while faculty librarians did (although all faculty positions in the library are non-tenure-track). To address this issue, and to provide more accurate job profiles in the University Staff classification system, the library partnered with UVA HR to create a librarian career ladder for the University Staff librarians. A small working group looked for other models of nonfaculty career ladders for librarians and were unable to find a comparable model. Using a model from the UVA School of Nursing, the working group created three new job profiles (librarian I, II, and III) and established the minimum qualifications for each, as well as expectations for professional involvement and contributions to the field. After creating the profiles, the group created the procedures for advancing through the ladder, which enabled us to map all professional librarians to the appropriate job profile as part of this review. By recognizing years of expertise and professional contributions, this new promotion model should help to better compensate and retain staff in the University Staff librarian job classification.

Year 2 Job Profiles

Library roles:	Librarian I, II, III (staff categories)
Other roles:	Administrative and Office Specialist III
	Engagement and Annual Giving Officer
	Facility Assistant Manager
	Finance Services Specialist I, II
	Finance Generalist, Senior Finance Generalist
	IT Project Manager I
	IT Specialist II
	Policy and Planning Specialist II
	Project Associate
	Senior Fiscal Technician

Figure 9.3. Year 2 job profiles

Also in the second year, we had to decide how to handle new employees hired in job profiles already reviewed. It ended up being easily addressed—we used the data from the compensation review results to determine the salary we could offer to maintain equity in job profiles that had been through the review. Consequently, we had confidence new employees were being paid an appropriate and equitable salary compared to their colleagues. One unanticipated issue that emerged in the second year was a policy hurdle: in reaction to the pandemic shutdown, the university froze all compensation increases in mid-March 2020. We were forced to delay acting on the recommendations from the compensation team until the following spring. After making the case to the provost that we needed to complete the four-year process to be equitable within the organization and to protect the salary set aside in a time of budget reduction, we were able to update the recommendations received the previous spring, add in the small number of new employees in the included profiles, and make equity adjustments in the spring of 2021.

While we had learned a lot during our first year in this process, year two of the review brought additional insights. Case in point, it was extremely important to involve University Staff librarians in developing the new career ladder, and we were fortunate to have an engaged working group who helped to develop the criteria for the three levels. Even so, the implications of salary recommendations based on placement in the ladder were confusing to many. The higher up the profile ladder, the lower an employee fell in the salary range for that profile, since years of experience is a criterion for each rank. There were also instances where we needed to revisit decisions due to new information regarding relevant experience. When this occurred, we collected additional information and made updates and salary increases. For instance, some questions were raised by staff who had foreign language skills and had been performing subject liaison duties for many years prior to being placed in a librarian role. Their earlier work was not included in the calculation of their experience as a librarian, but once we were alerted to the situation, we worked with their managers to revise their years of experience and amend their salary adjustments accordingly. In another case, an employee's years of experience at another institution had not been included in the data forwarded to UVA HR. After correcting for the omission, a new salary recommendation was developed. These examples highlight the importance of communication from everyone involved in the process, as well as clear definitions and the iterative nature of the review process.

Year Three: July 2021–April 2022

In the third year, we included faculty librarians, library technologists, and library managers (figure 9.4). As with Classified employees, faculty librarians needed to be matched to the most appropriate University Staff profile for their role, and the outcomes were more precise since we had created the University Staff career ladder in the prior year. After receiving salary recommendations for the faculty librarians, we revisited the adjustments from the previous year for University Staff librarians with comparable amounts of experience. In a few cases, additional adjustments to the University Staff librarian salaries were justified.

In addition to the library-specific roles, we also included many technical roles, including computer support technicians, multimedia professionals, web designers, communications specialists, project managers, and academic discipline–specific technology professionals (ADSTPs) such as GIS experts, statistical data analysts, and digital humanities specialists. For some of these profiles, we had relatively small numbers of library employees, so the equity reviews relied more heavily on salary comparisons with employees at the institution but outside of the library. Well-crafted position descriptions and their accurate match to appropriate job profiles was especially important so that the compensation team had confidence they were comparing library employees' salaries to those of employees doing similar work in another part of the university. Particularly in the information technology (IT) roles, we changed the job profiles of some employees to better align with the work they were doing.

Year 3 Job Profiles

Library roles:	Librarian II, III (faculty categories)
	Library Manager
	Library Technologist
Other roles:	ADSTP (Academic Discipline-Specific Technology Professional) Specialist
	Communications Generalist 3
	Computer Engineer 4
	Events and Venue Manager
	Executive Assistant
	Multimedia Creative Professional 3
	Museum Registrar
	Project Manager
	Software Engineer 2
	Stewardship and Donor Relations Manager
	Technical Support 2-5
	Web Developer 3

Figure 9.4. Year 3 job profiles

By now we have come to expect that each year will bring additional takeaways and insights. In year three we learned the importance of focusing on responsibilities rather than classification. We have a very complex set of job profiles for librarians spanning three distinct employment classification systems, each with its own set of policies and historic compensation practices. We have also identified some profiles that are very similar; for instance, a position that provides skilled expertise in a particular type of software or technology could be hired as a library technologist, an ADSTP, or a librarian, depending on their service focus and job duties. Each of these job profiles has a different salary range, and profiles in the IT job families typically earn more than profiles in the library job family. While our review process could not ignore or always adjust for structural differences in profile ranges, job families, or policy, we were able to provide the first ever equity review at our organization that focused on the duties of each employee and their experience in the role compared to others doing similar work.

Year Four: July 2022–April 2023

As we write this chapter, we have completed the data collection phase of the fourth year of the review. The final year includes highly skilled IT professionals, library leadership, and a small operational unit that was moved into the library this year (figure 9.5). We followed the same process for data collection, and the compensation team will work directly with the dean and the UVA HR business partner to review and approve any salary adjustments. At the conclusion of this process, we will have reviewed the salaries of everyone in the UVA Library employed prior to 2019. All employees hired since 2019 were either included in a review or they were hired at a salary level that is equitable with existing employees.

Year 4 Job Profiles

Library roles:	Associate University Librarian
	Deputy University Librarian
	Library Director
Other roles:	ADSTP (Academic Discipline-Specific Technology Professional) Senior
	Associate Dean for Administration
	Budget Manager
	Communications Director
	Director, Administration
	IT Director
	IT Manager
	Systems Engineer 4
	Software Engineer 4.5

Figure 9.5. Year 4 job profiles

Results

Staff retention was a key area we hope to see positively impacted by our salary equity review. To this end, in the most recent library climate survey conducted in the fall of 2022, 77 percent of UVA Library employees agreed that they were fairly compensated, with almost one-quarter of employees still awaiting the final review of this year's outcome. This statistic rose from 53 percent in 2020, although differences in the question construction make a direct comparison impossible. Additionally, 81 percent agreed that they were motivated to stay with the organization, compared to 66 percent in 2020. Our turnover is relatively low: we lost fourteen employees in 2022, ten of which were retirements. The four who left for other opportunities constitute about 2 percent of our workforce. While we do not know how much the compensation review has influenced these statistics, it is reasonable to conclude that it has had a positive impact on our retention and employee motivation to stay.

Conclusion and Takeaways

Doing a comprehensive salary equity review is a long, multifaceted process. Partnerships with our UVA HR business partner and the compensation team at the university continue to be critical to the success of this project. Compensation is a sensitive area where it is particularly important to be accurate, consistent, and fair. Providing valid market analysis and equity reviews that we could stand behind required us to trust and depend on the experts we were partnering with at UVA HR to apply best practices in salary analysis. However, for them to do their work, we needed to provide employee data not already in the HR system that was as uniform and accurate as possible. Establishing clear and consistent employee data on experience in the role, education, and current position descriptions before the beginning of the actual compensation analysis was tremendously beneficial. While changes to process infrastructure were necessary due to changes in circumstances and led to some variation in procedures from year to year, we recommend that the underpinning principles of the review remain consistent through the entire process.

Clear and frequent communication with all stakeholders throughout the process, and with managers in particular, is key to the success of a compensation review project. For example, it is important to communicate with managers from the beginning and clarify the different goals and outcomes between a compensation review for equity and the outcomes of a merit review for performance. We also recommend testing the data collection terms in advance; in our case, "experience related to the position" proved to be surprisingly subjective, and clarification was required to ensure equitable application. Staff will also have questions specific to their circumstances, even with consistent communication, and their managers are the first people that employees turn to with questions. In the first year, when we did not provide them with advance information, some managers felt ill-prepared to answer questions. In subsequent years, we gave managers more lead time, answered their questions before employees received letters, and saw better results. Since our process spanned multiple years, it was helpful to review the principles, definitions, and procedure just before the results of the compensation review were shared with employees each year. This helped to refresh everyone on why and how we were conducting the review.

We would also caution that it is unlikely that decades of compensation inequities can be completely erased in one review process. In our case, different employee classifications have had different compensation and merit structures, allowing some significant variations to develop over the years. We surfaced situations where employees with the same job and years of relevant experience were making less than others, including those from underrepresented groups, and this process allowed us to take corrective action. However, we did not try to neutralize all historical factors. We encountered a few salary anomalies that were explained by large retention offers in previous years, or past reductions in job responsibilities, such as someone moving from a managerial role to a nonmanagerial role, that did not result in reduced pay. We did not correct downward for these situations.

While the process we undertook helped ameliorate some of the systemic inequality at our library, it was not within our budget or power to completely correct these differences in every case. Be aware of university or state policies that could have an impact on decision-making as well—in our case, a 10 percent annual cap on salary increases needed to be considered in most cases.

While a comprehensive review across employee categories is very complex, it has been equally rewarding. As noted in the results, we have seen improved staff satisfaction and intention to remain with the organization. In future years, we plan to maintain equitable compensation practices by paying attention to appropriate placement in job profile salary ranges as we hire new personnel and by adjusting salaries proactively for significant changes in position responsibilities. We also intend to expand on our work and continue to collaborate with the UVA HR team to look at developing career paths for library employees who are not in librarian profiles.

Notes

1. Lisa Nagele-Piazza, "The Importance of Pay Equity," Society for Human Resource Management, February 21, 2020, https://www.shrm.org/hr-today/news/hr-magazine/spring2020/pages/importance-of-pay-equity.aspx; Kylie Ora Lobell, "How to Leverage Equity to Attract and Retain Employees," Society for Human Resource Management, July 12, 2022, https://www.shrm.org/resourcesandtools/hr-topics/compensation/pages/how-to-leverage-equity-to-attract-and-retain-employees.aspx.
2. Brad Federman, "Turning the Tide on the Talent Tsunami," *HRProfessionalsMagazine* (blog), July 26, 2021, https://hrprofessionalsmagazine.com/2021/07/26/turning-the-tide-on-the-talent-tsunami/; Lara Ewen, "Quitting Time," *American Libraries* 53, no. 6 (June 2022): 38–41.
3. Society for Human Resource Management, *Bridging the Pay Gap* (Alexandria, VA: Society for Human Resource Management, 2021), https://www.shrm.org/hr-today/trends-and-forecasting/research-and-surveys/documents/pay%20equity%20full%20report.pdf (page discontinued).
4. Nagele-Piazza, "Importance of Pay Equity."
5. Robert L. Armacost, "A Three-Pronged Approach to Evaluating Salary Equity among Faculty, Administrators, and Staff at a Metropolitan Research University" (paper presented at the Annual Forum for the Association for Institutional Research, Toronto, Ontario, June 2–5, 2002), https://eric.ed.gov/?id=ED474147; Society for Human Resource Management, "SHRM Research Shows Pay Equity Pays Off for Employers," news release, October 25, 2021, https://www.shrm.org/about-shrm/press-room/press-releases/pages/-shrm-research-shows-pay-equity-pays-off-for-employers.aspx; Lobell, "How to Leverage Equity"; Judith K. Pringle et al., "Gender Pay Equity and Wellbeing: An Intersectional Study of Engineering and Caring Occupations," *New Zealand Journal of Employment Relations* 42, no. 3 (December 2017): 29–45; Karen Hawley Miles and Nicole Katz, "Teacher Salaries: A Critical Equity Issue," *State Education Standard* 18, no. 3 (September 2018): 18–22; Cassandra Jones Havard, "Hidden Figures: Wage Inequity and Economic Insecurity for Black Women and Other Women of Color," *St. John's Law Review* 95, no. 4 (September 2022): 641–81.
6. Lori L. Taylor et al., "How to Do a Salary Equity Study: With an Illustrative Example from Higher Education," *Public Personnel Management* 49, no. 1 (March 2020): 57–82; Don Noel Smith, "Achieving Equity in Faculty Salaries: A Proven Model," *Planning for Higher Education* 36, no. 3 (April–June 2008): 56–66, https://www.scup.org/resource/achieving-equity-in-faculty-salaries/.
7. Federman, "Turning the Tide"; Ewen, "Quitting Time."
8. Joan McConkey et al., "Salary Equity: A Case Study," *College and Research Libraries* 54, no. 1 (January 1993): 33–41, https://doi.org/10.5860/crl_54_01_33; Scott Seaman, "Salary Compression: A Time-Series Ratio Analysis of ARL Position Classifications," *portal: Libraries and the Academy* 7, no. 1 (January 2007): 7–24, https://doi.org/10.1353/pla.2007.0012; Scott Seaman, Carol Krismann, and Nancy Carter, "Salary Market Equity at the University of Colorado at Boulder Libraries: A Case Study Follow-up," *College and Research Libraries* 64, no. 5 (September 2003): 390–400, https://doi.org/10.5860/crl.64.5.390; Brent M. Graves and Dale Kapla, "Salary Compression among University Faculty: A Review and Case Study of Remediation and Prevention in a Collective Bargaining Environment," *Journal of Collective Bargaining in the Academy* 10, no. 1 (2018): article 3, https://doi.

org/10.58188/1941-8043.1741; Bernadette M. López-Fitzsimmons and Kanu A. Nagra, "Implementing Excellence in Diversity, Equity, and Inclusion in the Library Workforce: Tips to Overcome Challenges," *College and Research Libraries News* 82, no. 7 (July/August 2021): 314–18, https://crln.acrl.org/index.php/crlnews/article/view/25036; Quinn Galbraith, Adam Henry Callister, and Heather Kelley, "Have Academic Libraries Overcome the Gender Wage Gap? An Analysis of Gender Pay Inequality," *College and Research Libraries* 80, no. 4 (May 2019): 470–84.
9. Gene Kinnaly, "Pay Equity, Support Staff, and ALA," *Library Mosaics* 13, no. 2 (March/April 2002): 8.
10. Farrell, Shannon L., and Aliqae Geraci. "Librarians and Compensation Negotiation in the Library Workplace." *Library Management* 38, no. 1 (January 2017): 45–64. https://doi.org/10.1108/LM-08-2016-0060.
11. Beverley Gass, "NCLA's Pay Equity Project: It's about More Than Loving to Be a Librarian!" *North Carolina Libraries* 67, no. 1/2 (2009): 17–19, http://www.ncl.ecu.edu/index.php/NCL/article/view/251 (page discontinued).
12. ALA-APA, "ALA-APA Salary Survey," accessed January 6, 2023, https://ala-apa.org/salary-survey/.
13. Suzie Allard, "Careers during COVID," *Library Journal* 146, no. 10 (October 2021): 36.
14. Carnegie Classification of Institutions of Higher Education, "University of Virginia-Main Campus," accessed April 14, 2023, https://carnegieclassifications.acenet.edu/institution/university-of-virginia-main-campus/.
15. UVA Policy Directory, "HRM-003: Employment of Administrative or Professional General Faculty Members," University of Virginia, accessed April 14, 2023, https://uvapolicy.virginia.edu/policy/HRM-003.
16. UVA Policy Directory, "HRM-021: Terms and Conditions of University Staff Employment," University of Virginia, accessed April 14, 2023, https://uvapolicy.virginia.edu/policy/HRM-021.
17. UVA Policy Directory, "PROV-004: Employment of Academic General Faculty Members (Tenure-Ineligible)," accessed April 14, 2023, https://uvapolicy.virginia.edu/policy/PROV-004.
18. UVA Policy Directory, "PROV-004."

Bibliography

ALA-APA. "ALA-APA Salary Survey." Accessed January 6, 2023. https://ala-apa.org/salary-survey/.
Allard, Suzie. "Careers during COVID." *Library Journal* 146, no. 10 (October 2021): 32–37.
Armacost, Robert L. "A Three-Pronged Approach to Evaluating Salary Equity among Faculty, Administrators, and Staff at a Metropolitan Research University." Paper presented at the Annual Forum for the Association for Institutional Research, Toronto, Ontario, June 2–5, 2002. https://eric.ed.gov/?id=ED474147.
Carnegie Classification of Institutions of Higher Education. "University of Virginia-Main Campus." Accessed April 14, 2023. https://carnegieclassifications.acenet.edu/institution/university-of-virginia-main-campus/.
Ewen, Lara. "Quitting Time." *American Libraries* 53, no. 6 (June 2022): 38–41.
Farrell, Shannon L., and Aliqae Geraci. "Librarians and Compensation Negotiation in the Library Workplace." *Library Management* 38, no. 1 (January 2017): 45–64. doi:https://doi.org/10.1108/LM-08-2016-0060.
Federman, Brad. "Turning the Tide on the Talent Tsunami." *HRProfessionalsMagazine* (blog), July 26, 2021. https://hrprofessionalsmagazine.com/2021/07/26/turning-the-tide-on-the-talent-tsunami/.
Galbraith, Quinn, Adam Henry Callister, and Heather Kelley. "Have Academic Libraries Overcome the Gender Wage Gap? An Analysis of Gender Pay Inequality." *College and Research Libraries* 80, no. 4 (May 2019): 470–84.
Gass, Beverley. "NCLA's Pay Equity Project: It's about More Than Loving to Be a Librarian!" *North Carolina Libraries* 67, no. 1/2 (2009): 17–19. https://www.ncl.ecu.edu/index.php/NCL/article/view/251.
Graves, Brent M., and Dale Kapla. "Salary Compression among University Faculty: A Review and Case Study of Remediation and Prevention in a Collective Bargaining Environment." *Journal of Collective Bargaining in the Academy* 10, no. 1 (2018): article 3. https://doi.org/10.58188/1941-8043.1741.
Havard, Cassandra Jones. "Hidden Figures: Wage Inequity and Economic Insecurity for Black Women and Other Women of Color." *St. John's Law Review* 95, no. 4 (September 2022): 641–81.
Kinnaly, Gene. "Pay Equity, Support Staff, and ALA." *Library Mosaics* 13, no. 2 (March/April 2002): 8–10.
Lobell, Kylie Ora. "How to Leverage Equity to Attract and Retain Employees." Society for Human Resource Management, July 12, 2022. https://www.shrm.org/resourcesandtools/hr-topics/compensation/pages/how-to-leverage-equity-to-attract-and-retain-employees.aspx.
López-Fitzsimmons, Bernadette M., and Kanu A. Nagra. "Implementing Excellence in Diversity, Equity, and Inclusion in the Library Workforce: Tips to Overcome Challenges." *College and Research Libraries News* 82, no. 7 (July/August 2021): 314–18. https://crln.acrl.org/index.php/crlnews/article/view/25036.
McConkey, Joan, Susan Anthes, Ellen Robertson, and Barbara Bintliff. "Salary Equity: A Case Study." *College and Research Libraries* 54, no. 1 (January 1993): 33–41. https://doi.org/10.5860/crl_54_01_33.
Miles, Karen Hawley, and Nicole Katz. "Teacher Salaries: A Critical Equity Issue." *State Education Standard* 18, no. 3 (September 2018): 18–22.
Nagele-Piazza, Lisa. "The Importance of Pay Equity." Society for Human Resource Management, February 21, 2020. https://www.shrm.org/hr-today/news/hr-magazine/spring2020/pages/importance-of-pay-equity.aspx.

Pringle, Judith K., Sharyn Davies, Lynne Giddings, and Judy McGregor. "Gender Pay Equity and Wellbeing: An Intersectional Study of Engineering and Caring Occupations." *New Zealand Journal of Employment Relations* 42, no. 3 (December 2017): 29–45.

Seaman, Scott. "Salary Compression: A Time-Series Ratio Analysis of ARL Position Classifications." *portal: Libraries and the Academy* 7, no. 1 (January 2007): 7–24. https://doi.org/10.1353/pla.2007.0012.

Seaman, Scott, Carol Krismann, and Nancy Carter. "Salary Market Equity at the University of Colorado at Boulder Libraries: A Case Study Follow-up." *College and Research Libraries* 64, no. 5 (September 2003): 390–400. https://doi.org/10.5860/crl.64.5.390.

Smith, Don Noel. "Achieving Equity in Faculty Salaries: A Proven Model." *Planning for Higher Education* 36, no. 3 (April–June 2008): 56–66. https://www.scup.org/resource/achieving-equity-in-faculty-salaries/.

Society for Human Resource Management. *Bridging the Pay Gap: Why Pay Equity Pays Off*. Alexandria, VA: Society for Human Resource Management, 2021. https://www.shrm.org/hr-today/trends-and-forecasting/research-and-surveys/documents/pay%20equity%20full%20report.pdf (page discontinued).

———. "SHRM Research Shows Pay Equity Pays Off for Employers." News release. October 25, 2021. https://www.shrm.org/about-shrm/press-room/press-releases/pages/-shrm-research-shows-pay-equity-pays-off-for-employers.aspx.

Taylor, Lori L., Joanna N. Lahey, Molly I. Beck, and Jeffrey E. Froyd. "How to Do a Salary Equity Study: With an Illustrative Example from Higher Education." *Public Personnel Management* 49, no. 1 (March 2020): 57–82.

UVA Policy Directory. "HRM-003: Employment of Administrative or Professional General Faculty Members." University of Virginia. Accessed April 14, 2023. https://uvapolicy.virginia.edu/policy/HRM-003.

———. "HRM-021: Terms and Conditions of University Staff Employment." University of Virginia. Accessed April 14, 2023. https://uvapolicy.virginia.edu/policy/HRM-021.

———. "PROV-004: Employment of Academic General Faculty Members (Tenure-Ineligible)." University of Virginia. Accessed April 14, 2023. https://uvapolicy.virginia.edu/policy/PROV-004.

CHAPTER 10

A Salary Study Model for Academic Libraries
Leveraging Strategic Salary Studies to Generate Library Employee Goodwill

Bridgit McCafferty and Shawna Kennedy-Witthar

Defining the Problem

Despite the recent and ubiquitous emergence of the Great Resignation in headlines, the underlying issue of worker dissatisfaction with compensation has been building for some time. As noted by Gordon in "American Inequality," wages in America, when adjusted for inflation, have not risen since the 1970s.[1] For lower-wage workers, these wages have, in fact, fallen. Moreover, whereas the increase in wages kept pace with worker productivity through the early 1970s, it no longer does—a fact Piketty demonstrated in *Capital in the Twenty-First Century*, arguing that the labor income inequality has never been higher in the United States.[2]

Though not a new phenomenon, pressures in the labor market following the COVID-19 pandemic have certainly exacerbated compensation issues in every industry, including libraries. When librarians and paraprofessional staff are presented with opportunities to leave libraries to secure better hourly wages outside of higher education, retaining and recruiting qualified candidates becomes problematic. For the lowest-level staffers, this can mean leaving the library to work at a fast-food establishment, many of which are now paying a minimum of $15 an hour. Most libraries have not kept up and are just starting to do the work necessary to be more competitive. While flexible work arrangements and other perks can counteract some of this, administrators cannot ignore that compensation is at the heart of the matter for many.

Compensation is a difficult problem for administrators. Often there is pressure from executive leaders to keep labor costs low, even while staff and faculty turnover is an ever-present and accelerating setback. Library deans and directors, often caught between these two forces, must approach the issue from two different directions: improving the situation on the ground for employees, while justifying and benchmarking these improvements to ensure executive leadership buy-in for the required changes. To accurately represent the needs of employees and demonstrate to executive leadership that adjustment in compensation is not a luxury but a necessity, library administrators should start by conducting a salary study, including a review of position descriptions, employee ranks, and market-driven compensation data. This data can then be used to show administrators how employees line up with these descriptions, ranks, and compensation.

Though this may seem like a function better suited to a human resources (HR) department, most libraries exist as part of a larger organization (e.g., university, city or county, corporation, hospital, etc.). This means that the HR professionals for the organization do not have the niche knowledge a library dean or director has about the hiring pressures in the field. Moreover, they typically do not know when it is or is not appropriate to compare library specialist wages at a municipal library to those at a university library, or how the job of a librarian at a community college might be different from that of a librarian who is a faculty member at a university. Dynamics unique to libraries—such as the divide between librarians and nonlibrarians, or the difference between public-service and technical-service librarians—are nuanced. For library salary studies, a library administrator is in a better place to lead on these issues. Even the salary data that informs such a study is niche, requiring some understanding of the field. Library deans and directors will have a better sense of where they are losing staff, especially lower-level staff, and the kinds of industries they compete with, including those that are not library-adjacent. As a result, library leaders gain a real advantage if they can exercise agency by completing or being heavily involved in such a study.

The Texas A&M University-Central Texas (A&M-Central Texas) University Library and Archives discovered this through trial and error during several salary studies over a ten-year period, some initiated by the library and others imposed on the library externally. Through these experiences, the A&M-Central Texas library created a model for how to complete these studies that it still uses today. The West Texas A&M University (WTAMU) Cornette Library, recognizing that it, too, needed to review salaries, decided to adapt this model to its institution to test how it works outside of A&M-Central Texas. The development of this model, and its efficacy, are explored throughout this chapter, providing a road map for libraries wishing to complete their own study to improve salaries.

Literature Review

The topic of salary studies has not been discussed much in the context of academic libraries. The most recent literature to cover related subjects in depth, relevant to libraries, is Singer and Francisco's *Developing a Compensation Plan for your Library* and Baldwin's *The Library Compensation Handbook*.[3] Cottrell also discusses unique issues relevant to library pay and employee retention, in the hope that managers will advocate for better compensation in libraries, though Cottrell does not describe explicitly a salary study process.[4] Broadening the scope to universities and faculty salary studies across institutions, there is a wider breadth of scholarship. For instance, Marchetti and Bailey's "The Importance of HOW in Faculty Salary Equity Studies" is a case study describing the creation of a collaborative, faculty-driven annual salary equity process at the Rochester Institute of Technology.[5] This transparent process was created using rubrics and evaluative criteria that clarified how salary decisions were being made at the institution. Similarly, Taylor and colleagues describe a salary study process across public organizations, giving the example of an institution of higher education as an illustrative case.[6] Though a little older, Herzog's "A Four-Step Faculty Compensation Model" is a forerunner to the process proposed for the current qualitative study, and therefore key, as it demonstrates the same approach taken in the proposed model.[7] Also notable is Haignere's *Paychecks*, a guidebook that details faculty salary equity studies.[8]

While salary studies in academic libraries are not a prevalent research topic, the broader subject of salaries in academic libraries is: most notably, Perret and Young's recent review of librarian salaries over time.[9] Perret and Young's study is especially important because they detail how librarian salaries at institutions that are not research-focused have slipped over two decades, in comparison to salaries at Association of Research Libraries (ARL) member institutions. Moreover, they show that starting salaries for librarians slipped compared to other types of institution faculty over a twenty-five-year period of time ending in 2011.[10] Davis also presents longitudinal data about salary expenditures in academic libraries between 2000 and 2009, looking at the percentage of overall library operating budgets made up of salaries and the salary ranges for different types of library positions at both academic and public libraries.[11] These trends toward lower compensation for library faculty have a real impact, as Heady and colleagues show: compensation is one major factor in librarian turnover at academic libraries.[12] Falcone and McCartin also identify compensation as especially significant in attracting new librarians.[13]

A second set of studies focuses on the cultural aspects of compensation in libraries. For instance, Farrell and Geraci analyze pay negotiations in academic libraries and how various factors related to who is more likely to negotiate higher salaries can lead to salary inequities.[14] Ettarh's "Vocational Awe and Librarianship" discusses the ways that reverence for the profession is used against librarians in the area of compensation—librarians are expected to do the job for love of the job, rather than fair pay.[15]

These cultural and social impacts are indicative more broadly of trends that are important to salary equity studies and fair compensation in libraries, especially for women and BIPOC librarians. As Blau and Kahn note, industry is an important factor in gender pay discrepancies, and as a traditionally pink collar profession, library employees are impacted by this economic reality.[16] This does not entirely explain salary discrepancies in libraries, however, since gaps between genders, and other racial and ethnic identities, persist within the field. In "Less Money, Less Children, and Less Prestige," Eva, Lê, and Sheriff show that female academic librarians in Canada make less than males, have fewer children, and are overrepresented in the lower faculty ranks, such as assistant librarian.[17] Galbraith, Merrill, and Outzen also show that salary differences continue to exist for women and BIPOC librarians, though they have shrunk over time.[18] Salary equity studies are one important way to combat this gendered wage gap across faculty, as Brown, Troutt, and Prentice argue in their follow-up study ten years after a salary equity review at a Canadian institution.[19] They show that following their earlier equity study, the gendered wage gap was eliminated for their faculty. Moreover, as Trotter, Zacur, and Stickney argue, salary transparency, advocated by the proposed salary study model, is an important method to address enduring pay discrepancies between genders and other minority statuses, such as race.[20] Lyons and Zhang show the impact of this transparency at Canadian universities, finding that it tends to increase pay equity.[21]

Finally, there are several data sources relevant to library salaries that are valuable for library administrators embarking on this kind of salary study. Some will be discussed throughout this chapter, and some are more specialized. The most important of these are the annual salary studies from the American Library Association's Allied Professional Association (ALA-APA) and the College and University Professional Association for Human Resources (CUPA-HR). Both surveys publish ranges of salaries for various types of library jobs, such as reference librarians or copy catalogers. The ARL also publishes an annual salary survey that may be of use to ARL libraries, as well as those that aspire to be members of ARL. Additionally, the Association of College and Research Libraries (ACRL) publishes annual benchmarking data about library spending, including average annual expenditures for HR, gathered through its annual "Academic Library Trends and Statistics Survey." Annual salary data broken down by region is also regularly published in the fall by *Library Journal*.

Addressing the Problem in Practice

Given the dearth of publications about salary studies in academic libraries, we endeavor to document a model for academic libraries that wish to pursue increased compensation through salary studies. This model was developed at A&M-Central Texas over the course of successive salary studies and was adapted to the WTAMU Cornette Library as a means of testing how effective and flexible it could be at a fellow institution. This model consists of ten steps, drawn from experience, as well as from Singer and Francisco's book about compensation plans and Baril and Donily's *Academic Library Job Descriptions*.[22] The proposed steps for this model are as follows:

1. Form a committee comprised of a small number of representative library employees to coordinate and manage the study. This group should have some autonomy from library administration to make decisions about how the study is carried out in order to build trust with the committee and library employees more broadly.
2. Survey library employees about current job duties.
3. Compare reported employee job duties to actual job descriptions.
4. Edit job descriptions to match actual duties or remove duties that fall outside of job descriptions.
5. Review classifications for employees to ensure they are fair, equitable, and accurately represent all employees in a class.
6. Review classifications assigned to each job description based on adjusted job description language.
7. Reclassify employees whose updated job descriptions place them in a different category.
8. Review pay bands for each classification against benchmarked, external data for the job descriptions assigned to that classification (e.g., data from CUPA-HR, ALA, ARL, etc.). When discrepancies arise, shift job descriptions to different classifications, or shift pay bands for classifications.
9. Review individual employees to determine where they fall in pay bands, based on experience, job duties, and other data.
10. Use this data to propose market-based salary adjustments to external administrators or funding agencies.

The proposed method for this salary study model is a committee made up of members from across the library staff. The purpose of this committee is to promote transparency and objectivity as the study is conducted. This collaborative approach also promotes buy-in by library staff so that salary changes do not seem like they are coming from only the library administration. By presenting this model, we hope it can be adapted by other libraries to guide similar studies, improving library employee compensation across the industry. The following collective case study documents the development of this model, as well as its application.

A&M-Central Texas University Library & Archives

The A&M-Central Texas University Library and Archives is a 27,000-square-foot library with approximately 100,000 physical books and 500,000 e-books. We are located in Killeen, Texas, and have about 3,000 students. We are a relatively new institution, having received initial, independent accreditation in 2013. Prior to 2013, we were a university center for Tarleton State University. The university is one of the only institutions in the country to offer only upper-division and graduate courses, relying on transfer students for the entirety of our enrollment. Our Carnegie Classification is medium as a master's institution.

As mentioned above, at A&M-Central Texas, the library has participated in four salary studies focused on shifting pay for staff and faculty. The first took place in 2014, with three subsequent salary studies since that time. Some of these were initiated by university or system leadership, and others were initiated by the library itself with an eye toward attracting and retaining staff. Notably, these were not associated with a stepped, annual raise structure, though they did create promotion ladders based on experience and competence.

2014 All Staff Salary Study

The first salary study, which took place in 2014, was a staff-wide effort that examined data from CUPA-HR, which reports salaries and wages at a variety of different institutions, allowing administrators to benchmark current and proposed salaries. This survey is quite useful for library staff and faculty because the generalized jobs listed accurately articulate professional and paraprofessional classifications in libraries. CUPA-HR statistics are also the gold standard for salary studies in higher education and accommodate benchmarking against a variety of salary measures.

The first step the library took when university administration announced the study was a review of current library positions to ensure that our staff were correctly classified for the level of work they were performing. This is extremely important, because staff—and especially paraprofessional staff—who are asked to perform duties outside of or above their pay grade have no chance of receiving a fair compensation adjustment in this type of study, since those adjustments will be based on their current job description. Many paraprofessionals in the library were especially impacted by this review of duties, as it turned out they should have been classified at higher levels than they were.

Even with the library's diligence in preparing job descriptions ahead of time, there was a marked disparity between the library administration's expectations of professional and paraprofessional staff salaries from that of the committee performing the salary study. This was largely due to the fact that HR professionals and administrators from other units, who were the primary members of the committee, did not understand library jobs, and especially the distinction between professional and paraprofessional staff. While in other units, jobs can be filled by people without the professional degree as long as they have an appropriate amount of experience in the field, librarians are more akin to counselors with a professional credential. Our HR staff found this distinction challenging.

Because the committee completing the salary study had difficulties understanding our positions and the library as a niche area of the university with a distinctive employment market and context, the library director had to step in and persuasively advocate for the staff in the library. This meant making sure that library staff were placed in the correct categories based on the CUPA salary study, as well as ensuring that the CUPA categories accurately represented the larger market in the area. To this end, one helpful tool was the ALA-APA annual salary survey. Especially when it came to paraprofessional salaries, this survey supplemented the data available through the CUPA survey to show where paraprofessional salaries might have been lower in CUPA than made sense for our institution.

This was where the review of position descriptions that the library completed prior to the beginning of the study was especially helpful. Many members of the staff would have been classified in lower categories with less competitive compensation if not for the revised position descriptions that accounted for expanded duties and responsibilities that many staff members had taken on over the years without receiving appropriate recognition. By ensuring that their position descriptions were closely correlated with what staff were actually doing, the library administration was able to successfully argue for many staff members, and especially paraprofessionals, being classified into higher ranges. For instance, we were able to classify someone who was formerly a library specialist I into a library specialist III based on experience and complexity of job duties. This ensured that staff salary adjustments were substantial and meaningful.

Ultimately, the library director had to step in during this study to ensure that the library was well represented. The end result was extremely positive, with multiple members of the library staff receiving significant and well-deserved raises. Though salaries were still on the low end, they were finally more competitive in the low-cost-of-living area where the university is located. Another bright spot of this survey was that we were able to receive funding from the university for raises, since the larger initiative was initially kicked off by the executive administration of the university. One drawback of this initiative was that it was primarily conducted outside of the library and the lack of transparency was distressing for the library staff, who were not confident that reclassifications would be made fairly and objectively.

2016 Faculty Study

The library was involved in a second salary study in 2016. This time it was initiated by the library while preparing documentation to request the transition of our librarians from staff to professional-track faculty. For this study, we again used the CUPA data. As with the prior salary study, each position was reviewed, and any unaccounted-for responsibilities were incorporated into the job description before the actual salary data was pulled. This ensured, again, that librarian salaries would be commensurate with current roles and duties, not those in place when individuals were hired many years prior.

After these position description reviews, the library director ran the CUPA data for each position. The goal was to get each librarian up to the thirtieth percentile salary listed for institutions with a master's Carnegie Classification. The thirtieth percentile was chosen because the other faculty on campus had recently been brought up to that threshold by a faculty salary study. As expected, when these numbers were calculated, they revealed that librarians were making well below the thirtieth percentile for CUPA data for comparable positions, and exceptionally below the fiftieth percentile, or average salary. The cost to bring all of the salaries up to the thirtieth percentile would be approximately $40,000—not a small amount for a modest, regional institution.

In addition to these calculations, the library director used the ACRL Library Trends survey data from the prior year to benchmark the library's annual spending on professional staff compared to the median average spent by other institutions in our Carnegie Classification. Because the library needed to request funding from the institution to raise salaries, this amount showed that the library was actually spending a lot less than was typical on HR. We also ran data analysis to show that staff-to-student ratios were on target or a little low compared to other, similar libraries at smaller institutions. This was specifically intended to combat the erroneous narrative in the institution's business offices that the library spent too much on staff salaries and hired too many staff. By being proactive in benchmarking library spending and hiring patterns before any questions were asked about them, library administration was able to shut down some concerns about the proposed raises before they were even mentioned.

Armed with the data, the library prepared a budget request to be considered during the university's annual budget hearings. The library also prepared documents for the Faculty Senate, receiving its approval and support for the proposed transition before the budget hearings took place. With the faculty on the side of our librarians, the library had built-in allies on the budget committee.

In this case, as in the previous one, the library administration was successful. By initiating this process within the library, involving library personnel in the process, and building a compelling narrative that was both rooted in data and benchmarked against other similar institutions, the library was able to control the process and improve the situation for librarians, who subsequently became professional-track faculty. Notably, the initial bump in pay that was funded by the university as a result of this transition was not the only improvement in compensation that was achieved through this process. Librarians were also able to pursue promotion in rank as professional-track faculty. Library administration ensured that the documentation submitted relevant to the requirements for each librarian rank and the process for promotion included stipulations that librarians would be boosted back to the thirtieth percentile salary range after each successful promotion, followed by an additional raise in a set amount for each rank. This helped create integrated opportunities to ensure librarian salaries were keeping pace with the changes in the hiring market into the future.

2017 PwC Study

The year after the librarians transitioned to faculty, the staff at the university were again reviewed through a salary study, this time initiated by the Texas A&M University System (A&M System). This study centralized all position descriptions and classifications across the entire system of eleven universities. The study also created a pay plan with grades and ranges for all of these positions that were regularized based on the cost of living in the regions for each system school. As faculty, our librarians were exempt from this study, but not our paraprofessional staff. Though the library was not as involved in this study as it was in the others, we made some decisions following the last salary study, in collaboration with our HR department, that helped ensure our staff were placed correctly through this process. The biggest of these was our commitment to keeping job descriptions current and appropriately reflective of the duties that each paraprofessional staff member was performing. If we had let job descriptions become outdated due to lack of attention over the years, our staff would have been classified at much lower levels than was equitable. Luckily, one feature of our university's annual evaluations is the annual review of position descriptions. Though this may seem like a tedious and routine part of the evaluation, our commitment to doing it properly has helped us in every salary study in which we have participated.

Another factor that helped us was that we ensured a library staff member was on the committee participating in the study. The position descriptions that came back were both technically detailed and specific, including duties that were clearly correlated to jobs like copy cataloger, interlibrary loan assistant, or acquisitions specialist; and were also appropriately broad, in that they listed a wide variety of tasks that might correspond to a paraprofessional staff member within a given classification. These tasks would not have been easy to organize and recognize for someone who had never worked in a library. Having a library staff member on the committee allowed us to identify collections of duties that might apply to individual specialists or coordinators with discrete duties, ensuring that they were appropriately compensated. This staff member was also skilled at recognizing when a staff member's job was best described by a position description outside of the suite directly correlated to libraries. For instance, the library staff member who handles payments, budgets, contracts, and other specialized acquisitions and financial tasks was classified as a business coordinator, a professional role that fit her job better than any of the library-specific classifications.

We were particularly lucky that we had a receptive, experienced HR department that recognized we needed this staff member on the committee. In part, the library achieved this accommodation because we had been able to successfully build an understanding with HR over the previous two salary initiatives, conveying to HR that the library field is unique and requires some expertise to navigate when it comes to these sorts of studies. We were also lucky that, for individuals whose wage fell below the range for their position, we received funding through the university to cover raises.

We have continued to use some of the things were learned when the new compensation and position classification system was created. We routinely review the position descriptions that came out of the study. This is especially important because several new levels of library paraprofessional positions were created through this study, which we can now use if needed. We also routinely look at positions outside of those listed specific to the library, since sometimes they better fit our roles and occasionally pay more. These types of positions are especially important when we need to hire someone with professional responsibilities, but who is not a librarian, for functions like IT and business workflow.

2022 Salary Study

The most recent salary study that the library has undertaken was a study of paraprofessional staff. In part, this study was necessary because we had to reorganize the library several times in response to people leaving during the pandemic and directly following. It was also directly related to the fact that hourly wages for low-skilled labor increased drastically in our area in the last few years, in part because of our proximity to the northern suburbs of Austin, Texas. Whereas Killeen was not previously considered an exurb of Austin, as housing prices skyrocket throughout the region, people are increasingly moving into the Killeen-Temple-Fort Hood metroplex. The library is currently paying an hourly wage lower than our local fast-food restaurants, even for some full-time paraprofessional employees. The library administration, recognizing that this is untenable, has committed to increasing hourly wages. This includes paraprofessionals at the lowest end of the wage scale, as well as some who make more, to avoid salary compression.

Again, the first thing we did during this process was review position descriptions. This review was very fruitful because it allowed us to also shift duties between staff. Because we reorganized many departments during the pandemic to meet new remote service needs and other requirements, the review helped us to identify duties that should have been moved during the reorganization, but for one reason or another were not.

The second part of this initiative was a little different than the previous salary studies we had completed. This time, we determined that we wanted all hourly workers to make more than $13 hourly. We came to this number based on the data for our region in the MIT Living Wage Calculator.[23] Per the calculator, the living wage for a single individual working full-time in our region is $12.86. We wanted all full-time staff to meet this rate, at a bare minimum. We also set a stretch goal of $15 per hour in the next couple of years. In prior studies, we had not set an hourly minimum; though we had taken into consideration a variety of contextual data, such as ALA's recommended minimum starting salary for a professional librarian, which is currently $45,282.[24] This time, however, we thought it was important to set a minimum hourly salary and a stretch goal because we were finding that we were no longer competing with only our local libraries for paraprofessional staff. Again, places like our local fast-food restaurants currently pay a fair bit more than we do, and although the environment in libraries is often an adequate draw, at the end of the day, if someone cannot pay their bills, they will have to accept a less desirable position elsewhere.

Once we identified these goals, we researched what local public and academic libraries are currently paying their staff. Several had recently raised their wages, and while we used to pay more than they did, we were now substantially behind. Because we pulled this data from our local region, we felt comfortable benchmarking our salaries a little higher than the median, though not by a substantial amount. Notably, most of our data came from public libraries, and we felt that, as an academic library, we sometimes have more complex research tasks associated with employment at our institution. We were able to gather this data through professional connections with these other libraries, though we also could have gathered it by perusing job boards for our state, and especially the Texas Library Association's Jobline.

For this study, we were planning to self-fund raises, since there is presently no extra money available through the university for this initiative. We were able to do this as a result of our reorganization. When we reviewed our positions, we found a few open positions that we reclassified lower prior to filling them because we were able to put professional librarians in charge of some functions or shift more advanced responsibilities to other positions. Notably, in this case, self-funding required a true commitment to improving salaries. As with many libraries, every resource is needed, and needed by more than one department. Putting money toward salaries means it will not be available to meet needs elsewhere. Equitable raises for staff, as well as reclassifications for staff who had taken on additional duties during the pandemic, made this our highest priority.

As with the other studies, we found many staff that were making less than they should have been, and several that were classified lower than they should be. We developed a plan to rectify this situation in several stages, with salary adjustments for all full-time staff occurring first, followed by raises for part-timers. Many were reclassified. The ones who were not reclassified received compensation for additional duties. We hope that this will help us to retain staff and demonstrate a recognition of their value.

One particular feature of this salary study was transparency. We involved our entire leadership team in the decision-making process for raises, used objective benchmarking data as we had learned to do with other studies, and were open and transparent with staff and faculty about what we were doing and planning to do in regard to salaries.

This transparency extended to honestly answering questions about salaries as people had them. We discovered that regular communication about our activities, transparency about our methods, and an openness to discussing compensation helped maintain morale, decrease stress, and maintain confidence in the process across our employees, even when difficult conversations arose as a result. Though we had been hesitant to lean so heavily into transparency in previous studies, doing so ended up improving the process immensely.

WTAMU Cornette Library

Cornette Library is an 88,900-square-foot 461,000-volume academic library on the campus of WTAMU in Canyon, Texas, about twenty miles from Amarillo in the Texas Panhandle. WTAMU is a Large Comprehensive Master's University with approximately 9,300 students, 7,000 of whom are classified as undergraduates. The university offers sixty undergraduate programs, thirty-eight master's degree programs, and two doctoral programs.

In August 2022, the library director at Cornette Library embarked on a salary study using the model described above, after recognizing that the steps taken at A&M-Central Texas could be replicated at WTAMU. To achieve this, WTAMU's plan was as follows:

- create an academic library salary study checklist (figure 10.1) based on A&M-Central Texas's salary study process;
- test this new checklist at WTAMU; and
- have library staff benefit from equity adjustments, if time and funds allowed.

Though WTAMU's last salary study, completed in the spring of 2021, led to equity adjustments for the majority of exempt and nonexempt staff, this process did not include a review of position descriptions, limiting its efficacy. This limitation, combined with the rate of inflation in the years following the COVID-19 pandemic, compelled the library administration to pursue a follow-up study.

To this end, the WTAMU library director, in consultation with the A&M-Central Texas library administration, created a draft of the academic library salary study checklist in the fall of 2022. WTAMU also created two Salary Study committees, the first consisting of one librarian and one soon-to-be librarian for the exempt employee salary study, and the second consisting of two nonexempt staff for the salary study relevant to nonexempt staff. The library director planned to participate with both groups to provide context and answer questions. As the committees formed, there was initial apprehension on the part of the WTAMU director about sharing salary information due to the difficult conversations this could engender. Because transparency with salary information was an important part of the process at A&M-Central Texas, the dean at A&M-Central Texas encouraged WTAMU to continue with this approach despite the apprehension.

> **Academic Library Salary Study Checklist**
> - Appoint an existing committee or create a committee to do the study.
> - Reach out to your campus HR department and develop a relationship, if you do not currently have one with HR.
> - Review what salary data is already available to you on your campus or within your System.
> - Review current position descriptions to make sure they accurately describe all major duties.
> - Survey your staff about their position, using a job analysis questionnaire.
> - Other questions to ask in analysis of position descriptions:
>   - ☐ Do the duties reflect the job classification?
>   - ☐ Does the position correlate better to a position description elsewhere on your campus or within your System?
>   - ☐ Do the position descriptions reflect clearly the path to advance?
> - Align positions with job categories in the CUPA-HR survey. Does the CUPA-HR data on positions reflect the larger job market in our area?
> - What are other local public and academic libraries paying? Set salaries, including paraprofessionals, slightly above the median for public libraries, because academic libraries often have more complex research tasks.
> - Analyze TLA Jobline and ALA's JobLIST postings. ALA's recommended minimum starting salary for a professional librarian is currently $45,282.
> - Allow for cost of living when doing salary comparisons—Use the Massachusetts Institute of Technology (MIT) Living Wage Calculator.
> - Other sources to inform your study:
>   - ☐ Do the ALA-APA annual salary survey positions reflect the larger job market in our area (good for historical perspective, but data is not current)? How does this information compare to the CUPA-HR data?
>   - ☐ Use ACRL Library Trends survey data from prior year to benchmark your library's annual spending on professional staff compared to the median average spent by other institutions in the same Carnegie Classification.
>   - ☐ Calculate professional staff to student ratios and compare to similar libraries in the ACRL Library Trends survey.
>   - ☐ Salary.com data
>   - ☐ Library IPEDS survey data
>   - ☐ OpenPayrolls.com

Figure 10.1. WTAMU library salary study checklist

Both WTAMU salary study committees met at the kickoff meeting in January 2023 where the project was explained and the time commitment discussed. During this gathering, the committees decided that, because they would be navigating a little-known task, operating as a single group would make better sense.

The January meeting was followed up quickly with e-mails thanking committee members for their attendance and their interest in the task they were about to undertake. A job analysis questionnaire from the book *Developing a Compensation Plan for Your*

Library by Singer and Laura Francisco,[25] the salary studies draft from A&M-Central Texas, and the draft of the academic library salary study checklist were also given to the committee. These items gave the members of the committee background on what A&M-Central Texas had done and what WTAMU wanted to achieve. The WTAMU library director also reiterated that the group would be learning a lot together, so all questions and observations were welcome. For the majority of the spring semester the committee met weekly. The committee undertook the salary study in two phases: a position description review (phase 1) and a salary review (phase 2).

The first focus of the committee, as mentioned in the checklist, was reviewing staff position descriptions to determine if they were classified into the wrong position level. The committee considered it important to gain staff input into this process. To this end, they decided to administer Singer and Francisco's questionnaire to all library employees.[26] The committee quickly reviewed the questionnaire's language, making only minor changes and additions, in order to get the study started. After the committee gained permission from ALA, which originally published the questionnaire, it was distributed to library staff to gauge their perceptions of all aspects of their job. Staff were asked to complete the questionnaire without looking at their position descriptions. The feedback from the questionnaire was enlightening.

While it quickly became apparent that answer choices in the questionnaire were not always geared to academic libraries, the amount of time staff devoted to special projects, the varied contact various library positions had with external entities, and the perceived lack of authority felt by library department heads were all telling from a management perspective. Moreover, the position description review revealed a few nonexempt positions and one librarian position required releveling and salary adjustments. Pursuing faculty status for librarians was discussed, and the committee agreed that this should be a conversation revisited at a later date by all librarians at the Cornette Library.

Continuing to follow the checklist, the committee began the salary review by seeking CUPA-HR data. The committee discovered that obtaining the CUPA report can be an expensive endeavor unless the university has an institutional membership and has previously purchased the CUPA reports you need. WTAMU has CUPA-HR membership but had not previously purchased the staff and librarian reports. Due to the expense and lack of clarity about what data would be received if purchased, the committee discussed alternatives for benchmarked salary data. The following tools were used to create datasets:

- salary postings at ALA's JobLIST, TLA's Jobline, and regional institutions in surrounding states (New Mexico, Oklahoma, Kansas, and Colorado);
- Salary.com data provided by the WTAMU HR department;
- OpenPayrolls.com;
- library IPEDS data; and
- the *Salary Budget by System Member* report by the A&M System Office of Budgets and Accounting.

In OpenPayrolls.com, committee members pulled salaries for active employees only from A&M System institutions, geographic peers, aspirant peers, and any additional, local libraries that they could find. In many cases they had to go to the institution's library staff directory to establish which positions were currently filled and which were vacant. A committee member created a spreadsheet with the regional salary data.

After reviewing this spreadsheet, the committee felt it was still missing important data. In the committee's quest for data granularity to more fully match the institution, the library director asked WTAMU's government documents librarian for assistance in finding better salary data for A&M System institutions. She was able to find the *Salary Budget by System Member* report from A&M System for the current year.[27] The committee member took the data from this report and created a spreadsheet that allowed for an easy comparison of librarian II and III salaries across similar A&M System institutions, such as Texas A&M International University and Tarleton State University, which is also a geographic peer. MIT's Living Wage Calculator was used to allow for cost-of-living adjustments to this data.[28]

This resulting spreadsheet was invaluable to our study, since the salary information for the A&M System institutions appeared more accurate than what was reported in Open-Payroll.com. The committee was also able to use Workday, the human capital management software used by the A&M System, to search positions from the other A&M System institutions when a clarification of duties was needed to establish a match.

Overall, the committee worked well for this salary study. The collaborative and transparent approach proved beneficial for morale and buy-in. Surprisingly, the majority of library salaries at WTAMU for professional librarians and nonexempt staff compared closely to our peer institutions within the A&M System. As mentioned earlier, some leveling was required, as well as equity adjustments for librarian II salaries to make these positions more competitive with system peers. Fortunately, the university provost offered the opportunity for the university to assist departments in funding equity adjustments. The library director was able to use limited library funds, along with university resources, to accomplish the equity adjustments flagged by the committee. Next steps in the future, as funding allows, will include addressing salary compression. The committee also plans to expand our salary study, adding the salary data from one aspirant peer.

Conclusion and Lessons Learned

Through this succession of salary studies at both A&M-Central Texas and WTAMU, we recognize that salaries and position descriptions are never a fixed point. They require constant evaluation and attention, because a faculty or staff member who is paid fairly in one year might easily slip the next. This is especially evident with librarians. After many years of reviewing data, the constant increase in librarian salaries is inescapable. By regularly participating in salary initiatives, both within and outside of the library,

library administrators can demonstrate to our employees that we recognize this fact and that we are willing to fight for them in the ways we are able to ensure fair compensation. This willingness to fight for fair compensation is excellent for morale, because, ultimately, compensation is a key indicator of an individual's worth to the institution. This is even more important if raises do not keep pace with inflation.

Another important takeaway is that, though being a good advocate may seem like it requires a combative approach to salary study committees, working with HR to make a case using data is a better approach. HR staff understand these concepts, though they may not be as familiar with libraries as a library dean or director. They are much more receptive to compensation adjustments if they are approached with mutual respect and an understanding that everyone is trying to do the right thing for the employees and the institution. One of the best ways to do this is to point them toward good data and to translate library roles to the roles of other, more typical employees at the university.

Similarly, though staff and faculty almost always desire whatever raise a library can give, the issue of salaries is not entirely linked to paying the most. We found that our employees wanted to know that we recognize the work they are doing and that they are being classified fairly for that work. Even if you pay lower than the median nationally, regularly revisiting position descriptions ensures employees are getting paid for the proper job. You should also revisit position descriptions and examine classifications whenever changes are made, large or small, to paraprofessional descriptions. In the salary studies at both A&M-Central Texas and WTAMU, we found that the people who were the most underpaid were routinely improperly classified. An institution can have the best-benchmarked pay grades and still be paying staff too little if the staff are broadly misclassified.

This points to another takeaway, which is that it does not help to try to fight against a pay plan. Library administrators need to learn how to work within it. Though externally imposed pay plans can be frustrating and feel like they take autonomy away from directors, they are becoming a more common reality in many kinds of libraries. Fighting against them will only transform HR into the enemy. Working within them to get the best situation for all library employees is a better approach and invites further collaboration with HR when bigger decisions are being made, such as large pay adjustment initiatives.

Similarly, though transparency around salaries can feel fraught for library leadership, a collaborative, objective approach to salaries, marked by regular and clear communication from administrators, is key. Though sometimes this can lead to difficult conversations, these conversations are important to ensuring equity and addressing concerns that can have a huge impact on whether an employee feels comfortable in their position. Consistent with other research on salary studies, transparency and objectivity are the enemy of inequity—when salaries are clear and consistent, the discussion becomes much easier.

Finally, library deans and directors need to know how to benchmark against other, similar libraries before they make any argument about salary structure. Administrators hear complaints about salaries every day, so these same complaints from a library director will not make much of an impact. Administrators *will* understand, however, data showing that wages are in the tenth percentile, or that the institution's library spends considerably less than other, similar libraries on HR.

Takeaways

- One committee is better than two—and all committees should focus on transparency and objectivity. Committees must include both librarians and paraprofessionals, as well as employees from a variety of work areas. Your committee should also include newer employees, along with older ones, since they bring fresh perspectives from outside the organization.
- Get to know your HR director. Your HR director will help you navigate things like your CUPA-HR membership and what reports may be available to you. They will also work with you to update position descriptions and can advocate for equity adjustments, if looped in on your intentions.
- Do not attempt, if possible, a salary study while trying to do extensive hiring or while contemplating a major reorganization. The WTAMU library administration was anticipating a hiring freeze, so the salary study and hiring were happening simultaneously, which was not ideal.
- A salary study committee is not only a good idea for transparency—it will also bring members of your staff together for a common goal and inform them about the way salary decisions are made in the library and at the university. This creates salary specialists within units of the library who can combat negative perceptions and low morale in situations where the staff do not have a good understanding of how compensation works.
- Even in-house salary studies are not free—budget for large expenses, such as CUPA-HR Reports.
- Revise the questionnaire from Singer and Francisco for academic library use or create your own.[29] Some of the terminology used in the questionnaire was more specific to public libraries.
- Make use of your staff expertise, such as your government documents librarian or a business librarian. Also, look for librarians who show promise as future leaders to work on this project—this is a committee that will test a lot of skills necessary for leadership, including discretion, objectivity, supervision, and organization.
- Salary studies and reviews of position descriptions should happen routinely and continually, since inflation, reorganization, and other changes happen all the time. For instance, WTAMU has decided to turn their salary review committee into a standing committee going forward.

- The job market has changed post-COVID and is continually changing due to inflation—do not use old data. The best salary studies benchmark against the freshest data.

Acknowledgement: Thank you to Bruce Wardlow, Chelsea Kuehler, Deanna Moore, and Jeff Farris, members of Cornette Library's Salary Study Committee, for their invaluable contribution to West Texas A&M University's library salary study.

Notes

1. Colin Gordon, "American Inequality: A Primer," in *Inequality in America: Interdisciplinary Perspectives*, ed. Barbara Hahn, Kerstin Schmidt, and Jasmin Falk (Heidelberg, Germany: Universitätsverlag Winter, 2017), 9–10.
2. Thomas Piketty, *Capital in the Twenty-First Century*, reprint ed. (Cambridge, MA: Belknap Press, 2017).
3. Paula Singer and Laura Francisco, *Developing a Compensation Plan for Your Library* (Chicago: American Library Association, 2009); David Baldwin, *The Library Compensation Handbook* (New York: Libraries Unlimited, 2003).
4. Terry Cottrell, "Moving On: Salaries and Managing Turnover," *Bottom Line* 24, no. 3 (2011): 187–91, https://doi.org/10.1108/08880451111186044.
5. Carol Marchetti and Margaret Bailey, "The Importance of HOW in Faculty Salary Equity Studies: Development and Impact of an ADVANCE Salary Equity Study and Workshop Series to Promote an Inclusive Academic Environment," *ADVANCE Journal* 3, no. 2 (2022), https://doi.org/10.5399/osu/ADVJRNL.3.2.5.
6. Lori L. Taylor et al., "How to Do a Salary Equity Study: With an Illustrative Example from Higher Education," *Public Personnel Management* 49, no. 1 (2020): 57–82, https://doi.org/10.1177/0091026019845119.
7. Serge Herzog, "A Four-Step Faculty Compensation Model: From Equity Analysis to Adjustment," *New Directions for Institutional Research* 2008, no. 140 (2008): 49–64, https://doi.org/10.1002/ir.269.
8. Lois Haignere, *Paychecks*, 2nd ed. (Washington, DC: American Association of University Professors, 2002).
9. Robert Perret and Nancy Young, "Economic Status of Academic Librarians," *portal: Libraries and the Academy* 11, no. 2 (2011): 703–15, https://doi.org/10.1353/pla.2011.0016.
10. Perret and Young, "Economic Status of Academic Librarians," 707.
11. Denise M. Davis, "Academic and Public Librarian Salaries and Library Staffing Expenditures Trends, 2000–2009," *Library Trends* 59, no. 1 (2010): 43–66, https://doi.org/10.1353/lib.2010.a407806.
12. Christina Heady et al., "Contributory Factors to Academic Librarian Turnover: A Mixed-Methods Study," *Journal of Library Administration* 60, no. 6 (2020): 579–99, https://doi.org/10.1080/01930826.2020.1748425
13. Andrea Falcone and Lyda Fontes McCartin, "Strategies for Retaining and Sustaining the Academic Librarian Workforce in Times of Crises," *Journal of Library Administration* 62, no. 4 (2022): 557–63, https://doi.org/10.1080/01930826.2022.2057132.
14. Shannon L. Farrell and Aliqae Geraci, "Librarians and Compensation Negotiation in the Library Workplace," *Library Management* 38, no. 1 (2017): 45–64, https://doi.org/10.1108/LM-08-2016-0060.
15. Fobazi Ettarh, "Vocational Awe and Librarianship: The Lies We Tell Ourselves," *In the Library with the Lead Pipe*, January 10, 2018, https://www.inthelibrarywiththeleadpipe.org/2018/vocational-awe/.
16. Francine D. Blau and Lawrence M. Kahn, "The Gender Wage Gap: Extent, Trends, and Explanations," *Journal of Economic Literature* 55, no. 3 (2017): 789–865, https://doi.org/10.1257/jel.20160995.
17. Nicole Eva, Mê-Linh Lê, and John Sheriff, "Less Money, Less Children, and Less Prestige: Differences between Male and Female Academic Librarians," *Journal of Academic Librarianship* 4, no. 5 (September 2021): article 102392, https://doi.org/10.1016/j.acalib.2021.102392.
18. Quinn Galbraith, Erin Merrill, and Olivia Outzen, "The Effect of Gender and Minority Status on Salary in Private and Public ARL Libraries," *Journal of Academic Librarianship* 44, no. 1 (2018): 75–80, https://doi.org/10.1016/j.acalib.2017.10.005.
19. Laura K. Brown, Elizabeth Troutt, and Susan Prentice, "Ten Years After: Sex and Salaries at a Canadian University," *Canadian Public Policy* 37, no. 2 (June 2011): 239–55, https://doi.org/10.3138/cpp.37.2.239.
20. Richard G. Trotter, Susan Rawson Zacur, and Lisa T. Stickney, "The New Age of Pay Transparency," *Business Horizons* 60, no. 4 (July–August 2017): 529–39, https://doi.org/10.1016/j.bushor.2017.03.011.
21. Elizabeth Lyons and Laurina Zhang, "Salary Transparency and Gender Pay Inequality: Evidence from Canadian Universities," *Strategic Management Journal* 44, no. 8 (2023): 2005–34, https://doi.org/10.1002/smj.3483.
22. Singer and Francisco, *Developing a Compensation Plan*; Kathleen Baril and Jennifer Donily, *Academic Library Job Descriptions*, CLIPP 6 (Chicago: Association of College and Research Libraries, 2021).

23. Amy K. Glasmeier, "Living Wage Calculator," Massachusetts Institute of Technology, accessed November 8, 2023, https://livingwage.mit.edu.
24. "Salary Negotiation," American Library Association-Allied Professional Association, accessed September 27, 2024, https://ala-apa.org/improving-salariesstatus/salary-negotiation/.
25. Singer and Francisco, *Developing a Compensation Plan*, 69–70.
26. Singer and Francisco, *Developing a Compensation Plan*, 69–70.
27. Texas A&M University System Office of Budgets and Accounting, *Salary Budget by System Member* (College Station: Texas A&M University System, 2023).
28. Glasmeier, "Living Wage Calculator."
29. Singer and Francisco, *Developing a Compensation Plan*, 69–70.

Bibliography

American Library Association-Allied Professional Association. "Salary Negotiation." Accessed September 27, 2024. https://ala-apa.org/improving-salariesstatus/salary-negotiation/.

Baldwin, David. *The Library Compensation Handbook: A Guide for Administrators, Librarians, and Staff*. New York: Libraries Unlimited, 2003.

Baril, Kathleen, and Jennifer Donily. *Academic Library Job Descriptions*. CLIPP 46. Chicago: Association of College and Research Libraries, 2021.

Blau, Francine D., and Lawrence M. Kahn. "The Gender Wage Gap: Extent, Trends, and Explanations." *Journal of Economic Literature* 55, no. 3 (2017): 789–865. https://doi.org/10.1257/jel.20160995.

Brown, Laura K., Elizabeth Troutt, and Susan Prentice. "Ten Years After: Sex and Salaries at a Canadian University." *Canadian Public Policy* 37, no. 2 (June 2011): 239–55. https://doi.org/10.3138/cpp.37.2.239.

Cottrell, Terry. "Moving On: Salaries and Managing Turnover." *Bottom Line* 24, no. 3 (2011): 187–91. https://doi.org/10.1108/08880451111186044.

Davis, Denise M. "Academic and Public Librarian Salaries and Library Staffing Expenditures Trends, 2000–2009." *Library Trends* 59, no. 1 (2010): 43–66. https://doi.org/10.1353/lib.2010.a407806.

Ettarh, Fobazi. "Vocational Awe and Librarianship: The Lies We Tell Ourselves." *In the Library with the Lead Pipe*, January 10, 2018. https://www.inthelibrarywiththeleadpipe.org/2018/vocational-awe/.

Eva, Nicole, Mê-Linh Lê, and John Sheriff. "Less Money, Less Children, and Less Prestige: Differences between Male and Female Academic Librarians." *Journal of Academic Librarianship* 4, no. 5 (September 2021): article 102392. https://doi.org/10.1016/j.acalib.2021.102392.

Falcone, Andrea, and Lyda Fontes McCartin. "Strategies for Retaining and Sustaining the Academic Librarian Workforce in Times of Crises." *Journal of Library Administration* 62, no. 4 (2022): 557–63. https://doi.org/10.1080/01930826.2022.2057132.

Farrell, Shannon L., and Aliqae Geraci. "Librarians and Compensation Negotiation in the Library Workplace." *Library Management* 38, no. 1 (2017): 45–64. https://doi.org/10.1108/LM-08-2016-0060.

Galbraith, Quinn, Erin Merrill, and Olivia Outzen. "The Effect of Gender and Minority Status on Salary in Private and Public ARL Libraries." *Journal of Academic Librarianship* 44, no. 1 (2018): 75–80. https://doi.org/10.1016/j.acalib.2017.10.005.

Glasmeier, Amy K. "Living Wage Calculator," Massachusetts Institute of Technology. Accessed November 8, 2023, https://livingwage.mit.edu.

Gordon, Colin. "American Inequality: A Primer." In *Inequality in America: Interdisciplinary Perspectives*, edited by Barbara Hahn, Kerstin Schmidt, and Jasmin Falk, 9–24. Heidelberg, Germany: Universitätsverlag Winter, 2017.

Haignere, Lois. *Paychecks: A Guide to Conducting Salary-Equity Studies for Higher Education Faculty*, 2nd ed. Washington, DC: American Association of University Professors, 2002.

Heady, Christina, Amy F. Fyn, Amanda Foster Kaufman, Allison Hosier, and Millicent Weber. "Contributory Factors to Academic Librarian Turnover: A Mixed-Methods Study." *Journal of Library Administration* 60, no. 6 (2020): 579–99. https://doi.org/10.1080/01930826.2020.1748425.

Herzog, Serge. "A Four-Step Faculty Compensation Model: From Equity Analysis to Adjustment." *New Directions for Institutional Research* 2008, no. 140 (2008): 49–64. https://doi.org/10.1002/ir.269.

Lyons, Elizabeth, and Laurina Zhang. "Salary Transparency and Gender Pay Inequality: Evidence from Canadian Universities." *Strategic Management Journal* 44, no. 8 (2023): 2005–34. https://doi.org/10.1002/smj.3483.

Marchetti, Carol, and Margaret Bailey. "The Importance of HOW in Faculty Salary Equity Studies: Development and Impact of an ADVANCE Salary Equity Study and Workshop Series to Promote an Inclusive Academic Environment." *ADVANCE Journal* 3, no. 2 (2022). https://doi.org/10.5399/osu/ADVJRNL.3.2.5.

Perret, Robert, and Nancy Young. "Economic Status of Academic Librarians." *portal: Libraries and the Academy* 11, no. 2 (2011): 703–15. https://doi.org/10.1353/pla.2011.0016.

Piketty, Thomas. *Capital in the Twenty-First Century*, reprint ed. Cambridge, MA: Belknap Press, 2017.
Singer, Paula, and Laura Francisco. *Developing a Compensation Plan for Your Library*. Chicago: American Library Association, 2009.
Taylor, Lori L., Joanna N. Lahey, Molly I. Beck, and Jeffrey E. Froyd. "How to Do a Salary Equity Study: With an Illustrative Example from Higher Education." *Public Personnel Management* 49, no. 1 (2020): 57–82. https://doi.org/10.1177/0091026019845119.
Texas A&M University System Office of Budgets and Accounting. *Salary Budget by System Member* (College Station: Texas A&M University System, 2023).
Trotter, Richard G., Susan Rawson Zacur, and Lisa T. Stickney. "The New Age of Pay Transparency." *Business Horizons* 60, no. 4 (July–August 2017): 529–539. https://doi.org/10.1016/j.bushor.2017.03.011.

CHAPTER 11

Employee Unions in Academic Libraries

Something Old and Something New

Bridgit McCafferty

In December 2023, Jason de Stefano, writing in the *Chronicle of Higher Education*, proclaimed the current moment "a golden age of academic unionization."[1] This was spurred by the recent surge in academic unions, and especially unionization for graduate students and contingent faculty. According to CUNY's *The State of the Unions 2023*, unionizing in higher education is ascendant—in fact, workers in higher education now make up a quarter of those in United Auto Workers union.[2] Moreover, recent strikes at the University of California System and Rutgers were some of the biggest in the history of higher education.[3]

Union support is on the rise both inside and outside of higher education. A Gallup survey published in 2021 reported that support for unions is at its highest since 1965.[4] Sixty-eight percent of Americans report favorable opinions toward labor unions, and approval for unions among 18-to-34-year-olds, the primary demographic for students in colleges and universities, was 77 percent, explaining the rapid rise in unionization by both graduate and undergraduate students.[5] Despite the fact that support of unions is at its highest in more than fifty years, the density of union membership in the US labor force continues to decrease.[6] The trend toward unionization in higher education is a particular bright spot in this narrative, compared to other industries.

Most of this union activity is happening on private campuses, though the biggest strikes have occurred at public sector colleges. Most of the unionization has focused on student workers, though a notable amount has involved postdoctoral researchers, contingent faculty, or other non-tenure-track positions.[7] This increase in unions for undergraduate and graduate student workers has had a particular impact on libraries, which are often some of the biggest employers of students on campuses, rivaling student resident assistants and cafeteria staff. This makes the impact of unionizing particularly prominent in libraries.

Though unions have been active in libraries for more than a century, they are relevant to innovative library management at the present moment in two ways. First, AFL-CIO reports that librarians and library workers with union representation make, on average, 37 percent more than those without.[8] For this reason, it recommends unionization as one strategy to improve salaries and benefits for library workers. Secondly, many library managers work with student workers and graduate students, making the most recent surge in union activity for these groups especially notable. As a result, understanding the history and relevance of unions, as well as the ways in which the union landscape is currently changing, is important.

Union History in Libraries

Though the rise of unions in higher education may seem like an ascendant phenomenon, the notion of library workers unionizing is an old idea. Milden tracks this history, demonstrating that the existence of unions in libraries goes back to the mid-1910s, when union activity began at the Library of Congress.[9] Milden contributes support for this unionization to the realities faced by women in pink collar professions, including harassment and discrimination.[10] The popularity of unions for library employees was an attempt to reckon with these issues, which were profound given the largely female workforce and predominantly male administrative class. He reports that the first library union was the New York Public Library Employee's Union, followed quickly by unions affiliated with AFL at other prominent public libraries, such as Boston and Washington, DC. Milden notes that librarian unions faced an uphill battle in a profession where unionization was depicted as going against the feminine nature of the work.[11]

Despite the fact that unions were not prominent in the early twentieth century for the library profession, the formation of unions and the topic of unions continued to be one of interest in some corners of the profession. For instance, the Library Unions Round Table was formed by members of the American Library Association in 1937,[12] shortly after the passage of the National Labor Relations Act, which established the right of workers to form unions without reprisal. This round table existed into the 1950s, and in some ways, it was a precursor to the current subcommittee of ALA-APA focused on unions in libraries.

Unions in higher education also have a long history. Like libraries, collective bargaining and discussions relevant to unionization began in higher education at the turn of the century. Unionization for faculty started in the early twentieth century, with the founding of the American Federation of Teachers in 1916, which quickly incorporated its first university chapter at Howard University in 1918.[13] Collective bargaining for nonacademic staff became prominent in the 1940s, starting at the University of Illinois.[14] These arrangements often dealt with specific groups of staff at universities, and especially nonacademic staff, such as janitors, service staff, and maintenance workers.[15]

Legal changes in the 1960s and 1970s that protected the right to unionize led to greater union activity on campuses, starting with President Kennedy's 1962 executive order No. 10988, which recognized the rights of public sector employees to unionize.[16] This led to a variety of laws across individual states that determined which public sector employees were eligible to unionize and in what contexts. Moreover, some scholars link the fundamental concepts of shared faculty governance and tenure to the foundational philosophies underpinning the union movement, as argued by Herbert, who pointed to the phrase "academic democracy" as a shared concept.[17] As this suggests, the role of faculty in advocating for leadership and employment considerations in higher education has a rich history.

Faculty and Staff Unions

Typically, when unions are discussed in the context of libraries and higher education, unions for full-time faculty and staff come to mind. This is especially true in parts of the country where there are strong public sector unions. In fact, as Hovekamp notes, though membership in unions has declined almost every year since the statistics were first tracked in 1983, union membership in the public sector is nearly four times as high compared to the private sector.[18] In fact, the highest rates of unionization are for workers in education, training, and library occupations, at 32.7 percent in 2023, the most recent year of data available.[19] Moreover, approximately 27 percent of public sector librarians were union members in 2023, up from 25 percent in 2022 and 23 percent in 2010.[20] Moreover, 39 percent of academic librarians responding to a 2015 survey reported current union membership, including 61.5 percent of tenure-track faculty librarians.[21] This means that there is a high potential for librarians working in states with a greater density of union membership to either manage workers who are in unions or to themselves be in unions.

Academic librarians are often linked with faculty in bargaining units. The connection is reinforced by ACRL's "Guideline on Collective Bargaining," which states that this is how librarians should be classified for collective bargaining arrangements.[22] For librarians at private institutions, the link with faculty may create an impediment to unionization, because the ability of private sector employees to unionize is determined by the National Labor Relations Board (NLRB). As a result, faculty unions at private institutions are governed by the 1980 Supreme Court ruling on NLRB v. Yeshiva University, 444 U.S. 672, which established that faculty may be exempt from unionization in situations where they meet certain managerial criteria. These criteria were expanded and clarified in 2014 when the full NLRB ruled on Pacific Lutheran University and Service Employees International

Union, Local 925, Case 19-RC-102521, 361 NLRB No. 157. The ruling specified that the managerial role of faculty at private institutions is determined primarily by their decision-making authority related to curriculum, enrollment, and finances, and secondarily by their role in academic policy and personnel decisions.[23] This means that librarians at many private institutions may not be permitted to unionize.

Public sector unions are not governed by these rules—instead, they follow state law and the rulings of state-level labor boards. As a result, the ability of faculty at public universities to unionize is heavily dependent on the state where they live. Some states are friendly to public sector unions, while others are limited in the impact that these unions can have, especially in some areas of the Sunbelt.

For those looking for a quick overview of this limited but valuable topic, Hovekamp's chapter "Unions in Academic Libraries" is a great resource.[24] She identifies AFT, the National Education Association, and the American Association of University Professors as the predominant unions for faculty at universities. Notably, these are not the most prominent unions for other types of employees, including students, who are largely represented by the United Auto Workers.[25] As Hovekamp notes, community colleges are much more likely to be unionized, compared to other types of institutions.[26] The particular strength of Hovekamp's chapter is the overview she provides relevant to union negotiations in academic settings. In particular, she discusses the formation of unions and the process of collective bargaining, including mandatory, permissive, and prohibited negotiation topics—or topics that the union must negotiate, could negotiate, and may not negotiate. She notes that unions start with interest in a specific union by employees at an institution, followed by a confidential employee vote about whether to join a union, and then the formation of a bargaining unit if the vote is successful. This bargaining unit then negotiates with the management of an organization every few years. The end goal of these negotiations is a written contract to which both management and the union are parties.[27] Notably, Hovekamp also published a study about organizational commitment at union and nonunion libraries, as well as research about job satisfaction and unionization among academic librarians.[28]

More current resources that deal with unions in both libraries and higher education include the journal *Progressive Librarian*, which is now on hiatus. Library unionizing was a regular topic of discussion in this journal, including updated entries from McCook titled "There Is Power in a Union," which reviewed union activities in libraries over the last year.[29] These reviews have extensive bibliographies with wide-ranging data, though most sources are news articles about union activities. *Progressive Librarian* also publishes a *Union Library Workers* blog, which it still regularly updates.

There have been some notable peer-reviewed articles related to collective bargaining and unions in libraries over the last couple of years since unionization has been resurgent in higher education, a trend noted by Hirsch, Macpherson, and Even in a special section of *The 2023 State of the Unions* focused on the recent success of unions in this industry.[30]

Mills and McCullough, for instance, found that most librarians who were members of unions participated as faculty and that these faculty librarians had a "large and persistent premium in their salary" even after taking tenure status into account.[31] Moreover, librarians perceived unions as benefiting them on several measures, including salary and worker protections. This study builds on an earlier one by Garcha and Phillips, which looked at library participation in unions.[32] Mills and McCullough also provided an exhaustive literature review reaching back to the 1970s and earlier.[33] Likewise, Applegate found a positive correlation between unionization and library salaries, though she reports that unionization does not lead to higher budgets for libraries on the whole, which results in unionized libraries spending more, proportionally, on salaries than those that are not unionized.[34] Aby reviewed the content of collective bargaining agreements in libraries, determining that faculty collective bargaining contracts often did not take into account the specific and niche needs of librarians.[35]

Braunstein and Russo discussed the fraught process of unionization for librarians at a public university in the United States,[36] which is related to the twenty-year case study by Spang documenting collective bargaining issues among librarians at Wayne State, who had wide-ranging debates about faculty status in conjunction with unionization.[37] Lee also published a case study focusing on Regis University.[38] *In Solidarity*, a collection focusing on labor activism in Canada, contains several articles about unions in libraries, including reviews of contract terms in collective bargaining agreements.[39]

Another strain of research relevant to librarians and unions features discussions about the role of librarians in unions and the impact a union can have on librarian involvement and satisfaction with administration. Applegate suggested that this strain of research represents the theory that librarians unionize when they are particularly displeased with their role in governance issues.[40] Spang and Kane explored the role of professional groups and unions in representing librarians, finding that these organizations sometimes compete or overlap, leading to a lack of clarity about who represents the needs of librarians relevant to status and governance.[41] Milton explored the importance of librarian involvement in faculty unions, where library interests are not always equally represented compared to teaching faculty,[42] a disparity that Spang and Kane also discuss.[43]

In higher education more broadly, the *Journal of Collective Bargaining in the Academy*,* published by the National Center for the Study of Collective Bargaining in Higher Education and the Professions, focuses on unions in higher education. The goal of this peer-reviewed journal is to advance scholarship focused on collective bargaining efforts at colleges and universities. It publishes special issues documenting conferences held by the center, in addition to regular issues focusing on historical and current trends relevant to this topic.

---

* *Journal of Collective Bargaining in the Academy* (JCBA), https://thekeep.eiu.edu/jcba/.

Student Unions

The most significant current trend in unionization, relevant to both libraries and higher education, is the trend toward student unions both at the undergraduate and graduate level, though graduate student unions are the most prominent. This new unionizing kicked off largely because of recent rulings from the NLRB. Prior to 2016, the NLRB had a tendency to issue new rulings about whether graduate students were eligible to form unions with every new presidential administration. The central question in these deliberations was whether or not graduate students are apprentices. This meant that efforts to unionize graduate students stalled every four or eight years when a new administration came in and reversed course. In 2016, the NLRB ruled that graduate students are eligible to unionize, and this ruling has remained in effect for eight years as of this writing, through both Republican and Democratic administrations.[44] As a result, it seems likely it will remain in force for the foreseeable future. This has led to a resurgence of unionizing for students in higher education, documented by Herbert, Apkarian, and van der Naald in *The 2023 State of the Unions*.[45]

Unlike faculty unions, student unions tend to impact librarians as employers more than as employees. For a basic overview of current trends in higher education, Herbert and Apkarian provide the history and recent movement in higher education unions for both faculty and graduate students.[46] Herbert and Apkarian later published a study of strikes, stoppages, and lockouts at higher education campuses between 2012 and 2018, which is valuable for contextualizing the impact of the current movement on operations at universities.[47] Herbert and van der Naald track the modern development of graduate student unions, characterizing this union movement as struggle between a surging class of workers who, traditionally, were not recognized as employees and were therefore denied the compensation and protections assigned to other employees at institutions of higher education.[48] To this end, they provide a detailed account of graduate student unionization efforts and trends between 2012 and 2019, including information about resistance to unionization by institutions of higher education. Herbert and van der Naald published an analysis of NLRB rule-making relevant to graduate students, including the most recent activity.[49] Cain published an *ASHE Higher Education Report* about faculty and graduate student unionization, which provides a more in-depth introduction to the topic.[50] Additionally, Cain wrote a history of labor movements in higher education that can help contextualize current trends.[51]

Some accounts and case studies of graduate student unionization have been published. Crow and Greene published a case study of graduate student unionization at Columbia University.[52] Whitford offers three case studies of student unionizing in higher education.[53] Additionally, student union organizing at individual institutions is documented in the *Chronicle of Higher Education*, which frequently reports on movements across the sector.

Related to this, McCarthy discussed the questions that student movements need to reckon with to achieve labor goals in his study about the rise in these movements.[54]

Another article of interest by Lafer posited that the increased corporatization of the modern university has led to a greater need for employee protections, especially for student employees.[55] In part, Lafer contended, this is due to the economic reality that graduate students cost as little as $5,000 annually and can do some work formerly performed by faculty. The potential savings for universities by hiring more graduate students with fewer faculty to supervise their work is a significant benefit in an era where state appropriations are growing smaller.[56] Rhoads and Rhoades discussed unions as a pushback against corporatization in higher education.[57] Kitchen also discussed corporatization and graduate student unions, including the way these unions may reinforce corporatization.[58] Another older article by Julius and Gumport discussed the reasons for and impacts of graduate student unionization across higher education.[59] Julius also recently wrote a valuable article about graduate unions from an employer's perspective, which may be of interest to librarians who supervise graduate student union members.[60] Notably, Kezar, DePaola, and Scott recently published a book-length study that delves into many of these same labor trends, including the gig economy in higher education.[61]

One theme in many of these publications is the sense that graduate student unions may have the potential to reawaken the latent labor movement in the United States. In an era where unions are on the decline in most industries, their striking rise in higher education, especially given that they have been organized by student labor, is an anomaly. Those who are interested in this angle might use Kitchen's research as a jumping-off point for further exploration.[62] *The 2023 State of the Unions* report also highlights the ascendent nature of graduate student unions.

Conclusion

Though all types of union organizing, and especially graduate student efforts, are ascendent in higher education, it is important to remember that unionization is not a straight line. Just recently, graduate students at Princeton University voted against forming a union.[63] This shows that each union movement is local, contending with issues on the ground at individual institutions. There is a recurring theme in the literature that unions tend to succeed best where they are most needed, suggesting that unions are a response in many cases to bad management or labor conditions. This is a reminder to managers that, whether or not an institution has a union, it is important to take employees into consideration and respond to their needs in a thoughtful, respectful way.

Nonetheless, analysis of the data shows that unionized faculty and staff tend to enjoy many benefits of their membership in unions and that unions are more positively regarded by librarians than the general population. Moreover, education is one of the most highly unionized sectors in the United States. As a result, no matter their position on unions, it is important for library workers and managers to understand their role and impact on the labor force in academic libraries.

Notes

1. Jason de Stefano, "This Is a Golden Age of Academic Unionization," *Chronicle of Higher Education*, December 8, 2023, https://www.chronicle.com/article/this-is-a-golden-age-of-academic-unionization.
2. William A. Herbert, Jacob Apkarian, and Joseph van der Naald, "Union Organizing and Strikes in Higher Education: The 2022–2023 Upsurge in Historical Context," special feature in *The State of the Unions 2023: A Profile of Organized Labor in New York City, New York State, and the United States*, by Ruth Milkman and Joseph van der Naald (CUNY Academic Works, 2023), 8, https://academicworks.cuny.edu/cgi/viewcontent.cgi?article=1020&context=slu_pubs.
3. Herbert, Apkarian, and van der Naald, "Union Organizing and Strikes in Higher Education," 6.
4. Meg Brenan, "Approval of Labor Unions at Highest Point since 1965," Gallup, September 2, 2021, https://news.gallup.com/poll/354455/approval-labor-unions-highest-point-1965.aspx.
5. Brenan, "Approval of Labor Unions."
6. Ruth Milkman and Joseph van der Naald, *The State of the Unions 2023* (CUNY Academic Works, 2023), 3–4. https://academicworks.cuny.edu/cgi/viewcontent.cgi?article=1020&context=slu_pubsMilkman and van der Naald.
7. Herbert, Apkarian, and van der Naald, "Union Organizing and Strikes in Higher Education," 6.
8. Department for Professional Employees, AFL-CIO, "Library Professionals: Facts and Figures," Factsheet, June 18, 2024, https://www.dpeaflcio.org/factsheets/library-professionals-facts-and-figures.
9. James W. Milden, "Women, Public Libraries, and Library Unions: The Formative Years," *Journal of Library History (1974–1987)* 12, no. 2 (1977): 150, https://www.jstor.org/stable/25540731.
10. Milden, "Women, Public Libraries, and Library Unions," 151.
11. Milden, "Women, Public Libraries, and Library Unions," 151.
12. Benedict Z. Hirsch. "Library Unions Round Table." *ALA Bulletin* 41, no. 9 (1947): 77-81, https://www.jstor.org/stable/25692802
13. William A. Herbert, "The History Books Tell It? Collective Bargaining in Higher Education in the 1940s," *Journal of Collective Bargaining in the Academy* 9 (2017): article 3, p. 19, https://doi.org/10.58188/1941-8043.1734.
14. Herbert, "History Books Tell It?" 3–4.
15. Herbert, "History Books Tell It?" 4.
16. Martin Halpern, "'From the Top Down or from the Bottom Up?' John F. Kennedy, Executive Order 10988, and the Rise of Public Employee Unionism," chap. 5 in *Unions, Radicals, and Democratic Presidents: Seeking Social Change in the Twentieth Century* (Westport, CT: Praeger, 2003), 80.
17. Herbert, "History Books Tell It?" 2.
18. Tina Maragou Hovekamp, "Unions in Academic Libraries," in *The Successful Academic Librarian: Winning Strategies from Library Leaders*, ed. Gwen Meyer Gregory (Medford, NJ: Information Today, 2005), 111.
19. US Bureau of Labor Statistics, "Union Members—2023," news release, January 23, 2024, pp. 8–9, https://www.bls.gov/news.release/pdf/union2.pdf.
20. Barry T. Hirsch, David A. Macpherson, and William E. Even, "Union Membership, Coverage, Density, and Employment by Occupation, 1983–2023," Union Membership and Coverage Database from the CPS, accessed June 26, 2024, https://www.unionstats.com/occ/occ_index.html
21. Chloe Mills and Ian McCullough, "Academic Librarians and Labor Unions: Attitudes and Experiences," *portal: Libraries and the Academy* 18, no. 4 (2018): 805–29, https://doi.org/10.1353/pla.2018.0046
22. Association of College and Research Libraries, "Guideline on Collective Bargaining," Guidelines, Standards, and Frameworks, accessed June 26, 2024, https://www.ala.org/acrl/standards/guidelinecollective.
23. William A. Kaplin et al., *The Law of Higher Education*, 6th ed. (San Francisco: John Wiley & Sons, 2019), 239–45.
24. Hovekamp, "Unions in Academic Libraries."
25. Milkman and van der Naald, *State of the Unions 2023*.
26. Hovekamp, "Unions in Academic Libraries," 114.
27. Hovekamp, "Unions in Academic Libraries," 116–19.
28. Tina Maragou Hovekamp, "Organizational Commitment of Professional Employees in Union and Nonunion Research Libraries," *College and Research Libraries* 55, no. 4 (1994): 297–307, https://crl.acrl.org/index.php/crl/article/viewFile/14901/16347; Tina Maragou Hovekamp, "Unionization and Job Satisfaction among Professional Library Employees in Academic Research Institutions," *College and Research Libraries* 56, no. 4 (1995): 341–50, https://crl.acrl.org/index.php/crl/article/download/14983/16429.
29. Kathleen de la Pena McCook, "There Is Power in a Union—2009–2010," *Progressive Librarian* 34/35, (Fall 2010): 76–87, 106, ProQuest.

30. Milkman and van der Naald, *State of the Unions 2023*, 27.
31. Mills and McCullough, "Academic Librarians and Labor Unions," 815.
32. Rajinder Garcha and John C. Phillips, "US Academic Librarians: Their Involvement in Union Activities," *Library Review* 50, no. 3 (2001): 122–27, https://doi.org/10.1108/00242530110386825.
33. Mills and McCullough, "Academic Librarians and Labor Unions."
34. Rachel Applegate, "Who Benefits? Unionization and Academic Libraries and Librarians," *Library Quarterly* 79, no. 4 (2009): 456, https://doi.org/10.1086/605383.
35. Stephen H. Aby, "Library Faculty and Collective Bargaining: An Exploration," in *Advances in Library Administration and Organization*, ed. D. E. Williams, J. M. Nyce, and J. Golden (Bingley, UK: Emerald Group Publishing, 2009), 290–91, https://doi.org/10.1108/S0732-0671(2009)0000028009.
36. Stephanie Braunstein and Michael F. Russo, "The Mouse That Didn't Roar: The Difficulty of Unionizing Academic Librarians at a Public American University," in *In Solidarity: Academic Librarian Labour Activism and Union Participation in Canada*, ed. Jennifer Dekker and Mary Kandiuk (Sacramento, CA: Library Juice Press, 2014), 251–76.
37. Lothar Spang, "Collective Bargaining and Faculty Status: A Twenty-Year Case Study of Wayne State University Librarians," *College and Research Libraries* 54, no. 3 (1993): 241–53, https://doi.org/10.5860/crl_54_03_241.
38. Janet Lee, "Contract Equity for Librarians at Regis University," *Library Personnel News*, March–April 1993, 3–5.
39. Jennifer Dekker and Mary Kandiuk. *In Solidarity: Academic Librarian Labour Activism and Union Participation in Canada* (Sacramento, California: Library Juice Press, 2013).
40. Applegate, "Who Benefits," 446.
41. Lothar Spang and William P. Kane, "Who Speaks for Academic Librarians? Status and Satisfaction Comparisons between Unaffiliated and Unionized Librarians on Scholarship and Governance Issues," *College and Research Libraries* 58, no. 5 (1997): 446–62, https://doi.org/10.5860/crl.58.5.446.
42. Suzanne Milton, "Librarians: Key Players in Faculty Unions," *Alki* 21, no. 3 (2005): 5–7.
43. Spang and Kane, "Who Speaks for Academic Librarians?" 449.
44. William A. Herbert and Joseph van der Naald, "A Different Set of Rules? NLRB Proposed Rule Making and Student Worker Unionization Rights," *Journal of Collective Bargaining in the Academy* 11 (2020): article 1, https://doi.org/10.58188/1941-8043.1867
45. Herbert, Apkarian, and van der Naald, "Union Organizing and Strikes in Higher Education."
46. William A. Herbert and Jacob Apkarian, "Everything Passes, Everything Changes: Unionization and Collective Bargaining in Higher Education," *Perspectives on Work* 21 (2017): 30–35, https://lerawebillinois.web.illinois.edu/index.php/LERAMR/article/view/3146/3118
47. William A. Herbert and Jacob Apkarian, "You've Been with the Professors: An Examination of Higher Education Work Stoppage Data, Past and Present," *Employee Relations and Employee Policy Journal* 23 (2019): 249–77, https://www.researchgate.net/profile/William-Herbert/publication/345387079_You%27ve_Been_with_the_Professors_An_Examination_of_Higher_Education_Work_Stoppage_Data_Past_and_Present/links/5fa556fe458515157befcc5b/Youve-Been-with-the-Professors-An-Examination-of-Higher-Education-Work-Stoppage-Data-Past-and-Present.pdf.
48. William A. Herbert and Joseph van der Naald, "Graduate Student Employee Unionization in the Second Gilded Age," chap. 11 in *Revaluing Work(ers): Toward a Democratic and Sustainable Future*, ed. Tobias Schulze-Cleven and Todd E. Vachon (Champaign: University of Illinois, 2021), https://books.google.com/books/about/Revaluing_Work_ers.html?id=rgk7AAAACAAJ.
49. Herbert and van der Naald, "A Different Set of Rules?"
50. Timothy Reese Cain, "Campus Unions: Organized Faculty and Graduate Students in U.S. Higher Education," special issue, *ASHE Higher Education Report* 43, no. 3 (2017): 7–163, https://doi.org/10.1002/aehe.20119.
51. Timothy Reese Cain, "Collective Bargaining and Committee A: Five Decades of Unionism and Academic Freedom," *Review of Higher Education* 44, no. 1 (2020): 57–85, https://doi.org/ 10.1353/rhe.2020.0035.
52. Andrea Crow and Alyssa Greene, "Mobilizing Academic Labor: The Graduate Workers of Columbia Unionization Campaign," in *Women Mobilizing Memory*, ed. Ayşe Gül Altýnay, Maria José Contreras, Marianne Hirsch, Jean Howard, Banu Karaca, and Alisa Solomon (New York: Columbia University Press, 2020), https://www.jstor.org/stable/10.7312/alti19184.14.
53. Heidi Whitford, "The Role of Graduate Student Unions in the Higher Education Landscape," *New Directions for Higher Education* 2014, no. 167 (2014): 17–29, https://doi.org/10.1002/he.20102.
54. Michael A. McCarthy, "Occupying Higher Education: The Revival of the Student Movement," *New Labor Forum* 21, no. 2 (2012): 50–55, https://www.jstor.org/stable/43681978.
55. Gordon Lafer, "Graduate Student Unions: Organizing in a Changed Academic Economy," *Labor Studies Journal* 28, no. 2 (2003): 25–43, https://doi.org/10.1177/0160449X0302800202.
56. Lafer, "Graduate Student Unions," 26–27.
57. Robert A. Rhoads and Gary Rhoades, "Graduate Employee Unionization as Symbol of and Challenge to the Corporatization of U.S. Research Universities," *Journal of Higher Education* 76, no. 3 (2005): 243–75, https://doi.org/10.1080/00221546.2005.11772282.

58. Deeb-Paul Kitchen, II, "On Graduate Unions and Corporatization," *Journal of Collective Bargaining in the Academy* 2, no. 1 (2010): article 1, https://thekeep.eiu.edu/cgi/viewcontent.cgi?article=1003&context=jcba.
59. Daniel J. Julius and Patricia J. Gumport, "Graduate Student Unionization: Catalysts and Consequences," *Review of Higher Education* 26, no. 2 (2003): 187–216, ProQuest.
60. Daniel J. Julius, "The Current Status of Graduate Student Unions: An Employer's Perspective," *Journal of Collective Bargaining in the Academy* 14, no. 1 (2023): 78–97, https://thekeep.eiu.edu/cgi/viewcontent.cgi?article=1905&context=jcba
61. Adrianna Kezar, Tom DePaola, and Daniel T. Scott, *The Gig Academy* (Baltimore, MD: Johns Hopkins University Press, 2019).
62. Deeb-Paul Kitchen, II, "Can Graduate Students Re-energize the Labor Movement?," *Thought and Action* 47 (Fall 2014): 47–62, https://eric.ed.gov/?id=EJ1047969.
63. Adrienne Lu, "Two Votes on Unionization at Princeton, Two Different Results," *Chronicle of Higher Education*, June 14, 2024, https://www-chronicle-com.tamuct.idm.oclc.org/article/two-votes-on-unionization-at-princeton-two-different-results.

Bibliography

Aby, Stephen H. "Library Faculty and Collective Bargaining: An Exploration." In *Advances in Library Administration and Organization*, edited by D. E Williams, J. M. Nyce, and J. Golden, 283–321. Bingley, UK: Emerald Group Publishing, 2009. https://doi.org/10.1108/S0732-0671(2009)0000028009.

Applegate, Rachel. "Who Benefits? Unionization and Academic Libraries and Librarians." *Library Quarterly* 79, no. 4 (2009): 443–63. https://doi.org/10.1086/605383.

Association of College and Research Libraries. "Guideline on Collective Bargaining." Guidelines, Standards, and Frameworks. Accessed June 26, 2024. https://www.ala.org/acrl/standards/guidelinecollective.

Braunstein, Stephanie, and Michael F. Russo. "The Mouse That Didn't Roar: The Difficulty of Unionizing Academic Librarians at a Public American University." In *In Solidarity: Academic Librarian Labour Activism and Union Participation in Canada*, edited by Jennifer Dekker and Mary Kandiuk, 251–76. Sacramento, CA: Library Juice Press, 2014. EBSCOhost.

Brenan, Meg. "Approval of Labor Unions at Highest Point since 1965." Gallup, September 2, 2021. https://news.gallup.com/poll/354455/approval-labor-unions-highest-point-1965.aspx.

Cain, Timothy Reese. "Campus Unions: Organized Faculty and Graduate Students in U.S. Higher Education." Special issue, *ASHE Higher Education Report* 43, no. 3 (2017): 7–163. https://doi.org/10.1002/aehe.20119.

———. "Collective Bargaining and Committee A: Five Decades of Unionism and Academic Freedom." *Review of Higher Education* 44, no. 1 (2020): 57–85. https://doi.org/10.1353/rhe.2020.0035.

Crow, Andrea, and Alyssa Greene. "Mobilizing Academic Labor: The Graduate Workers of Columbia Unionization Campaign." In *Women Mobilizing Memory*, edited by Ayşe Gül Altýnay, Maria José Contreras, Marianne Hirsch, Jean Howard, Banu Karaca, and Alisa Solomon, 192–205. New York: Columbia University Press, 2020. https://www.jstor.org/stable/10.7312/alti19184.14.

Dekker, Jennifer, and Mary Kandiuk. *In Solidarity : Academic Librarian Labour Activism and Union Participation in Canada*. Sacramento, California: Library Juice Press, 2013.

Department for Professional Employees, AFL-CIO. "Library Professionals: Facts and Figures." Factsheet, June 18, 2024. https://www.dpeaflcio.org/factsheets/library-professionals-facts-and-figures.

de Stefano, Jason. "This Is a Golden Age of Academic Unionization." *Chronicle of Higher Education*, December 8, 2023. https://www.chronicle.com/article/this-is-a-golden-age-of-academic-unionization.

Garcha, Rajinder, and John C. Phillips. "US Academic Librarians: Their Involvement in Union Activities." *Library Review* 50, no. 3 (2001): 122–27. https://doi.org/10.1108/00242530110386825.

Halpern, Martin. "'From the Top Down or from the Bottom Up?' John F. Kennedy, Executive Order 10988, and the Rise of Public Employee Unionism." Chap. 5 in *Unions, Radicals, and Democratic Presidents: Seeking Social Change in the Twentieth Century*. Westport, CT: Praeger, 2003.

Herbert, William A. "The History Books Tell It? Collective Bargaining in Higher Education in the 1940s." *Journal of Collective Bargaining in the Academy* 9 (2017): article 3. https://doi.org/10.58188/1941-8043.1734.

Herbert, William A., and Jacob Apkarian. "Everything Passes, Everything Changes: Unionization and Collective Bargaining in Higher Education." *Perspectives on Work* 21 (2017): 30–35. https://lerawebillinois.web.illinois.edu/index.php/LERAMR/article/view/3146/3118.

———. "You've Been with the Professors: An Examination of Higher Education Work Stoppage Data, Past and Present." *Employee Relations and Employee Policy Journal* 23 (2019): 249–77. https://www.researchgate.net/profile/William-Herbert/publication/345387079_You%27ve_Been_with_the_Professors_An_Examination_of_Higher_Education_Work_Stoppage_Data_Past_and_Present/links/5fa556fe458515157befcc5b/

Youve-Been-with-the-Professors-An-Examination-of-Higher-Education-Work-Stoppage-Data-Past-and-Present.pdf.

Herbert, William A., Jacob Apkarian, and Joseph van der Naald. "Union Organizing and Strikes in Higher Education: The 2022–2023 Upsurge in Historical Context." Special feature in *The State of the Unions 2023: A Profile of Organized Labor in New York City, New York State, and the United* States, by Ruth Milkman and Joseph van der Naald, 6–11. CUNY Academic Works, 2023. https://academicworks.cuny.edu/cgi/viewcontent.cgi?article=1020&context=slu_pubs.

Herbert, William A., and Joseph van der Naald. "A Different Set of Rules? NLRB Proposed Rule Making and Student Worker Unionization Rights." *Journal of Collective Bargaining in the Academy* 11 (2020): article 1. https://doi.org/10.58188/1941-8043.1867.

———. "Graduate Student Employee Unionization in the Second Gilded Age." Chap. 11 in *Revaluing Work(ers): Toward a Democratic and Sustainable Future*, edited by Tobias Schulze-Cleven and Todd E. Vachon,. Champaign: University of Illinois, 2021. https://books.google.com/books/about/Revaluing_Work_ers.html?id=rgk7AAAACAAJ.

Hirsch, Barry T., David A. Macpherson, and William E. Even. "Union Membership, Coverage, Density, and Employment by Occupation, 1983–2023." Union Membership and Coverage Database from the CPS. Accessed June 26, 2024. https://www.unionstats.com/occ/occ_index.html.

Hirsch, Benedict Z.. "Library Unions Round Table." *ALA Bulletin* 41, no. 9 (1947): 77–81. https://www.jstor.org/stable/25692802.

Hovekamp, Tina Maragou. "Organizational Commitment of Professional Employees in Union and Nonunion Research Libraries." *College and Research Libraries* 55, no. 4 (1994): 297–307. https://crl.acrl.org/index.php/crl/article/viewFile/14901/16347.

———. "Unionization and Job Satisfaction among Professional Library Employees in Academic Research Institutions." *College and Research Libraries* 56, no. 4 (1995): 341–50. https://crl.acrl.org/index.php/crl/article/download/14983/16429.

———. "Unions in Academic Libraries." In *The Successful Academic Librarian: Winning Strategies from Library Leaders*, edited by Gwen Meyer Gregory, 111–24. Medford, NJ: Information Today, 2005. ProQuest.

Julius, Daniel J. "The Current Status of Graduate Student Unions: An Employer's Perspective." *Journal of Collective Bargaining in the Academy* 14, no. 1 (2023): 78–97. https://thekeep.eiu.edu/cgi/viewcontent.cgi?article=1905&context=jcba

Julius, Daniel J., and Patricia J. Gumport. "Graduate Student Unionization: Catalysts and Consequences." *Review of Higher Education* 26, no. 2 (2003): 187–216. ProQuest.

Kaplin, William A., Barbara A. Lee, Neal H. Hutchens, and Jacob H. Rooksby. *The Law of Higher Education: A Comprehensive Guide to Legal Implications of Administrative Decision Making*, 6th ed. San Francisco: Jossey Bass, 2019.

Kezar, Adrianna, Tom DePaola, and Daniel T. Scott. *The Gig Academy: Mapping Labor in the Neoliberal University*. Baltimore, MD: Johns Hopkins University Press, 2019.

Kitchen, Deeb-Paul, II. "Can Graduate Students Re-energize the Labor Movement?" *Thought and Action* 47 (Fall 2014): 47–62. https://eric.ed.gov/?id=EJ1047969.

———. "On Graduate Unions and Corporatization." *Journal of Collective Bargaining in the Academy* 2 (2010): article 1. https://thekeep.eiu.edu/cgi/viewcontent.cgi?article=1003&context=jcba.

Lafer, Gordon. "Graduate Student Unions: Organizing in a Changed Academic Economy." *Labor Studies Journal* 28, no. 2 (2003): 25–43. https://doi.org/10.1177/0160449X0302800202.

Lee, Janet. "Contract Equity for Librarians at Regis University." *Library Personnel News*, March–April 1993, 3–5.

Lu, Adrienne. "Two Votes on Unionization at Princeton, Two Different Results." *Chronicle of Higher Education*, June 14, 2024. https://www.chronicle.com/article/two-votes-on-unionization-at-princeton-two-different-results.

McCarthy, Michael A. "Occupying Higher Education: The Revival of the Student Movement." *New Labor Forum* 21, no. 2 (2012): 50–55. https://www.jstor.org/stable/43681978.

McCook, Kathleen de la Pena. "There Is Power in a Union—2009–2010." *Progressive Librarian* 34/35 (Fall 2010): 76–87, 106. ProQuest.

Milden, James W. "Women, Public Libraries, and Library Unions: The Formative Years." *Journal of Library History (1974–1987)* 12, no. 2 (1977): 150–158. https://www.jstor.org/stable/25540731.

Milkman, Ruth, and Joseph van der Naald. *The State of the Unions 2023: A Profile of Organized Labor in New York City, New York State, and the United States*. CUNY Academic Works, 2023. https://academicworks.cuny.edu/cgi/viewcontent.cgi?article=1020&context=slu_pubs.

Mills, Chloe, and Ian McCullough. "Academic Librarians and Labor Unions: Attitudes and Experiences." *portal: Libraries and the Academy* 18, no. 4 (2018): 805–29. https://doi.org/10.1353/pla.2018.0046.

Milton, Suzanne. "Librarians: Key Players in Faculty Unions." *Alki* 21, no. 3 (2005): 5–7.

Rhoads, Robert A., and Gary Rhoades. "Graduate Employee Unionization as Symbol of and Challenge to the Corporatization of U.S. Research Universities." *Journal of Higher Education* 76, no. 3 (2005): 243–75. https://doi.org/10.1080/00221546.2005.11772282.

Spang, Lothar. "Collective Bargaining and Faculty Status: A Twenty-Year Case Study of Wayne State University Librarians." *College and Research Libraries* 54, no. 3 (1993): 241–53. https://doi.org/10.5860/crl_54_03_241.

Spang, Lothar, and William P. Kane. "Who Speaks for Academic Librarians? Status and Satisfaction Comparisons between Unaffiliated and Unionized Librarians on Scholarship and Governance Issues." *College and Research Libraries* 58, no. 5 (1997): 446–62. https://doi.org/10.5860/crl.58.5.446.

US Bureau of Labor Statistics. "Union Members—2023." News release. January 23, 2024. https://www.bls.gov/news.release/pdf/union2.pdf.

Whitford, Heidi. "The Role of Graduate Student Unions in the Higher Education Landscape." *New Directions for Higher Education* 2014, no. 167 (2014): 17–29. https://doi.org/10.1002/he.20102.

Part II
Work Culture and Organization

Employee Morale

CHAPTER 12

Wellness Initiatives in Academic Libraries

Dawn M. Harris, Bridgit McCafferty, Sandra Yvette Desjardins, and Johnnie Porter

Faculty and staff are among the most valuable resources at any academic library, and employee benefits are one of the largest expenditure categories for organizations. For this reason, it is advantageous for libraries to assist employees in bettering and preserving their health to improve their quality of life and the library's bottom line. This obviously includes physical health, but also emotional, social, and mental wellness. Programs that target wellness can be large, fully funded, and involve extensive planning, but they can also be one-off events that target a specific element of health. While wellness encompasses many types of services and programs, the difference better health can make for library employees is argument enough that a wellness program is essential in all types of libraries.

We were first drawn to this topic because, at the Texas A&M University-Central Texas (A&M-Central Texas) University Library and Archives, we encourage our staff to practice a healthy work-life balance. Our goal is to provide a supportive environment by creating a culture that values our employees and their well-being. Before the pandemic, we had monthly group events, as well as a library health and wellness newsletter. During the pandemic, we increased our wellness programs to include not only physical, but also mental health tips. Since the pandemic concluded, we continue to use some of these more popular programs, while trying to increase face-to-face engagement. We are constantly assessing our health and wellness programs to make necessary changes so that they continue to evolve.

We believe a strong wellness program keeps our employees happy and engaged, which leads to lower staff turnover. Within the library we have tried many types of programs, such as salad potlucks, a newsletter with healthy recipes and tips, staff birthday celebrations tailored to individual preferences, and a variety of social events targeted at morale. When the pandemic started and we shifted to 100 percent remote work, we realized that we needed to increase engagement among our staff to compensate for physical isolation. We tested numerous initiatives that adhered to COVID restrictions. There were many successful events, as well as some that were less popular. These included shelter-in-place tips, museum websites that allowed virtual tours, online games and jigsaw puzzles, desk yoga, and an employee spotlight section in our monthly newsletters. We also sent out Monday motivational memes, played trivia on Tuesdays, and had virtual dessert parties.

Both during and after the pandemic, our university's wellness initiatives, available to all employees, were extremely helpful. For instance, we encourage our team to take advantage of our university wellness release time program, which provides thirty minutes during normal work hours, up to three times a week, of release time for participation in physical, mental, or emotional wellness activities. Our human resource department also regularly hosts step challenges, as well as fruit-themed activities and exercise programming. It also hosts webinars and lunch-and-learn sessions focused on health topics and allows flexible work arrangements (FWAs) so employees can work from home one or two days a week. All of these contribute to the wellness of our employees in the library, as well as across the university.

Our experiences both during and after the pandemic inspired us to better understand the types of wellness programs offered at academic libraries and how these discrete programs impact employee well-being. The research presented in this chapter will not only improve the programs offered at our university library, but it will also add to a growing body of literature and may inspire and inform other institutions looking to improve employee health and wellness initiatives.

Problem Definition

Popular media often portray librarians sitting at a desk, stamping books, and adding due dates to cards. At times, librarians are seen completing physical tasks, like shelving; but overall, the stereotype of librarianship as a sedentary profession has permeated the collective consciousness because it is very often true. Many librarians do not move around enough, and this inactivity can negatively impact librarians in several ways, particularly in terms of physical and mental health.

In "The Dangers of Sedentary Work," Foulis discusses recent research that shows "that sitting for long periods can incur bad health outcomes such as heart disease, type 2 diabetes and even cancer."[1] She goes on to discuss the importance of movement and mobility, especially in the form of work breaks. Walking away from a workstation not only provides an opportunity to increase blood circulation, which can help eliminate toxins from the body, but also has the added benefit of giving a person space to mentally decompress and come back to their task with greater focus.

The impact of sedentary and work-related stress on employees and organizations can be profound. The World Health Organization defines work-related stress as "the response people… have when presented with work demands and pressures that are not matched to their knowledge and abilities and which challenge their ability to cope."[2] In terms of the financial burden these stressors cause on society, Hassard and colleagues found that, annually, "the total estimated cost of work-related stress was observed to range from $221.3 million to upward of $187 billion."[3]

Given the staggering financial burden that workplace-related stress can cause, many workplaces have started to adopt health and wellness programs. These programs are typically designed to alleviate a particular issue, like offering wellness release time so people feel encouraged to take work breaks. Employers also offer other incentive programs, such as financial coaching, opportunities for employees to join committees focused on workplace culture, or exercise groups. Paid leave for designated wellness activities, like leave as an incentive for preventative care, can also motivate employees.

In her book *Fostering Wellness in the Workplace*, Newman discusses the service component of librarianship and how it impacts the overall health and wellness of those in the profession.[4] She describes the dedication of librarians when offering health and wellness resources to their patrons, but notes that they frequently do not have the same self-awareness or insight to use those resources for themselves. She emphasizes the growing need for health and wellness programs geared toward librarians, who often struggle with low morale, as well as complaints of burnout and toxic work environments.[5] In "An Investigation of Factors Impacting the Wellness of Academic Library Employees," Lo and Herman echo this sentiment when they discuss how library employees frequently feel overwhelmed at work, which can lead to unhealthy habits.[6] Waltz writes that "librarianship was struggling with issues of burnout, low morale, and low engagement prior to 2020, although the COVID-19 pandemic highlighted and exacerbated these issues."[7]

This points to an important reality that we also discovered at A&M-Central Texas: the effects of the COVID-19 pandemic focused the spotlight on work-life balance in libraries. Townsend and Bugg studied perceptions of work-life balance in an urban academic library and proposed that, in this context, "work-life balance covers a wide range of individual experiences, including personal and professional responsibilities, the impact of organizational culture on the individual, health and wellness, and policy development."[8] Academic libraries, in particular, are in a unique position to offer services to help their staff improve these experiences in their professional lives and at home, since they are nested in larger universities and colleges that often already offer a wealth of wellness services and because they are led by administrators with experience integrating evidence-based practices into library operations.

Over the last decade, these programs have grown in importance, especially following recommendations from the Centers for Disease Control and Prevention related to wellness programs and physical activity in the workplace. This growth is demonstrated by the fact that most colleges have fitness facilities that employees can use at a discounted rate, and many employers have adopted health-related wellness programs, like walking challenges, that help establish healthy habits and foster camaraderie. Additionally, there are usually a plethora of on-site or online resources available that can help with mental health and overall well-being, like counseling sessions and daycare facilities. However, despite the variety of services currently available, many librarians continue to struggle with maintaining healthy habits or tackling mental health issues associated with psychologically demanding jobs that require intensely focused, sedentary work. To help libraries improve well-being for their employees, this chapter will evaluate current health and wellness programs that are available for academic library employees and offer suggestions for future directions that library managers can take when establishing or expanding health and wellness programs.

Literature Review

While workplace wellness has been the topic of a great deal of literature, studies related to wellness for library employees, and more specifically academic library employees, are a bit sparse. Newman's book is the most important resource on this subject, since it is directly related.[9] Other titles are more loosely affiliated. They discuss mindfulness or workplace culture, which are related to elements of wellness. These include *The 360 Librarian*, *Recipes for Mindfulness in Your Library*, *The Dysfunctional Library*, and *Cultivating Civility*.[10] Hudson-Vitale and Miller Waltz also wrote a recent article discussing wellness for remote library teams, no doubt inspired by the pandemic.[11]

Notably, there are a plethora of articles about wellness programs in libraries for patrons, which echoes Newman's observation that the profession is so focused on the wellness of communities that the wellness of employees is often overlooked. Also notable is the work of the American Library Association's Allied Professional Association, which has wellness as one of its subgroups. This organization defines wellness as having eight elements: emotional, environmental, financial, intellectual, occupational, physical, spiritual, and social.[12] While this chapter will not focus specifically on any given element, it will encompass all of these when discussing wellness for employees.

Wellness programs at universities are better researched, especially in the last decade. For instance, one resource that is particularly useful for institutions looking to implement a new wellness program is *The Healthy Campus Framework* by the American College Health Association.[13] This tool models how a wellness program might look for academic libraries, as it is specifically geared toward colleges and universities. Tapps, Symonds, and Baghurst also provide an overview of the steps to complete a needs assessment for employee wellness on a university campus, which could be adapted to a library.[14] The US Office of Personnel Management, whose mission is to empower federal agencies to deliver pioneering work-life programs, is another good resource when establishing or modifying wellness programs.[15]

The use and value of wellness programs at universities have also been studied. In their study about wellness programs at the university level, Yuen and colleagues found that about half of public universities and colleges offer employee wellness programs.[16] In contrast, less than a third of private colleges, private universities, and junior colleges do—although about 60 percent of this latter group with more than 500 employees offered such a program.[17] Mathien and colleagues surveyed university employees to gauge interest in certain types of wellness programs, finding that physical activity, nutrition, and lifestyle wellness activities were the most desired. They also found that time, scheduling, and motivation were all barriers to using such a program.[18] Hill-Mey and colleagues found that a lack of communication about the wellness programs available at a given institution was an additional barrier to university employee participation.[19]

The value of these programs has been studied in both universities and libraries. For instance, Jenkins and Sherman demonstrate that employees who participated in wellness programming or a health risk assessment at a large, midwestern university had a lower rate of turnover.[20] This aligns with Martin's findings that tied health and wellness to engagement, based on study respondents' comments on reasons for decreased engagement.[21] Dement and colleagues found that employees who participated in wellness programs at one university saved an estimated $35, on average, every month, with a return on investment for every dollar spent on wellness programming of $2.53.[22] The Texas Department of State Health Services notes, "Within the first year of implementing evidence-based wellness programs, employers can see increased productivity, reduced absenteeism, and lower turnover."[23]

There are also reports of employee benefits as a result of specific wellness programs within libraries. One example is Zucker and colleagues, who discovered that labyrinth (meditative) walking benefited employees, faculty, and staff by lowering blood pressure and pulse rates and creating feelings of relaxation and happiness.[24] Casucci and Baluchi suggest that "mindfulness and exercise, such as yoga, can help mitigate burnout," in their article about offering free yoga classes in a health sciences library.[25] Casucci and colleagues found that game intervention, or gamifying wellness activities with competition and positive rewards to increase motivation for continued participation, can create a better social environment and encourage engagement.[26]

The precise nature of this wellness impact on employees may be difficult to pin down. In a large clinical trial at the University of Illinois at Urbana-Champaign, Reif and colleagues found that, while wellness program participation increased the reported incidence of employees having a primary care physician as well as improving employee beliefs about their health in relation to a host of medical markers, there were no significant impacts on biometrics, medical diagnoses, or medical use.[27] This suggests that some impacts of wellness participation may be more mental than directly physical. This seems to be determined by the workplace culture, whether evidence-based programs are implemented, and the execution of programs, according to a meta-analysis by Goetzel and colleagues.[28]

Though wellness programs within the library can help improve employee perceptions of each of the elements identified by ALA—APA, programs require effort, intent, and monetary investment. Zula discusses guidelines for successful wellness programs and states "organizations must be more diligent about engaging and involving leadership" so that these programs support the mission and goals of the institution.[29] Without administrators at the highest levels championing wellness work and keeping an eye toward how they serve the overall needs of the institution, intentionality can become difficult and, as a result, monetary support might not be forthcoming. Varman and Justice note that trying to create these programs without funding can be difficult.[30]

In our study, we examined which programs are currently available in academic libraries, which programs library employees wanted to have available, and which of those currently offered programs were most important to academic library employees. We hope to get a better understanding of how these programs are currently being used and how libraries might expand their offerings in the future.

Wellness Survey

Methodology

To evaluate the frequency and importance of wellness programs, we used an online survey with sixteen questions. The first group of questions asked participants to report whether they had access to, used, or would use wellness programs from twenty-two designated categories: on-campus health screenings and services; paid leave designated for wellness; tobacco cessation services; stress reduction services; mental health services; social wellness activities; healthy food options on campus and at campus events; physical activity opportunities; financial incentives to participate in healthy activities or maintain a healthy lifestyle; sleep wellness activities; employee assistance programs (EAPs); appropriate facilities for lactation and pumping; FWAs; educational events targeted at health and wellness; health and wellness challenges; health coaching; diet and nutrition services; access to health- and wellness-focused apps; policies limiting after-hours work communications; on-site daycare for dependent children; health and wellness certifications; nature-focused wellness activities; and other.

We also asked participants whether their supervisor made participating in the services difficult and the importance of each service in their lives using a five-point Likert scale that ranged from not important to absolutely essential. Finally, we included open-ended questions about which programs worked the best and worst at their library, as well as a set of demographic questions.

Drawing from several sources, we created a taxonomy of wellness. In his article, "Health Wellness Programs—An Introduction and a Resource," Nason lists ten examples of wellness programs:

> (1) employer provided fitness facilities or the employer's reimbursement of all or a portion of the membership costs to a fitness facility; (2) educational programs (e.g., written communications, on-

line programs or meetings on health topics such as exercise, diet, stress reduction, substance abuse, etc.); (3) smoking cessation programs; (4) employer sponsored social events and sports (e.g., healthy cooking classes, softball and basketball teams, walking or exercise programs and running clubs); (5) diagnostic testing programs; (6) health risk assessments; (7) employer provided preventive care (e.g., employer provided flu shots); (8) workplace modifications (such as increasing healthy food options at canteens or dining facilities, offering stand up desks, and programming elevators to skip floors); (9) activity tracking or activity challenges through wearable monitoring devices; and (10) disease management activities.[31]

This, of course, is not an exhaustive list, but we used it as a jumping-off point for the wellness categories in our survey. The taxonomy used for the survey also drew from the Texas Department of State Health Services wellness categories from its 2020 study.[32] We believe our list encompasses most types of wellness programs and services, though undoubtedly some were left out.

We received institutional review board approval as an exempt project through A&M-Central Texas. We sent this survey through the Association of College and Research Libraries e-mail discussion list, as well as the TLA e-mail discussion list for the College and University Libraries Division. It ran in May and June of 2023. Participants accessed the online survey, posted in Qualtrics, via these solicitations. Before entering the survey, participants were directed to a consent document. They were also thanked for completing the survey.

The survey garnered 200 responses, but only 136 were complete enough to be included in the dataset. Of these responses, 76.5 percent ($n = 104$) came from librarians at universities, with 21.3 percent ($n = 29$) from community colleges. Most respondents ($n = 114$, 83.8%) were professional librarians, with the rest being either paraprofessionals or other types of exempt staff. The majority were fully or mostly on-campus ($n = 118$, 86.8%), with only 3.6 percent ($n = 5$) that were remote more than half of their time. Most respondents were white ($n = 105$, 77.2%), with the next highest category being those who identified as more than one race ($n = 11$, 8.1%), as Black or African American ($n = 8$, 5.9%), or as Hispanic or Latino(a) ($n = 6$, 4.4%). The majority also identified as women ($n = 109$, 80.1%), with 9.6 percent ($n = 13$) identifying as male and 5.1 percent ($n = 7$) identifying as nonbinary or other. The average age of respondents was 44.4 ($SD = 10.90$) years, the average length of time in their current job was 9.6 years ($SD = 9.39$), and the average time working for their current supervisor was 4.1 years ($SD = 4.29$).

Before we ran the data, responses that were determined to be significantly incomplete were removed. For the quantitative data, we used a combination of Excel and SPSS. With SPSS, we ran frequency and other descriptive statistics. For the open-ended questions, we coded responses with three independent raters using the twenty-two categories predefined for the study, as well as several additional codes that arose from our review process. These included a code related to concerns about body-shaming in wellness programs and one about marketing wellness programs, which we will discuss later. Codes were discussed until raters reached consensus.

Results

Our findings for the first set of questions focused on the frequencies of program availability, use, and need (table 12.1). Questions one, two, and four were concerned with which wellness programs were available, which were being utilized, and which programs that were not offered would be desired. When queried about the availability of specific wellness programs, respondents reported that the five most common programs offered at their organizations were social wellness activities ($n = 102, 75\%$), physical activity opportunities ($n = 99, 73\%$), EAPs ($n = 97, 71\%$), mental health services ($n = 96, 71\%$), and FWAs ($n = 95, 70\%$). The least common were policies limiting after-hours work communications ($n = 7, 5\%$), sleep wellness activities ($n = 18, 13\%$), on-site daycare for dependent children ($n = 26, 19\%$), nature-focused wellness activities ($n = 31, 23\%$), and access to health- and wellness-focused apps ($n = 34, 25\%$).

Table 12.1. Full results for availability of wellness programs.

Availability of Wellness Programs

Type of Wellness Program	Percentage of Respondents Reporting Program Availability	Number of Respondents Reporting Program Availability
Access to Health- and Wellness-Focused Apps	25%	34
Appropriate Facilities for Lactation and Pumping	43%	58
Diet and Nutrition Services	28%	38
Educational Events Targeted at Health and Wellness	57%	78
Employee Assistance Programs	71%	97
Financial Incentives to Participate in Healthy Activities or Maintain a Healthy Lifestyle	33%	45
Flexible Work Arrangements	70%	95
Health and Wellness Certifications	41%	56
Health and Wellness Challenges	60%	81
Health Coaching	26%	35
Healthy Food Options on Campus and at Campus Events	57%	77
Mental Health Services	71%	96
Nature-Focused Wellness Activities	23%	31
On-Site Daycare for Dependent Children	19%	26
On-Site Health Screenings and Services	69%	94
Other	4%	5
Paid Leave Designated for Wellness	38%	51
Physical Activity Opportunities	73%	99
Policies Limiting After-Hours Work Communications	5%	7

Table 12.1. Full results for availability of wellness programs.

Availability of Wellness Programs

Type of Wellness Program	Percentage of Respondents Reporting Program Availability	Number of Respondents Reporting Program Availability
Sleep Wellness Activities	13%	18
Social Wellness Activities	75%	102
Stress Reduction Services	46%	62
Tobacco Cessation Services	43%	59

Regarding what programs were being utilized (table 12.2), respondents reported most often taking advantage of FWAs ($n = 83$, 61%); social wellness activities ($n = 81$, 60%); on-site health screenings and services ($n = 77$, 57%); physical activity opportunities ($n = 55$, 40%); and healthy food options on campus and at campus events ($n = 52$, 38%). They least often participated in tobacco cessation services ($n = 2$, 1%), policies limiting after-hours work communications ($n = 3$, 2%), sleep wellness activities ($n = 5$, 4%), health coaching ($n = 6$, 4%), and on-site daycare for dependent children ($n = 5$, 4%).

Table 12.2. Full results for the use of wellness programs

Use of Wellness Programs

Type of Wellness Program	Percentage of Respondents Reporting Program Use	Number of Respondents Reporting Program Use
Access to Health- and Wellness-Focused Apps	10%	14
Appropriate Facilities for Lactation and Pumping	7%	10
Diet and Nutrition Services	10%	14
Educational Events Targeted at Health and Wellness	24%	33
Employee Assistance Programs	22%	30
Financial Incentives to Participate in Healthy Activities or Maintain a Healthy Lifestyle	21%	28
Flexible Work Arrangements	61%	83
Health and Wellness Certifications	21%	29
Health and Wellness Challenges	32%	44
Health Coaching	4%	6
Healthy Food Options on Campus and at Campus Events	38%	52
Mental Health Services	18%	24
Nature-Focused Wellness Activities	11%	15
On-Site Daycare for Dependent Children	4%	5
On-Site Health Screenings and Services	57%	77
Other	2%	3
Paid Leave Designated for Wellness	34%	46
Physical Activity Opportunities	40%	55
Policies Limiting After-Hours Work Communications	2%	3

Table 12.2. Full results for the use of wellness programs

Use of Wellness Programs

Type of Wellness Program	Percentage of Respondents Reporting Program Use	Number of Respondents Reporting Program Use
Sleep Wellness Activities	4%	5
Social Wellness Activities	60%	81
Stress Reduction Services	19%	26
Tobacco Cessation Services	1%	2

As to what the respondents wanted to see offered by their organizations (table 12.3), paid leave designated for wellness ($n = 60$, 44%), policies limiting after-hours work communications ($n = 52$, 38%), nature-focused wellness activities ($n = 50$, 37%), stress reduction services ($n = 48$, 35%), and financial incentives to participate in healthy activities or maintain a healthy lifestyle ($n = 46$, 34%) garnered the most interest. Programs for tobacco cessation services ($n = 5$, 4%), EAPs ($n = 16$, 12%), educational events targeted at health and wellness ($n = 16$, 12%), appropriate facilities for lactation and pumping ($n = 18$, 13%), and health and wellness challenges ($n = 17$, 13%) scored the lowest in terms of programs that respondents wanted.

Table 12.3. Full results for which wellness programs are wanted.

Demand for Wellness Programs

Type of Wellness Program	Percentage of Respondents Reporting Program Demand	Number of Respondents Reporting Program Demand
Access to Health- and Wellness-Focused Apps	14%	19
Appropriate Facilities for Lactation and Pumping	13%	18
Diet and Nutrition Services	29%	39
Educational Events Targeted at Health and Wellness	12%	16
Employee Assistance Programs	12%	16
Financial Incentives to Participate in Healthy Activities or Maintain a Healthy Lifestyle	34%	46
Flexible Work Arrangements	24%	33
Health and Wellness Certifications	21%	29
Health and Wellness Challenges	13%	17
Health Coaching	19%	26
Healthy Food Options on Campus and at Campus Events	23%	31
Mental Health Services	18%	25
Nature-Focused Wellness Activities	37%	50
On-Site Daycare for Dependent Children	28%	38

Table 12.3. Full results for which wellness programs are wanted.

Demand for Wellness Programs		
Type of Wellness Program	Percentage of Respondents Reporting Program Demand	Number of Respondents Reporting Program Demand
On-Site Health Screenings and Services	22%	30
Other	3%	4
Paid Leave Designated for Wellness	44%	60
Physical Activity Opportunities	18%	24
Policies Limiting After-Hours Work Communications	38%	52
Sleep Wellness Activities	22%	30
Social Wellness Activities	15%	20
Stress Reduction Services	35%	48
Tobacco Cessation Services	4%	5

The third question on the survey queried respondents about how easy or difficult their supervisor made it for them to participate in health and wellness programs. This question used a five-point scale, from extremely difficult to extremely easy. Responses for this question had a mean of 4.32 ($SD = 1.09$), suggesting that supervisors make it fairly easy for respondents to participate in programs.

The fourth question on this survey asked respondents to rate the importance of each health and wellness program category using a five-point scale, from not important to absolutely essential (table 12.4). Based on the mean for each of these ratings, the most important programs were FWAs ($M = 4.46$, $SD = 0.98$); mental health services ($M = 4.26$, $SD = 0.91$); paid leave designated for wellness activities ($M = 4.14$, $SD = 1.08$); healthy food options on campus and at campus events ($M = 4.04$, $SD = 1.16$); and EAPs ($M = 4$, $SD = 1.09$). Each of these had a mean rating higher than four. Other highly rated services included physical activity opportunities ($M = 3.88$, $SD = 1.08$), on-site health screenings ($M = 3.83$, $SD = 1.04$), appropriate facilities for lactation and pumping ($M = 3.8$, $SD = 1.51$), stress reduction services ($M = 3.72$, $SD = 1.06$), and social wellness activities ($M = 3.7$, $SD = 1.12$).

The programs that were rated as least important were access to health and wellness apps ($M = 2.71$, $SD = 1.23$), tobacco cessation services ($M = 2.73$, $SD = 1.41$) and sleep wellness activities ($M = 2.93$, $SD = 1.18$), which all had a mean score lower than three. Ratings for several services were neutral, indicating that they were also less important than other services. These included health and wellness challenges ($M = 3.01$, $SD = 1.12$); health coaching ($M = 3.05$, $SD = 1.16$); educational events targeted at health and wellness ($M = 3.14$, $SD = 1.03$); diet and nutrition services ($M = 3.21$, $SD = 1.18$); and nature-focused wellness programs ($M = 3.28$, $SD = 1.11$).

Table 12.4. Mean scores for importance of wellness programs.

Importance of Wellness Programs

Wellness Program Type	Mean Importance	Standard Deviation
Access to Health- and Wellness-Focused Apps	2.71	1.23
Appropriate Facilities for Lactation and Pumping	3.80	1.51
Diet and Nutrition Services	3.21	1.18
Educational Events Targeted at Health and Wellness	3.14	1.03
Employee Assistance Programs	4.00	1.09
Financial Incentives to Participate in Healthy Activities or Maintain a Healthy Lifestyle	3.40	1.26
Flexible Work Arrangements	4.46	0.98
Health and Wellness Certifications	3.52	1.06
Health and Wellness Challenges	3.01	1.12
Health Coaching	3.05	1.16
Healthy Food Options on Campus and at Campus Events	4.04	1.16
Mental Health Services	4.26	0.91
Nature-Focused Wellness Activities	3.28	1.11
On-Site Daycare for Dependent Children	3.60	1.55
On-Site Health Screenings and Services	3.83	1.04
Paid Leave Designated for Wellness	4.14	1.08
Physical Activity Opportunities	3.88	1.08
Policies Limiting After-Hours Work Communications	3.46	1.31
Sleep Wellness Activities	2.93	1.18
Social Wellness Activities	3.70	1.12
Stress Reduction Services	3.72	1.06
Tobacco Cessation Services	2.73	1.41

In terms of the qualitative data, the frequencies and percentages for each response were analyzed following coding. There were 77 responses, with 120 identified codes, for our open-ended question about wellness programs that worked well. Within these responses, the wellness programs that were reported to work the best were FWAs ($n = 13$, 17%) and health and wellness challenges ($n = 13$, 17%), with on-site health screenings and services ($n = 11$, 14%) and education events targeted at health and wellness ($n = 11$, 14%) ranked next, followed closely behind by stress reduction services ($n = 10$, 13%).

There were 64 responses, with 90 identified codes, on our open-ended question about programs that worked poorly. Of the programs that respondents reported as working poorly, it is worth noting that the top two categories fell under "non-applicable" ($n = 11$, 17%) and "other" ($n = 9$, 14%). These categories encompassed a variety of responses that did not fall within the scope of the coding schema but provided valuable insight, oftentimes indicating that the participant did not have experience with a particular wellness program. As for those programs that respondents identified as having worked poorly, health and wellness challenges ($n = 7$, 11%), financial incentives to participate in healthy activities or maintain a healthy lifestyle ($n = 7$, 11%), and social wellness activities ($n = 7$, 11%) topped the list, followed closely by educational events targeted at health and wellness

(n = 6, 9%). In terms of reasons why some participants perceived that wellness programs worked poorly, many indicated that a lack of marketing or communication (n = 5, 8%) may have played a role in the failures. Moreover, many respondents expressed a concern about weight loss programs and body-shaming (n = 7, 11%), rivaling the frequency of the most poorly performing programs.

Discussion

When looking at the "Available-Use-Want" trio of wellness programs questions, a few interesting results merited discussion. Considering the work-at-home requirements for many employees during the early days of the COVID-19 pandemic and the increased emphasis on work-life balance following this experience, the availability of FWAs suggests that library administrators acknowledged and responded to an increased desire for work-life balance on the part of employees. Not surprisingly, employees who are offered this incentive take full advantage of it. Unfortunately, there are still some employees who do not have the luxury of this program, since nearly one-fourth would like the option. In terms of overall work-life balance, few respondents had policies limiting after-hours work communication, but many indicated that they wanted this. However, few used the perk when available, which is perhaps an indicator of how difficult cutting off communication after hours can be in libraries, which are often open during nonstandard hours.

The ability to take care of health screenings on-site can be a boon to time management, and organizations have responded by offering this program with high employee participation. However, providing paid leave for wellness, while highly desired by employees, is much more infrequently available. Notably, one-third of respondents took advantage of this program when it was available.

The age-old stereotype of library employees as quiet and shy is somewhat negated by the high number of social wellness programs available and the parallel high number of employees who are engaging in these programs. This emphasis on social wellness might also be a reaction to social distancing that employees encountered during pandemic protocol.

Mental health services and EAPs come in as a fairly standard wellness program, but unfortunately, according to respondents, are not highly utilized. Tobacco cessation services are offered in less than half of queried employees' organizations, but they are also rarely used or desired. Finally, stress reduction activities, on-site daycare for dependent children, and sleep wellness activities are infrequently available and infrequently used when available. Less than one-quarter of those without the daycare benefit expressed interest in having it, which might indicate that many respondents did not have small children. While this suggests that these kinds of programs might not be important to library employees broadly speaking, they likely have outsize importance for employees who need them—and might even enable some working mothers to continue to work.

As far as perceiving the ability to use these services, our data demonstrated that library employees think their supervisors make it relatively easy for them to participate in health and wellness activities. Since supervisors are not a barrier to using programs, marketing and communication might be the real issue in persuading employees to use wellness programs, which is reflected in our qualitative data.

In relation to the importance of various wellness programs, the data suggests that FWAs, mental health services, paid leave in support of health and wellness, healthy food options, and EAPs are viewed as important or essential for library employees. Notably, at least four of these options provide the employee with autonomy in how and when they are used. FWAs, paid wellness leave, healthy food on campus, and EAPs all leave it to the employee to determine how and why they will take advantage of the provided opportunity. This is consistent with our findings related to the "available-want-use" trio of questions. Mental health services, stress reduction services, and social wellness activities are often aligned with each other and point to a possible need for services that combat burnout and promote a professional community in libraries, echoing Newman's observations on library work environments. Opportunities for physical activity and on-site health screenings and services were also popular, indicating that wellness programs that save library employees time by allowing them to take care of exercise or health visits easily during the day are appreciated, since they contribute to work-life balance.

Programs that were not important or of little importance included those that were niche or uncommon, such as health and wellness apps, tobacco cessation, sleep wellness services, and nature activities. These programs also received little use or demand in earlier sections of our survey, with the exception of nature activities, which were high in demand. Notably, the other lower rated programs tended to be more prescriptive than the higher rated ones. For instance, health challenges and coaching are often regimented, with rules and directives that employees have to follow. Educational events require library employees to participate in activities they may not otherwise attend, and diet and nutrition services frequently involve the end goal of losing weight, something that several respondents felt uncomfortable about in our qualitative data due to the prevalence of body-shaming. This suggests that prescriptive programs that focus on negative health activities or that require participation in specific activities are not ideal. Interestingly, some of these programs, such as health challenges, were popular in other sets of questions, indicating they were used and generally liked, but not deemed important in the way other programs were on this measure.

In terms of the qualitative data, the researchers originally created a coding schema that encompassed the twenty-two wellness program options that were available as choices on the survey. As researchers began assigning appropriate codes to the participants' responses, it was evident that there were several responses that did not fall within the existing coding schema, and three additional codes were added. These codes included a "no" or "non-applicable" category for responses where participants had nothing further to add or instances in which participants had not engaged in that type of wellness program. Additionally, a "body image" category was created, which included responses that referenced "fat shaming" or "body positivity." Lastly, a "communication and marketing" category was included, since many respondents' commented on how these two components potentially played a role in why particular wellness programs failed, or why they were not as successful as they could have been. As mentioned above, both body-shaming and communication became recurrent themes in our qualitative data and merit further examination in future studies.

Conclusions and Best Practices

Librarianship is often a desk-bound, emotionally draining occupation, a fact discussed at length in Newman's *Fostering Wellness in the Workplace*,[33] so providing employees with ample and varied opportunities for wellness is fundamental to ensuring physical, mental, and emotional well-being. Moreover, the literature about wellness programs across higher education demonstrates that employee participation in wellness programs can result in belonging, negate unhealthy habits, lessen burnout, and reverse low morale.

While our study did not look at the impact of these programs on employee satisfaction, our results suggest that libraries looking to initiate or expand wellness activities should focus on flexible programs that let librarians set their own goals and increase work-life balance. These include FWAs, EAPs, release time for wellness activities, healthy food options on campus, and on-site checkups and other health services, which library employees ranked as both highly used and important. These flexible programs are especially valuable because library employees work varying schedules, including evenings and weekends, so they allow as many employees to participate as possible. Programs that are overly prescriptive or focus on negative health practices should be avoided, since they are not favored by most library employees, especially when workers feel judged for their weight or bad habits—a fact that was especially evident in our qualitative data, but also reflected in the programs that respondents deemed unimportant.

For those looking to implement wellness programs, Zula suggests five strategic activities that help ensure the success of such programs: (1) effective and efficient communication, (2) leadership engagement and commitment, (3) relationships and partnerships to leverage resources, (4) accessible and involved employees, and (5) relevance as well as continuous improvement.[34] These tactics are important whether the program is aimed at an individual unit of a library, an entire library, or the whole academic institution.

Communication is first on this list, and for good reason. Administrators should pay special attention to relaying information about the program, including its purpose. This fact came up again and again in our qualitative data, where employees reported that failed programs were not sufficiently advertised or seemed superficial, as well as in the study by Hill-Mey and colleagues, who reported that lack of communication was a barrier to employee participation.[35] Without a clear objective, programs are wasted effort, because employees, who are limited in the amount of time they can spend on wellness,[36] will not make time to participate. As suggested by Goetzel and colleagues, wellness programs are more successful when they are rooted in the research and evidence-based best practices that ensure they have a real and substantial impact on employee health.[37] In addition to communicating the purpose of the program, it is also important to provide complete and detailed information to employees, to include who, what, where, and when. A unified method of notification such as a blanket e-mail gives everyone the same information at the same time, rather than the scattershot results that word-of-mouth provides.

Another particularly important facet of implementing a program is encouraging staff input and suggestions during the planning process so that it meets the individualized needs of employees and fits with the work culture, another important factor of success noted by Goetzel and colleagues.[38] This is especially important, because more flexible programs that allow employees to set and target their own wellness and work-life balance goals are valued by employees. In addition to buy-in from staff, leaders should also communicate buy-in so employees know they are encouraged to participate. Leaders can show their support in many ways, including designating resources and time toward the program; offering input about the program; and sending an e-mail urging participation. Library administrators can also help convey that leadership is invested in employee wellness by participating themselves because it will make lower-level staff feel more comfortable spending time on wellness during the workday.

While a program might be successful without incentives, even small rewards can motivate a more reluctant employee. Creative partnerships between departments and outside organizations might be used to offer these carrots, which stimulate attendance. Competition could be a valuable addition to incentives, or used in the place of incentives, even if only bragging rights are awarded in the end. However, leadership should keep an eye on competition to ensure that it does not become detrimental to staff morale or unity.

Once the program is operational, administrators should incorporate assessment activities to demonstrate the program's effectiveness and improve any weaknesses. To this end, surveying employees about the value of the program and their impression of its effectiveness can provide the program planners with invaluable input concerning its continuation and any future plans. This will also provide data that can justify the output of resources required to run the program.

Program planners should strive to make wellness programs educational, fun, inviting, and rewarding. To assure inclusivity, planners need to present programs that appeal to employees regardless of their work mode, whether it is in-person, remote, or hybrid. Providing a wide variety of events will help to keep participants interested and engaged. In addition, planners should seize all opportunities to tie the program and its events to employees' physical, emotional, and mental well-being.

Lessons Learned

During our study of the availability and usage of employee wellness programs in academic libraries, we identified the following insights:

- Administrative backing and buy-in are a must and need to be acquired early in the planning process.
- Ample planning, to include which programs are desired, should take place with a wide variety of stakeholders.
- Communicate, communicate, communicate!
- Make sure some types of programs are available to all employees, regardless of work modality or shift work.
- Make sure employees are provided with adequate time to participate.
- Watch out for and eliminate appearances of body-shaming.
- Do not define wellness targets that prescribe only one way of being healthy.
- Keep competition light-hearted.

Notes

1. Maia Foulis, "The Dangers of Sedentary Work," *Canadian Occupational Safety*, October 18, 2021, https://www.thesafetymag.com/ca/topics/occupational-hygiene/the-dangers-of-sedentary-work/313466.
2. World Health Organization, "Occupational Health: Stress at the Workplace," October 19, 2020, https://www.who.int/news-room/questions-and-answers/item/ccupational-health-stress-at-the-workplace.
3. Juliet Hassard et al., "The Cost of Work-Related Stress to Society: A Systemic Review," *Journal of Occupational Health Psychology* 23, no. 1 (2018): 1, https://doi.org/10.1037/ocp0000069.
4. Bobbi Newman, *Fostering Wellness in the Workplace* (Chicago: ALA Editions, 2022), 9.
5. Newman, *Fostering Wellness*, 40.
6. Leo S. Lo and Bethany Herman, "An Investigation of Factors Impacting the Wellness of Academic Library Employees," *College and Research Libraries* 78, no. 6 (2017): 795, https://crl.acrl.org/index.php/crl/article/view/16736.
7. Rebecca Miller Waltz, "In Support of Flourishing: Practices to Engage, Motivate, Affirm, and Appreciate," *International Information and Library Review* 53, no. 4 (2021): 334, https://doi.org/10.1080/10572317.2021.1990564.
8. Tamara Townsend and Kimberley Bugg, "Perceptions of Work–Life Balance for Urban Academic Librarians: An Exploratory Study," *Journal of Library Administration* 60, no. 5 (2020): 498, https://doi.org/10.1080/01930826.2020.1729624.
9. Newman, *Fostering Wellness*.
10. Tammi Owens and Carol A. Daul-Elhindi, *The 360 Librarian* (Chicago: Association of College and Research Libraries, 2019); Madeleine Charney, Jenny Colvin, and Richard J. Moniz, eds., *Recipes for Mindfulness in Your Library* (Chicago: ALA Editions, 2019); Jo Henry, Joe Eshleman, and Richard Moniz, *The Dysfunctional Library* (Chicago: ALA Editions, 2018); Jo Henry, Joe Eshleman, and Richard Moniz, *Cultivating Civility* (Chicago: ALA Editions, 2020).
11. Cynthia Hudson-Vitale and Rebecca Miller Waltz, "Caring for Our Colleagues: Wellness and Support Strategies for Remote Library Teams," *College and Research Libraries News* 81, no. 10 (November 2020): 494, https://doi.org/10.5860/crln.81.10.494.
12. American Library Association—Allied Professional Association, "ALA-APA Wellness," accessed November 7, 2023, https://ala-apa.org/wellness/.
13. American College Health Association, *The Healthy Campus Framework* (Silver Spring, MD: American College Health Association, 2023), https://www.acha.org/wp-content/uploads/2024/06/The_Healthy_Campus_Framework.pdf.

14. Tyler Tapps, Matthew Symonds, and Timothy Baghurst, "Assessing Employee Wellness Needs at Colleges and Universities: A Case Study," *Cogent Social Sciences* 2, no. 1 (2016): article 1250338, https://doi.org/10.1080/23311886.2016.1250338.
15. US Office of Personnel Management, "Health & Wellness," accessed October 12, 2023, https://www.opm.gov/policy-data-oversight/worklife/health-wellness/.
16. Hon K. Yuen et al., "Prevalence and Characteristics of Campus-Based Employee Wellness Programs among United States Accredited Colleges and Universities," *Work: A Journal of Prevention, Assessment and Rehabilitation* 68, no. 4 (2021): 1049–57, https://doi.org/10.3233/wor-213435.
17. Yuen et al., "Campus-Based Employee Wellness Programs."
18. Rebecca G. Mathien et al., "Rationale for Participation in University Worksite Wellness Programs," *Journal of American College Health*, January 2023: 1–9, https://doi.org/10.1080/07448481.2022.2155827.
19. Patricia E. Hill-Mey et al., "A Focus Group Assessment to Determine Motivations, Barriers and Effectiveness of a University-Based Worksite Wellness Program," *Health Promotion Perspectives* 3, no. 2 (2013): 154, https://doi.org/10.5681%2Fhpp.2013.019.
20. Kristi Rahrig Jenkins and Bruce W. Sherman, "Wellness Program Nonparticipation and Its Association with Employee Turnover," *American Journal of Health Promotion* 34, no. 5 (2020): 559–62, https://doi.org/10.1177/0890117120907867.
21. Jason Martin, "Workplace Engagement of Librarians and Library Staff," *Journal of Library Administration* 69, no. 1 (2020): 35, https://doi.org/10.1080/01930826.2019.1671037.
22. John M. Dement et al., "Impacts of Workplace Health Promotion and Wellness Programs on Health Care Utilization and Costs," *Journal of Occupational and Environmental Medicine* 57, no. 11 (2015): 1159.
23. Texas Department of State Health Services, *Implementation and Participation in State Agency Worksite Wellness* (Austin: Texas Health and Human Services, 2020), 3, https://www.dshs.texas.gov/sites/default/files/2020_State_Agency_Worksite_Wellness_Report.pdf.
24. Donna M. Zucker et al., "The Effects of Labyrinth Walking in an Academic Library," *Journal of Library Administration* 56, no. 8 (2016): 966, https://doi.org/10.1080/01930826.2016.1180873.
25. Tallie Casucci and Donna Baluchi, "A Health Sciences Library Promotes Wellness with Free Yoga," *Journal of the Medical Library Association* 107, no. 1 (2019): 86, https://doi.org/10.5195/jmla.2019.475.
26. Tallie Casucci et al., "A Workplace Well-Being Game Intervention for Health Sciences Librarians to Address Burnout," *Journal of the Medical Library Association* 108, no. 4 (2020): 613, https://doi.org/10.5195/jmla.2020.742.
27. Julian Reif et al., "Effects of a Workplace Wellness Program on Employee Health, Health Beliefs, and Medical Use: A Randomized Clinical Trial," *JAMA Internal Medicine* 180, no. 7 (2020): 952–60, https://doi.org/10.1001/jamainternmed.2020.1321.
28. Ron Z. Goetzel et al., "Do Workplace Health Promotion (Wellness) Programs Work?" *Journal of Occupational and Environmental Medicine* 56, no. 9 (2014): 927–34, https://doi.org/10.1097/JOM.0000000000000276.
29. Ken Zula, "Workplace Wellness Programs: A Comparison between Best Practice Guidelines and Implementation," *Journal of Applied Business Research* 30, no. 3 (2014): 790, https://doi.org/10.19030/jabr.v30i3.8564.
30. Beatriz G. Varman and Adela V. Justice, "The Unfunded Worksite Wellness Program," *Journal of Hospital Librarianship* 15, no. 3 (2015): 284–95, https://doi.org.10.1080/15323269.2015.1049065
31. Johnathan Nason, "Health Wellness Program—An Introduction and a Resource," JD Supra, July 23, 2018, https://www.jdsupra.com/legalnews/health-wellness-programs-an-77295/.
32. Texas Department of State Health Services, *Implementation and Participation*, B-4.
33. Newman, *Fostering Wellness*.
34. Zula, "Workplace Wellness Programs," 787.
35. Hill-Mey et al., "Focus Group Assessment," 163.
36. Mathien et al., Cochran "Rationale for Participation," 7.
37. Goetzel et al., "Do Workplace Health Promotion (Wellness) Programs Work?" 927.
38. Goetzel et al., "Do Workplace Health Promotion (Wellness) Programs Work?" 927.

Bibliography

American College Health Association. *The Healthy Campus Framework*. Silver Springs, MD: American College Health Association, 2023. https://www.acha.org/wp-content/uploads/2024/06/The_Healthy_Campus_Framework.pdf.
American Library Association—Allied Professional Association. "ALA-APA Wellness." Accessed November 7, 2023. https://ala-apa.org/wellness/.
Casucci, Tallie, and Donna Baluchi. "A Health Sciences Library Promotes Wellness with Free Yoga." *Journal of the Medical Library Association* 107, no. 1 (2019): 80–88. https://doi.org/10.5195/jmla.2019.475.

Casucci, Tallie, Amy B. Locke, Autumn Henson, and Fares Qeadan. "A Workplace Well-Being Game Intervention for Health Sciences Librarians to Address Burnout." *Journal of the Medical Library Association* 108, no. 4 (2020): 605–17. https://doi.org/10.5195/jmla.2020.742.

Charney, Madeleine, Jenny Colvin, and Richard J. Moniz, eds. *Recipes for Mindfulness in Your Library: Supporting Resilience and Community Engagement*. Chicago: ALA Editions, 2019.

Dement, John M., Carol Epling, Julie Joyner, and Kyle Cavanaugh. "Impacts of Workplace Health Promotion and Wellness Programs on Health Care Utilization and Costs." *Journal of Occupational and Environmental Medicine* 57, no. 11 (2015): 1159–69.

Foulis, Maia. "The Dangers of Sedentary Work." *Canadian Occupational Safety,* October 18, 2021. https://www.thesafetymag.com/ca/topics/occupational-hygiene/the-dangers-of-sedentary-work/313466.

Goetzel, Ron Z., Rachel Mosher Henke, Maryam Tabrizi, Kenneth R. Pelletier, Ron Loeppke, David W. Ballard, Jessica Grossmeier, et al. "Do Workplace Health Promotion (Wellness) Programs Work?" *Journal of Occupational and Environmental Medicine* 56, no. 9 (2014): 927–34. https://doi.org/10.1097/JOM.0000000000000276.

Hassard, Juliet, Kevin R. H. Teoh, Gintare Visockaite, Philip Dewe, and Tom Cox. "The Cost of Work-Related Stress to Society: A Systemic Review." *Journal of Occupational Health Psychology* 23, no. 1 (2018), 1–17. https://doi.org/10.1037/ocp0000069.

Henry, Jo, Joe Eshleman, and Richard Moniz. *Cultivating Civility: Practical Ways to Improve a Dysfunctional Library*. Chicago: American Library Association, 2020.

———. *The Dysfunctional Library: Challenges and Solutions to Workplace Relationships*. Chicago: American Library Association, 2018.

Hill-Mey, Patricia E., Ray M. Merrill, Karol L. Kumpfer, Justine Reel, and Beverly Hyatt-Neville. "A Focus Group Assessment to Determine Motivations, Barriers and Effectiveness of a University-Based Worksite Wellness Program." *Health Promotion Perspectives* 3, no. 2 (2013): 154–64. https://doi.org/10.5681%2Fhpp.2013.019.

Hudson-Vitale, Cynthia, and Rebecca Miller Waltz. "Caring for Our Colleagues: Wellness and Support Strategies for Remote Library Teams." *College and Research Libraries News* 81, no. 10 (November 2020): 494–97. https://doi.org/10.5860/crln.81.10.494.

Jenkins, Kristi Rahrig, and Bruce W. Sherman. "Wellness Program Nonparticipation and Its Association with Employee Turnover." *American Journal of Health Promotion* 34, no. 5 (2020): 559–62. https://doi.org/10.1177/0890117120907867.

Lo, Leo S., and Bethany Herman. "An Investigation of Factors Impacting the Wellness of Academic Library Employees." *College and Research Libraries* 78, no. 6 (2017): 789–811. https://crl.acrl.org/index.php/crl/article/view/16736.

Martin, Jason. "Workplace Engagement of Librarians and Library Staff." *Journal of Library Administration* 60, no. 1 (2020): 22–40. https://doi.org/10.1080/01930826.2019.1671037.

Mathien, Rebecca G., Beth Cochran, Aimee K. Johnson, and A. Laura Dengo. "Rationale for Participation in University Worksite Wellness Programs." *Journal of American College Health*, January 2023: 1–9. https://doi.org/10.1080/07448481.2022.2155827.

Miller Waltz, Rebecca. "In Support of Flourishing: Practices to Engage, Motivate, Affirm, and Appreciate." *International Information and Library Review* 53, no. 4 (2021): 333-40. https://doi.org/10.1080/10572317.2021.1990564.

Nason, Johnathan. Health Wellness Programs—An Introduction and a Resource. JD Supra, July 23, 2018. https://www.jdsupra.com/legalnews/health-wellness-programs-an-77295/.

Newman, Bobbi. *Fostering Wellness in the Workplace: A Handbook for Libraries*. Chicago: ALA Editions, 2022.

Owens, Tammi, and Carol A. Daul-Elhindi. *The 360 Librarian: A Framework for Integrating Mindfulness, Emotional Intelligence, and Critical Reflection in the Workplace*. Chicago: Association of College and Research Libraries, 2019.

Reif, Julian, David Chan, Damon Jones, Laura Payne, and David Molitor. "Effects of a Workplace Wellness Program on Employee Health, Health Beliefs, and Medical Use: A Randomized Clinical Trial." *JAMA Internal Medicine* 180, no. 7 (2020): 952–60. https://doi.org/10.1001/jamainternmed.2020.1321.

Tapps, Tyler, Matthew Symonds, and Timothy Baghurst. "Assessing Employee Wellness Needs at Colleges and Universities: A Case Study." *Cogent Social Sciences* 2, no. 1 (2016): article 1250338. https://doi.org/10.1080/23311886.2016.1250338.

Texas Department of State Health Services. *Implementation and Participation in State Agency Worksite Wellness*. Austin: Texas Health and Human Services, 2020. https://www.dshs.texas.gov/sites/default/files/2020_State_Agency_Worksite_Wellness_Report.pdf.

Townsend, Tamara, and Kimberley Bugg. "Perceptions of Work–Life Balance for Urban Academic Librarians: An Exploratory Study." *Journal of Library Administration* 60, no. 5 (2020): 493–511. https://doi.org/10.1080/01930826.2020.1729624.

US Office of Personnel Management. "Health & Wellness," Accessed October 12, 2023. https://www.opm.gov/policy-data-oversight/worklife/health-wellness/.

Varman, Beatriz G., and Adela V. Justice. "The Unfunded Worksite Wellness Program." *Journal of Hospital Librarianship* 15, no. 3 (2015): 284–95. https://doi.org/10.1080/15323269.2015.1049065.

World Health Organization. "Occupational Health: Stress at the Workplace." October 19, 2020. https://www.who.int/news-room/questions-and-answers/item/ccupational-health-stress-at-the-workplace.

Yuen, Hon K., Sarah W. Becker, Michelle T. Ellis, and Joi Moses. "Prevalence and Characteristics of Campus-Based Employee Wellness Programs among United States Accredited Colleges and Universities." *Work: A Journal of Prevention, Assessment and Rehabilitation* 68, no. 4 (2021): 1049–57. https://doi.org/10.3233/wor-213435.

Zucker, Donna M., Jeungok Choi, Matthew N. Cook, and Janet Brennan Croft. "The Effects of Labyrinth Walking in an Academic Library." *Journal of Library Administration* 56, no. 8 (2016): 957–73. https://doi.org/10.1080/01930826.2016.1180873.

Zula, Ken. "Workplace Wellness Programs: A Comparison between Best Practice Guidelines and Implementation." *Journal of Applied Business Research* 30, no. 3 (2014): 783–92. https://doi.org/10.19030/jabr.v30i3.8564..

CHAPTER 13

Offering More Than Just a Desk and Chair
Combatting Librarian Burnout

Jennifer Batson, Kelly Williams, Margaret Dawson, and Sandra Yvette Desjardins

Burnout occurs when multiple factors combine to interfere with an individual's ability to engage with their work in a positive way. Characterized by exhaustion, cynicism, and feelings of inefficacy, burnout can have serious consequences for both employees and employers.[1] The issue of burnout gained national attention during the 2021 Great Resignation that followed COVID-19 lockdowns, during which approximately one in five employees quit their jobs citing low pay, lack of opportunity, and lack of respect.[2] However, combating burnout and promoting psychological well-being at work is neither a new problem nor limited to medical staff and teachers: research demonstrating burnout among librarians and staff in academic libraries extends back to the eighties, and the problem persists today.

As many workplaces evolve to meet changing job expectations and new realities in digital work and information access, libraries too will benefit from finding ways to avoid employee burnout and increase positive work engagement in a changing information environment. This chapter will provide an overview of workplace factors that can lead to burnout and those that encourage engagement. These include autonomy, work-life balance (WLB), feelings of competence, and psychological safety. The chapter concludes with ideas for combating burnout and promoting librarian and staff engagement in academic libraries.

Problem Definition

Burnout negatively affects employees in multiple ways that, in turn, impact the functioning of the organization where they work. Consequences for the employees, in this case librarians and library staff, include adverse effects on mental health, physical health, and job performance. Librarians and library staff work in a wide range of specialties, from teaching to technical services, reference, and more. While job descriptions might differ, all employees are impacted by the balance of job demands, resources to meet those demands, and personal needs for growth and satisfaction.

To better understand how librarians and library staff in our geographic area are experiencing burnout and engagement, we sought approval from the university institutional review board to send an anonymous survey, included in the appendix, to employees at three local academic libraries. The survey asked respondents if they had personal experiences with burnout and how it affected them and their job performance. They were asked for personal observations about factors that contribute to burnout or engagement. Fourteen people responded. Their comments are included in the chapter to provide perspective on how burnout is affecting librarians and library staff currently active in the field. The goal is to understand how to achieve a work environment where employees thrive and produce the best possible outcomes for themselves and the organization they work for.

Literature Review
Overview of Burnout

In his 1975 paper, "The Staff Burn-Out Syndrome in Alternative Institutions," psychiatrist Herbert J. Freudenberger identified a condition where "dedicated and committed" volunteers in a free clinic became exhausted and physically unwell.[3] Freudenberger explained that for the burnt-out worker, "the harder he works, the more frustrated he is, the more exhausted… the more cynical in outlook and behavior… and, of course the less effective in the very things he so wishes to accomplish."[4]

Other researchers quickly expanded on the topic. Working from interviews, surveys, and observations of people from a wide range of service jobs, Christina Maslach, Susan Jackson, and Michael Leiter defined burnout as a "psychological syndrome of emotional exhaustion, depersonalization, and reduced personal accomplishment that can occur among individuals who work with other people in some capacity."[5] In 1981 they published the Maslach Burnout Inventory (MBI), where Maslach, Jackson, and Leiter noted that, although it is related to job satisfaction, wellness, and morale, burnout is a specific and separate phenomenon.[6]

Researchers in subsequent years developed alternative instruments to measure aspects of burnout. The Copenhagen Burnout Inventory (CBI), from Tage Kristensen and colleagues, groups evaluative questions into personal burnout, work-related burnout, and client-centered burnout.[7] The Oldenburg Burnout Inventory, from 1999, measures both exhaustion and disengagement from work.[8] More recently, the 2017 Stanford Professional Fulfillment Index, designed with physicians in mind, assesses both burnout and professional fulfillment.[9] Research using these and other assessment tools has frequently focused on public service jobs such as health care workers, teachers, police, and other similar professions. However, burnout is not limited to human services positions and may occur in a wide range of occupations.[10]

In spite of the general social acceptance of the term *burnout*, it was not until 2019 that the World Health Organization (WHO) recognized it as an occupational phenomenon and adopted the 11th Revision of the *International Classification of Diseases* (ICD-11) description. The ICD-11 definition identifies three key characteristics: "feelings of energy depletion or exhaustion; increased mental distance from one's job, or feelings of negativism or cynicism related to one's job; and reduced professional efficacy."[11] Recognition by the WHO supports the understanding that burnout is a serious condition of importance to both employees and employers.

Still, there are physical and emotional effects of burnout not clearly identified in the standard definition. Echoing Freudenberger's observations, a 2008 study by Ulla Peterson, Evangelia Demerouti, and colleagues found complaints of neck pain, anxiety, poor memory, and poor sleep among workers experiencing burnout.[12] A three-year study published in 2011 also observed respiratory diseases and gastrointestinal infections.[13] The evidence for serious effects of burnout continues to grow. Neurological research from 2022 using wearable devices to measure physiological markers showed a connection between burnout, physical activity, heart rate, and executive functions.[14] Burnout, researchers noted, "is linked with inefficient EF [executive function] in everyday life," affecting working memory, task monitoring, emotional control, stress regulation, and other metacognitive abilities.[15]

Key Burnout Studies in Academic Libraries

As interest in burnout grew, researchers began investigating how it pertained to specific vocations. In one of the earliest accounts of burnout research, Smith and Nelson administered a survey to 262 academic librarians. The survey questions pertained to job characteristics and personal information. The authors also included questions from the Forbes Burnout Survey.[16] No respondents met the burnout threshold, and only five registered "mild burnout." The researchers concluded that academic librarians were not prone to burnout. Rather, the authors contended, academic librarians enjoyed their jobs and the challenges they posed.[17] Further, in the authors' estimation, those academic librarians who did suffer from burnout simply had not yet learned how to relax.[18]

Over a decade later, in 1996, Mary Ann Affleck investigated burnout among bibliographic instruction librarians with very different results. In her research, Affleck surveyed 142 bibliographic librarians using the MBI and a role questionnaire. She found that 8.5 percent of that population was experiencing the full syndrome of burnout, "exhibiting high levels of emotional exhaustion, depersonalization, and diminished sense of personal accomplishment."[19] The findings also suggested that while many of these bibliographic librarians were not suffering from the full syndrome of burnout, many were susceptible to eventually falling victim to it due to their high scores in one or more of the MBI's subcategories or dimensions.[20]

In 2008, after experiencing the full burnout syndrome, Kevin Harwell, a business librarian, shared some of his experiences and strategies for managing burnout on a personal and organizational level. In 2013 he published a follow-up study of burnout and job engagement among a sample of business librarians that found a 13.4 percent occurrence of burnout.[21] In his article, Harwell argued that it is possible to understand where an employee may fall within the burnout spectrum by using Maslach's "job-person fit," a model that considers workload, control, reward, community, fairness, and values to determine how well or poorly a person fits with their job. Per Harwell, "The more doubtful the fit, the more likely the person will experience burnout. A strong fit in these areas indicates a greater likelihood that the person is engaged in work."[22] In essence, the more a person can positively check off the boxes of Maslach's job-person fit theory, the more content they will be at work—and the less likely they will be to develop burnout.

In a similar study conducted by Nardine in 2019, liaison and subject librarians were surveyed using the MBI and the Areas of Worklife Survey. This study found that many of these librarians ranked "lack of personal agency" as the most significant cause of their burnout.[23] Personal agency, as defined by Alper, typically involves a person's ability to feel as though they are the one causing or generating an action and that they have the ability to influence their own actions and life circumstances.[24] In her study, Nardine found that these librarians did not feel as though they had control over their work environments, which was contributing to their burnout. It is worth noting, however, that there was a positive correlation between institutional and personal values, and personal efficacy, both of which were attributed to having the potential to offset symptoms of burnout for these librarians.[25]

Most recently, Wood and colleagues published an article about librarian burnout using the CBI. They selected this assessment tool because the MBI was not available in the public domain, it was not cross-culturally sensitive, and, rather than measuring burnout with a simple, unidimensional score, it instead measured it on a multidimensional score.[26] The CBI, in their estimation, was a better instrument to measure burnout, and they discovered that the work-related CBI scores of the 1,628 participants surveyed reflected that "academic librarians are, generally speaking, in a state of burnout."[27] They also found that "demographic factors such as gender, age, and years in the profession are also tied to the prevalence and severity of burnout."[28] Female academic librarians, they concluded, experience more gender-driven work-life imbalances, while male librarians are more likely to encounter age-driven work-life balance problems.[29]

Overall, much of the research illustrates that librarians of all varieties are struggling with burnout. Many librarians suffer from the full syndrome of burnout, and others appear to be susceptible to it. On a bright note, evidence also suggests that there are many cost-effective personal and organizational interventions and mitigating factors that can help individuals reduce the effects of burnout.

Engagement

The concept of engagement was introduced by William Kahn in 1990. It is considered to be the opposite of burnout. Khan explained that people engaged with their work are involved physically, cognitively, and emotionally.[30] "Work contexts," he noted, "mediated by people's perceptions, create the conditions in which they personally engage or disengage."[31] Engaged employees characterize their work as challenging rather than stressful.[32] More recently, Pradarelli, Shimizu, and Smink noted the positive association between engagement and well-being.[33] Two different schools of thought have continued to theorize about the nature of engagement. The first believes that engagement, demonstrated by high levels of energy, involvement, and efficacy, is at the opposite end at the spectrum from burnout [34] while the second hypothesizes that engagement is independent from burnout.[35]

Engagement in the library workplace has appeared in more recent literature. For instance, in 2020, Jason Martin used the Utrecht Work Engagement Scale to survey library employees. He described engagement as the opposite of burnout, with vigor, dedication, and absorption all being key components.[36] Engaged employees have better mental and physical health, demonstrate more initiative, and are more effective, which undoubtedly creates positive outcomes for their employer.[37] Martin found the components of workplace engagement in libraries to be workload, work fit, work expectations, recognition, meaning, leadership, health, and culture and environment.[38]

Key Theories on the Causes of Burnout

Generally, research on burnout points to essential human needs not being met. Abraham Maslow was an early theorist on the connection between motivation and basic human needs. His 1943 work posits a hierarchy of needs working from physiological needs at the base, to security, then social needs, esteem, and self-actualization.[39] The evolution of needs-based theories continued with Herzberg's Two-Factor Theory, McClelland's Theory of Needs, the ERG Theory,[40] and Ryan and Deci's Self-Determination Theory. Self-determination theory, for example, proposes that well-being and motivation depend on three basic psychological needs: competence, relatedness, and autonomy.[41] Much of the research on burnout, engagement, job satisfaction, morale, and wellness draws from these theories, highlighting that work is not all about the paycheck.

For example, while researching both burnout and engagement, Arnold Bakker and Evangelia Demerouti looked at situational and individual factors to develop their theory, the Job Demands—Resources Model. Their model proposes a need for balance between job demands and job resources.[42] Job demands include characteristics such as role ambiguity, workload, work pressure, conflict, unfairness, and lack of autonomy. Resources include characteristics such as having a voice in decisions; the ability to engage in job crafting; receiving constructive feedback and recognition from supervisors; engaging in significant tasks with some variability; and receiving support from coworkers. Job resources "fulfill basic psychological needs, such as the need for autonomy, relatedness, and competence"[43] Bakker, Demerouti, and Sanz-Vergel's research demonstrates that job demands are a strong indicator of burnout while job resources predict engagement.[44]

Four job characteristics that can act as demands or resources depending on the degree to which they are present are autonomy; WLB; the degree of self-efficacy and competence; and the degree of trust and support. For example, a poor WLB stresses and drains the individual and is thus a demand. A positive WLB bolsters the employee, acting as a resource. These may become intertwined as each can impact another. For instance, an adequate degree of trust and support allows employees to set limits that create a positive WLB. Similarly, receiving the trust of a supervisor can confirm feelings of competence. Of course, the reciprocal could also occur. Micromanagement could undermine autonomy and degrade feelings of competence.

Autonomy

Autonomy is defined as independence in "what, when, and how [employees] perform their work."[45] It allows people to feel a level of control and personal investment in outcomes, rather than feeling coerced to meet imposed expectations. When present, autonomy acts as a positive resource contributing to engagement. However, a lack of autonomy, as Nardine's study indicates, acts as a demand on the employee and contributes to burnout.[46] The ability to make decisions about factors that affect a person's working environment and success impacts morale, self-efficacy, fairness, and motivation. All are closely tied to burnout. The need for autonomy applies to workers in any position, public-facing or not. Employers who allow some autonomy have found that not only do employees benefit, the organization they work for also benefits from having more proactive, confident, and committed employees.[47] Library instruction is especially fraught with a lack of independence. Andrea Baer's article on information literacy instruction includes a comment that "I go back and forth between feeling like a guest in someone's else's classroom with little autonomy as a professional… who can set standards for how and what I will teach."[48] In any position, it is hard to feel satisfaction when there is not a balance between expectations and control.

Work-Life Balance

WLB can be defined in many ways. For the purpose of this chapter, we will define it as an individual's ability to successfully balance and intertwine their personal and professional lives in a way that benefits them.[49] A positive WLB results in growth and success at both work and home. Often, when that balance is not maintained and the individual cannot satisfy one or both roles, burnout is the result. WLB can be difficult to maintain, and many factors potentially contribute to an imbalance, including scheduling, employer expectations, gender roles, and expected obligations.

The academic setting, with its intense demands for both students and staff, can be a field where employees become overwhelmed, ultimately leading to an improper WLB. According to Kinman and Johnson, "there is evidence that achieving a healthy work-life balance can be particularly challenging for academics, leading to health problems, job dissatisfaction, and high turnover in the sector."[50] Students can have information needs at any time of day, so academic libraries are usually one of the few departments on college and university campuses that are open during nonstandard working hours. This is true even when the library is understaffed. The need to constantly be available to students and coworkers can tether library staff to their devices in order to meet the needs of all parties, even to the detriment of themselves. Employers expecting this level of availability can infringe on staff's nonwork responsibilities and obligations, leading to an unhappy home life—which can contribute in turn to an unhappy work life.

WLB can be significantly affected by social identities and status.[51] Gender roles and expected obligations are also contributing factors to improper WLB.[52] Research has shown a clear distinction in the WLB between genders, between single versus married coworkers,[53] and between employees with and without children. Even though all genders report having issues with WLB, those who identify with household duties associated with women report having higher levels of improper WLB.[54] Employees that do not have the textbook nuclear family also tend to have different expectations and demands placed on them.[55]

Large amounts of improper WLB lead to negative consequences for both employee and employer. The consequences can affect employee engagement, commitment, retention, and productivity. Generally speaking, engaged employees are productive, committed, and steadfast employees. Engaged employees view their organization and its values with high esteem and strive to work with their colleagues to ensure goals are met and productivity is at its highest. These beliefs and actions do not take place when employees feel as though they do not have time for critical personal activities. Instead, they can become disengaged and unsatisfied employees, leading to less productivity, commitment, and, eventually, higher turnover rates.[56]

Feelings of Competency

Self-efficacy, or perceived competence, as defined by Bandura, refers to an individual's belief in their capacity to execute behaviors necessary to produce specific performance attainments.[57] According to Carey and Forsyth, self-efficacy reflects a person's confidence in their ability to exert control over their motivation, behavior, and social environment.[58] These cognitive self-evaluations influence all manner of human experience, including the goals for which people strive, the amount of energy expended toward goal achievement, and the likelihood of attaining particular levels of behavioral performance. Conversely, a lack of confidence can compromise competence. According to Maddux, "Those with low self-efficacy also will respond to difficulties with increased anxiety, which usually disrupts performance, thereby further lowering self-efficacy, and so on."[59] The workplace environment can enhance or diminish these feelings of competence.

Supervisors who are willing to provide professional development opportunities, support, rewards, and assignments that fit well with the employees' ability can raise self-efficacy.[60] In his article, Lunenburg noted that "the most important source of self-efficacy is past performance. Employees who have succeeded on job-related tasks are likely to have more confidence to complete similar tasks in the future."[61]

Psychological Safety—Trust, Support, and Recognition

Trust can be categorized as library staff having the belief that their administration will make their physical and psychological welfare a priority. This can mean providing resources, giving positive feedback, or respecting contributions and ideas. Unsurprisingly, a lack of this administrative support, trust, and recognition can contribute to burnout in academic library staff. Trust is eroded, for example, when a patron or student brings a problem or situation to the administration, and then the library staff's answer is said to be incorrect. Staffing decisions can also affect trust, as they did during the COVID-19 pandemic, when some library staffers were working with the public while those above them were at home. In a *Library Journal* article, librarians expressed how they were expected to return to work in person during the pandemic even though it "had a side dose of potential death."[62] Employees need to trust that their leaders are as engaged in their own jobs as they expect subordinates to be.

Library employees also want their leaders to trust them to do their jobs and treat them as professionals that are knowledgeable in their position.[63] Lack of support, whether monetary or emotional, is another contributor to burnout. The concept of doing more with less has been prevalent in the library workplace for many years now. Martin found that understaffing was a "cause for low morale."[64] A lack of recognition for hard work and achievements can also lead to burnout. Martin found that compensation was tied to recognition, since librarians and library staff stated how they were underpaid and how difficult it was to survive with a high student loan debt.[65] He also found that respondents who worked with patrons had higher engagement and satisfaction in their work. This could be attributed to patrons offering thanks and appreciation to librarians and library staff after being helped. Conversely, those who did not work with patrons needed to receive that validation and recognition from their administration, and often felt that they were not appreciated.

Another factor tying into the need for recognition is the idea that librarianship is a calling or a vocation, and therefore the job gives fulfillment and does not need recognition. This "vocational awe" discourages criticism. Promoting the idea that librarianship is a higher-level calling suggests that library staff should not complain or ask for more resources. Ettarh and Vidas have called for library staff to dismantle this awe and see their profession as one that needs sufficient support, such as adequate staffing.[66]

Method

After receiving approval from the university's institutional review board, an eight-question survey was sent to librarians and staff at three Central Texas university libraries (see appendix for the complete list of questions). Due to the potential for responses to reveal concerns about a work environment or reflect negatively on coworkers, the responses were submitted anonymously and any characteristics that could connect respondents to a specific library were removed before inclusion in the results.

Respondents were asked whether they were experiencing the three primary symptoms of burnout: energy depletion; negativism or cynicism about the job; or feeling a lack of accomplishment. If they said yes, they were asked how those symptoms affected their overall well-being. If they responded no, they were asked if there was a factor that they felt helped them avoid burnout. We also selected four key areas that needs-based theories hypothesize are contributors to burnout or engagement and asked for personal observations. These job characteristics were the following: the degree of autonomy an employee has; the WLB a job allows; the degree of self-efficacy and competence an employee feels; and the degree of trust and support employees receive.

Results

Of the fourteen respondents, eight said they were currently experiencing, or had previously experienced, one or all of the symptoms in the ICD-11 definition for burnout. Three responses from the survey group mentioned work-related feelings of depression. Two mentioned feeling tired or exhausted. Cynicism was mentioned specifically by two respondents, while another reflected on doubting that a best effort would have a positive outcome. A fourth mentioned increased mental distance at work. One individual noted that guilt and anxiety over negative work-related feelings had interfered with sleep and wellness. Yet another respondent mentioned that going to work each day had become a struggle. The comment "When I feel stretched too far, I can't give people and tasks the attention I would like" summed up some of the tension between too many demands and the desire to do a good job. More than one person commented on a causal link between work experiences and negative effects on self-confidence, personal relationships, and relationships with coworkers.

We also received feedback on positive experiences. Four participants reflected on factors that helped them avoid burnout and engage with their work. Respondents mentioned supportive coworkers and trusted supervisors. Having a degree of control was also important, as one reply mentioned being able to take time to de-stress, and another mentioned being able to make independent decisions about what to do when.

Autonomy

Several of our respondents specifically commented on how autonomy, or a lack thereof, affected them at work. On the positive side, one library employee commented that while their general job responsibilities had not changed, they currently "have more ability to make decisions… and there is less anxiety about being second-guessed.… This helps me feel excited [about my job]." The change in the level of autonomy enabled this librarian to shift from frustration to engagement. Another response indicated that "it is important to me to have some space to make my own decisions about where to put my time and attention, or how to approach a project within the larger requirements of the position." "Managements' confidence in a worker's ability greatly increases confidence while lowering anxiety," contributed another library employee. Not all respondents were positive about the level of autonomy they experience. Not having autonomy "caused me to second guess my own abilities" commented one person. Others mentioned micromanagement by coworkers or supervisors.

Work-Life Balance

Survey responses indicated how damaging an imbalance between work and personal life can be. One library employee commented on how work-related burnout affected their personal life and contributed to struggles with depression. Time to be there for elderly parents or children was clearly a critical element of WLB. Our survey participants reported having to work on projects and tasks nights and weekends, resulting in inadequate time with loved ones. Others generally reported work concerns spilling over into personal time and the home. Respondents commented on the need to set boundaries and leave work problems at work.

Feelings of Competency

Several of our respondents mentioned having their self-confidence undermined rather than built up by micromanagement and a lack of positive, constructive feedback. Not surprisingly, these feelings translated into other negative consequences. "The lack of a feeling of accomplishment seemed to feed into feeling tired…" commented one person. "Constantly feeling overwhelmed and unable to accomplish your duties can be very daunting and depressing," commented another. A third mentioned losing self-confidence and self-respect. A lack of training coupled with negative feedback undermined another participant's confidence.

On the other hand, we also had several responses that supported the idea that librarians are invested in continuous improvement. One librarian mentioned their appreciation for a supervisor who supports staff participation in classes and other learning opportunities. Another person expressed a desire for increased training. A third commented that "training that lets me expand my knowledge and abilities keeps me interested and excited about my job." This bolsters the idea that librarians and library staff respond well to positive feedback and new opportunities for growth, and, in fact, these can counter job demands that might otherwise push an employee toward burnout.

Psychological Safety—Trust, Support, and Recognition

We had several responses reinforcing the importance of trust, support, and recognition in the workplace. Respondents said that psychological safety "is huge." They commented that "feeling like you matter… and can freely share your ideas is really important… [it] makes for happier employees," and "I feel like my organization does a great job of promoting an atmosphere where most people feel safe to be themselves, ask questions, and share ideas." Another explained that "working in a positive environment where employees treat each other with kindness and respect makes a huge difference." This level of psychological safety leads to employees becoming more engaged and committed to their jobs.[67] As these comments suggest, support that reinforces positive emotions can contribute exponentially to a decrease in levels of burnout.[68]

One respondent in the authors' survey summed it up well by stating, "Trust is essential." Other comments showed that trust is noted and valued. Examples include: "I do feel appreciated and trusted by both our administration and my colleagues"; and "members of my organization show appreciation for my work effort and value me as an employee."

The survey showed that while some library staff do feel supported at their workplace, others do not. When asked, "Do you feel like you belong and are trusted?" some participants responded with an unequivocal "no." Others mentioned unfair work distributions and gossip undermining trust in leadership. Still others voiced a need for more staff and clearer job descriptions and workflows. One respondent described a lack of support from human resources when faced with a possible library personality conflict. Library staff are given more duties and there are fewer people to fulfill those tasks, which leads to feelings of being overworked and burned out.

The survey responses indicated that recognition is important to the well-being of library employees. As one person stated, "just a thanks or casual comment goes a long way." Other participants felt that they were not appreciated and valued, and it had negative impacts on their feelings about work.

Conclusion

As the critical effects of burnout and engagement are better understood, more employers are looking for tactics to create an optimal work environment. Job demands are a part of any work experience, including work in academic libraries, but initiatives and personal interactions can give employees the resources to deal with these demands.

Wellness programs are one way to increase resources. Our survey asked whether respondents worked at places with wellness programs and whether these had an effect on burnout symptoms, but we did not receive any responses. Wellness initiatives focus on individual and group health challenges, activities, and goals. They can lead to increased physical activity and introduce other stress-relief tools, such as mindfulness or breathing techniques, that are positively related to well-being and reduced levels of stress.[69]

The introduction of flexible scheduling and alternative work locations has also proven to be another successful initiative in terms of combating employee burnout. The COVID-19 pandemic required many employers to allow employees to work from home. As businesses returned to normal operating procedures, employers realized that allowing employees a measure of autonomy in scheduling or work locations could assist with preventing burnout and increasing engagement. The continuation of this practice post-pandemic allows employees to practice self-leadership and occupational well-being, both of which combine to develop work-based psychological safety for employees.[70]

For the specific job characteristics that we identified, there are more narrowly focused ideas. For example, allowing employees to have a voice in creating clear, concise standard operating procedures ensures consistency and bolsters employee confidence. Standard operating procedures can also help with cross-training, another important element in boosting employee confidence and autonomy. Promoting training generally supports self-efficacy and growth.

Many job demands are requirements that individual employees are not able to change, but there are some steps that might help create a healthier situation. For example, employees can engage in a practice called "job crafting," or making choices about what direction they want to take their jobs. Employees can also take a proactive approach in regaining their WLB by setting boundaries. Detaching from work when not at work, controlling the ways in which their work life overlaps with their personal life, and ensuring they place as much importance on their personal life as they do their work life are all individual steps.[71] As one of our survey respondents mentioned, "Communication is very helpful." Indeed, our survey indicates that librarians and library staff engage when they feel heard and when they are getting clear and fair work distribution and feedback.

A broader concept taking root in workplaces is the importance of meeting the needs of employees rather than expecting them to be satisfied regardless of the work requirements or environment. Having engaged employees means moving beyond envisioning employment as a transactional relationship between employer and employee. Employers benefit when engagement and motivation are increased, and this happens when physiological, security, social, and esteem needs are satisfied. Meeting these needs leads to employees ultimately becoming self-actualized in their positions.[72] Being self-actualized, or feeling that one is fulfilling one's potential and playing an important role, leads to employees becoming fully engaged, with positive attitudes, high job satisfaction, productivity, and commitment.

While it is tempting to look for institution-wide solutions, the research we reviewed and our survey responses indicated that improvement may not involve complex or expensive new initiatives. Rather, supervisors need to provide the resources employees need so that they can become engaged with the work they do. In 2008, Harwell suggested fairness, choice and control, recognition, and support would lead to positive outcomes.[73] Demerouti and colleagues make the case that this path remains a good one, and they caution that supervisors should focus on providing actual job resources and not just trying to change how people perceive their working conditions.[74]

Although there is some individual variability, burnout is an occupational phenomenon, tied to actual job conditions.[75] The way to avoid burnout is to "provide adequate job design and not try to change people's perceptions and interpretations of their working conditions."[76] Participants in our survey reinforced this, indicating that autonomy, WLB, feeling competent, and psychological safety at work do indeed make a crucial difference in whether library employees feel excited about the work they do, or tired, disenchanted, and demoralized.

Appendix

Survey Questions—Burnout in the Academic Library—Causes and Prevention

QUESTION 1

The 11th edition of the *International Classification of Diseases* (ICD-11) defines burnout as characterized by

> 1) feelings of energy depletion or exhaustion; 2) increased mental distance from one's job, or feelings of negativism or cynicism related to one's job; and 3) a sense of ineffectiveness and lack of accomplishment.[77]

As it relates to your work, would you say you currently experience any of these symptoms, or have you experienced them in a previous work experience?

QUESTION 2

Can you explain further which of those characteristics apply and how they affect(ed) your well-being?

QUESTION 3

If you have not experienced these symptoms, do you think there was anything about the work environment that helped you avoid them?

QUESTION 4

Can you explain further regarding any effects on your ability to fully engage with your job or library patrons?

QUESTION 5

Are there any specific factors/policies at work that contributed to these symptoms of burnout?

QUESTION 6—YES OR NO

Has your workplace changed any policies or started any new programs to promote mental and physical wellness at work?

QUESTION 7

Were they helpful? If so, how, and if not, why?

QUESTION 8

Observations on your experience with any of the following would be welcome:

8a. Psychological safety at work (the belief you can be yourself, ask questions, share ideas…)

8b. Autonomy (you can make some decisions about how and when you accomplish work responsibilities)

8c. Belonging/Trust (you are appreciated and valued by administration and/or colleagues)

8d. Competence (you believe you do your job well and want to continue to improve)

8e. Resources/Support (you have the personal and material support you need to do your job well)

8f. Work-life balance (you have a reasonable amount of personal time, and work requirements do not adversely affect your personal time/time with family and friends)

Notes

1. Christina Maslach and Susan E. Jackson, "The Measurement of Experienced Burnout," *Journal of Occupational Behaviour* 2, no. 2 (April 1981): 99, https://doi.org/10.1002/job.4030020205; ICD-11 for Mortality and Morbidity Statistics, "QD85 Burnout," accessed January 25, 2023, https://icd.who.int/browse/2024-01/mms/en#129180281.
2. Kim Parker and Julianna Menasce Horowitz, "Majority of Workers Who Quit a Job in 2021 Cite Low Pay, No Opportunities for Advancement, Feeling Disrespected," Pew Research Center, accessed January 25, 2023, https://www.pewresearch.org/ft_22-03-09_resignation-featured-image/ (page discontinued).
3. Herbert J. Freudenberger, "The Staff Burn-Out Syndrome in Alternative Institutions," *Psychotherapy: Theory, Research, Practice, Training* 12, no. 1 (1975): 73, https://doi.org/10.1037/h0086411.
4. Freudenberger, "Staff Burn-Out Syndrome," 74.
5. Christina Maslach, Susan E. Jackson, and Michael P. Leiter, "Maslach Burnout Inventory, Third Edition," in *Maslach Burnout Inventory: Manual and Non-reproducible Instrument and Scoring Guides*, 3rd ed. (Mind Garden, 2010), 192, https://www.researchgate.net/profile/Christina-Maslach/publication/277816643_The_Maslach_Burnout_Inventory_Manual/links/5574dbd708aeb6d8c01946d7/The-Maslach-Burnout-Inventory-Manual.pdf.
6. Maslach, Jackson, and Leiter, "Maslach Burnout Inventory," 203.
7. Tage S. Kristensen et al., "The Copenhagen Burnout Inventory: A New Tool for the Assessment of Burnout," *Work and Stress* 19, no. 3 (July 2005): 192–207.
8. Evangelia Demerouti et al., "The Job Demands–Resources Model of Burnout," *Journal of Applied Psychology* 86, no. 3 (June 2001): 500, EBSCOhost.
9. Mickey Trockel et al., "A Brief Instrument to Assess Both Burnout and Professional Fulfillment in Physicians: Reliability and Validity, including Correlation with Self-Reported Medical Errors, in a Sample of Resident and Practicing Physicians," *Academic Psychiatry* 42, (December 2017): 19, https://doi.org/10.1007/s40596-017-0849-3.
10. Demerouti et al., "Jobs Demands–Resources Model of Burnout," 499.
11. ICD-11 for Mortality and Morbidity Statistics, "QD85 Burnout."
12. Ulla Peterson et al., "Burnout and Physical and Mental Health among Swedish Healthcare Workers," *Journal of Advanced Nursing* 62, no. 1 (2008): 84. https://doi.org/10.1111/j.1365-2648.2007.04580.x.
13. Arnold B. Bakker, Evangelia Demerouti, and Ana Isabel Sanz-Vergel, "Burnout and Work Engagement: The JD–R Approach," *Annual Review of Organizational Psychology and Organizational Behavior* 1, no. 1 (2014): 396, https://doi.org/10.1146/annurev-orgpsych-031413-091235.
14. Mia Pihlaja et al., "Occupational Burnout Is Linked with Inefficient Executive Functioning, Elevated Average Heart Rate, and Decreased Physical Activity in Daily Life—Initial Evidence from Teaching Professionals," *Brain Sciences* 12, no. 12 (2022): 1736, 1728, https://doi.org/10.3390/brainsci12121723.
15. Pihlaja et al., "Occupational Burnout," 1736.

16. Nathan M. Smith and Veneese C. Nelson, "Burnout: A Survey of Academic Reference Librarians (Research Note)," *College and Research Libraries* 44, no. 3 (May 1983): 245–50, https://doi.org/10.5860/crl_44_03_245.
17. Smith and Nelson, "Burnout," 247.
18. Smith and Nelson, "Burnout," 249.
19. Mary Ann Affleck, "Burnout among Bibliographic Instruction Librarians," *Library and Information Science Research* 18, no. 2 (Spring 1996): 178, https://doi.org/10.1016/S0740-8188(96)90018-3.
20. Affleck, "Burnout," 178.
21. Kevin Harwell, "Burnout and Job Engagement among Business Librarians," *Library Leadership and Management* 27, no. 1/2 (January 2013): 1–19, https://llm.corejournals.org/llm/article/view/2084.
22. Harwell, "Burnout and Job Engagement," 3.
23. Jennifer Nardine, "The State of Academic Liaison Librarian Burnout in ARL Libraries in the United States," *College and Research Libraries* 80, no. 4 (2019): 508, https://doi.org/10.5860/crl.80.4.508.
24. Sinan Alper, "Personal Agency," in *Encyclopedia of Personality and Individual Differences*, ed. Virgil Zeigler-Hill and Todd K. Shackelford (Cham, Switzerland: Springer International, 2020), 3500–3502, https://doi.org/10.1007/978-3-319-24612-3_1871.
25. Nardine, "State of Academic Liaison Librarian Burnout."
26. Barbara A. Wood et al., "Academic Librarian Burnout: A Survey Using the Copenhagen Burnout Inventory (CBI)," *Journal of Library Administration* 60, no. 5 (2020): 512–31, https://doi.org/10.1080/01930826.2020.1729622.
27. Wood et al., "Academic Librarian Burnout," 520.
28. Wood et al., "Academic Librarian Burnout," 520.
29. Wood et al., "Academic Librarian Burnout," 525.
30. William A. Kahn, "Psychological Conditions of Personal Engagement and Disengagement at Work," *Academy of Management Journal* 33, no. 4 (December 1990): 694, https://www.jstor.org/stable/256287.
31. Kahn, "Psychological Conditions," 695.
32. Bakker, Demerouti, and Sanz-Vergel, "Burnout and Work Engagement," 391.
33. Jason C. Pradarelli, Naomi Shimizu, and Douglas S. Smink, "Important Terms in Wellbeing," in *Wellbeing*, ed. Eugene Kim and Brenessa Lindeman, (New York: Springer, 2020), 24.
34. Michael P. Leiter and Christina Maslach, "A Mediation Model of Job Burnout," in *Research Companion to Organizational Health Psychology*, ed. Alexander-Stamatios G. Antonio and Cary L. Cooper (Cheltenham: Edward Elgar, 2005), 544.
35. Wilmar B. Schaufeli, Marisa Salanova, Vicente González-Romá, and Arnold B. Bakker, "The Measurement of Engagement and Burnout: A Two Sample Confirmatory Factor Analytic Approach," *Journal of Happiness Studies* 3, no. 1 (2002): 85-88, https://doi.org/10.1023/A:1015630930326.
36. Jason Martin, "Workplace Engagement of Librarians and Library Staff," *Journal of Library Administration* 60, no. 1 (2020): 23, https://doi.org/10.1080/01930826.2019.1671037.
37. Martin, "Workplace Engagement," 24.
38. Martin, "Workplace Engagement," 37.
39. Abraham H. Maslow, *Motivation and Personality*, 3rd ed. (Harper and Row, 1987).
40. Mushtaq Ahmad, Amjid Khan, and Muhammad Arshad, "Major Theories of Job Satisfaction and Their Use in the Field of Librarianship," *Library Philosophy & Practice*, (September 2021): 2-7, EBSCOhost.
41. Richard M. Ryan and Edward L. Deci, *Self-Determination Theory* (New York: Guilford, 2018), 10.
42. Arnold B. Bakker and Evangelia Demerouti, "Job Demands—Resources Theory: Taking Stock and Looking Forward," *Journal of Occupational Health Psychology* 22, no. 3 (July 2017): 273–85, https://doi.org/10.1037/ocp0000056.
43. Bakker, Demerouti, and Sanz-Vergel, "Burnout and Work Engagement," 399.
44. Bakker, Demerouti, and Sanz-Vergel, "Burnout and Work Engagement," 393.
45. Miriam L. Matteson, Yue Ming, and David E. Silva, "The Relationship between Work Conditions and Perceptions of Organizational Justice among Library Employees," *Library and Information Science Research* 43, no. 2 (April 2021): article 101093, p. 2, https://doi.org/10.1016/j.lisr.2021.101093.
46. Nardine, "State of Academic Liaison Librarian Burnout."
47. Ryan and Deci, *Self-Determination Theory*, 541; Matteson, Ming, and Silva, "Relationship between Work Conditions," 2.
48. Andrea Baer, "Librarians' Development as Teachers," *Journal of Information Literacy* 15, no. 1 (2021): 44, https://doi.org/10.11645/15.1.2846.
49. Dawn Culpepper et al., "Who Gets to Have a Life? Agency in Work-Life Balance for Single Faculty," *Equity and Excellence in Education* 53, no. 4 (2020): 532, https://doi.org/10.1080/10665684.2020.1791280; Amadeja Lamovšek et al., "The Key to Work–Life Balance Is (Enriched) Job Design? Three-Way Interaction Effects with Formalization and Adaptive Personality Characteristics," *Applied Research in Quality of Life* 18 (2023): 647–76, https://doi.org/10.1007/s11482-022-10100-9.
50. Gail Kinman and Sheena Johnson, "Special Section on Well-Being in Academic Employees," *International Journal of Stress Management* 26, no. 2 (2019): 159, https://doi.org/10.1037/str0000131.

51. Culpepper et al., "Who Gets to Have a Life?" 532.
52. Culpepper et al., "Who Gets to Have a Life?" 532–33.
53. Culpepper et al., "Who Gets to Have a Life?" 533.
54. Culpepper et al., "Who Gets to Have a Life?" 548
55. Culpepper et al., "Who Gets to Have a Life?" 542
56. Nor Siah Jaharuddin and Liyana Nadia Zainol, "The Impact of Work-Life Balance on Job Engagement and Turnover Intention," *South East Asian Journal of Management* 13, no. 1 (2019): article 7, p. 108, https://doi.org/10.21002/seam.v13i1.10912.
57. Albert Bandura, "Self-Efficacy: Toward a Unifying Theory of Behavioral Change," *Psychological Review* 84, no. 2 (1977): 193, https://doi.org/10.1037/0033-295X.84.2.191.
58. Michael P. Carey and Andrew D. Forsyth, "Teaching Tip Sheet: Self-Efficacy," 2009, https://www.apa.org/pi/aids/resources/education/self-efficacy.
59. James E. Maddux, "Self-Efficacy: The Power of Believing You Can," in *The Oxford Handbook of Positive Psychology*, ed. Shane J. Lopez and C. R. Snyder (Oxford: Oxford University Press, 2009), 281, https://doi.org/10.1093/oxfordhb/9780195187243.013.0031.
60. Fred C. Lunenburg, "Self-Efficacy in the Workplace: Implications for Motivation and Performance," *International Journal of Management, Business, and Administration* 14, no. 1 (2011): 3, http://www.nationalforum.com/Electronic%20Journal%20Volumes/Lunenburg%2C%20Fred%20C.%20Self-Efficacy%20in%20the%20Workplace%20IJMBA%20V14%20N1%202011.pdf.
61. Lunenberg, "Self-Efficacy in the Workplace," 3.
62. Jennifer A. Dixon, "Feeling the Burnout," *Library Journal*, March 7, 2022, https://www.libraryjournal.com/story/Feeling-the-Burnout.
63. Alma Ortega, *Academic Libraries and Toxic Leadership* (Oxford, UK: Elsevier Science & Technology, 2017), 5, ProQuest.
64. Martin, "Workplace Engagement," 35.
65. Martin, "Workplace Engagement," 34.
66. Fobazi Ettarh and Chris Vidas, "'The Future of Libraries': Vocational Awe in 'Post-COVID World,'" *Serials Librarian* 82, no. 1–4, (2022): 20, https://doi.org/10.1080/0361526X.2022.2028501.
67. Sjöblom Kirsi, Soile Juutinen, and Anne Mäkikangas, "The Importance of Self-Leadership Strategies and Psychological Safety for Well-Being in the Context of Enforced Remote Work," *Challenges* 13, no. 1 (2022): article 14, p. 4, https://doi.org/10.3390/challe13010014.
68. Sjöblom, Juutinen, and Mäkikangas, "Importance of Self-Leadership Strategies," 13.
69. Clément Ginoux, Sandrine Isoard-Gautheur, and Philippe Sarrazin, "'Workplace Physical Activity Program' (WOPAP) Study Protocol: A Four-Arm Randomized Controlled Trial on Preventing Burnout and Promoting Vigor," *BMC Public Health* 19, no. 1 (2019): 301–2, https://doi.org/10.1186/s12889-019-6598-3.
70. Sjöblom, Juutinen, and Mäkikangas, "Importance of Self-Leadership Strategies," 4.
71. Lamovšek et al., "Key to Work–Life Balance?"
72. Bibi Alajmi and Hessah Alasousi, "Understanding and Motivating Academic Library Employees: Theoretical Implications," *Library Management* 40, no. 3/4 (2019): 204–5, https://doi.org/10.1108/LM-10-2017-0111.
73. Kevin Harwell, "Burnout Strategies for Librarians," *Journal of Business & Finance Librarianship* 13 no. 3, 381, https://doi.org/10.1080/08963560802183021.
74. Demerouti et al., "Job Demands–Resources Model of Burnout," 510.
75. World Health Organization, "Burn-out an 'Occupational Phenomenon': International Classification of Diseases," news release, May 28, 2018, https://www.who.int/news/item/28-05-2019-burn-out-an-occupational-phenomenon-international-classification-of-diseases.
76. Demerouti et al., "Job Demands–Resources Model of Burnout," 510.
77. ICD-11 for Mortality and Morbidity Statistics, "QD85 Burnout."

Bibliography

Affleck, Mary Ann. "Burnout among Bibliographic Instruction Librarians." *Library and Information Science Research* 18, no. 2 (Spring 1996): 165–83. https://doi.org/10.1016/S0740-8188(96)90018-3.

Ahmad, Mushtaq, Amjid Khan, and Muhammad Arshad. "Major Theories of Job Satisfaction and Their Use in the Field of Librarianship." *Library Philosophy & Practice*, (November 2021): 1–17. EBSCOhost.

Alajmi, Bibi, and Hessah Alasousi. "Understanding and Motivating Academic Library Employees: Theoretical Implications." *Library Management* 40, no. 3/4 (2019): 203–14. https://doi.org/10.1108/LM-10-2017-0111.

Alper, Sinan. "Personal Agency." In *Encyclopedia of Personality and Individual Differences*, edited by Virgil Zeigler-Hill and Todd K. Shackelford, 3500–02. Cham, Switzerland: Springer International, 2020. https://doi.org/10.1007/978-3-319-24612-3_1871.

Baer, Andrea. "Librarians' Development as Teachers." *Journal of Information Literacy* 15, no. 1 (2021): 26–53. https://doi.org/10.11645/15.1.2846.

Bakker, Arnold B., and Evangelia Demerouti. "Job Demands—Resources Theory: Taking Stock and Looking Forward." *Journal of Occupational Health Psychology* 22, no. 3 (July 2017): 273–85. https://doi.org/10.1037/ocp0000056.

Bakker, Arnold B., Evangelia Demerouti, and Ana Isabel Sanz-Vergel. "Burnout and Work Engagement: The JD–R Approach." *Annual Review of Organizational Psychology and Organizational Behavior* 1, no. 1 (2014): 389–411. https://doi.org/10.1146/annurev-orgpsych-031413-091235.

Bandura, Albert. "Self-Efficacy: Toward a Unifying Theory of Behavioral Change." *Psychological Review* 84, no. 2 (1977): 191–215. https://doi.org/10.1037/0033-295X.84.2.191.

Carey, Michael P., and Andrew D. Forsyth. "Teaching Tip Sheet: Self-Efficacy." 2009. https://www.apa.org/pi/aids/resources/education/self-efficacy.

Culpepper, Dawn, Courtney Lennartz, KerryAnn O'Meara, and Alexandra Kuvaeva. "Who Gets to Have a Life? Agency in Work-Life Balance for Single Faculty." *Equity and Excellence in Education* 53, no. 4 (2020): 531–50. https://doi.org/10.1080/10665684.2020.1791280.

Demerouti, Evangelia, Arnold B. Bakker, Friedhelm Nachreiner, and Wilmar B. Schaufeli. "The Job Demands–Resources Model of Burnout." *Journal of Applied Psychology* 86, no. 3 (June 2001): 499–512. EBSCOhost.

Dixon, Jennifer A. "Feeling the Burnout." *Library Journal*. March 7, 2022. https://www.libraryjournal.com/story/Feeling-the-Burnout.

Ettarh, Fobazi, and Chris Vidas. "'The Future of Libraries': Vocational Awe in a 'Post-COVID' World." *Serials Librarian* 82, no. 1–4 (2022): 17–22. https://doi.org/10.1080/0361526X.2022.2028501.

Freudenberger, Herbert J. "The Staff Burn-Out Syndrome in Alternative Institutions." *Psychotherapy: Theory, Research, Practice, Training* 12, no. 1 (1975): 73–82. https://doi.org/10.1037/h0086411.

Ginoux, Clément, Sandrine Isoard-Gautheur, and Philippe Sarrazin. "'Workplace Physical Activity Program' (WOPAP) Study Protocol: A Four-Arm Randomized Controlled Trial on Preventing Burnout and Promoting Vigor." *BMC Public Health* 19, no. 1 (2019): 289–305. https://doi.org/10.1186/s12889-019-6598-3.

Harwell, Kevin. "Burnout Strategies for Librarians." *Journal of Business & Finance Librarianship*, 13 no. 3 (2008): 379–390. https://doi.org/10.1080/08963560802183021

Harwell, Kevin. "Burnout and Job Engagement among Business Librarians." *Library Leadership and Management* 27, no. 1/2 (January 2013): 1–19. https://llm.corejournals.org/llm/article/view/2084.

ICD-11 for Mortality and Morbidity Statistics. "QD85 Burnout." Accessed January 25, 2023. https://icd.who.int/browse/2024-01/mms/en#129180281.

Jaharuddin, Nor Siah, and Liyana Nadia Zainol. "The Impact of Work-Life Balance on Job Engagement and Turnover Intention." *South East Asian Journal of Management* 13, no. 1 (2019): article 7. https://doi.org/10.21002/seam.v13i1.10912.

Kahn, William A. "Psychological Conditions of Personal Engagement and Disengagement at Work." *Academy of Management Journal* 33, no. 4 (December 1990): 692–724. https://www.jstor.org/stable/256287.

Kinman, Gail, and Sheena Johnson. "Special Section on Well-Being in Academic Employees." *International Journal of Stress Management* 26, no. 2 (2019): 159–61. https://doi.org/10.1037/str0000131.

Kristensen, Tage S., Marianne Borritz, Ebbe Villadsen, and Karl B. Christensen. "The Copenhagen Burnout Inventory: A New Tool for the Assessment of Burnout." *Work and Stress* 19, no. 3 (July 2005): 192–207.

Lamovšek, Amadeja, Matej Černe, Ivan Radević, and Katerina Božič. "The Key to Work–Life Balance Is (Enriched) Job Design? Three-Way Interaction Effects with Formalization and Adaptive Personality Characteristics." *Applied Research in Quality of Life*, 18 (2023): 647–76. https://doi.org/10.1007/s11482-022-10100-9.

Leiter, Michael, and Christina Maslach. "A Mediation Model of Job Burnout." In *Research Companion to Organizational Health Psychology*, 544-564. Cheltenham: Edward Elgar, 2005.

Lunenburg, Fred C. "Self-Efficacy in the Workplace: Implications for Motivation and Performance." *International Journal of Management, Business, and Administration* 14, no. 1 (2011). http://www.nationalforum.com/Electronic%20Journal%20Volumes/Lunenburg%2C%20Fred%20C.%20Self-Efficacy%20in%20the%20Workplace%20IJMBA%20V14%20N1%202011.pdf.

Maddux, James E. "Self-Efficacy: The Power of Believing You Can." In *The Oxford Handbook of Positive Psychology*, edited by Shane J. Lopez and C. R. Snyder, 277–287. Oxford, UK: Oxford University Press, 2009. https://doi.org/10.1093/oxfordhb/9780195187243.013.0031.

Martin, Jason. "Workplace Engagement of Librarians and Library Staff." *Journal of Library Administration* 60, no. 1 (2020): 22–40. https://doi.org/10.1080/01930826.2019.1671037.

Maslach, Christina, and Susan E. Jackson. "The Measurement of Experienced Burnout." *Journal of Occupational Behaviour* 2, no. 2 (April 1981): 99–113. https://doi.org/10.1002/job.4030020205.

Maslach, Christina, Susan E. Jackson, and Michael P. Leiter. "Maslach Burnout Inventory, Third Edition." In *Maslach Burnout Inventory: Manual and Non-reproducible Instrument and Scoring Guides*, 3rd ed., 191–218. Mind Garden,

2010. https://www.researchgate.net/profile/Christina-Maslach/publication/277816643_The_Maslach_Burnout_Inventory_Manual/links/5574dbd708aeb6d8c01946d7/The-Maslach-Burnout-Inventory-Manual.pdf.

Maslow, Abraham H. *Motivation and Personality*, 3rd ed. New York: Harper and Row, 1987.

Matteson, Miriam L., Yue Ming, and David E. Silva. "The Relationship between Work Conditions and Perceptions of Organizational Justice among Library Employees." *Library and Information Science Research* 43, no. 2 (April 2021): article 101093. https://doi.org/10.1016/j.lisr.2021.101093.

Nardine, Jennifer. "The State of Academic Liaison Librarian Burnout in ARL Libraries in the United States." *College and Research Libraries* 80, no. 4 (2019): 508–24. https://doi.org/10.5860/crl.80.4.508.

Ortega, Alma. *Academic Libraries and Toxic Leadership*. Oxford, UK: Elsevier Science & Technology, 2017. ProQuest.

Parker, Kim, and Julianna Menasce Horowitz. "Majority of Workers Who Quit a Job in 2021 Cite Low Pay, No Opportunities for Advancement, Feeling Disrespected." Pew Research Center. Accessed January 25, 2023. https://www.pewresearch.org/ft_22-03-09_resignation-featured-image/ (page discontinued).

Pihlaja, Mia, Pipsa P. A. Tuominen, Jari Peräkylä, and Kaisa M. Hartikainen. "Occupational Burnout Is Linked with Inefficient Executive Functioning, Elevated Average Heart Rate, and Decreased Physical Activity in Daily Life—Initial Evidence from Teaching Professionals." *Brain Sciences* 12, no. 12 (2022): 1723–1739. https://doi.org/10.3390/brainsci12121723.

Peterson, U., Demerouti, E., Bergström, G., Samuelsson, M., Åsberg, M. and Nygren, Å. "Burnout and physical and mental health among Swedish healthcare workers." *Journal of Advanced Nursing* 62, no. 1 (2008): 84–95. https://doi.org/10.1111/j.1365-2648.2007.04580.x.

Pradarelli, Jason C., Naomi Shimizu, and Douglas S. Smink. "Important Terms in Wellbeing." In *Wellbeing*, edited by Eugene Kim and Brenessa Lindeman, 23–30. New York: Springer, 2020.

Ryan, Richard M., and Edward L. Deci. *Self-Determination Theory: Basic Psychological Needs in Motivation, Development, and Wellness*. New York: Guilford, 2018.

Schaufeli, Wilmar B., Marisa Salanova, Vicente González-romá, and Arnold B. Bakker. "The Measurement of Engagement and Burnout: A Two Sample Confirmatory Factor Analytic Approach." *Journal of Happiness Studies* 3, no. 1 (2002): 71-92. https://doi.org/10.1023/A:1015630930326.

Sjöblom, Kirsi, Soile Juutinen, and Anne Mäkikangas. "The Importance of Self-Leadership Strategies and Psychological Safety for Well-Being in the Context of Enforced Remote Work." *Challenges* 13, no. 1 (2022): article 14. https://doi.org/10.3390/challe13010014.

Smith, Nathan M., and Veneese C. Nelson. "Burnout: A Survey of Academic Reference Librarians (Research Note)." *College and Research Libraries* 44, no. 3 (May 1983): 245–50. https://doi.org/10.5860/crl_44_03_245.

Trockel, Mickey, Bryan Bohman, Emi Lesure, Maryam S. Hamidi, Dana Welle, Laura Roberts, and Tait Shanafelt. "A Brief Instrument to Assess Both Burnout and Professional Fulfillment in Physicians: Reliability and Validity, including Correlation with Self-Reported Medical Errors, in a Sample of Resident and Practicing Physicians." *Academic Psychiatry* 42, (December 2017): 11–24. https://doi.org/10.1007/s40596-017-0849-3.

Wood, Barbara A., Ana B. Guimaraes, Christina E. Holm, Sherrill W. Hayes, and Kyle R. Brooks. "Academic Librarian Burnout: A Survey Using the Copenhagen Burnout Inventory (CBI)." *Journal of Library Administration* 60, no. 5 (2020): 512–31. https://doi.org/10.1080/01930826.2020.1729622.

World Health Organization. "Burn-out an 'Occupational Phenomenon': International Classification of Diseases." News release. May 28, 2018. https://www.who.int/news/item/28-05-2019-burn-out-an-occupational-phenomenon-international-classification-of-diseases.

CHAPTER 14

Damp, Dark, and Dull
Addressing the Impact of Library Workspace Woes on Health, Productivity, and Morale

Melinda H. Berg, Janet Chan, Janet Schalk, and Ann Coppola

Where, how, and the conditions in which people work are currently under intense scrutiny. The COVID-19 pandemic forced an examination of the health and safety of the workplace. The rise of remote work has prompted greater discussion of how workspaces affect employee productivity, morale, and engagement. The Great Resignation has drawn more attention to employee satisfaction and has made recruitment and retention challenging.[1] Administrators and managers often acknowledge that their employees are the most valuable resources of their organizations and recognize the importance of providing a healthy work environment.[2] Nevertheless, while there are many factors that affect employee well-being, physical space considerations are an often neglected piece of the puzzle. Libraries are no exception.

    The public-facing areas of libraries are typically prioritized and thoughtfully planned with the needs of end users in mind, as demonstrated by the yearly "Library Design Showcase" issue of *American Libraries* magazine, which features beautiful profiles of newly built or renovated libraries. The showcase highlights innovative design, including gorgeous common spaces, inventive use of art, magnificent views, sustainable building practices, and other laudable architectural achievements. However, despite employee wellness being an elevated concern since COVID-19 and the Great Resignation, the 2022 issue made no mention of library staff workspaces or the critical behind-the-scenes facility infrastructure that plays a role in the day-to-day lives of library workers.[3] Limited funding often necessitates library administrators weigh the merit of design or renovation projects against competing needs. Sadly, improvements to staff spaces often end up cut from tight budgets.[4]

Traditionally, library employees face many barriers to job satisfaction. Low wages, stress, burnout, compassion fatigue, emotional labor, and the phenomenon of vocational awe can all take their toll.[5] The scant research available specifically focusing on library employees "highlights that negative impacts to wellbeing are alarmingly globally reported by librarians… and the effective promotion of positive wellbeing seems imperative."[6] Given these additional challenges and the current difficult employment climate, library stakeholders cannot afford to overlook ways in which they can optimize work environments. Bolstering the wellness of workers helps to attract and retain quality employees, which is essential to providing the best service possible to users.

This chapter will examine the effects of physical workspaces on library employees' health, job satisfaction, and performance through a framework commonly used in general office space studies: indoor environmental quality, spatial factors, and socio-spatial factors.[7] Due to the public nature of libraries, an additional category of safety and security will also be discussed. Finally, the role of administration in incorporating these considerations into workplace culture, policies, and partnerships will be addressed. Library buildings vary widely, and employees' needs and preferences are diverse. There are no universal recommendations; however, practical suggestions will be offered that can be implemented based on each library's distinct needs.

Literature Review

Although there is a robust volume of research describing the influence of the physical library environment on end users, the design literature for library staff spaces is limited.[8] In a case study of an academic library, environmental comfort was found to be the most common negative issue of the physical work environment, followed by acoustics and window access.[9] Environmental comfort encompassed temperature, ventilation, and indoor air quality. This finding is corroborated in a survey of library workers that found that poor air conditioning was the second most frequently cited item identified as bothersome.[10] Additionally, library staff areas are often perceived as a source of stress, which can influence employee performance and service delivery.[11]

General office building studies are more prevalent than the limited research specific to libraries but reflect similar challenges. The literature identifies three primary areas that impact employee performance and satisfaction. Indoor environmental quality research examines features of light, air quality, temperature, and acoustics. Spatial factors refer to design, layout, and physical features. Socio-spatial factors consider the interactions between workers and their space and can be divided into the categories of autonomy, territoriality, and privacy.[12] Notably, in a study of university staff, the features of the physical work environment were found to be one of the most significant predictors of retention.[13]

Workspaces can also be a cause of physical and mental health complaints. The World Health Organization has identified noncommunicable diseases as the source of 70 percent of total disease burden in the workplace.[14] Sick building syndrome is a compilation of indoor environmental factors that lead to physical symptoms that usually resolve upon leaving a building.[15] Common sources of sick building syndrome include poor ventilation, indoor air pollutants, and biological contaminants like mold or pollen, which can disturb systems throughout the body.[16] Light, thermal comfort, and office design are strongly associated with mental health indicators, and improvements to these features can contribute positively to employees' mental health.[17] A synopsis of research study results is presented in table 14.1.

Table 14.1. Synopsis of research study results

Attribute	Results
Light	• Natural light is preferred.[a] • Blue-white bright light is associated with increased productivity and concentration.[b]
Temperature	• Uncomfortable temperatures can increase stress and fatigue.[c]
Air Quality	• Poor air quality decreases concentration.[d]
Acoustics	• Background noise can affect concentration.[e]
Office Design	• Private offices decrease distractions. • Open offices decrease productivity.[f]

a. Antal Haans, "The Natural Preference in People's Appraisal of Light," *Journal of Environmental Psychology* 39 (September 2014): 52, 56, https://doi.org/https://doi.org/10.1016/j.jenvp.2014.04.001.
b. Peter R. Mills, Susannah C. Tomkins, and Luc J. M. Schlangen, "The Effect of High Correlated Colour Temperature Office Lighting on Employee Wellbeing and Work Performance," *Journal of Circadian Rhythms* 5 (2007): article 2, p. 8, https://doi.org/10.1186/1740-3391-5-2.
c. Lisanne Bergefurt et al., "The Physical Office Workplace as a Resource for Mental Health—A Systematic Scoping Review," *Building and Environment* 207, part A (January 2022): article 108505, p. 8, https://doi.org/10.1016/j.buildenv.2021.108505.
d. Jan Pejtersen et al., "Effect of Renovating an Office Building on Occupants' Comfort and Health," *Indoor Air* 11, no. 1 (March 2001): 22, https://doi.org/10.1034/j.1600-0668.2001.011001010.x.
e. Bergefurt et al., "Physical Office Workplace," 8; Sonja Di Blasio et al., "A Cross-Sectional Survey on the Impact of Irrelevant Speech Noise on Annoyance, Mental Health and Well-being, Performance and Occupants' Behavior in Shared and Open-Plan Offices," *International Journal of Environmental Research and Public Health* 16, no. 2 (2019): article 280, p. 12, https://doi.org/10.3390/ijerph16020280; Anil Mital, James D. McGlothlin, and Hamid F. Faard, "Noise in Multiple-Workstation Open-Plan Computer Rooms: Measurements and Annoyance," *Journal of Human Ergology* 21, no. 1 (1992): 80, https://doi.org/10.11183/jhe1972.21.69.
f. Aram Seddigh et al., "Concentration Requirements Modify the Effect of Office Type on Indicators of Health and Performance," *Journal of Environmental Psychology* 38 (2014): 172, https://doi.org/10.1016/j.jenvp.2014.01.009; Iris De Been and Marion Beijer, "The Influence of Office Type on Satisfaction and Perceived Productivity Support," *Journal of Facilities Management* 12, no. 2 (2014): 150, https://doi.org/10.1108/JFM-02-2013-0011.

Table 14.1. Synopsis of research study results

Attribute	Results
Plants and Greenery	• Increase productivity and decrease stress.[g]
Windows	• Contribute to openness but can also be a visual distraction.[h]
Autonomy	• Freedom to adjust workspace increases productivity.[i]
Territoriality	• Personalization of workspace promotes meaningfulness and community.[j]
Privacy	• Sustained unregulated stimuli adversely affect productivity.[k]

g. Bergefurt et al., "Physical Office Workplace," 8; Nalise Hähn, Emmanuel Essah, and Tijuana Blanusa, "Biophilic Design and Office Planting: A Case Study of Effects on Perceived Health, Well-Being and Performance Metrics in the Workplace," *Intelligent Buildings International* 13 no. 4 (2020): 250, https://doi.org/10.1080/17508975.2020.1732859; Fatima Felgueiras et al., "A Systematic Review of Environmental Intervention Studies in Offices with Beneficial Effects on Workers' Health, Well-Being and Productivity," *Atmospheric Pollution Research* 13, no. 9 (2022): article 101513, p. 14, https://doi.org/10.1016/j.apr.2022.101513.
h. Melina Forooraghi, Antonio Cobaleda-Cordero, and Maral Babapour Chafi, "A Healthy Office and Healthy Employees: A Longitudinal Case Study with a Salutogenic Perspective in the Context of the Physical Office Environment," *Building Research and Information* 50, no. 1–2 (2022): 141–42, https://doi.org/10.1080/09613218.2021.1983753.
i. Candido, Christhina, Prithwi Chakraborty, and Dian Tjondronegoro, "The Rise of Office Design in High-Performance, Open-Plan Environments," *Buildings* 9, no. 4 (2019): article 100, p.10, https://doi.org/10.3390/buildings9040100.
j. Forooraghi, Cobaleda-Cordero, and Chafi, "Healthy Office," 148.
k. Janetta McCoy and Gary W. Evans, "Physical Work Environment," in *Handbook of Work Stress*, ed. Julian Barling, E. Kevin Kelloway, and Michael R. Frone. (Thousand Oaks, CA: SAGE, 2005) 220.

Office environments can also be a challenge for those living with chronic conditions or disabilities, both visible and invisible. A survey of librarians working with chronic conditions found that 26% of respondents had changed or left their jobs due to their chronic condition, and 46% had more than one type of chronic condition.[18] These librarians cited psychological ailments as the most prevalent (42%), followed by autoimmune disorders and migraines. Thirty-five percent of the librarians requested physical workplace accommodations, with the most common requests being ergonomic workstations, assistive technology, and environmental changes.[19] Although simple adjustments can facilitate an employee's ability to perform their job, the equipment must be compatible with the workplace. A qualitative study found that even when accommodations are granted, they can produce mixed results. One librarian in this study described the experience of having hearing-related assistive technology which picked up a local radio station.[20] Attention to the needs of employees working with chronic conditions may help retention efforts and reduce the financial and human costs of employee turnover.

Indoor Environmental Quality

The dusty smell associated with old bookshops and libraries may bring nostalgic comfort to readers, but it may also bring significant health concerns over time. Indoor air quality is increasingly recognized as a principal factor in human health, especially as humans spend more and more of their time inside.[21] The COVID-19 pandemic has further reinforced the importance of indoor air quality. The Environmental Protection Agency has identified many short- and long-term health effects caused by indoor air pollution, ranging from eye, nose, and throat irritation and respiratory ailments to cancer, heart disease, and even death. Of course, the nature of the ailment depends on the type of pollutant: the life-threatening dangers of asbestos, carbon monoxide, and radon gas are well-documented and immediate concerns.[22] However, more common library pollutants like dust, fungal spores (mold), bacteria, and particulate matter can aggravate or contribute to chronic health conditions such as asthma, respiratory infections, allergies, and more.[23] Even in environments with small amounts of pollution, this can add up to significant exposure over time.[24] While individuals vary in tolerance and more research is needed about the precise role of the immune system and pollutants, the larger health community agrees that minimizing the level of long-term exposure to indoor pollutants is important for overall human health.[25]

Indoor air pollution can come from many sources, but the most likely sources in a library setting are from outdoor air pollution, dust, pests, mold, harsh chemicals, and even copy/print/fax machines. For most of these sources, the first line of defense is a robust, well-maintained heating, ventilation, and air conditioning (HVAC) system that uses high-efficiency particulate air (HEPA) filters. This is coupled with diligent cleaning, including dusting with a damp cloth (instead of a traditional duster), and vacuuming regularly (preferably with a vacuum also featuring a HEPA filter). Keeping the humidity level below 60 percent is also strongly recommended to reduce the risk of mold growth.[26] Major HVAC system upgrades are costly and may take considerable time and advocacy work. In the meantime, older libraries may supplement their existing HVAC systems with portable air cleaners, sometimes called air purifiers or air sanitizers. When used properly, they will reduce the number of hazardous particulates in the air and contribute to improvements in respiratory health. However, these popular home appliances are not a panacea; despite frequent marketing claims, no home air cleaner can completely purify the air. They do not substitute for mold remediation, ventilation, and regular cleaning.[27] The Environmental Protection Agency recommends looking for a device that is appropriately sized for the room, has a high clean air delivery rate, contains a gas filter, and avoids ozone production. This is often achieved with a HEPA filter, an activated carbon filter, and UV lights with specialized lamp coatings. The effectiveness of the device also requires monitoring the filter and replacing as recommended.[28]

Like air quality, lighting is an equally important environmental factor. Exposure to low-glare natural light has been shown to be beneficial to productivity, physical and mental health, and overall well-being.[29] The many psychological benefits of natural light are well documented, but "many libraries try to save the 'best' areas in the library—those with natural light and a window—for patron space, relegating staff to interior offices and rooms without windows."[30] While exterior windows are not always possible, interior rooms can still benefit from borrowed light by incorporating glass walls that allow light to pass through.[31] However, since interior glass can be incredibly expensive to add later, the time to install it is during construction. This makes thorough space planning before any construction or remodeling essential.[32] The feeling of being on display and the amount of light let in can be regulated to accommodate individual preferences by using frosted glass or window coverings that can be adjusted as needed.[33] Finally, Schlipf and Moorman point out: "Library staff can be particularly unhappy when condemned to windowless subterranean spaces without natural light.... Basement spaces are no bargain. They cost nearly as much as upper floors, they are unnecessarily depressing, and they tend to flood."[34]

The ideal work temperature varies among individuals, so finding a temperature that is comfortable for everyone can seem nearly impossible. In buildings with one central thermostat, temperature can fluctuate throughout the space depending on the location of windows and other physical features. Often, thermostat controls are housed in a maintenance or facilities department with regulation of the thermostat beyond the control of library staff.[35] Temperatures outside the range of 65 to 72 degrees Fahrenheit have been associated with decreased productivity and concentration.[36] Errors have been shown to increase in environments that are perceived as too cold, while cognitive functions decrease when too warm.[37] In libraries that cannot accommodate individual temperature preferences, space heaters (with safety features) and fans can be used to adjust individual work areas so that staff can be comfortable and productive.

A core part of the library workspace that is often overlooked is facility infrastructure and maintenance and its impact on indoor environmental quality. Facility infrastructure includes things like HVAC systems, temperature and humidity controls, electrical and water systems, elevators, safety equipment, and more. Routine maintenance like changing light bulbs, air and water filters, cleaning, effective pest control, and attention to air quality and mold issues are essential for not only comfort, but also health and safety. These factors may be less noticeable when a building is new but can often fall by the wayside as buildings age, administrations change, and priorities shift. Whether an institution is large or small, caring for the physical library will almost certainly require coordination with a facilities or maintenance team. Usually, these staff members are responsible for multiple buildings and are not directly under the purview of the library, so it is important to develop good working relationships.[38] Knowing how facility departments do their work and acknowledging their important role in keeping the library safe and comfortable will make it easier to ask questions and initiate changes when needed. Facilities experts Brian

Atkins and Adrian Brooks warn that "if a facility is not managed properly, it can impact organizational performance and productivity. Conversely, a well-managed facility can enhance performance by contributing towards the optimal working environment."[39] Failure to maintain the facility poses physical risks not only to staff, but also to patrons—and may open the institution to liability risk.[40] In short, a library cannot afford to overlook the everyday work of facility infrastructure maintenance.

Safety and Security

Simply put, library workers cannot do their best work in spaces where they do not feel safe, whether it be from possible Occupational Safety and Health Administration (OSHA) violations or security concerns. Library staff should consult with their facilities team immediately to remedy conditions that could be unsafe. These include, but are not limited to, fire and trip hazards, water leaks, elevator problems, and blocked doors. Procedures for annual safety reviews, routine inspections, and equipment tests are often mandated by a patchwork of codes and laws that vary between state, county, and building type. For instance, the Florida Department of Education requires all public educational buildings (including academic libraries) follow the State Requirements for Educational Facilities, which guide all aspects of building construction and maintenance, from financial planning to building design to inspection requirements.[41] Library staff do not need to know all of these regulations in detail, but they should take the opportunity to ask questions, learn from these inspections, and do their own part to maintain safety. Assisting facilities staff by maintaining an organized, uncluttered workspace (which makes cleaning easier and more effective), paying attention to potential fire hazards (such as excessive extension cord use or heating elements), and being aware of door policies (know which ones should be open, stay locked, have appropriate clearances, etc.) builds goodwill with the facilities team and makes their jobs easier, keeping the library a safer place for all.

As public spaces that welcome patrons and protect privacy, libraries are in a tricky position when it comes to building security. While libraries are generally considered a safe place, staff are not immune to threats, assaults, or even murder.[42] In a time of growing concern about community violence, political threats, and mass shootings, library workers need an environment that has a security plan in place appropriate for their building. However, decision-makers need to approach security, especially guards, in their libraries carefully. Overpoliced communities may feel intimidated or unwelcome in the presence of security officers. Any implementation of security staff will need to be managed carefully with the community and staff as partners.[43] Security cameras are another powerful tool and should be considered carefully in disclosed locations to protect privacy. While there is no way to completely prevent such terrible acts, employees should practice active shooter response and lockdown procedures as part of their emergency preparedness routine.[44] Security can be a difficult and controversial topic but cannot be disregarded when considering library workspaces. This subject is vast, but the Association of College and Research Libraries offers many useful resources for safety and security planning.[45]

Emergency infrastructure may not be foremost in the mind when considering the optimal physical workspace, but when the need arises, there is nothing more important. Due to the public nature of libraries, staff need to feel confident that they can respond appropriately in an emergency and utilize equipment like fire extinguishers, first aid kits, and automated external defibrillator (AED) machines. OSHA emergency guidelines are numerous and detailed but should be considered a minimum benchmark for safety standards. For instance, they require employers to have an "emergency action plan" that details procedures for reporting an emergency, evacuation procedures and routes, and emergency medical procedures.[46] Other guidelines include state building and fire codes that detail specifications for fire alarms, emergency exit locations, elevator requirements, and much more. While most regulations require some type of emergency training for staff, the reality is that most sessions are dull, infrequent, and often interrupt seemingly more relevant work. Nonetheless, training is important for emergency equipment and procedures to be effective. Small-group, hands-on training, paired with routine drills, question-and-answer sessions, and even role-play scenarios will increase the likelihood that staff will remember their training in an emergency.[47]

Spatial Factors

Many of the library buildings in use today were designed and constructed before the health consequences of indoor environments were well understood.[48] Numerous library employees work or know someone who works in a less than ideal setting: a damp windowless basement, a former closet, or an office designed for one that currently holds multiple people. Budgets always seem to be tight, so cutting corners on employee-only areas may seem to make sense, but at what long-term cost? Employee workspaces are often shoehorned into impossibly small areas with no access to natural light or rooms that were never designed for staff use in the first place.[49] Non-ergonomic workstations that are too small or poorly laid out can place employees at risk for adverse physical and mental health outcomes, such as repetitive motion injuries, or the exacerbation of chronic illnesses and conditions.[50]

Private workspaces, which have been associated with less workplace distraction, may be ideal, but are usually not feasible for all library workers.[51] Priority should go to employees working with confidential information or rare or expensive materials that require securable private space. Depending on job responsibilities, some positions may also need room for specialized equipment or storage.[52] Open offices and shared work areas may save on construction costs but have been proven to be expensive in the long term due to increased sick days, decreased productivity, lower job satisfaction, higher turnover, and hindering the recruitment of new employees.[53] However, given that many libraries have no alternative other than open floorplans, it is crucial to try to minimize the negative effects on workers. Some recommendations include using cubicles or modular office system furniture that can be reconfigured as needed, ensuring panels between workstations are high enough to provide privacy and minimize noise and distractions, placing desks and computers so that they do not face one another, and providing enough clearance between partitions and the ceiling for adequate air circulation.[54] Practical space planning for libraries also incorporates enough open floor space for book trucks,[55] accessible routes to accommodate persons with various disabilities,[56] and enough room for social distancing if it becomes necessary to help minimize the spread of disease.[57] As difficult as it may seem, given that library buildings may be in use for decades, it is also advisable to try to plan for future needs and growth in headcount.[58]

Restorative areas should be provided for workers whenever possible since they can positively contribute to staff's mental health.[59] Many library employees eat on site and should have a relaxing, welcoming space with comfortable furniture for breaks.[60] At a minimum, a refrigerator and microwave should be supplied along with adequate seating for eating alone or as a group.[61] Access to pleasing outdoor environments are particularly beneficial because of the positive effects of nature.[62] Use of a private multipurpose office can serve many functions, such as a sickroom, a meditation or prayer space, a lactation room, or a place to make phone calls or hold virtual meetings that require privacy.[63]

In building design, form and function are equally important. Aesthetics should not be overlooked as they play a vital role in creating a productive space people want to work in.[64] Biophilic design, which can be described as "indoor environments that reference nature in both obvious and subtle ways… to improve people's mental and physical well-being,"[65] has been gaining popularity in office spaces.[66] There is substantial evidence that this design philosophy can enhance productivity, mitigate stress, improve well-being, promote collaboration, and increase employee satisfaction.[67] According to Kellert and Calabrese, these principles can be applied in three primary ways: (1) direct experience of nature, (2) indirect experience of nature, and (3) experience of space and place.[68] This can be achieved by incorporating plant life, air flow, natural materials and light, open sightlines, colors and patterns inspired by nature, views of the outdoors, or even something as simple as scenic artwork.

Furnishings and finishings may seem inconsequential, but since library staff spend much of their day sitting at a desk working at a computer, they can have a huge impact on employee well-being and productivity.[69] Furnishings should be ergonomically designed to support the physical health and comfort of workers, meet the diverse needs of staff, and minimize the development of musculoskeletal disorders.[70] Investing in quality, durable, reconfigurable furnishings allows for flexibility, especially in shared workspaces, and such furnishings can be rearranged as necessary to serve future needs.[71] Breakroom furniture should be comfortable and functional rather than the shabby hand-me-downs no longer fit for public use found in many libraries.[72] Research has also shown color has an impact on productivity. Although the optimal color varies by individual,[73] a fresh coat of paint is a cost-effective way to brighten up a dull space.

Architects, planners, and designers are increasingly aware of their role in supporting human health and well-being through the buildings they design.[74] There is a growing interest in architectural practice and research using evidence-based design (EBD).[75] The Center for Health Design defines EBD as "the process of basing decisions about the built environment on credible research to achieve the best possible outcomes."[76] While most often used in health-care facilities, these methodologies can be applied to any type of building, including libraries.[77] Universal design, another important topic to design-focused stakeholders, can be described as "a process that enables and empowers a diverse population by improving human performance, health and wellness, and social participation."[78] A high level of usability not only supports workers with disabilities, but it also helps to increase efficiency, productivity, morale, and safety for all staff, as well as attracting and retaining diverse employees.[79] There are many excellent sources for more information related to spatial factors, including the National Institute of Building Science's Whole Building Design Guide, the US Green Building Council's LEED Certification Guide, and the WELL Building Standard.[80]

Socio-Spatial Factors

Administrators play a key role in managing socio-spatial factors, or the interactions between office space and users. Policies governing privacy, autonomy, and territoriality, as well as accessibility and ergonomics are usually set at the administrative level of a library or parent institution.[81] It is often necessary for administrators to liaise with departments outside of the library, making good working relationships essential. Since individual staff may have little input or control over policies, it is incumbent upon library leadership to address workspace woes as it "signals to employees that their workplace cares about their overall health and well-being and helps to improve staff satisfaction and reduce turnover, absences, and presenteeism" and demonstrates that employees are cared for on an individual basis.[82] Privacy can increase staff productivity by keeping interruptions to a minimum but is not always possible.[83] When open workspaces are the only option, consider creating policies that can make a shared space function better, such as allowing employees to stagger or flex their schedules so fewer people occupy the room at one time. Administrators should also ensure access to a dedicated breakroom or lounge area and create a culture that encourages taking breaks away from one's desk.

Autonomy and territoriality, the concept of individuality, ownership, and belonging in the workplace, are also contributing factors to job satisfaction and mental health. Administrators must create and support policies that empower workers to improve their personal workspaces and recognize the importance of personalization. Allowing personal expression with decor, artwork, photographs, and so on is an easy way to give staff a sense of autonomy and territoriality.[84] Employers who are sensitive to these kinds of needs may see higher rates of retention due to employee satisfaction.

The socio-spatial aspects of workspaces also include accessibility and ergonomics. Many, if not all, institutions have a department dedicated to managing these issues, but most often they are intended to address the needs of students rather than providing guidance or assistance to employees. Human resources departments are frequently tasked with handling accessibility and ergonomics needs but, depending on the institution, may not have the proper training or resources. To reduce barriers for employees with disabilities, library administrators can work with institution-wide leadership to implement accessibility policies that not only provide clear guidance but that also do so inclusively, in a manner that recognizes and normalizes the need for such policy.[85] Three examples of what inclusive accessibility policies may look like are (1) regularly auditing the workspace, including surveying staff for practical feedback and observations; (2) requiring managers to participate in annual professional development training with detailed action plans for use in the library; and (3) yearly individual reviews to discuss employees' evolving needs. Like accessibility, ergonomic policies should also be clearly defined and communicated to staff during onboarding. There should be an open-door policy for employees to share changing needs that require an adjustment to their work area.[86] The US Department of Labor's Office of Disability Employment Policy's website and the European Union OSHA's "Conversation Starters for Workplace Discussions about Musculoskeletal Disorders" provide additional helpful information on these topics.[87]

Conclusion

Working in a space that functions well and is aesthetically pleasing can have a significant positive impact on the health, morale, and productivity of library workers and may increase job satisfaction, lower turnover, and positively impact the recruitment of new employees.[88] Since people now spend approximately 90 percent of their time indoors, the effects of the built environment on human well-being cannot be ignored.[89] Also, given high levels of retirement and people leaving the library profession during COVID-19 and the Great Resignation, the impact of physical space issues on recruitment and retention should not be overlooked.[90] Modern building designers understand their role in supporting human health, and various methodologies and programs exist that can help libraries apply these principles. It is possible to design library workspaces that are comfortable, safe, well-maintained, and beneficial for the people who work in them. Library administrators and leaders have a responsibility to understand the effects of the physical environment on employees, create a culture of wellness, and craft policies that support workers' physical and mental health. As the needs and functions of libraries continue to evolve, it will be imperative to seek opportunities to provide healthy, flexible spaces that meet the needs of patrons and employees alike.[91]

Key Takeaways

- Allocate budget money annually for employee space enhancements even if it is only a small amount. A fresh coat of paint can have a big impact.
- Incorporate biophilic design principles.
- Solicit input from staff and make physical workspace assessments a routine ongoing process.
- Adopt policies that empower employees to address workspace concerns.
- Address accessibility and ergonomic needs as part of the onboarding and review processes.
- Allow adjustments to physical spaces to support a comfortable work environment.
- Provide ergonomic equipment and furniture: desks, keyboards, chairs, and so on.
- Allow personalization of workspaces.
- Avoid built-in furniture when possible. Reconfigurable options better serve changing long-term needs.
- Make sure cubicle walls are high enough for privacy and noise reduction but low enough to allow air circulation.
- Allow space heaters (with safety features) or fans for individual temperature comfort.
- When space planning, consider future needs, including growth in headcount.
- Take advantage of borrowed light whenever possible.
- Ensure enough clearance in workspaces for wheelchair access and book trucks.
- Use adjustable window coverings on interior and exterior windows to provide privacy and light modulation.
- Ensure thorough regular cleaning takes place including dusting and vacuuming.
- Encourage the use of breakrooms and ensure they are a relaxing space with comfortable furniture.
- Establish good working relationships with facilities/maintenance and other institution-wide departments.
- Create policies that help shared workspaces function better, such as flex or staggered schedules and access to private space when needed.
- Conduct regular safety inspections. Have the proper safety equipment (fire extinguishers, first aid kits, AED machines) and ensure staff know their locations and are trained in their use.

- Plan layouts so that desks and computers do not face one another to increase privacy.
- Address safety hazards immediately.
- Keep humidity levels stable and below 60 percent to help prevent mold growth.
- Ensure safety plans including evacuation procedures are in place, known by all staff, and practiced regularly.
- Provide access to pleasing outdoor space to enjoy the health benefits of nature.
- Properly maintain HVAC systems and supplement with quality portable air cleaners as needed.
- Make sure employee-only areas can be secured in case of emergency.
- Create a culture of wellness and craft policies that support it.

After reading this chapter, evaluate the employee areas in your library with a fresh perspective. How does the space make you feel? Inspired or discouraged? Focused or distracted? Comfortable or stressed? Energized or drained? What small changes can you implement that may have a significant positive impact on the employees in your library?

Notes

1. Lara Ewen, "Quitting Time," *American Libraries*, June 1, 2022, https://americanlibrariesmagazine.org/2022/06/01/quitting-time/.
2. Hirbod Norouzianpour, "Architectural Interventions to Mitigate Occupational Stress among Office Workers," *Enquiry* 17, no. 2 (2020): 22, https://doi.org/10.17831/enq:arcc.v16i2.1069.
3. Sallyann Price, "2022 Library Design Showcase," *American Libraries*, September/October 2022, https://americanlibrariesmagazine.org/2022/09/01/2022-library-design-showcase/.
4. Allison Head, *Planning and Designing Academic Library Learning Spaces* (Project Information Literacy, 2016): 19, https://projectinfolit.org/pubs/library-space-study/pil_libspace-study_2016-12-06.pdf.
5. Jennifer A. Bartlett, "New and Noteworthy: You Too, Can Prevent Librarian Burnout," *Library Leadership and Management* 32, no. 2 (2018): 1–3, https://doi.org/10.5860/llm.v32i2.7301; Susan Carter et al, "'What About Us?' Wellbeing of Higher Education Librarians," *Journal of Academic Librarianship* 49, no 1 (January 2023): article 102619, p. 2, https://doi.org/10.1016/j.acalib.2022.102619; Edward M. Corrado, "Low Morale and Burnout in Libraries," *Technical Services Quarterly* 39, no. 1 (2002): 37–45, https://doi.org/10.1080/07317131.2021.2011149; Jennifer A. Dixon, "Feeling the Burnout: Library Workers Are Facing Burnout in Greater Numbers and Severity—and Grappling with It as a Systemic Problem," *Library Journal*, March 2022, 44, EBSCOhost Academic Search Premier; Fobazi Ettarh and Chris Vidas, "The Future of Libraries: Vocational Awe in a 'Post-Covid' World," *Serials Librarian* 82, no. 1–4 (2022): 19–20, https://doi.org/10.1080/0361526x.2022.2028501; Ewen, "Quitting Time," 38; Patricia Katopol, "Enough Already: Compassion Fatigue," *Library Leadership and Management* 30, no. 2 (2015): 1–3, https://llm.corejournals.org/llm/article/view/7177; Bobbi L. Newman, *Fostering Wellness in the Workplace* (Chicago: ALA Editions, 2022), 66–68; Ellen I. Shupe, Stephanie K. Wambaugh, and Reed J. Bramble, "Role-Related Stress Experienced by Academic Librarians," *Journal of Academic Librarianship* 41, no. 3 (May 2015): 268, https://doi.org/10.1016/j.acalib.2015.03.016.
6. Carter et al., "'What About Us?'" 2.
7. Michael Roskams and Barry Haynes, "Environmental Demands and Resources: A Framework for Understanding the Physical Environment for Work," *Facilities* 39, no. 9–10 (2021): 654, https://doi.org/10.1108/F-07-2020-0090.
8. Neda Abbasi, Kenn Fisher, and Robert Gerrity, "Designing Better Workspaces for Academic Library Staff Case Study of University of Queensland Library," *New ARCH—International Journal of Contemporary Architecture* 5, no. 1 (April 2018): 1, https://the-new-arch.net/index.php/journal/article/view/53.
9. Abbasi, Fisher, and Gerrity, "Designing Better Workspaces," 13.
10. Bridget Juniper, Patricia Bellamy, and Nicola White, "Evaluating the Well-Being of Public Library Workers," *Journal of Librarianship and Information Science* 44, no. 2 (June 2012): 112, https://doi.org/10.1177/0961000611426442.

11. Abbasi, Fisher, and Gerrity, "Designing Better Workspaces," 14; Charles Albert Bunge, "Stress in the Library," *Library Journal*, September 15, 1987, 48-49. EBSCOhost Academic Search Complete.
12. Melina Forooraghi et al., "Scoping Review of Health in Office Design Approaches." *Journal of Corporate Real Estate* 22, no. 2 (2020): 170–71. https://doi.org/10.1108/JCRE-08-2019-0036.
13. Odunayo Salau et al., "The Impact of Workplace Environments on Retention Outcomes of Public Universities in Southern Nigeria," *SAGE Open* 10, no. 2 (2020): 11, https://doi.org/10.1177/2158244020930767.
14. J. Wolf et al., *Preventing Disease through a Healthier and Safer Workplace* (Geneva, Switzerland: World Health Organization, 2018), 7, https://www.who.int/publications/i/item/9789241513777.
15. Andrew Smith and Michael Pitt, "Sustainable Workplaces and Building User Comfort and Satisfaction," *Journal of Corporate Real Estate* 13, no. 3 (2011): 148, https://doi.org/10.1108/14630011111170436.
16. US Environmental Protection Agency, *Indoor Air Facts No. 4 (revised): Sick Building Syndrome*, February 1991, 1–2, https://www.epa.gov/sites/default/files/2014-08/documents/sick_building_factsheet.pdf.
17. Daan Kropman et al., "The Business Case for a Healthy Office; a Holistic Overview of Relations between Office Workspace Design and Mental Health," *Ergonomics* 66, no. 5 (2023): 669, https://doi.org/10.1080/00140139.2022.2108905.
18. Susan Rathbun-Grubb, "Voices of Strength: A Survey of Librarians Working with Chronic Illnesses or Conditions," *Journal of Library Administration* 61, no. 1 (2021): 46, 49, https://doi.org/10.1080/01930826.2020.1845546.
19. Rathbun-Grubb, "Voices of Strength," 48.
20. Joanne Oud, "Systemic Workplace Barriers for Academic Librarians with Disabilities," *College and Research Libraries* 80, no. 2 (March 2019): 185, https://doi.org/10.5860/crl.80.2.169.
21. World Health Organization, *WHO Guidelines for Indoor Air Quality: Dampness and Mould*, ed. Elisabeth Heseltine and Jerome Rosen (Copenhagen, Denmark: World Health Organization, 2009), 1, https://iris.who.int/bitstream/handle/10665/164348/9789289041683-eng.pdf.
22. US Environmental Protection Agency, "Introduction to Indoor Air Quality," last modified December 5, 2022, https://www.epa.gov/indoor-air-quality-iaq/introduction-indoor-air-quality.
23. María Elena Báez Flores et al., "Fungal Spore Concentrations in Indoor and Outdoor Air in University Libraries, and Their Variations in Response to Changes in Meteorological Variables," *International Journal of Environmental Health Research* 24, no. 4 (2014): 320–21, https://doi.org/10.1080/09603123.2013.835029.
24. World Health Organization, *WHO Global Air Quality Guidelines: Particulate Matter (PM2.5 and PM10), Ozone, Nitrogen Dioxide, Sulphur Dioxide, and Carbon Monoxide* (Geneva, Switzerland: World Health Organization, 2021), 9–10, https://apps.who.int/iris/bitstream/handle/10665/345329/9789240034228-eng.pdf.
25. World Health Organization, *WHO Global Air Quality Guidelines*, 9–10.
26. World Health Organization, *WHO Global Air Quality Guidelines*, 12.
27. US Environmental Protection Agency, *Guide to Air Cleaners in the Home*, 2nd ed. July 2018. https://www.epa.gov/sites/default/files/2018-07/documents/guide_to_air_cleaners_in_the_home_2nd_edition.pdf.
28. US Environmental Protection Agency, "Sources of Indoor Particulate Matter," last modified December 12, 2022, https://www.epa.gov/indoor-air-quality-iaq/sources-indoor-particulate-matter-pm.
29. Fred Schlipf and John A. Moorman, *The Practical Handbook of Library Architecture* (Chicago: ALA Editions, 2018), 659; Jacqueline C. Vischer, "The Effects of the Physical Environment on Job Performance: towards a Theoretical Model of Workspace Stress," *Stress and Health* 23, no. 3 (August 2007): 178, https://doi.org/10.1002/smi.1134; Newman, *Fostering Wellness*, 25; Norouzianpour, "Architectural Interventions," 30; Peter R. Mills, Susannah C. Tomkins, and Luc J. M. Schlangen, "The Effect of High Correlated Colour Temperature Office Lighting on Employee Wellbeing and Work Performance," *Journal of Circadian Rhythms* 5 (2007): article 2, p. 2, https://doi.org/10.1186/1740-3391-5-2; Terri Peters and Kristen D'Penna. "Biophilic Design for Restorative University Learning Environments: A Critical Review of Literature and Design Recommendations," *Sustainability* 12, no. 17 (2020): article 706, p. 12, https://doi.org/10.3390/su12177064.
30. Newman, *Fostering Wellness*, 25.
31. Schlipf and Moorman, *Practical Handbook*, 657, 659–60.
32. Schlipf and Moorman, *Practical Handbook*, 657.
33. Schlipf and Moorman, *Practical Handbook*, 660.
34. Schlipf and Moorman, *Practical Handbook*, 659.
35. Newman, *Fostering Wellness*, 22.
36. Rokas Valančius and Andrius Jurelionis, "Influence of Indoor Air Temperature Variation on Office Work Performance," *Journal of Environmental Engineering and Landscape Management* 21, no.1 (2013): 24, https://doi.org/10.3846/16486897.2012.721371.
37. Newman, *Fostering Wellness*, 23.
38. US Environmental Protection Agency, *An Office Building Occupant's Guide to Indoor Air Quality* (Office of Air and Radiation, October 1997), https://www.epa.gov/sites/default/files/2014-08/documents/occupants_guide.pdf.
39. Brian Atkins and Adrian Brooks, *Total Facility Management*, 5th ed. (Hoboken, NJ: John Wiley & Sons, 2021), 4.

40. Jerry Nichols and Rebekkah Smith Aldrich, *Handbook for Library Trustees of New York State*, 2018 ed. (Bellport, NY: Suffolk Cooperative Library System, 2018), 36–37, https://niogatrustees.org/handbook/Handbook%20for%20Library%20Trustees%20of%20New%20York%20State%20-%202018%20edition.pdf.
41. Florida Department of Education, Office of Educational Facilities, *State Requirements for Educational Facilities, 2014*. (Tallahassee, FL: Office of Educational Facilities, November 4, 2014), https://www.fldoe.org/core/fileparse.php/7738/urlt/srefrule14.pdf.
42. Kelly Clark, "Keep Library Workers Safe," *American Libraries*, April 23, 2019, https://americanlibrariesmagazine.org/2019/04/23/keep-library-workers-safe/.
43. Ben Robinson, "No Holds Barred: Policing and Security in the Public Library," *In the Library with the Lead Pipe*, December 11, 2019, https://www.inthelibrarywiththeleadpipe.org/2019/no-holds-barred/.
44. Steven Bell, "Creating a More Secure Academic Library: Even the Heart of the Campus Needs Protection," *Library Issues* 33, no. 1 (2012), https://www.academia.edu/9610198/Creating_a_More_Secure_Academic_Library_Even_the_Heart_of_the_Campus_Needs_Protection.
45. Association of College and Research Libraries, "Academic Library Building Design: Resources for Planning: Safety and Security," last updated March 2021, https://acrl.libguides.com/c.php?g=459032&p=3138024.
46. Occupational Safety and Health Administration, *Training Requirements in OSHA Standards*, US Department of Labor, 2015, 5–6, https://www.osha.gov/sites/default/files/publications/osha2254.pdf.
47. Guy Robertson, "Emergency Management Training for Your Library: The Joys of Tabletopping," *Feliciter* 60, no. 1 (2014): 33. EBSCOhost Academic Search Premier.
48. Newman, *Fostering Wellness*, 20.
49. Newman, *Fostering Wellness*, 19; Schlipf and Moorman, Practical Handbook, 655–57.
50. Newman, *Fostering Wellness*, 21; Rathburn-Grubb, "Voices of Strength," 43; Schlipf and Moorman, *Practical Handbook*, 657.
51. Aram Seddigh et al., "Concentration Requirements Modify the Effect of Office Type on Indicators of Health and Performance," Journal of Environmental Psychology 38 (June 2014): 172, https://doi.org/10.1016/j.jenvp.2014.01.009.
52. Schlipf and Moorman, *Practical Handbook*, 656.
53. Iris De Been and Marion Beijer, "The Influence of Office Type on Satisfaction and Perceived Productivity Support," *Journal of Facilities Management* 12, no. 2 (2014): 150, https://doi.org/10.1108/JFM-02-2013-0011; Anil Mital, James D. McGlothlin, and Hamid F. Faard, "Noise in Multiple-Workstation Open-Plan Computer Rooms: Measurements and Annoyance," *Journal of Human Ergology* 21, no. 1 (1992): 80, https://doi.org/10.11183/jhe1972.21.69; Newman, *Fostering Wellness*, 63; Seddigh et al., "Concentration Requirements," 172; Lisanne Bergefurt et al., "The Physical Office Workplace as a Resource for Mental Health—A Systematic Scoping Review," *Building and Environment* 207, part A (January 2022): article 108505, pp. 2–3, 8–9, https://doi.org/10.1016/j.buildenv.2021.108505; Vischer, "Effects of the Physical Environment," 175.
54. Newman, *Fostering Wellness*, 63–64.
55. Schlipf and Moorman, *Practical Handbook*, 667.
56. National Institute of Building Sciences, "Office," Whole Building Design Guide, last modified December 3, 2019, https://www.wbdg.org/space-types/office.
57. Louis Gagnon, Stephanie Gagnon, and Jessica Lloyd, "Social Distancing Causally Impacts the Spread of SARS-CoV-2: A U.S. Nationwide Event Study," *BMC Infectious Diseases* 22, no. 1 (2022): article 787, pp. 9–10, https://doi.org/10.1186/s12879-022-07763-y.
58. Schlipf and Moorman, *Practical Handbook*, 5.
59. Abbasi, Fisher, and Gerrity, "Designing Better Workspaces," 13, 16.
60. Schlipf and Moorman, *Practical Handbook*, 682–87; Newman, *Fostering Wellness*, 65.
61. Schlipf and Moorman, *Practical Handbook*, 683–84.
62. Norouzianpour, "Architectural Interventions," 31–32; Peters and D'Penna, "Biophilic Design," 2, 10.
63. Schlipf and Moorman, *Practical Handbook*, 689.
64. Head, *Planning and Designing*, 22; National Institute of Building Sciences, "Office"; Newman, *Fostering Wellness*, 27–28.
65. Katharine Schwab, "What Is Biophilic Design and Can It Really Make You Happier and Healthier?" Fast Company, April 11, 2019, https://www.fastcompany.com/90333072/what-is-biophilic-design-and-can-it-really-make-you-happier-and-healthier.
66. Schwab, "What Is Biophilic Design?"; William Browning, Catherine Ryan, and Joseph Clancy, *14 Patterns of Biophilic Design* (New York: Terrapin Bright Green, 2014), https://www.terrapinbrightgreen.com/reports/14-patterns/#nature-health-relationships.
67. Bergefurt et al., "Physical Office Workplace," 8; Browning, Ryan, and Clancy, *14 Patterns of Biophilic Design*; Nalise Hähn, Emmanuel Essah, and Tijuana Blanusa, "Biophilic Design and Office Planting: A Case Study of Effects on Perceived Health, Well-Being and Performance Metrics in the Workplace," *Intelligent Buildings International* 13 no. 4 (2020): 250, https://doi.org/10.1080/17508975.2020.1732859; Fatima Felgueiras et al., "A Systematic Review of Environmental Intervention Studies in Offices with Beneficial Effects on Workers' Health, Well-Being and

Productivity," *Atmospheric Pollution Research* 13, no. 9 (2022): article 101513, p. 14, https://doi.org/10.1016/j.apr.2022.101513; Kropman et al., "Business Case," 668; Stephen R. Kellert and Elizabeth F. Calabrese, "The Practice of Biophilic Design," 2015, 8, http://www.biophilic-design.com; Norouzianpour, "Architectural Interventions," 24–25; Schwab, "What Is Biophilic Design?"

68. Kellert and Calabrese, "Practice of Biophilic Design," 9.
69. Newman, *Fostering Wellness*, 2; National Institute of Building Sciences, "Office."
70. National Institute of Building Sciences, "Office"; Newman, Fostering Wellness, 20–22; Occupational Safety and Health Administration, *Training Requirements*; Schlipf and Moorman, *Practical Handbook*, 662–64.
71. Schlipf and Moorman, *Practical Handbook*, 663.
72. Newman, *Fostering Wellness*, 65; **Schlipf and Moorman**, *Practical Handbook*, 687.
73. Zara Poursafar, Lewlyn L. R. Rodrigues, and Sriram K.V., "Architectural Design Model for Office Interior to Suit Personality Types and to Enhance Productivity," *International Journal of Recent Technology and Engineering* 8, no. 2 (2019): 1918–19, https://www.doi.org/10.35940/ijrte.B1855.078219.
74. Norouzianpour, "Architectural Interventions," 27.
75. Peters and D'Penna, "Biophilic Design for Restorative University," 2.
76. Center for Health Design, "About EBD," accessed January 19, 2023. https://www.healthdesign.org/certification-outreach/edac/about-ebd.
77. Elisa Alfonsi, Stefano Capolongo, and Maddalena Buffoli, "Evidence Based Design and Healthcare: An Unconventional Approach to Hospital Design," *Annali di Igiene: Medicina Preventiva e di Comunità* 26, no. 2 (2014): 137, https://doi.org/10.7416/ai.2014.1968.
78. Edward Steinfeld and Jordana L. Maisel, *Universal Design* (Hoboken, NJ: Wiley, 2012), 29, ProQuest Ebook Central.
79. WBDG Accessible Committee, Jordana L. Maisel, and Molly Ranahan, "Beyond Accessibility to Universal Design," Whole Building Design Guide, last modified April 29, 2022, https://www.wbdg.org/design-objectives/accessible/beyond-accessibility-universal-design.
80. National Institute of Building Sciences, "Whole Building Design Guide," last updated 2022, https://www.wbdg.org/; US Green Building Council, "Mission and Vision," accessed January 6, 2023, https://www.usgbc.org/about/mission-vision; International WELL Building Institute, "WELL Building Standard," accessed December 27, 2022, https://standard.wellcertified.com/well.
81. Roskams and Haynes, "Environmental Demands and Resources," 654.
82. Newman, *Fostering Wellness*, 61, 26, 76.
83. Seddigh, "Concentration Requirements," 172.
84. Roskams and Haynes, "Environmental Demands and Resources," 658.
85. Oud, "Systemic Workplace Barriers," 189.
86. Joanne O. Crawford et al., "Musculoskeletal Health in the Workplace," *Best Practice and Research: Clinical Rheumatology* 34, no. 5 (October 2020): article 101558, p. 10, https://doi.org/10.1016/j.berh.2020.101558.
87. US Department of Labor, Office of Disability Employment Policy home page, accessed April 28, 2023, https://www.dol.gov/agencies/odep; European Agency for Safety and Health at Work, *Conversation Starters for Workplace Discussions about Musculoskeletal Disorders* (Birmingham, UK: Royal Society for the Prevention of Accidents, 2019), https://osha.europa.eu/sites/default/files/Conversation_starters.pdf.
88. Abbasi, Fisher, and Gerrity, "Designing Better Workspaces, 9, 13; Bergefurt et al, "Physical Office Workplace, 2, 8–9; De Been and Beijer, "Influence of Office Type," 150; Felgueiras et al., "A Systematic Review," 14; Hähn, Essah, and Blanusa, "Biophilic Design and Office Planting," 250; Kropman et al., "Business Case," 668-69; Iqra Hafeez et al., "Impact of Workplace Environment on Employee Performance: Mediating Role of Employee Health," *Business Management and Education* 17, no. 2 (2019):186, https://doi.org/10.3846/bme.2019.10379. Janetta McCoy and Gary W. Evans, "Physical Work Environment," in *Handbook of Work Stress*, ed. Julian Barling, E. Kevin Kelloway, and Michael R. Frone. (Thousand Oaks, CA: SAGE, 2005) 220; Mital, McGlothlin, and Faard, "Noise in Multiple-Workstation," 80; Newman, *Fostering Wellness*, 19–20, 28, 63; National Institute of Building Sciences, "Whole Building Design Guide."
89. US Environmental Protection Agency, "Indoor Air Quality: What Are the Trends in Indoor Air Quality and Their Effects on Human Health?" last modified September 7, 2021, https://www.epa.gov/report-environment/indoor-air-quality.
90. Ewan, "Quitting Time," 38–39.
91. Norouzianpour, "Architectural Interventions," 29.

Bibliography

Abbasi, Neda, Kenn Fisher, and Robert Gerrity. "Designing Better Workspaces for Academic Library Staff: Case Study of University of Queensland Library." *New ARCH—International Journal of Contemporary Architecture* 5, no. 1 (April 2018): 9–16. https://the-new-arch.net/index.php/journal/article/view/53.

Alfonsi, Elisa, Stefano Capolongo, and Maddalena Buffoli. "Evidence Based Design and Healthcare: An Unconventional Approach to Hospital Design." *Annali di Igiene: Medicina Preventiva e di Comunità* 26, no. 2 (2014): 137–43. https://doi.org/10.7416/ai.2014.1968.

Association of College and Research Libraries. "Academic Library Building Design: Resources for Planning: Safety and Security." Last updated March 2021. https://acrl.libguides.com/c.php?g=459032&p=3138024.

Atkins, Brian, and Adrian Brooks. *Total Facility Management*, 5th ed. Hoboken, NJ: John Wiley & Sons, 2021.

Báez Flores, María Elena, Pável Gaxiola Medina, Sylvia Páz Díaz Camacho, Magdalena de Jesús Uribe Beltrán, María del Carmen de la Cruz Otero, Ignacio Osuna Ramírez and Martín Ernesto Tiznado Hernández. "Fungal Spore Concentrations in Indoor and Outdoor Air in University Libraries, and Their Variations in Response to Changes in Meteorological Variables." *International Journal of Environmental Health Research* 24, no. 4 (2014): 320–40, https://doi.org/10.1080/09603123.2013.835029.

Bartlett, Jennifer A. "New and Noteworthy: You Too, Can Prevent Librarian Burnout." *Library Leadership and Management* 32, no. 2 (2018): 1–4. https://llm.corejournals.org/llm/article/view/7301.

Bell, Steven. "Creating a More Secure Academic Library: Even the Heart of the Campus Needs Protection." *Library Issues* 33, no. 1 (2012). https://www.academia.edu/9610198/Creating_a_More_Secure_Academic_Library_Even_the_Heart_of_the_Campus_Needs_Protection.

Bergefurt, Lisanne, Minou Weijs-Perree, Rianne Appel-Meulenbroek, and Theo Arentze. "The Physical Office Workplace as a Resource for Mental Health—A Systematic Scoping Review." *Building and Environment* 207, part A (January 2022): article 108505. https://doi.org/10.1016/j.buildenv.2021.108505.

Browning, William, Catherine Ryan, and Joseph Clancy. *14 Patterns of Biophilic Design: Improving Health and Well-Being in the Built Environment*." New York: Terrapin Bright Green, 2014. https://www.terrapinbrightgreen.com/reports/14-patterns/.

Bunge, Charles Albert. "Stress in the Library." *Library Journal*, September 15, 1987. EBSCOhost Academic Search Complete.

Candido, Christhina, Prithwi Chakraborty, and Dian Tjondronegoro. "The Rise of Office Design in High-Performance, Open-Plan Environments." *Buildings* 9, no. 4 (2019): article 100. https://doi.org/10.3390/buildings9040100.

Carter, Susan, Cecily Andersen, Michelle Turner, and Lorraine Gaunt. "'What About Us?' Wellbeing of Higher Education Librarians." *Journal of Academic Librarianship* 49, no 1 (January 2023): article 102619. https://doi.org/10.1016/j.acalib.2022.102619.

Center for Health Design. "About EBD." Accessed January 19, 2023. https://www.healthdesign.org/certification-outreach/edac/about-ebd.

Clark, Kelly. "Keep Library Workers Safe." *American Libraries*, April 23, 2019. https://americanlibrariesmagazine.org/2019/04/23/keep-library-workers-safe/.

Corrado, Edward M. "Low Morale and Burnout in Libraries." *Technical Services Quarterly* 39, no. 1 (2002): 37–48. https://doi.org/10.1080/07317131.2021.2011149.

Crawford, Joanne O., Danielle Berkovic, Jo Erwin, Sarah M. Copsey, Alice Davis, Evanthia Giagloglou, Amin Yazdani, Jan Hartvigsen, Richard Graveling, and Anthony Woolf. "Musculoskeletal Health in the Workplace." *Best Practice and Research: Clinical Rheumatology* 34, no. 5 (October 2020): article 101558. https://doi.org/10.1016/j.berh.2020.101558.

De Been, Iris, and Marion Beijer. "The Influence of Office Type on Satisfaction and Perceived Productivity Support." *Journal of Facilities Management* 12, no. 2 (2014): 142–57. https://doi.org/10.1108/JFM-02-2013-0011.

Di Blasio, Sonja, Louena Shtrepi, Giuseppina Emma Puglisi, and Arianna Astolfi. "A Cross-sectional Survey on the Impact of Irrelevant Speech Noise on Annoyance, Mental Health and Well-Being, Performance and Occupants' Behavior in Shared and Open-Plan Offices." *International Journal of Environmental Research and Public Health* 16, no. 2 (2019): 280. https://doi.org/10.3390/ijerph16020280.

Dixon, Jennifer A. "Feeling the Burnout: Library Workers Are Facing Burnout in Greater Numbers and Severity—and Grappling with It as a Systemic Problem." *Library Journal*, March 2022. EBSCOhost Academic Search Premier.

Ettarh, Fobazi, and Chris Vidas. "The Future of Libraries: Vocational Awe in a 'Post-COVID' World." *Serials Librarian* 82, no. 1–4 (2022): 17–22. https://doi.org/10.1080/0361526x.2022.2028501.

European Agency for Safety and Health at Work. *Conversation Starters for Workplace Discussions about Musculoskeletal Disorders: An EU-OSHA Resource for Workplaces*. Birmingham, UK: Royal Society for the Prevention of Accidents, 2019. https://osha.europa.eu/sites/default/files/Conversation_starters.pdf.

Ewen, Lara. "Quitting Time." *American Libraries*, June 1, 2022. https://americanlibrariesmagazine.org/2022/06/01/quitting-time/.

Felgueiras, Fatima, Liliana Cunha, Zenaida Mourão, André Moreira, and Marta F. Gabriel. "A Systematic Review of Environmental Intervention Studies in Offices with Beneficial Effects on Workers' Health, Well-Being and Productivity." *Atmospheric Pollution Research* 13, no. 9 (2022): article 101513. https://doi.org/10.1016/j.apr.2022.101513.

Florida Department of Education, Office of Educational Facilities. *State Requirements for Educational Facilities, 2014.* Tallahassee, FL: Office of Educational Facilities, November 4, 2014. https://www.fldoe.org/core/fileparse.php/7738/urlt/srefrule14.pdf.

Forooraghi, Melina, Antonio Cobaleda-Cordero, and Maral Babapour Chafi. "A Healthy Office and Healthy Employees: A Longitudinal Case Study with a Salutogenic Perspective in the Context of the Physical Office Environment." *Building Research and Information* 50, no. 1–2 (2022): 134–51. https://doi.org/10.1080/09613218.2021.1983753.

Forooraghi, Melina, Elke Miedema, Nina Ryd, and Holger Wallbaum. "Scoping Review of Health in Office Design Approaches." *Journal of Corporate Real Estate* 22, no. 2 (2020): 155–80. https://doi.org/10.1108/JCRE-08-2019-0036.

Gagnon, Louis, Stephanie Gagnon, and Jessica Lloyd. "Social Distancing Causally Impacts the Spread of SARS-CoV-2: A U.S. Nationwide Event Study." *BMC Infectious Diseases* 22, no. 1 (2022): article 787. https://doi.org/10.1186/s12879-022-07763-y.

Haans, Antal. "The Natural Preference in People's Appraisal of Light." *Journal of Environmental Psychology* 39 (September 2014): 51–61. https://doi.org/https://doi.org/10.1016/j.jenvp.2014.04.001.

Hafeez, Iqra, Yingjun Zhu, Saba Hafeez, Rafiq Mansoor, and Khaliq U. Rehman. "Impact of Workplace Environment on Employee Performance: Mediating Role of Employee Health." *Business Management and Education* 17, no. 2 (2019): 173–93. https://doi.org/10.3846/bme.2019.10379.

Hähn, Nalise, Emmanuel Essah, and Tijuana Blanusa. "Biophilic Design and Office Planting: A Case Study of Effects on Perceived Health, Well-Being and Performance Metrics in the Workplace." *Intelligent Buildings International* 13 no. 4 (2020): 241–60. https://doi.org/10.1080/17508975.2020.1732859.

Head, Allison. *Planning and Designing Academic Library Learning Spaces: Expert Perspectives of Architects, Librarians, and Library Consultants.* Project Information Literacy, 2016. https://projectinfolit.org/pubs/library-space-study/pil_libspace-study_2016-12-06.pdf.

International WELL Building Institute. "WELL Building Standard." Accessed December 27, 2022. https://standard.wellcertified.com/well.

Juniper, Bridget, Patricia Bellamy, and Nicola White. "Evaluating the Well-Being of Public Library Workers." *Journal of Librarianship and Information Science* 44, no. 2 (June 2012): 108–17. https://doi.org/10.1177/0961000611426442.

Katopol, Patricia. "Enough Already: Compassion Fatigue." *Library Leadership and Management* 30, no. 2 (2015): 1–5. https://llm.corejournals.org/llm/article/view/7177.

Kellert, Stephen R., and Elizabeth F. Calabrese. "The Practice of Biophilic Design." 2015. http://www.biophilic-design.com.

Kropman, Daan, Rianne Appel-Meulenbroek, Lisanne Bergefurt, and Pascale LeBlanc. "The Business Case for a Healthy Office: A Holistic Overview of Relations between Office Workspace Design and Mental Health." *Ergonomics* 66, no. 5 (2023): 658–75. https://doi.org/10.1080/00140139.2022.2108905.

McCoy, Janetta Mithell, and Gary W. Evans. "Physical Work Environment." In *Handbook of Work Stress*, edited by Julian Barling, E. Kevin Kelloway, and Michael R. Frone, 219–45. Thousand Oaks, CA: SAGE, 2005.

Mills, Peter R., Susannah C. Tomkins, and Luc J. M. Schlangen. "The Effect of High Correlated Colour Temperature Office Lighting on Employee Wellbeing and Work Performance." *Journal of Circadian Rhythms* 5 (2007): article 2. https://doi.org/10.1186/1740-3391-5-2.

Mital, Anil, James D. McGlothlin, and Hamid F. Faard. "Noise in Multiple-Workstation Open-Plan Computer Rooms: Measurements and Annoyance." *Journal of Human Ergology* 21, no. 1 (1992): 69–82. https://doi.org/10.11183/jhe1972.21.69.

National Institute of Building Sciences. "Office." Last modified December 3, 2019. https://wbdg.org/space-types/office.

———. "Whole Building Design Guide." Last modified 2022. https://www.wbdg.org/.

Newman, Bobbi L. *Fostering Wellness in the Workplace: A Handbook for Libraries.* Chicago: ALA Editions, 2022.

Nichols, Jerry, and Rebekkah Smith Aldrich. *Handbook for Library Trustees of New York State*, 2018 ed. Bellport, NY: Suffolk Cooperative Library System, 2018. https://niogatrustees.org/handbook/Handbook%20for%20Library%20Trustees%20of%20New%20York%20State%20-%202018%20edition.pdf.

Norouzianpour, Hirbod. "Architectural Interventions to Mitigate Occupational Stress among Office Workers." *Enquiry* 17, no. 2 (2020): 21–40. https://doi.org/10.17831/enq:arcc.v16i2.1069.

Occupational Safety and Health Administration. *Training Requirements in OSHA Standards.* US Department of Labor, 2015. https://www.osha.gov/sites/default/files/publications/osha2254.pdf.

Oud, Joanne. "Systemic Workplace Barriers for Academic Librarians with Disabilities." *College and Research Libraries* 80, no. 2 (March 2019): 169–94. https://doi.org/10.5860/crl.80.2.169.

Pejtersen, Jan, Henrik Brohus, Carl Erik Hyldgaard, Jan Bach Nielsen, Ole Valbjorn, Pernille Hauschildt, Soren K. Kjaergaard, and Peder Wolkoff. "Effect of Renovating an Office Building on Occupants' Comfort and Health." *Indoor Air* 11, no. 1 (March 2001): 10–25. https://doi.org/10.1034/j.1600-0668.2001.011001010.x.

Peters, Terri, and Kristen D'Penna. "Biophilic Design for Restorative University Learning Environments: A Critical Review of Literature and Design Recommendations." *Sustainability* 12, no. 17 (2020): article 7064. https://doi.org/10.3390/su12177064.

Poursafar, Zara, Lewlyn L. R. Rodrigues, and K. V. Sriram. "Architectural Design Model for Office Interior to Suit Personality Types and to Enhance Productivity." *International Journal of Recent Technology and Engineering* 8, no. 2 (2019): 1916–21. https://www.doi.org/10.35940/ijrte.B1855.078219.

Price, Sallyann. "2022 Library Design Showcase." *American Libraries,* September/October 2022. https://americanlibrariesmagazine.org/2022/09/01/2022-library-design-showcase/.

Rathbun-Grubb, Susan. "Voices of Strength: A Survey of Librarians Working with Chronic Illnesses or Conditions." *Journal of Library Administration* 61, no. 1 (2021): 42–57. https://doi.org/10.1080/01930826.2020.1845546.

Robertson, Guy. "Emergency Management Training for Your Library: The Joys of Tabletopping." *Feliciter* 60, no. 1 (2014): 30–35. EBSCOhost Academic Search Premier.

Robinson, Ben. "No Holds Barred: Policing and Security in the Public Library." *In the Library with the Lead Pipe,* December 11, 2019. https://www.inthelibrarywiththeleadpipe.org/2019/no-holds-barred/.

Roskams, Michael, and Barry Haynes. "Environmental Demands and Resources: A Framework for Understanding the Physical Environment for Work." *Facilities* 39, no. 9–10 (2021): 652–66, https://doi.org/10.1108/F-07-2020-0090.

Salau, Odunayo, Rowland Worlu, Adewale Osibanjo, Anthonia Adeniji, Hezekiah Falola, Maxwell Olokundun, Stephen Ibidunni, Tolulope Atolagbe, Joy Dirisu, and Opeyemi Ogueyungbo. "The Impact of Workplace Environments on Retention Outcomes of Public Universities in Southern Nigeria." *SAGE Open* 10, no. 2 (2020). https://doi.org/10.1177/2158244020930767.

Schlipf, Fred, and John A. Moorman. *The Practical Handbook of Library Architecture: Creating Building Spaces That Work.* Chicago: ALA Editions, 2018.

Schwab, Katharine. "What Is Biophilic Design and Can It Really Make You Happier and Healthier?" Fast Company, April 11, 2019. https://www.fastcompany.com/90333072/what-is-biophilic-design-and-can-it-really-make-you-happier-and-healthier.

Seddigh, Aram, Erik Berntson, Christina Bodin Danielson, and Hugo Westerlund. "Concentration Requirements Modify the Effect of Office Type on Indicators of Health and Performance." *Journal of Environmental Psychology* 38 (June 2014): 167–74. https://doi.org/https://doi.org/10.1016/j.jenvp.2014.01.009.

Shupe, Ellen I., Stephanie K. Wambaugh, and Reed J. Bramble. "Role-Related Stress Experienced by Academic Librarians." *Journal of Academic Librarianship* 41, no. 3 (May 2015): 264–69. https://doi.org/10.1016/j.acalib.2015.03.016.

Smith, Andrew, and Michael Pitt. "Sustainable Workplaces and Building User Comfort and Satisfaction." *Journal of Corporate Real Estate* 13, no. 3 (2011): 144–56. https://doi.org/10.1108/14630011111170436.

Steinfeld, Edward, and Jordana L. Maisel. *Universal Design: Creating Inclusive Environments.* Hoboken, NJ: Wiley, 2012. ProQuest Ebook Central.

US Department of Labor, Office of Disability Employment Policy home page. Accessed April 28, 2023. https://www.dol.gov/agencies/odep.

US Environmental Protection Agency. *Guide to Air Cleaners in the Home,* 2nd ed. July 2018. https://www.epa.gov/sites/default/files/2018-07/documents/guide_to_air_cleaners_in_the_home_2nd_edition.pdf.

———. *Indoor Air Facts No. 4 (revised): Sick Building Syndrome.* February 1991. https://www.epa.gov/sites/default/files/2014-08/documents/sick_building_factsheet.pdf.

———. "Indoor Air Quality: What Are the Trends in Indoor Air Quality and Their Effects on Human Health?" Last modified September 7, 2021. https://www.epa.gov/report-environment/indoor-air-quality.

———. "Introduction to Indoor Air Quality." Last modified December 5, 2022. https://www.epa.gov/indoor-air-quality-iaq/introduction-indoor-air-quality.

———. *An Office Building Occupant's Guide to Indoor Air Quality.* Office of Air and Radiation. October 1997. https://www.epa.gov/sites/default/files/2014-08/documents/occupants_guide.pdf.

———. "Sources of Indoor Particulate Matter." Last modified December 12, 2022. https://www.epa.gov/indoor-air-quality-iaq/sources-indoor-particulate-matter-pm.

US Green Building Council. "Mission and Vision." Accessed January 6, 2023. https://www.usgbc.org/about/mission-vision.

Valančius, Rokas, and Andrius Jurelionis. "Influence of Indoor Air Temperature Variation on Office Work Performance." *Journal of Environmental Engineering and Landscape Management* 21, no. 1 (2013): 19–25. https://doi.org/10.3846/16486897.2012.721371.

Vischer, Jacqueline C. "The Effects of the Physical Environment on Job Performance: Towards a Theoretical Model of Workspace Stress." *Stress and Health* 23, no. 3 (August 2007): 175–84. https://doi.org/10.1002/smi.1134.

WBDG Accessible Committee, Jordana L. Maisel, and Molly Ranahan. "Beyond Accessibility to Universal Design." Whole Building Design Guide. Last modified April 29, 2022. https://www.wbdg.org/design-objectives/accessible/beyond-accessibility-universal-design.

Wolf, J., A. Prüss-Ustün, I. Ivanov, S. Mudgal, C. Corvalán, R. Bos, M. Neira. *Preventing Disease through a Healthier and Safer Workplace.* Geneva, Switzerland: World Health Organization, 2018. https://www.who.int/publications/i/item/9789241513777.

World Health Organization, *WHO Global Air Quality Guidelines: Particulate Matter (PM$_{2.5}$ and PM$_{10}$), Ozone, Nitrogen Dioxide, Sulphur Dioxide, and Carbon Monoxide*. Geneva, Switzerland: World Health Organization, 2021. https://apps.who.int/iris/bitstream/handle/10665/345329/9789240034228-eng.pdf.

———. *WHO Guidelines for Indoor Air Quality: Dampness and Mould*. Edited by Elisabeth Heseltine and Jerome Rosen. Copenhagen, Denmark: World Health Organization, 2009. https://iris.who.int/bitstream/handle/10665/164348/9789289041683-eng.pdf.

Flexible Work Arrangements

CHAPTER 15

The New Normal

An Empirical Examination of Remote Work in Academic Libraries

Lisa Kallman Hopkins, Andria F. Schwegler, Rebecca L. Hopkins, and Bridgit McCafferty

Trust and communication are crucial factors for successful leadership and workplace relationships. When organizational trust is established, outcomes include greater focus on productive tasks, commitment to the organization, intention to remain with the organization, and compliance with the organization's strategic plan.[1] Communication is critical in trust-building for any relationship, especially between leadership and coworkers. This is particularly true in remote working situations, where a lack of social interaction and support, coupled with the unique challenges of supervisory monitoring, may increase chances for miscommunication and feelings of isolation. This chapter investigates the relationship between organizational trust and a library employee's need satisfaction, efficacy, and intention to remain in the job, in relation to the ability to choose one's work modality.

Since the 1980s, digital technology has made remote work—also known as telework, e-working, work from home, telecommuting, alternative work location, mobile work, and flexible workplace—an increasingly attractive alternative for many knowledge workers. It offers a myriad of benefits, including flexibility and cost savings for both employees and employers, increased productivity, as well as improved recruitment and retention of staff.[2] In their examination of approximately 6.5 million documents generated over the past twenty years relating to flexible working arrangements (FWAs), of which remote work is a subset, Amirul and Shaari found the overwhelming consensus to be that FWAs have a positive relationship with work-life balance, employee health and happiness, and productivity.[3] Despite this significant amount of research on the subject, until recently there was little focus on how librarians and other information professionals engage with remote work.[4] This lack of information changed in 2020 when the COVID-19 pandemic and its concomitant nationwide stay-at-home orders provided the unique opportunity to examine the rapid shift to remote work for what were traditionally in-person, patron-serving organizations. Many scholars have leveraged this opportunity to research the impact flexible work modalities have on academic libraries, one such in-person, patron-serving organization.

Almost twenty years ago, Robertson wrote about the possible impact of a catastrophic pandemic on libraries, predicting a shift to electronic devices, wireless systems, and conference calls to continue providing services and remain effective.[5] As Robertson envisioned, the COVID-19 pandemic mandated hurried and radical response throughout society, and libraries experienced dramatic shifts in workplace locations, methodology, and organizational structure. Now three years since the start of the pandemic, many of these changes have become permanent, facilitated by advances in accessibility to electronic resources, workplace communication technology, team collaboration tools, and shifting expectations. Frederick and Wolff-Eisenberg surveyed library directors in the Ithaka S+R US Library Survey in 2020, reporting that more than half of responding academic library directors anticipated the need to allow library workers to continue to work from home after the pandemic.[6] In other words, the genie is out of the bottle, and remote work for library workers is here to stay. This new reality impacts library policies, workflows, and programming, and many libraries must re-examine the hastily constructed organizational conditions, work structures, and managerial expectations to support library workers while working remotely. Libraries need to transition from an emergency reaction and make-do frame of mind to implementing an intentional, carefully planned infrastructure that utilizes the myriad tools currently available to leverage the benefits of remote work.

This chapter will contribute to the unfolding literature and the patterns that have begun to present themselves by discussing the qualities of academic libraries that contribute to creating effective remote work contexts by answering two foundational questions: (1) How are academic libraries incorporating remote work since the COVID-19 pandemic? and (2) How is remote work related to communication and perceptions of trust and satisfaction in the workplace?

Literature Review
Work Modality—Working from Home

Millions of Americans were sent home to work in March 2020 as state governors issued stay-at-home orders to slow the spread of the novel coronavirus disease 2019 (COVID-19). Though a few states began reopening by the end of April 2020, some states remained on lockdown through June 2021.[7] Few sectors of the economy were spared the impact of this sudden change. Individuals who never dreamed of working from home found themselves scrambling to transform spare rooms and kitchen tables into home offices. In January 2021, the National Council on Compensation Insurance, citing the US Census Bureau and Bureau of Labor Statistics, stated that before the pandemic 6 percent of employed individuals worked primarily from home, and three-quarters of Americans had never worked from home. By May 2020, 35 percent of employed individuals reported working from home in the prior four weeks.[8]

This abrupt adaptation transformed expectations and upended norms across the labor force. One of the most profound outcomes of the stay-at-home orders was the realization that FWAs, specifically working from home, were not only possible, but were beneficial—for both employee and employer. Kelliher and Anderson observed that knowledge workers who worked remotely reported enhanced concentration on individual tasks, better work-life balance, an appreciation of fewer distractions and commutes, and overall seemed "more satisfied with their job, more committed to their organizations, and experienced less stress linked to day-to-day demands of the office."[9] According to Antonacopoulou and Georgiadou, the pandemic created the opportunity for "radical rethinking" about how and where work can be accomplished and the meaningfulness of work maintained and sustained. They wrote, "There is ample evidence that working remotely (e.g., from home) is working well, to the extent that it entrusts 'workers' to deliver the allocated tasks without being monitored," and it frees these same workers from the surveillance of targets meant to measure productivity and performance.[10]

Remote Work in Libraries

While FWAs, in the form of flexible shifts, compressed workweeks, job sharing, and, to some extent telecommuting, had been explored in academic libraries prior to the pandemic, the scant research available prior to 2020 reveals it was not a widespread experience for most library workers.[11] Green distributed two post-pandemic surveys that together provide unique and valuable insights about the paradigm shift in academic library work conditions. The first survey was distributed in July 2021 and sought librarians' expectations regarding material acquisitions, remote work arrangements, and staffing in the areas of resource description and discovery. The second survey, investigating librarians' work modality options and preferences, was distributed in October 2022. The earlier survey revealed an estimated 96 percent of survey respondents felt their duties could be performed either fully or partially remotely,[12] an insight gleaned during the work-from-home requirement the previous year. The second survey revealed that the "academic library segment of the U.S. workforce is among those that have adopted hybrid work modalities on a regular basis."[13] Green's pair of studies signal a new direction in academic librarians' practices, preferences, and which jobs they believed can be accomplished from home.[14]

To accommodate the realization that remote work is a logical and viable option for academic librarians, research is needed to inform practices in how this work can be effectively carried out. Adapting a remote work definition from Illegems and Verbeke as "an arrangement in which a librarian works from home or a satellite location outside of the main office/campus for at least one full day a week,"[15] Hickey and Tang provide practical coaching for academic librarians who are remote workers, remote supervisors, or supervising a remote worker.[16] They insist "developing an effective communication strategy that allows you to listen actively and respond authentically is key to building trust" in a remote supervisory situation.[17] Going forward, remote work provides an "opportunity to develop excellence in an environment where our students, faculty, and staff are increasingly geographically distributed" and allows libraries to be "leaders in the use of technology in the context of higher education."[18] Similarly, Hosoi, Reiter, and Zabel conducted interviews with leaders of academic libraries in fall 2020, finding that many respondents acknowledged the reality, based on their experience during the COVID-19 pandemic, that "most library work does not require physical presence," and flexible work will be an expectation rather than an exception that will significantly impact future recruitment and retention of library workers.[19] Circulation manager Obenauf discussed the challenges, benefits, and practical solutions of working remotely while managing on-site employees, emphasizing these critical variables for success: the use of tools, such as cloud-based drives for resource sharing (e.g., Outlook or Google), productivity platforms (e.g., Slack or Trello), videoconferencing software (e.g., Zoom, WebEx, or Microsoft Teams), and traditional communication tools (e.g., phone and e-mail), as well as trusting staff to know and do their jobs.[20] Gentry asserts that technology exists to make remote work feasible for library workers, but libraries have been "reluctant to embrace telework, citing a need for employees to be with library collections."[21] However, FWAs—including those with remote work options—do not preclude this desire, especially with the increasing number of digital collections.

Overall, the studies cited above investigated most areas of the library, including circulation, reference and instruction, technical services, and digital collections. The results support remote working at least part time, and now, three years after library employees experienced the ability to work from home, many want to hold onto it—and with good reason. Green found that the employees who prefer remote work claim it benefits the areas of their life that matter most, including their "physical, mental and economic wellbeing, as well as their productivity and quality of life."[22]

Agency in Choosing Work Modality

Many studies, both pre- and post-pandemic, examine the importance of allowing workers to choose their preferred work modality. In their systematic review of FWAs across a variety of job types since the 1970s, De Menezes and Killiher observed that remote working may have a positive impact on worker performance—but only when the worker has a positive perception about remote working.[23] In other words, it is the *availability* of FWAs, regardless of whether the employee takes advantage of them, that is related to job satisfaction, organizational commitment, and indirectly to job performance.[24] Choudhury insists employees should have the ability to choose their work modality, citing a 2015 finding by Nicholas Bloom:

> When employees opted in to [work from home (WFH)] policies, their productivity increased by 13%. When, nine months later, the same workers were given a choice between remaining at home and returning to the office, those who chose the former saw even further improvements: They were 22% more productive than they had been before the experiment. This suggests that people should probably determine for themselves the situation (home or office) that fits them best.[25]

Waizenegger and colleagues explored how the requirement to work from home due to COVID-19 affected team collaboration.[26] They evaluated the effect of *everybody* working from home and uncovered some surprising findings—namely, that teams were able to use technological means to collaborate and achieve their team goals, and businesses realized increased productivity, reduced communication barriers, and integrated remote e-workers.[27] The study celebrated productivity, collaboration, successful communication, and connectivity, but it did not examine the well-being of individuals who would not have wanted to work from home had the pandemic not been a threat. Though these employees did not have much choice during the COVID-19 pandemic, the emergency pivot to remote work was nonetheless associated with positive outcomes for them—perhaps as a favored alternative to unemployment or illness.

Now that the COVID-19 virus is endemic in the population, Green urges academic library deans or directors to support remote work *if desired by the employee*, observing that many libraries will operate in a hybrid model, with "some employees working fully remotely, some fully on site, and many working somewhere in between, depending on the nature of the employee's work and the employee's work modality preference."[28] Green emphasizes that the choice itself is important, because "such empowerment can boost employee morale, productivity, and wellbeing."[29] Employees who are offered the chance to engage in remote work and other FWAs feel fortunate, trusted, and supported, making them more likely to feel loyalty toward the organization.[30]

Employee-Organization Relationship Impacted by Work Modality

Charalampous and colleagues engaged in a rigorous, systematic review of remote working research to answer this question: "Does e-working remotely link to knowledge workers' work-related well-being, and if so, how is the link different to each of the work-related well-being's dimensions (i.e., affective, social, cognitive, professional, and psychosomatic)?"[31] They identified more than 3,000 peer-reviewed, English language articles published between 1995 and 2017 about knowledge employees who were e-working remotely. The final sixty-three eligible studies involved 37,553 individuals and provided some practical implications: namely, that a "sense of trust [that an] individual will appropriately conduct their work duties outside an office environment can increase [their] loyalty and organizational commitment." They further argued that "good communications between remote e-workers and their office-based colleagues needs to be encouraged."[32] As a result, the importance of building trust in the organization via open communication and fostering employees' autonomy, relatedness, and competence (concepts from self-determination theory) are critical variables in need of further investigation as they relate to remote work.

COGNITIVE AND AFFECTIVE TRUST IN SUPERVISORS, SUBORDINATES, AND COWORKERS

In their seminal work, Mayer, Davis, and Schoorman defined trust as "the willingness of a party to be vulnerable to the actions of another party based on the expectation that the other will perform a particular action important to the trustor, irrespective of the ability to monitor or control that other party."[33] In their discussion of "trickle-up" leadership, Fulmer and Ostroff define trust in leadership as "a psychological state of willingness to accept vulnerability based on positive expectations of a leader that derive in part from trustworthiness perceptions."[34] Trust in leadership is related to positive outcomes in attitudes, behaviors, and employee performance.[35] Yang and Mossholder stress the importance of interactions between supervisor and subordinate for "motivating and energizing positive work behavior," stating further that

> affective trust [based on socioemotional elements for interpersonal interactions] in management and affective trust in supervisor significantly predicted affective organizational commitment, and a combination of cognitive trust [based on salient characteristics for task-related interactions] in management and affective trust in supervisor was predictive of employees' overall job satisfaction.[36]

Trust matters a great deal to employees and should be treated as essential by those in leadership roles.

One of the most important indicators of employee trust in both top management and immediate supervisor is the amount of information received. Ellis and Shockley-Zalabak urge leaders to "consciously think about the frequency of their messages" and how that information is delivered.[37] Fulmer and Ostroff echoed this need for communication to facilitate trust in management, observing that trust can be cultivated throughout the organization through positive interactions with leaders.[38] Perceptions of support and "interpersonal justice" help to develop trust in supervisors and impact one's commitment to the organization.[39] Jaiswal and colleagues wrote extensively about organizational trust and its significant impact on remote employee performance, stating: "It is crucial for leaders and managers to be the torchbearers for enhancing the trust of employees in the telework context."[40]

TRUST DURING REMOTE WORK

Organizational trust, especially trust in leadership and between coworkers, is critical in a remote working situation. Over twenty years ago, Raghuram and colleagues wrote about trust and communication for virtual employees, observing that it is not enough to provide virtual employees with laptops and "set them free into a virtual work mode"; they must also be provided with an opportunity to connect with one another, and trust must be generated through trust-building activities and ensuring social connections and communication in order to bridge distance.[41] In her 2001 article "Building Trust and Collaboration in a Virtual Team," Holton agrees that "trust develops through frequent and meaningful interaction," and that creating trust with remote workers is a challenge that an increasing number of organizational leaders will face.[42] The themes of two-way trust and effective communication to build trust should not be underestimated as they come up again and again in the literature, beginning with Amirul and Shaari's history of FWAs.[43]

Despite the importance of trust in an organization, supervisors may struggle to trust employees who are not working in the same modality as they are. In their article "Remote Managers Are Having Trust Issues," Parker, Knight, and Keller warn that a worker who is being micromanaged will feel mistrusted, which will lower their perception that they are performing their job well. They urge supervisors to manage remote workers by results (work outputs) versus when and how they work (inputs).[44] Zorc frames this as "measuring deliverables, not hours."[45] Other ways to establish trust with remote employees include employee onboarding, team projects, allowing workers to choose work modality, expecting cameras to be on during virtual meetings, daily group stand-ups, and dress standards.[46]

Munir and colleagues observed that the need for trust in remote work is not limited to leadership, because when coworkers cannot observe each other's actions, they must rely on trust to combat doubt and suspicion.[47] As a result, trust based on relationships established while employees were in person together may not be sustained when working remotely.[48] Grant, Wallace, and Spurgeon noted both that communication and support from colleagues were critical factors to ensure successful remote working, and building trust and a strong relationship with management often coincided with the perception that they were performing well in their job.[49] In their unique study about mistrust, Lanaj and colleagues examined the impact of mistrust—which they define as "negative expectations about others' intentions and behavior"—on employees' resources and behaviors.[50] They found that trust and communication between coworkers is important in helping them navigate uncertainty and share information.

Communication

Communication is a consistent theme in the literature that is positively associated with organizational trust and psychological safety ("the belief that the workplace is safe for interpersonal risk taking"[51]) in the workplace. However, effective means to promote and engage in supportive and informative communication in an organization that includes remote work have yet to be fully determined. Employers and employees are still learning *how* to communicate when colleagues are remote or working in a combination of remote and on-site roles. They are also learning how to translate common communication types, from social or water-cooler talk to one-to-one or group meetings to formats that make sense in remote work contexts.

Research reveals communication challenges associated with remote work. On a survey about work modality preferences administered in October 2022, Green noted that participants who preferred on-site work when remote work was available cited communication-related reasons, including the perception that they miss out on workplace conversations when they are remote.[52] To address these challenges, for remote workers to feel connected, there need to be trust-building activities and a high level of social communication.[53] Trust develops through frequent and meaningful interactions, where people can share their individual insights and concerns.[54]

Communication from supervisors or top leadership is critical, and developing an effective communication strategy[55] that allows active listening and authenticity is the key to building two-way trust.[56] Receiving constructive and positive communication from managers and leaders strengthens trust in management. As a result, in alternative work modalities, supervisors must find a way to reveal their true selves to subordinates through computer-mediated means.[57] Managerial communication must convey managers' clear expectations and express appreciation and encouragement.[58] To do so, technology and communication tools, also known as information communication tools (ICT), can be leveraged to simulate a team environment virtually,[59] as frequent and effective use of ICT is a key to reducing negative consequences of remote working.[60]

Expectedly, interaction patterns using ICT differ from in-person communication. In their study "Together, Apart: Communication Dynamics among Academic Librarians during the COVID-19 Pandemic," Nash and colleagues found that 51 percent of respondents felt less connected as a result of their move to remote work, and 37 percent reported that the shift to remote work had a negative effect on the communication dynamics of their teams.[61] In their study on social talk and remote collegiality during the pandemic, Bleakely and colleagues found that casual conversation facilitates collaboration and leads to increased job satisfaction.[62] They further observed that videoconferencing for social talk and workplace communication can be effective but may be more formal than natural face-to-face conversations (speakers tend to interrupt each other less frequently on videoconferencing), body language and behavioral cues are harder to navigate, and folks may multitask while they are on a video call in a way they would not in person. Because videoconferencing is almost always planned and social talk is usually spontaneous, instant messaging is often used to find availability for social video conference calls, bridging the gap.[63]

Though the decrease in informal, impromptu communication between colleagues can lead to a sense of isolation, which has long-term effects on commitment and loyalty to the organization, this decline is not inevitable.[64] Social calls via ICT can be planned, and hybrid communication techniques that mix face-to-face meetings, which promote team cohesion and achieve efficient planning and goal setting, with "high virtuality tools" for "action team processes" have been demonstrated as effective.[65] These strategies are important for gathering and conveying information, and failure to find adequate means to effectively do so when people are on-site, remote, or hybrid can be detrimental to the organization. Ellis and Shockley-Zalabak found that timely and clear dissemination of a broad range of organizational and job-related information—such as "how employees are evaluated, how decisions that affect employees are made, organizational policies, pay and benefits, promotion and advancement opportunities, and long-term strategies of the organization"—is an important variable strongly related to trust in both upper leadership and direct supervisors.[66] Raghuram and colleagues assert that distance can be bridged through trust and organizational connectedness "by insuring that virtual workers remain connected with respect to important information that may affect their careers."[67]

Taken together, online communication, time management, and trust-building practices will take the place of direct observation in the supervision of remote workers, but it requires training and a shift in the way supervision has always been done.[68] Employees must take responsibility, as well, to remain vigilant in communicating with their supervisors to compensate for fewer face-to-face interactions when working remotely.[69] This increased responsibility respects employees' autonomy and ability to exercise control over their work conditions, qualities that are positively associated with work outcomes.

Job Autonomy and Satisfaction

In their influential work *Intrinsic Motivation and Self-Determination in Human Behavior,* Deci and Ryan defined self-determination theory as a theory of motivation that is concerned with intrinsic motivation, or the "innate, natural propensity to engage one's interests and exercise one's capacities" and the harmful effects of extrinsic motivation, rewards, or controls.[70] *When applied within work situations, Deci and Ryan suggest that increasing self-determination in work entails welcomes individuals' qualities such as creativity, independence, autonomy, and flexibility.*[71] Chiniara and Bentein further this by stating that individuals want to fulfill their "innate psychological needs for autonomy, competence and relatedness… deemed essential… for functioning and actualizing their full potential and growth." They further argue that leaders can build trustworthy relationships by creating a "psychologically safe and fair climate where employees strongly feel they can be themselves, make their own decisions, and feel connected with others."[72]

Austin-Egole, Iheriohanma, and Nwokorie used self-determination theory as the framework for their study in how the employee-driven and employer-driven FWA affect employees' level of commitment and performance. They determined that employees who choose FWA, especially when it is employee-driven and "designed to aid the work-life balance," are often "well-motivated, self-sufficient, self-disciplined, well-organized and good communicators, hence they tend to generate higher performance."[73] They urge employers to find ways to support FWAs that match employers' and employees' needs, as they improve quality of life for the employee and organizational performance for the employer. In their study about job characteristics in telecommuting, Vander Elst and colleagues found that the number of days of remote work did not directly relate to work-related well-being; instead, they found that higher levels of social support, participation in decision-making, and task autonomy were directly related to well-being. Stating these findings succinctly, they concluded, "Our results seem to suggest that not the extent of telecommuting, but rather the way in which the job—including telecommuting—is characterized (e.g., level of autonomy, contact with colleagues), is predictive of employee well-being."[74]

Objectives

The goals of this research are to examine the availability of remote work in academic libraries, perceptions of efficacy of remote work, and working relationships in the context of remote work. Given the literature described above, it is predicted that library employees will want access to remote work options and perceive them as effective given experience with remote work during the pandemic. Work characteristics of communication and trust among colleagues will be associated with higher levels of satisfaction, psychological safety, and intention to remain in the current job. Further, those working remotely are expected to have higher levels of trust in their organizations than those not working remotely. This study will also investigate reasons why jobs include remote work, assess challenges libraries face with remote work, and examine communication mediums employees use on the job. Results of this research can be used to inform working conditions in libraries to support remote work, and library administrators may use this information to make recommendations for workplace improvements.

Method
Participants

A total of 334 librarians consented to participate in the study, but 20 responses were removed because participants completed less than 15 percent of the survey. The final sample included 314 librarians who held positions as professional librarians ($n = 264$, 84.08%), other professionals ($n = 29$, 9.24%), and paraprofessionals ($n = 21$, 6.69%). Respondents ranged in age from 22 to 89 years with a mean of 44 years. The majority of the sample was White ($n = 236$, 75.16%) and identified as female ($n = 235$, 74.84%), with 31 identifying as male (9.87%) and 7 identifying as other genders (2.23%).

The majority of the sample worked in university or college libraries ($n = 294$, 93.63%), with the rest at community colleges ($n = 18$, 5.73%) or other academic libraries ($n = 2$, .64%). The structural model that best described the library in which participants worked included flat ($n = 47$, 14.97%), hierarchical ($n = 236$, 75.16%), task-oriented ($n = 21$, 6.69%), and other ($n = 10$, 3.18%). Participants' years in their current job ranged from 1 to 40, with the average time in their current position as 7.89 ($SD = 8.10$) years with 4.04 ($SD = 4.12$) years reporting to their current supervisor, ranging from 0 to 30 years. Over half the sample ($n = 175$, 55.73%) had supervisory responsibilities over other employees.

Materials
WORK MODALITY

In addition to the reported demographic and work role variables, participants indicated availability of remote work for their position, their supervisor's position, and their subordinates' positions if they were a supervisor. Those who did not have remote work available for their position indicated whether they wanted to work remotely on a Likert-type scale ranging from 1 (*strongly disagree*) to 7 (*strongly agree*). All participants rated whether they would be as effective working remotely as in person and if the library would function as well if they worked remotely as in person from 1 (*strongly disagree*) to 7 (*strongly agree*). Participants who had remote work available reported if they were currently working remotely, how long they have worked remotely in their current position (*years, months*), how many hours per week they work remotely on average, whether their employer made accommodations to help them work remotely, and whether their job included remote work when they were hired. All participants responded to open-ended prompts about the *best parts* and *biggest challenges* of working remotely. Responses on these items were coded by three independent raters and discussed until agreement was reached. A total of 17 codes were derived from the open-ended responses and are presented in table 15.1. Finally, participants who reported their position had changed to include remote work indicated why they continued working remotely after the pandemic. Participants who were not currently working remotely explained why they were not working remotely.

Table 15.1. Codes for open-ended responses to best parts and challenges of remote work

Best Parts	Challenges
1. Don't work remote	1. Only work remote
2. Flexible time and time savings	2. Predictable schedule (Time)
3. Physical comfort/convenience at home	3. Inferior technology/office at home
4. Avoiding commute issues	4. Lack of access to on campus perks
5. Cost savings	5.
6. Meal convenience	6.
7. Increased quality of life (psychological)	7. Decreased quality of life (psychological)
8. Decreased mental health concerns	8. Increased mental health concerns
9. Improved physical health management	9. Decreased physical health management
10. Better work conditions at home	10. Better work conditions at work
11. Organizational trust for remote work	11. Lack of organizational trust for remote work
12. More focus on projects/tasks at home	12. More focus on projects/tasks at work
13. Positive norms/expectations for remote work from colleagues, students	13. Negative norms/expectations for remote work from colleagues, students
14.	14. Difficulty planning own remote work
15. Point-of-service needs online	15. Point-of-service needs in library
16.	16. Management responsibilities
17.	17. Difficulty establishing relationships with peers

COMMUNICATION

Communication medium and efficacy were measured with a scale adapted from the Cultivating Innovative Workplaces survey.[75] Participants selected how often they communicated with their supervisor, coworkers, and if applicable, subordinates (*never, quarterly, monthly, bi-weekly, weekly, 1–2 times a week, daily*). Participants then adjusted slide bars to represent the percentage, out of 100 percent, they used each of the following mediums: in-person, phone calls, videoconferencing, e-mail, mobile phone texting, workplace online chat, collaborative documents, or other. Finally, participants rated the efficacy of each medium when communicating with colleagues from 1 (*not at all effective*) to 7 (*very effective*).

PSYCHOLOGICAL SAFETY

A revised version of the Supportive Learning Environment survey assessed psychological safety.[76] This five-item measure evaluated how well each statement described participants' sense of safety in terms of speaking up about issues, talking about problems and challenges, and assurance after making mistakes from 1 (*highly inaccurate*) to 5 (*highly accurate*; Cronbach's alpha = .85). Three questions from Bolick's Cultivating Innovative Workplaces survey were adapted to examine the relationship between the participant and their supervisor regarding how well the employee felt their supervisor is satisfied with their work, understands job-related problems, and recognizes their potential from 1 (*never*) to 5 (*always*).[77]

TRUST

Trust in leadership was assessed via Yang and Mossholder's scales.[78] Participants reported perceptions of affective and cognitive trust in their supervisors, coworkers, and subordinates by indicating their level of agreement on a 5-point Likert scale ranging from 1 (*strongly disagree*) to 5 (*strongly agree*). Consistent with Yang and Mossholder's results, Cronbach's alphas indicated high reliability ranging from .92 to .96.[79]

JOB SATISFACTION AND INTENTION TO STAY

Job satisfaction was measured as the extent autonomy, competence, and relatedness needs were met,[80] rated on 7-point Likert scales from 1 (*very dissatisfied*) to 7 (*very satisfied*). Cronbach's alpha for each scale was high (autonomy .96, competence .94, relatedness .90). Participants' intention to stay in their current position was measured with the item "I intend to stay at my current job in the library" on a 7-point Likert scale, from 1 (*extremely unlikely*) to 7 (*extremely likely*).[81]

Procedure

The present study was reviewed and approved as an exempt project by the university's institutional review board. Librarians were recruited via the ALA and TLA e-mail discussion lists. The online survey was disseminated through Qualtrics from January 2023 to March 2023. Participants were provided definitions of supervisor, coworker, subordinates, and remote work (i.e., working in a physical location that is not a central location operated by your employer). At the completion of the survey, participants were thanked for participating and exited from the survey.

Results
Descriptive Statistics

Overall, participants reported high levels of cognitive and affective trust in their supervisors, subordinates, and coworkers, as all means were above the scale midpoint. Repeated measures *t* tests revealed that participants reported significantly higher cognitive trust than affective trust for subordinates and coworkers but not for supervisors (see figure 15.1).

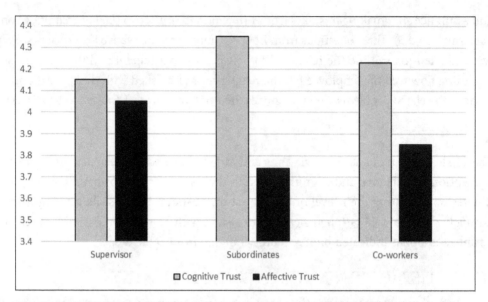

Figure 15.1. Differences in cognitive and affective trust by work group. p = .02.

A repeated measures one-way analysis of variance revealed that participants reported significantly higher autonomy need satisfaction than competence need satisfaction, and both of these measures were significantly higher than relatedness need satisfaction (see figure 15.2).

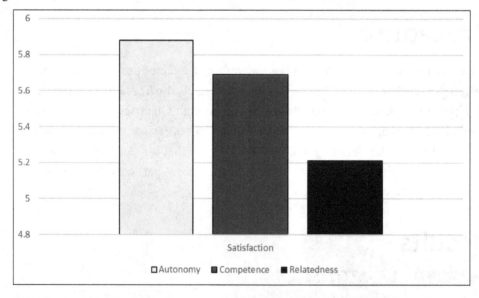

Figure 15.2. Differences in perceptions of need satisfaction

Overall, participants reported moderate levels of psychological safety ($M = 3.85$, $SD = .84$) and indicated they were likely to remain at their current job in the library ($M = 5.85$, $SD = 1.76$).

Bivariate Correlations among Study Variables

Pearson correlation coefficients among the cognitive and affective trust scales for all work groups (supervisor, subordinates, coworkers) were significant and positive. Pearson correlation coefficients among the satisfaction subscales (i.e., autonomy, competence, relatedness) were significant and positive. Psychological safety was significantly positively correlated with all trust and satisfaction scales. Intention to stay in the current job was significantly positively correlated with all study variables.

Communication

Most participants reported communicating with all work groups weekly or more frequently (see table 15.2).

Table 15.2. Rank and frequency of communication endorsed by number of participants (percentage) by work group

Rank and Frequency	Supervisor (n = 291)	Subordinates (n = 162)	Coworkers (n = 291)
1. Never	11 (3.8)	2 (1.2)	7 (2.4)
2. Quarterly	9 (3.1)	2 (1.2)	3 (1.0)
3. Monthly	23 (7.9)	4 (2.5)	12 (4.1)
4. Biweekly	31 (10.7)	10 (6.2)	20 (6.9)
5. Weekly	42 (14.4)	17 (10.5)	36 (12.4)
6. 1–2 Times a Week	78 (26.8)	35 (21.6)	64 (22.0)
7. Daily	97 (33.3)	92 (56.8)	149 (51.2)

Spearman correlation coefficients revealed that rank of communication frequency with subordinates was not related to any variables except frequency of communication with coworkers ($r = .29, p < .001, n = 162$) and supervisor ($r = .16, p = .05, n = 162$). Frequency of communication with supervisor was positively associated with relatedness need satisfaction ($r = .15, p = .01, n = 285$), psychological safety ($r = .17, p < .01, n = 291$), cognitive trust in supervisor ($r = .30, p < .001, n = 289$), affective trust in supervisor ($r = .26, p < .001, n = 289$), affective trust in coworkers ($r = .12, p = .05, n = 285$), and frequency of communication with coworkers ($r = .27, p < .001, n = 290$).

Frequency of communication with coworkers was positively associated with relatedness need satisfaction ($r = .19, p = .002, n = 285$), cognitive trust in coworkers ($r = .13, p = .03, n = 285$), affective trust in coworkers ($r = .23, p < .001, n = 285$), and intention to stay in the job ($r = .19, p < .001, n = 284$).

The largest percentage of time spent communicating in all work groups was via in-person conversations and e-mail (i.e., approximately 30% of the time each). Synchronous online tools for videoconferencing and chat were used less frequently (i.e., approximately 10–15% of the time). Participants across all groups reported using phone calls, mobile phone text messaging, and collaborative documents infrequently (i.e., less than 5% of the time). Supervisors reported spending more time in face-to-face communications and less time in video calls with subordinates than subordinates perceived they did.

When rating efficacy of communication, many participants did not rate communication types they did not use, so a one-way analysis of variance was performed on the efficacy of the most frequently used communication types. In-person communication was rated as significantly more effective than videoconferencing, e-mail, and online chat, which did not differ from each other (see figure 15.3).

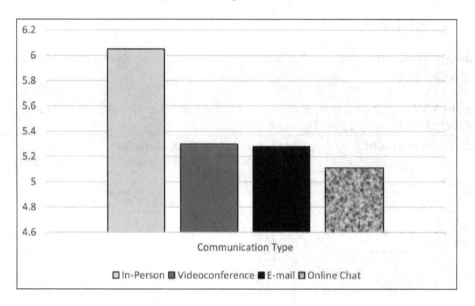

Figure 15.3. Perceived efficacy of communication type

Remote Work

Remote work at the library was available to 229 (72.93%) respondents, whereas 85 (27.07%) participants indicated it was not available to them. The groups did not differ on any study variables except autonomy need satisfaction [$M = 6.06$, $SD = 1.17$ vs. $M = 5.39$, $SD = 1.59$, $t(104.14) = -3.34$, $p = .001$, $d = .52$] and psychological safety [$M = 3.95$, $SD = .79$ vs. $M = 3.59$, $SD = .93$, $t(123.52) = -3.07$, $p = .003$, $d = .44$] with those having the ability to work remotely rating these variables significantly higher than those who did not.

LIBRARIANS WITHOUT REMOTE WORK OPTIONS.

Overall, employees who did not have remote work available somewhat agreed that they would be as effective working remotely at the library as they were working in person ($M = 4.52$, $SD = 2.33$); however, they neither agreed nor disagreed with the statement that the library would function just as well if they worked remotely as in person ($M = 3.93$, $SD = 2.33$).

Participants were grouped into those who agreed that they wanted to work remotely ($n = 51$, $M = 6.08$, $SD = .87$) and those who did not ($n = 34$, $M = 2.32$, $SD = 1.22$). Independent samples t test revealed that those who did not want to work remotely reported significantly lower scores that they would be as effective working remotely as they were in person compared to those who did want to work remotely. Those who did not want to work remotely reported significantly lower scores that the library would function just as well if they were remote compared to those who wanted to work remotely (see figure 15.4).

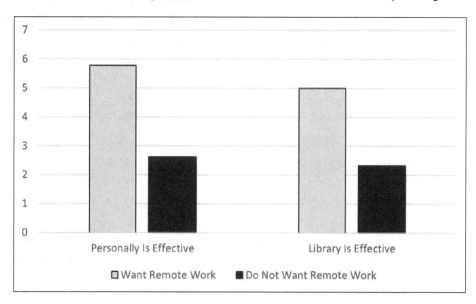

Figure 15.4. Perceptions of efficacy of remote work by preference to work remotely

For those who did not have remote work available to them, 81 participants provided a response to the open-ended prompt regarding what they believed would be the *best parts of working remotely*. These responses generated 193 codes. The most frequently reported perceived benefits were flexible time and time savings ($n = 35$, 18.13%), avoiding commute issues ($n = 32$, 16.58%), and better work conditions at home ($n = 24$, 12.44%). Physical comfort and convenience at home ($n = 18$, 9.33%) and improved quality of life working from home ($n = 18$, 9.33%) were also noted, along with cost savings ($n = 14$, 7.25%). Regarding perceptions of what would be the *biggest challenges of working remotely*, 76 participants responded, which resulted in 136 codes. The most frequently reported challenges were providing point-of-service needs in the library for both intrapersonal ($n = 28$, 20.59%) and physical objects ($n = 17$, 12.50%) in addition to concerns about negative norms and expectations associated with remote work held by colleagues and patrons ($n = 20$, 14.71%). Better work conditions at work ($n = 13$, 9.56%) and difficulty establishing relationships to fulfill both social ($n = 10$, 7.35%) and professional needs ($n = 10$, 7.35%) were also noted.

LIBRARIANS WITH REMOTE WORK OPTIONS.

Overall, employees who had remote work available to them agreed that they were as effective working remotely at the library as they were working in person ($M = 5.58$, $SD = 1.64$), and they agreed that the library functioned just as well when they worked remotely as in person ($M = 5.59$, $SD = 1.69$).

For those who had remote work available, 218 participants provided a response to the open-ended prompt regarding what they believed were the *best parts of working remotely*. These responses generated 674 codes. The most frequently reported benefits were flexible time and time savings ($n = 118$, 17.51%), avoiding commute issues ($n = 111$, 16.47%), and better work conditions at home ($n = 104$, 15.43%). Physical comfort and convenience at home ($n = 66$, 9.79%) and improved quality of life working from home ($n = 66$, 9.79%) were also noted, along with having more ability to focus on projects/tasks at home ($n = 42$, 6.23%).

Regarding perceptions of the *biggest challenges of working remotely*, 217 participants responded, which resulted in 446 codes. The most frequently reported challenges were difficulty establishing relationships to fulfill professional needs ($n = 77$, 17.26%), concerns about negative norms and expectations associated with remote work held by colleagues and patrons ($n = 56$, 12.56%), and better work conditions at work ($n = 45$, 10.09%). Difficulty establishing relationships to fulfill social needs ($n = 40$, 8.97%), inferior technology/office at home ($n = 39$, 8.74%), and providing point-of-service needs in the library for intrapersonal tasks ($n = 36$, 8.07%) were also noted.

Of those with remote work available, 98 (42.79%) were not currently working remotely, and 130 (56.77%) were.

LIBRARIANS CURRENTLY WORKING REMOTELY

Those who were currently working remotely agreed that they were as effective working remotely at the library as they were working in person ($M = 6.24$, $SD = 1.06$), and they agreed that the library functioned just as well when they worked remotely as in person ($M = 6.37$, $SD = 1.08$).

Of those currently working remotely, 38 (29.23%) indicated that when they were initially hired their job included remote work, whereas 92 (70.77%) indicated it did not. Only 9 (6.98%) participants indicated that their job was modified to enable remote work. Spearman correlations revealed that the number of hours worked remotely per week was not correlated with communication frequency rank for supervisors or subordinates, but it was negatively correlated with communication frequency rank for coworkers ($n = 120$, $r = -25$, $p = .005$), such that the more librarians worked remotely, the less communication they had with their coworkers. The number of hours worked remotely per week was positively correlated with cognitive trust in subordinates ($r = .25$, $p = .05$, $n = 63$) but was not correlated with any other study variables. Of those who were currently working remotely, 124 participants indicated *why their position changed to include remote work, or why they continued remote work after the pandemic*, which resulted in 345 codes. The most frequent responses noted the COVID-19 pandemic ($n = 76$, 22.03%) and changes in organizational policies or programs ($n = 66$, 19.13%) as reasons for their shift to or continuation with remote work. Participants also indicated that characteristics of the job ($n = 51$, 14.78%) and changes in personal preferences ($n = 42$, 12.17%) made remote work better than being in the library. In addition, changes in employers' norms and expectations ($n = 40$, 11.59%) and employee advocacy/negotiations ($n = 23$, 6.67%) supported the continuation of remote work.

LIBRARIANS NOT CURRENTLY WORKING REMOTELY

Those who were not currently working remotely only somewhat agreed that they were as effective working remotely at the library as they were working in person ($M = 4.68$, $SD = 1.84$) and that the library functioned just as well when they worked remotely as in person ($M = 4.55$, $SD = 1.81$).

Compared to those who were not currently working remotely, those currently working remotely reported significantly higher perceptions that they were as effective working remotely as they were in person [$t(144.27) = -7.48, p < .001, d = 1.08$] and that the library functioned just as well when they worked remotely as in person [$t(147.91) = -8.83, p < .001, d = 1.26$]. Contrary to expectations, independent samples t tests indicated that participants who were not currently working remotely did not differ from those who were on any study variables including cognitive and affective trust.

Of the employees who had remote work available but were not working remotely, 91 indicated *why they were not currently working remotely*, which resulted in 174 codes. The most frequent explanation was that though they were not currently working remotely on a regular basis, the option was available if needed for appointments, inclement weather, illness, or other needs ($n = 36$, 20.69%). Participants also indicated a personal preference not to work remotely ($n = 23$, 13.22%), citing concerns regarding a lack of organizational trust for remote work ($n = 20$, 11.49%), needs to be in the library to perform management duties ($n = 19$, 10.92%), and nonspecific point-of-service needs in the library ($n = 15$, 8.62%) in addition to those related to interpersonal obligations in the library ($n = 14$, 8.05%).

Trust

Participants were categorized into high (i.e., scores 4 or above) vs. low (i.e., scores less than 4) levels of trust on each of the trust scales. Independent samples t tests revealed that participants who indicated high cognitive trust reported significantly higher scores than those who reported low cognitive trust in their supervisors on need satisfaction (autonomy, competence, relatedness), psychological safety, and intention to stay in their current job (see figure 15.5).

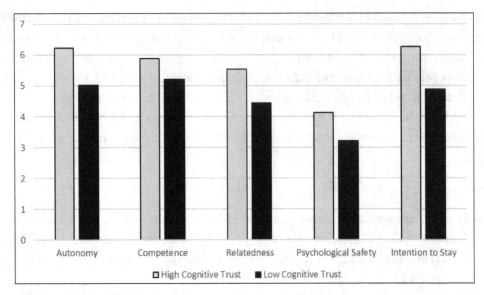

Figure 15.5. Differences in low vs. high cognitive trust in supervisor on study variables

Similar results with significant differences on all variables were obtained when participants were categorized into high vs. low levels of (1) affective trust in their supervisors, (2) cognitive trust in coworkers, (3) affective trust in coworkers, and (4) cognitive trust in subordinates. However, when participants were split by high vs. low levels of affective trust in subordinates, the only comparison that was statistically significant was relatedness need satisfaction with those high in affective trust in their subordinates reporting significantly higher scores ($n = 81$, $M = 5.79$, $SD = 1.06$) than those low in trust [$n = 76$, $M = 4.90$, $SD = 1.45$), $t(136.87) = -4.35$, $p < .001$, $d = .70$].

Discussion

The COVID-19 pandemic clearly impacted expectations for work in academic libraries, and a return to pre-pandemic assumptions appears unlikely and ineffective. The emergency pivot to remote work altered perceptions of how work can be performed, as most libraries now make some form of remote work available to employees. At the time of data collection, nearly three-fourths of the sample had remote work available, and over 40 percent currently worked in a remote capacity, having done so for just over two years, which coincided with the declaration of a nationwide emergency and closures associated with the pandemic.[82] This finding has significant implications not only for remote workers, but also for their supervisors, subordinates, and colleagues, as well as students and university colleagues outside of the library.

Study participants' explanations for why they currently worked remotely indicated that the pandemic and associated organizational changes led to the shift. Though most participants did not start in a job with remote work options, very few reported that their positions were modified to accommodate remote work, indicating that many positions were already conducive to remote work for at least some portion of the job. This is corroborated by Green's finding that 96 percent of survey participants believed their positions could be performed remotely at least part of the time.[83]

Efficacy of Remote Work Options

Having remote work available was associated with heightened perceptions of autonomy need satisfaction and a sense of psychological safety at work. Though not statistically significant after correcting for multiple comparisons, relatedness need satisfaction and intention to stay in the current job also trended in this direction. The flexibility that remote work brings is valued by librarians, providing them a sense of security and control over their work lives.

Having remote work options available, however, should not be interpreted as requiring remote work. The desirability of remote work varied considerably. Though the majority had remote work opportunities and a full 60 percent of the sample who did not have remote work available to them wanted it, the remaining portion did not want remote work. Perceptions of the efficacy of remote work were directly related to whether librarians wanted it. Those who wanted remote work believed it would be significantly more effective both for themselves and the library than those who did not want to work remotely.

Conclusions about the efficacy of remote work should not be determined based on assumptions or traditional ways of performing tasks. These determinations may be better informed by considering the duties associated with the job and how they can be carried out most productively. Librarians themselves are a valuable source of information to inform these decisions. Both those with and without remote work options generated the same benefits of working remotely to include flexible time and time savings, avoiding commute issues, better work conditions, physical comfort and conveniences, and improved quality of life. Those with experience working from home also noted having more ability to focus on projects at home compared to being in the library. These benefits are consistent with the higher autonomy need satisfaction reported by librarians who work remotely and may underlie the higher ratings of psychological safety as well. They may also factor into an employee's intentions to remain in the current job, a relationship employers may want to examine as a way to retain employees.

In addition to employees' perceptions, the task requirements of the job need to be objectively considered in relation to the online capabilities available in the library. Many duties that librarians described performing were well suited for remote work. For example, a respondent listed the following potential remote work activities: "online projects, create videos, do virtual reference, work on web pages, book orders, etc." Observing that reference and instruction roles provide opportunities for remote work, one respondent stated, "Many key elements of my group's core work (instruction and research) could be accomplished remotely even pre-pandemic, such as lesson/event planning or research guide and instruction module creation." Similarly, another respondent indicated that the reference and instruction team "worked completely from home, monitoring reference via chat and doing instruction virtually." Other respondents reported that working with digital collections provided opportunities to work from home: "Since a portion of my position includes working with digital resources, these duties can be completed remotely, making me eligible for a hybrid schedule."

On the other hand, some duties were not conducive to remote work. Participants who had remote work available described the challenges they faced, including difficulty establishing relationships to fulfill professional and social needs and concerns about negative norms and expectations associated with remote work held by colleagues and patrons. For some respondents, on-site work provided better work conditions as a result of inferior technology and too many domestic distractions at home. Another challenge was the ability to provide point-of-service needs in the library when working with patrons, concerns that were echoed by librarians who did not have remote work available. Examples of obstacles to remote work included: "Little to no access to the physical materials that are the sole materials I work with in my job," and "Most of my job involves instruction using historic books, artifacts, and archives, which is much less effective when done digitally/remotely." A particularly poignant response was:

> I felt so isolated during the pandemic, which was compounded by my spouse working from home, and my child attending school virtually. Even before the pandemic, and before my spouse worked remotely, I knew that I could not effectively work from home. Again, in special collections, even with electronic access to files, and considerable material digitized, there are just some tasks that require being on site—the bulk of the work as the department head, really; almost everything to do with supporting researchers during in-person visits; managing the reading room; physically managing collections and making sure there are no facilities issues, etc. I just need to be in person, in my workspace, in order to work effectively.

As reflected in this comment, many supervisors reported that, as a manager, they felt compelled to be on-site to support their staff, the library, or those who could not work remotely. Given that in-person communication was rated as the most effective medium, and participants frequently reported difficulty establishing relationships, administrators should work to disrupt these negative assumptions about effective managerial communication and support the use of online platforms for synchronous communication.

Despite these examples, challenges of remote work were not the most frequently mentioned reasons when librarians who were not currently working remotely described why. Many indicated that a remote work option was, in fact, available if needed (e.g., appointments, illness), and many stated personal preferences for not working remotely. Concerns regarding a lack of organizational trust for remote work were noted beyond the expected challenges of needing to be in the library to perform management duties and provide other services that required an in-person presence. However, ratings of trust in relationships in the organization were not related to whether employees engaged in remote work.

Based on the data, the hybrid work schedule that most librarians reported in this study appears an effective balance for the variety of job demands most librarians have. Given the widespread availability of remote work options, the demand for them, and the positive qualities reported by those who have them, administrators are well advised to consider providing them to improve employee retention and work-life balance. Notably, negative norms associated with remote work were consistent themes in the open-ended comments despite the prevalence of remote work for the library employees in our sample. Administrators need to be cognizant of and sensitive to these negative assumptions and actively mitigate them in their workplaces to support those who work remotely.

Revising Communication to Support Remote Work

Being two years into the pandemic at the time of data collection, librarians in the sample relied on in-person conversations and e-mail as their primary forms of communication. Unexpectedly, online forms of synchronous communication, including videoconference and online chat, were used infrequently. Given the popularity of online communication platforms (e.g., Zoom, Microsoft Teams, WebEx), librarians may be underutilizing opportunities to collaborate synchronously with colleagues while working remotely, consistent with the finding that as the number of hours working remotely increased, communication frequency with coworkers decreased. Research is needed regarding whether comprehensive packages that combine videoconferencing with online chat and collaborative documents will be rated as highly—or higher—as in-person communication in the future after increased adoption and familiarity. Study results suggest this may be likely, as those who never had in-person interactions with their supervisors and coworkers did not differ from those who did on study variables (i.e., trust, need satisfaction, psychology safety, and intention to remain in the job). Online synchronous meetings that enable attendees to interact in real time, access interactive digital files instead of static photocopies, and work collaboratively on documents during meetings instead of asynchronously afterward may replace in-person meetings for some work groups and activities.

In addition to increasing efficiency on project completion, these online synchronous tools may close interpersonal gaps when working remotely, enabling colleagues to create more engaged, personal connections than asynchronous e-mail communications, a potential benefit especially for those who have no in-person interactions with colleagues (e.g., those who are remote to campus). These tools increase communication with supervisors and coworkers, which was associated with increases in relatedness need satisfaction. In addition, given that increased frequency of communication was related to higher levels of cognitive and affective trust in supervisors and coworkers, online synchronous communication tools may be particularly valuable for remote work.

Trust

As predicted, trust was an important moderator for all study variables. Those reporting higher levels of trust (i.e., cognitive or affective) in supervisors or coworkers had higher levels of need satisfaction (autonomy, competence, relatedness), psychological safety, and intention to stay in their current job. These results are consistent with prior research that found that "affective trust in supervisor appeared more important to the accomplishment of behavioral outcomes… [which] underscores the importance of interpersonal interactions with the supervisor for motivating and energizing positive work behavior on the part of subordinates,"[84] and "when employees feel that the organization cares for them, their trust in the organization will grow manifold, leading to enhanced performance. [Further,] as traditional organizational structures pave the way for telework, trust becomes an even more important antecedent for a high-performance workforce."[85]

Contrary to predictions, whether participants worked remotely was unrelated to trust (both cognitive and affective) in colleagues (supervisors, subordinates, coworkers). In-person interactions with colleagues, which were prevalent across all work groups in this sample, may be masking the expected relationship for those who work remotely. Work groups with less frequent in-person interactions (and few synchronous online interactions) may demonstrate the expected relationship that higher levels of trust in colleagues are associated with higher levels of remote work; however, future research is needed to support this claim.

Takeaways

- Libraries should provide the option for remote work when possible based on job demands and allow employees to decide how much remote work is effective for them.
- Library workers who are working in person or remotely use the same communication methods. In other words, there is an underutilization of videoconferencing, which would mitigate communication barriers. Libraries must assess how well their IT staff can support remote workers. On the survey, 10 percent of comments indicated better conditions on-site than at home, and over 8 percent mentioned inferior technology at home.
- Most library jobs can accommodate at least a hybrid remote work schedule, as almost no respondents indicated their jobs were modified for remote work, and most respondents were successfully completing their jobs remotely.

- Administrators and other library employees should advocate for unbiased norms regarding remote work. Remote workers are not inherently effective or ineffective—rather, tasks and workflows are more or less suited to alternative work modalities. Library workers who regularly engage in such tasks and workflows should help make that determination.
- Communication frequency remains the same whether workers are remote or on site. Frequency of communication with supervisor reveals a high correlation with trust, relatedness, and satisfaction.
- Library employees should abandon the urge to go back to the old normal. Work can be restructured to accommodate work modality preference, including remote work; not all job functions are conductive to remote work, but many are, so the choice to work remotely on a hybrid basis is advantageous.
- Remote workers must leverage online synchronous communication modes to create social opportunities for coworkers to connect.

Notes

1. Kurt T. Dirks and Donald L. Ferrin, "Trust in Leadership: Meta-analytic Findings and Implications for Research and Practice," *Journal of Applied Psychology* 87, no. 4 (2002): 611, https://doi.org/10.1037/0021-9010.87.4.611.
2. Vittorio Di Martino and Linda Wirth, "Telework: A New Way of Working and Living," *International Labour Review* 129, no. 5 (1990): 538.
3. Sharifa Amirul and Sharija Che Shaari, "An Overview: Twenty Years of Flexible Working Arrangements," *Advances in Business Research* 7, no. 2 (2021): 28.
4. Daniel Hickey and Neely Tang, "Theoretical and Applied Approaches to Remote Work for Academic Reference and Instruction Librarians," in *Library Staffing for the Future (Advances in Library Administration and Organization, vol. 34)*, ed. Samantha Schmehl Hines and Marcy Simons (Bingley, UK: Emerald Group Publishing, 2015), 187.
5. Guy Robertson, "Pandemic Perspective: How an Outbreak Could Affect Libraries," *Feliciter* 52, no. 3 (2006): 112.
6. Jennifer K. Frederick and Christine Wolff-Eisenberg, *Academic Library Strategy and Budgeting during the COVID-19 Pandemic: Results from the Ithaka S+R US Library Survey 2020* (New York: Ithaka S+R, 2020), 26.
7. David J. Sencer, "CDC Museum COVID-19 Timeline," US Centers for Disease Control and Prevention, last reviewed March 15, 2023, https://www.cdc.gov/museum/timeline/covid19.html.
8. Patrick Coate, "Remote Work before, during, and after the Pandemic," National Council on Compensation Insurance, January 25, 2021, https://www.ncci.com/SecureDocuments/QEB/QEB_Q4_2020_RemoteWork.html.
9. Clare Kelliher and Deirdre Anderson, "Doing More with Less? Flexible Working Practices and the Intensification of Work," *Human Relations* 63, no. 1 (2010): 91, https://doi.org/10.1177/0018726709349199.
10. Elena P. Antonacopoulou and Andri Georgiadou, "Leading through Social Distancing: The Future of Work, Corporations and Leadership from Home," *Gender, Work and Organization* 29, no. 2 (2020): concluding paragraph.
11. Mihoko Hosoi, Lauren Reiter, and Diane Zabel, "Reshaping Perspectives on Flexible Work: The Impact of COVID-19 on Academic Library Management," *portal: Libraries and the Academy* 21, no. 4 (October 2021): 696, ProQuest.
12. Ashlea Green, "Post Covid-19: Expectations for Academic Library Collections, Remote Work, and Resource Description and Discovery Staffing," *Journal of Academic Librarianship* 48, no. 4 (July 2022): article 102564, p. 8, https://doi.org/10.1016/j.acalib.2022.102564.
13. Ashlea Green, "Academic Library Employees and Their Work Modality Options and Preferences," *Journal of Academic Librarianship* 49, no. 5 (September 2023): article 102764, p. 7, https://doi.org/10.1016/j.acalib.2023.102764.
14. Green, "Academic Library Employees," 8.
15. Viviane Illegems and Alain Verbeke, *Moving Towards the Virtual Workplace* (Cheltenham, UK: Edward Elgar, 2003), 20.
16. Hickey and Tang, "Theoretical and Applied Approaches," 192–98.
17. Hickey and Tang, "Theoretical and Applied Approaches," 197.
18. Hickey and Tang, "Theoretical and Applied Approaches," 198.

19. Hosoi, Reiter, and Zabel, "Reshaping Perspectives on Flexible Work," 707.
20. Sarah Edwards Obenauf, "Remote Management of Library Staff: Challenges and Practical Solutions," *Journal of Academic Librarianship* 47, no. 5 (2021): 2–3.
21. Laura M. Gentry, "Digital Collections at a Distance: Telework during the COVID-19 Pandemic," *Library Resources and Technical Services* 65, no. 2 (2021): 66.
22. Green, "Academic Library Employees," 7.
23. Lilian M. De Menezes and Clare Killiher, "Flexible Working and Performance: A Systematic Review of the Evidence for a Business Case," *International Journal of Management Review* 13, no. 4 (2011): 459–60.
24. De Menezes and Killiher, "Flexible Working and Performance," 464.
25. Prithwiraj (Raj) Choudhury, "Our Work-from-Anywhere Future," *Harvard Business Review*, November–December 2020, 3rd unnumbered page, https://hbr.org/2020/11/our-work-from-anywhere-future.
26. Lena Waizenegger et al., "An Affordance Perspective of Team Collaboration and Enforced Working from Home during COVID-19," *European Journal of Information Systems* 29, no. 4 (2020): 430, https://doi.org/10.1080/0960085X.2020.1800417.
27. Waizenegger et al., "Affordance Perspective of Team Collaboration," 429, 438.
28. Green, "Academic Library Employees," 11.
29. Green, "Academic Library Employees," 11.
30. Elaine Berkery et al., "On the Uptake of Flexible Working Arrangements and the Association with Human Resource and Organizational Performance Outcomes," *European Management Review* 14, no. 2 (Summer 2017): 176, https://doi.org/10.1111/emre.12103.
31. Maria Charalampous et al., "Systematically Reviewing Remote E-Workers' Well-Being at Work: A Multidimensional Approach," *European Journal of Work and Organizational Psychology* 28, no. 1 (2019), 51, https://doi.org/10.1080/1359432X.2018.1541886.
32. Charalampous et al., "Systematically Reviewing Remote E-Workers' Well-Being," 69.
33. Roger C. Mayer, James H. Davis, and F. David Schoorman, "An Integrative Model of Organizational Trust," *Academy of Management* 20, no. 3 (1995): 712, https://www.jstor.org/stable/258792; Charalampous et al., "Systematically Reviewing Remote E-Workers' Well-Being."
34. C. Ashley Fulmer and Cheri Ostroff, "Trust in Direct Leaders and Top Leaders: A Trickle-Up Model," *Journal of Applied Psychology* 102, no. 4 (2017): 649, https://doi.org/10.1037/apl0000189.
35. Dirks and Ferrin, "Trust in Leadership," 621.
36. Jixia Yang and Kevin W. Mossholder, "Examining the Effects of Trust in Leaders: A Bases-and-Foci Approach," *Leadership Quarterly* 21 (2010): 59.
37. Kathleen Ellis and Pamela Shockley-Zalabak, "Trust in Top Management and Immediate Supervisor: The Relationship to Satisfaction, Perceived Organizational Effectiveness, and Information Receiving," *Communication Quarterly* 49, no. 4 (2001): 393, https://doi.org/10.1080/01463370109385637.
38. Fulmer and Ostroff, "Trust in Direct Leaders," 654.
39. Pedro Neves and Antonio Caetano, "Social Exchange Processes in Organizational Change: The Roles of Trust and Control," *Journal of Change Management* 6, no. 4 (2006): 361.
40. Akanksha Jaiswal et al., "Teleworking: Role of Psychological Well-Being and Technostress in the Relationship between Trust in Management and Employee Performance," *International Journal of Manpower* 45, no. 1 (2024): 53, 62, https://doi.org/10.1108/IJM-04-2022-0149.
41. Sumita Raghuram et al., "Factors Contributing to Virtual Work Adjustment," *Journal of Management* 27, no. 3 (2001): 384, 401.
42. Judith A. Holton, "Building Trust and Collaboration in a Virtual Team," *Team Performance Management: An International Journal* 7, no. 3/4 (2001): 36.
43. Amirul and Shaari, "An Overview," 33.
44. Sharon K. Parker, Caroline Knight, and Anita Keller, "Remote Managers Are Having Trust Issues," *Harvard Business Review*, Summer 2021, 154, 156, 157.
45. Tony Zorc, "Establishing a New Definition of Trust with Remote Employees," *Leadership Excellence*, August 2021, 43.
46. Zorc, "Establishing a New Definition of Trust," 42–43.
47. Yasin Munir et al., "Workplace Isolation in Pharmaceutical Companies: Moderating Role of Self-Efficacy," *Social Indicators Research* 126, no. 3 (2016): 1160–62, https://doi.org/10.1007/s11205-015-0940-7.
48. Graham Sewell and Laurent Taskin, "Out of Sight, Out of Mind in a New World of Work? Autonomy, Control, and Spatiotemporal Scaling in Telework," *Organization Studies* 36, no. 11 (2015): 1521, https://doi.org/10.1177/0170840615593587.
49. Christine A. Grant, Louise M. Wallace, and Peter C. Spurgeon, "An Exploration of the Psychological Factors Affecting Remote E-worker's Job Effectiveness, Well-Being and Work-Life Balance," *Employee Relations* 35, no. 5 (2013): 539, 542.
50. Klodiana Lanaj et al., "Daily Mistrust: A Resource Perspective and Its Implications for Work and Home," *Personnel Psychology* 71 (2018): 548.

51. M. Lance Frazier et al., "Psychological Safety: A Meta-analytic Review and Extension," *Personnel Psychology* 70, no. 1 (2017): 114.
52. Green, "Academic Library Employees, 13.
53. Amirul and Shaari, "An Overview," 31; Raghuram et al., "Factors Contributing to Virtual Work Adjustment," 401; Sandy D. Staples, John S. Hulland, and Christopher A. Higgins, "A Self-Efficacy Theory Explanation for the Management of Remote Workers in Virtual Organizations," *Organization Science* 10, no. 6 (1999): 772, https://doi.org/10.1287/orsc.10.6.758; Wendy Wang, Leslie Albert, and Qin Sun, "Employee Isolation and Telecommuter Organizational Commitment," *Employee Relations* 42, no. 3 (2020): 620, https://doi.org/10.1108/ER-06-2019-0246.
54. Holton," Building Trust and Collaboration," 36.
55. Amirul and Shaari, "An Overview," 33; Staples, Hulland, and Higgins, "A Self-Efficacy Theory Explanation," 772.
56. Jaiswal et al., "Teleworking."
57. Yung-Kai Yang and Wen-Shan Lin, "How to Enhance Workplace Climate through Telework Communication Approaches in Organization during the Era of Changes? Evidences of Authentic Leaders," *Asia Pacific Management Review* 28 (2023): 110–19.
58. Hosoi, Reiter, and Zabel," Reshaping Perspectives on Flexible Work," 706.
59. Gentry, "Digital Collections at a Distance," 66.
60. Sewell and Taskin, "Out of Sight, Out of Mind," 1521; Staples, Hullard, and Higgins, "A Self-Efficacy Theory Explanation," 773.
61. Maryellen Nash et al., "Together, Apart: Communication Dynamics among Academic Librarians during the COVID-19 Pandemic," *College and Research Libraries* 83, no. 6 (November 2022): 954, https://crl.acrl.org/index.php/crl/article/view/25010/33596.
62. Anna Bleakley et al., "Bridging Social Distance during Social Distancing: Exploring Social Talk and Remote Collegiality in Video Conferencing," *Human-Computer Interaction* 37, no. 5 (2022): 404.
63. Bleakley et al., "Bridging Social Distance," 406, 421.
64. Christopher Bolick, "Cultivating Innovative Workplaces in a World Transforming: Cross-sectional Survey Research Exploring How the 2020 Shift to Remote Work Reshaped Managerial Relationships, Innovative Behaviors, and a Sense of Psychological Safety within a Work Unit," PhD diss., College of Professional Studies of Northeastern University, 2020, 131, 140, ProQuest 28158002.
65. Jessica R. Mesmer-Magnus et al., "A Meta-analytic Investigation of Virtuality and Information Sharing in Teams," *Organizational Behavior and Human Decision Processes* 115, no. 2 (July 2011): 222.
66. Ellis and Shockley-Zalabak, "Trust in Top Management," 393.
67. Raghuram et al., "Factors Contributing to Virtual Work Adjustment," 384.
68. Dimitrina Dimitrova, "Controlling Teleworkers: Supervision and Flexibility Revisited," *New Technology, Work and Employment* 18, no. 3 (November 2003): 193, https://doi.org/10.1111/1468-005X.00120; Bin Wang et al., "Achieving Effective Remote Working during the COVID-19 Pandemic: A Work Design Perspective," *Applied Psychology: An International Review* 70, no. 1 (2021): 51, https://doi.org/10.1111/apps.12290.
69. Timothy D. Golden, "The Role of Relationships in Understanding Telecommuter Satisfaction," *Journal of Organizational Behavior* 27, no. 3 (2006): 334, https://doi.org/10.1002/job.369.
70. Edward L. Deci and Richard M. Ryan, eds., *Intrinsic Motivation and Self-Determination in Human Behavior* (New York: Plenum Press, 1985), 43.
71. Deci and Ryan, *Intrinsic Motivation and Self*-Determination, 294.
72. Myriam Chiniara and Kathleen Bentein, "Linking Servant Leadership to Individual Performance: Differentiating the Mediating Role of Autonomy, Competence and Relatedness Need Satisfaction," *Leadership Quarterly* 27, no. 1 (2016): 125, 136.
73. Ifeyinwa Stella Austin-Egole, E. B. J. Iheriohanma, and Chinedu Nwokorie, "Flexible Working Arrangements and Organizational Performance: An Overview," *Journal of Humanities and Social Science* 25, no. 5 (May 2020): concluding paragraph.
74. Tinne Vander Elst et al., "Not Extent of Telecommuting, But Job Characteristics as Proximal Predictors of Work-Related Well-Being," *Journal of Occupational and Environmental Medicine* 59, no. 10 (2017): e185, https://doi.org/10.1097/JOM.0000000000001132.
75. Bolick, "Cultivating Innovative Workplaces."
76. David A. Garvin, Amy C. Edmondson, and Francesca Gino, "Is Yours a Learning Organization?" *Harvard Business Review*, March 2008, 109–16.
77. Bolick, "Cultivating Innovative Workplaces."
78. Yang and Mossholder, "Examining the Effects of Trust."
79. Yang and Mossholder, "Examining the Effects of Trust."
80. Chiniara and Bentein, "Linking Servant Leadership to Individual Performance."
81. Icek Ajzen, "Constructing a Theory of Planned Behavior Questionnaire," TPB Questionnaire Construction (University of Massachussetts Amherst, 2019). https://people.umass.edu/aizen/pdf/tpb.measurement.pdf.
82. Sencer, "CDC Museum COVID-19 Timeline."
83. Green, "Post-COVID-19," 8.

84. Yang and Mossholder, "Examining the Effects of Trust," 59.
85. Jaiswal et al., "Teleworking," unnumbered page 5.

Bibliography

Ajzen, Icek. "Constructing a Theory of Planned Behavior Questionnaire." TPB Questionnaire Construction. University of Massachusetts Amherts, 2019. https://people.umass.edu/aizen/pdf/tpb.measurement.pdf

Amirul, Sharifa, and Sharija Che Shaari. "An Overview: Twenty Years of Flexible Working Arrangements." *Advances in Business Research* 7, no. 2 (2021): 27–41.

Antonacopoulou, Elena P., and Andri Georgiadou. "Leading through Social Distancing: The Future of Work, Corporations and Leadership from Home." *Gender, Work and Organization* 29, no. 2 (2020): 1–19.

Austin-Egole, Ifeyinwa Stella, E. B. J. Iheriohanma, and Chinedu Nwokorie. "Flexible Working Arrangements and Organizational Performance: An Overview." *Journal of Humanities and Social Science* 25, no. 5 (May 2020): 50–59.

Berkery, Elaine, Michael J. Morley, Siobhan Tiernan, Helen Purtill, and Emma Parry. "On the Uptake of Flexible Working Arrangements and the Association with Human Resource and Organizational Performance Outcomes." *European Management Review* 14, no. 2 (Summer 2017): 165–83. https://doi.org/10.1111/emre.12103.

Bleakley, Anna, Daniel Rough, Justin Edwards, Philip Doyle, Odile Dumbleton, Leigh Clark, Sean Rintel, Vincent Wade, and Benjamin R. Cowan. "Bridging Social Distance during Social Distancing: Exploring Social Talk and Remote Collegiality in Video Conferencing." *Human-Computer Interaction* 37, no. 5 (2022): 404–32.

Bolick, Christopher. "Cultivating Innovative Workplaces in a World Transforming: Cross-sectional Survey Research Exploring How the 2020 Shift to Remote Work Reshaped Managerial Relationships, Innovative Behaviors, and a Sense of Psychological Safety within a Work Unit." PhD diss., College of Professional Studies of Northeastern University, 2020. ProQuest 28158002.

Charalampous, Maria, Christine A. Grant, Carlo Tramontano, and Evie Michailidis. "Systematically Reviewing Remote E-Workers' Well-Being at Work: A Multidimensional Approach. *European Journal of Work and Organizational Psychology* 28, no. 1 (2019): 51–73. https://doi.org/10.1080/1359432X.2018.1541886.

Chiniara, Myriam, and Kathleen Bentein. "Linking Servant Leadership to Individual Performance: Differentiating the Mediating Role of Autonomy, Competence and Relatedness Need Satisfaction." *Leadership Quarterly* 27, no. 1 (2016): 124–41.

Choudhury, Prithwiraj (Raj). "Our Work-from-Anywhere Future." *Harvard Business Review*, November–December 2020. https://hbr.org/2020/11/our-work-from-anywhere-future.

Coate, Patrick. "Remote Work before, during, and after the Pandemic." National Council on Compensation Insurance, January 25, 2021. https://www.ncci.com/SecureDocuments/QEB/QEB_Q4_2020_RemoteWork.html.

Deci, Edward L., and Richard M. Ryan, eds. *Intrinsic Motivation and Self-Determination in Human Behavior*. New York: Plenum Press, 1985.

De Menezes, Lilian M., and Clare Killiher. "Flexible Working and Performance: A Systematic Review of the Evidence for a Business Case." *International Journal of Management Review* 13, no. 4 (2011): 452–74.

Di Martino, Vittorio, and Linda Wirth. "Telework: A New Way of Working and Living." *International Labour Review* 129, no. 5 (1990): 529–54.

Dimitrova, Dimitrina. "Controlling Teleworkers: Supervision and Flexibility Revisited." *New Technology, Work and Employment* 18, no. 3 (November 2003): 181–95. https://doi.org/10.1111/1468-005X.00120.

Dirks, Kurt T., and Donald L. Ferrin. "Trust in Leadership: Meta-analytic Findings and Implications for Research and Practice." *Journal of Applied Psychology* 87, no. 4 (2002): 611–28. https://doi.org/10.1037/0021-9010.87.4.611.

Ellis, Kathleen, and Pamela Shockley-Zalabak. "Trust in Top Management and Immediate Supervisor: The Relationship to Satisfaction, Perceived Organizational Effectiveness, and Information Receiving." *Communication Quarterly* 49, no. 4 (2001): 382–98. https://doi.org/10.1080/01463370109385637.

Frazier, M. Lance, Stav Fainshmidt, Ryan L. Klinger, Amir Pezeshkan, and Veselina Vracheva. "Psychological Safety: A Meta-analytic Review and Extension." *Personnel Psychology* 70, no. 1 (2017): 113–65.

Frederick, Jennifer K., and Christine Wolff-Eisenberg. *Academic Library Strategy and Budgeting during the COVID-19 Pandemic: Results from the Ithaka S+R US Library Survey 2020* New York: Ithaka S+R, 2020. https://doi.org/10.18665/sr.314507.

Fulmer, C. Ashley, and Cheri Ostroff. "Trust in Direct Leaders and Top Leaders: A Trickle-Up Model. *Journal of Applied Psychology* 102, no. 4 (2017): 648–57. https://doi.org/10.1037/apl0000189.

Garvin, David A., Amy C. Edmondson, and Francesca Gino. "Is Yours a Learning Organization?" *Harvard Business Review*, March 2008, 109–16.

Gentry, Laura M. "Digital Collections at a Distance: Telework during the COVID-19 Pandemic." *Library Resources and Technical Services* 65, no. 2 (2021): 65–75. https://doi.org/10.5860/lrts.65n2.65-75.

Golden, Timothy D. "The Role of Relationships in Understanding Telecommuter Satisfaction." *Journal of Organizational Behavior* 27, no. 3 (May 2006): 319–40. https://doi.org/10.1002/job.369.

Grant, Christine A., Louise M. Wallace, and Peter C. Spurgeon. "An Exploration of the Psychological Factors Affecting Remote E-worker's Job Effectiveness, Well-Being and Work-Life Balance." *Employee Relations* 35, no. 5 (2013): 527–46. https://doi.org/10.1108/ER-08-2012-0059.

Green, Ashlea. "Academic Library Employees and Their Work Modality Options and Preferences." *Journal of Academic Librarianship* 49, no. 5 (September 2023): article 102764. https://doi.org/10.1016/j.acalib.2023.102764.

———. "Post Covid-19: Expectations for Academic Library Collections, Remote Work, and Resource Description and Discovery Staffing." *Journal of Academic Librarianship* 48, no. 4 (July 2022): article 102564. https://doi.org/10.1016/j.acalib.2022.102564.

Hickey, Daniel, and Neely Tang. "Theoretical and Applied Approaches to Remote Work for Academic Reference and Instruction Librarians." In *Library Staffing for the Future (Advances in Library Administration and Organization, vol. 34)*, edited by Samantha Schmehl Hines and Marcy Simons, 177–200. Bingley, UK: Emerald Group Publishing, 2015. https://doi.org/10.1108/S0732-067120150000034008.

Holton, Judith A., "Building Trust and Collaboration in a Virtual Team," *Team Performance Management: An International Journal* 7, no. 3/4 (2001): 36–47.

Hosoi, Mihoko, Lauren Reiter, and Diane Zabel. "Reshaping Perspectives on Flexible Work: The Impact of COVID-19 on Academic Library Management." *portal: Libraries and the Academy* 21, no. 4 (October 2021): 695–713. ProQuest.

Illegems, Viviane, and Alain Verbeke. *Moving Towards the Virtual Workplace: Managerial and Societal Perspectives on Telework*. Cheltenham, UK: Edward Elgar, 2003.

Jaiswal, Akanksha, Santoshi Sengupta, Madhusmita Panda, Lopamudra Hati, Verma Prikshat, Parth Patel, and Syed Mohyuddin. "Teleworking: Role of Psychological Well-Being and Technostress in the Relationship between Trust in Management and Employee Performance." *International Journal of Manpower* 45, no. 1 (2024): 49–71. https://doi.org/10.1108/IJM-04-2022-0149.

Kelliher, Claire, and Deirdre Anderson. "Doing More with Less? Flexible Working Practices and the Intensification of Work." *Human Relations* 63, no. 1 (2010): 83–106. https://doi.org/10.1177/0018726709349199.

Lanaj, Klodiana, Peter H. Kim, Joel Koopman, and Fadel K. Matta. "Daily Mistrust: A Resource Perspective and Its Implications for Work and Home." *Personnel Psychology* 71 (2018): 545–70.

Mayer, Roger C., James H. Davis, and F. David Schoorman. "An Integrative Model of Organizational Trust." *Academy of Management* 20, no. 3 (1995): 709–34. https://www.jstor.org/stable/258792.

Mesmer-Magnus, Jessica R., Leslie A. DeChurch, Miliani Jimenez-Rodriguez, Jessica Wildman, and Marissa Shuffler. "A Meta-analytic Investigation of Virtuality and Information Sharing in Teams." *Organizational Behavior and Human Decision Processes* 115, no. 2 (July 2011): 214–25.

Munir, Yasin, Saif-Ur-Rehman Khan, Misbah Sadiq, Imran Ali, Yacoub Hamdan, and Esha Munir. "Workplace Isolation in Pharmaceutical Companies: Moderating Role of Self-Efficacy." *Social Indicators Research* 126, no. 3 (2016): 1157–74. https://doi.org/10.1007/s11205-015-0940-7.

Nash, Maryellen, Barbara Lewis, Jessica Szempruch, Stephanie Jacobs, and Susan Silver. "Together, Apart: Communication Dynamics among Academic Librarians during the COVID-19 Pandemic." *College and Research Libraries* 83, no. 6 (November 2022): 946–65. https://crl.acrl.org/index.php/crl/article/view/25010/33596.

Neves, Pedro, and Antonio Caetano. "Social Exchange Processes in Organizational Change: The Roles of Trust and Control." *Journal of Change Management* 6, no. 4 (2006): 351–64.

Obenauf, Sarah Edwards. "Remote Management of Library Staff: Challenges and Practical Solutions." *Journal of Academic Librarianship* 47, no. 5 (2021): 1–3.

Parker, Sharon K., Caroline Knight, and Anita Keller. "Remote Managers Are Having Trust Issues. *Harvard Business Review*, Summer 2021, 154–58.

Raghuram, Sumita, Raghu Garud, Batia Wisenefeld, and Vipin Gupta. "Factors Contributing to Virtual Work Adjustment." *Journal of Management* 27, no. 3 (2001): 383–405.

Robertson, Guy. "Pandemic Perspective: How an Outbreak Could Affect Libraries." *Feliciter* 52, no. 3 (2006): 111–13.

Sencer, David J. "CDC Museum COVID-19 Timeline." US Centers for Disease Control and Prevention. Last reviewed March 15, 2023. https://www.cdc.gov/museum/timeline/covid19.html.

Sewell, Graham, and Laurent Taskin. "Out of Sight, Out of Mind in a New World of Work? Autonomy, Control, and Spatiotemporal Scaling in Telework." *Organization Studies* 36, no. 11 (2015): 1507–29. https://doi.org/10.1177/0170840615593587.

Staples, Sandy D., John S. Hulland, and Christopher A. Higgins. "A Self-Efficacy Theory Explanation for the Management of Remote Workers in Virtual Organizations." *Organization Science* 10, no. 6 (1999): 758–76. https://doi.org/10.1287/orsc.10.6.758.

Vander Elst, Tinne, Ronny Verhoogen, Maarten Sercu, Anja Van den Broeck, Elfi Baillien, and Lode Godderis. "Not Extent of Telecommuting, but Job Characteristics as Proximal Predictors of Work-Related Well-Being." *Journal of Occupational and Environmental Medicine* 59, no. 10 (2017): e180–e186. https://doi.org/10.1097/JOM.0000000000001132.

Waizenegger, Lena, Brad McKenna, Wenjie Cai, and Taino Bendz. "An Affordance Perspective of Team Collaboration and Enforced Working from Home during COVID-19." *European Journal of Information Systems* 29, no. 4 (2020): 429–42. https://doi.org/10.1080/0960085X.2020.1800417.

Wang, Bin, Yukun Liu, Jing Qian, and Sharon K. Parker. "Achieving Effective Remote Working during the COVID-19 Pandemic: A Work Design Perspective." *Applied Psychology: An International Review* 70, no. 1 (2021): 16–59. https://doi.org/10.1111/apps.12290.

Wang, Wendy, Leslie Albert, and Qin Sun. "Employee Isolation and Telecommuter Organizational Commitment." *Employee Relations* 42, no. 3 (2020): 609–25. https://doi.org/10.1108/ER-06-2019-0246.

Yang, Jixia, and Kevin W. Mossholder. "Examining the Effects of Trust in Leaders: A Bases-and-Foci Approach." *Leadership Quarterly* 21 (2010): 50–63.

Yang, Yung-Kai, and Wen-Shan Lin. "How to Enhance Workplace Climate through Telework Communication Approaches in Organization during the Era of Changes? Evidences of Authentic Leaders." *Asia Pacific Management Review* 28 (2023): 110–19.

Zorc, Tony. "Establishing a New Definition of Trust with Remote Employees." *Leadership Excellence*, August 2021, 42–43.

CHAPTER 16

Flexible Work Empowers

An Inclusive Strategy for Recruitment and Retention of Academic Librarians

Dana Reijerkerk and Kristen J. Nyitray

This chapter provides a rationale and conceptual framework for emplacing flexible work arrangements (FWAs) in academic libraries within larger discussions of equity, inclusion, and diversity (EID). Flexible work arrangements have been used in libraries for more than three decades. This approach to human resource management is mutually beneficial; as employer and employee needs change over time, work tasks and where they are completed vary. During the COVID-19 pandemic, interest in FWAs increased exponentially. In libraries, implementation was largely used to maintain public services, instruction, and access to library resources, and not deployed as an inclusive workplace practice.

The authors make a case for recalibrating and normalizing FWAs as a strategy for inclusiveness. Inclusion takes into account a spectrum of diverse life experiences and feelings of professional belonging. In the workplace, inclusivity is grounded in relationships: it is "two-way accountability wherein each person must grant and accept inclusion from others."[1] The chapter provides an overview of multidisciplinary literature about the benefits and challenges of implementing FWAs in library contexts and delves into the intersections of academic librarianship, FWAs, and EID. In the sections that follow, the authors describe how libraries can make FWAs the norm and not the exception. Practical steps offered include engaging in ideation activities and conducting workplace culture–mapping exercises to identify elements of inclusivity that resonate at the local level. By embracing FWAs, organizations can authentically embody inclusiveness.

Problem Definition

The COVID-19 pandemic heightened collective consciousness about FWAs. Examples of FWAs are flextime, remote work, compressed work weeks, job sharing, and phased retirements.[2] FWAs in academic libraries are not a new concept, although historical touchstones concerning FWAs are forgotten in library professional memory. For more than three decades, alternative schedules and locations have been a human resource strategy in libraries for temporary, short-term, or piloted special arrangements to perform work.[3] Although FWAs are advantageous to the organization and employee, a review of library literature reveals that they have an ambiguous and uneven history. While FWAs are more prevalent today, they are frequently granted with a revocation caveat and discontinued if deemed to undermine operational efficiencies or compromise continuous service. This conditional stance disempowers the employee and perpetuates the notion that FWAs are not inherently mutual. In essence, librarianship's reluctance to embrace FWAs for long-term and permanent use has obscured their potential as a strategy for inclusive recruitment and retention in academic librarians.

Inclusivity in EID creates a sense of belonging for employees in the workplace.[4] Implementing FWAs is an inclusive practice to create an engaged workforce. The American Library Association (ALA) defines inclusion as "an environment in which all individuals are treated fairly and respectfully; are valued for their distinctive skills, experiences, and perspectives; have equal access to resources and opportunities; and can contribute fully to the organization's success."[5] Experiencing agency over work boosts morale and contributes to an inclusive workplace culture. However, diversity initiatives are not going to be effective if people of diverse identities do not feel included. A 2022 national study looking at demographics of library professionals confirmed little progress in advancing diversity in the workplace. According to the Department for Professional Employees, AFL-CIO, "the librarian profession suffers from a persistent lack of racial and ethnic diversity that has not changed significantly over the past fifteen years."[6] Summary statistics compiled in 2021 revealed a lack of progress despite commitments to EID initiatives: 83 percent of librarians are white; median earnings for women are 81.5 percent of men's; the field is less diverse than other education professions; and, overall, it is an older workforce. While the same report does not address FWAs in discussions of how employees accomplish work, it points out that library professionals have little autonomy and influence in decision-making activities. These findings allude to the pressing need to embed stronger measures of *inclusiveness* in the profession and in librarian human resource management.

FWAs are a responsive approach to address existing deep-seated EID issues and to remedy conditions that cause groups to feel excluded. Further, studies have shown that

FWAs increase productivity and are a desired work benefit among younger professionals and underrepresented groups.[7] Investment in FWAs demonstrates trust and commitment to creating work conditions that mutually benefit the employer and the employee. Practical application of FWAs can be accomplished through customizable employment with "flexibility around the job tasks rather than the location or the schedule."[8] This thought shift recognizes that diversity in the library workforce presents in many forms, including age, experiences, gender expressions, race, and ethnicities. Flexible work provides people with disabilities with more equitable access to employment opportunities. By integrating FWAs, institutions can build and cultivate a culturally diverse workforce, one with greater potential to be productive and successful.[9] Without adapting and changing the status quo, libraries risk being unable to recruit and retain talent. Implications include recruitment failures, systemic low morale, and voluntary attrition of early career and experienced librarians.

Literature Review

To retain and recruit academic librarians, Reiter and Zabel contend "managers need to consider flexibility as a tool to attract and support an engaged multigenerational workforce."[10] A review of the literature reveals that academic libraries have yet to present compelling studies of investment in FWAs or assessments of their routine use. Writings focused on inclusiveness are limited, as is clear articulation of its expression in library professional guidelines and policies. This literature review includes contributions to these discussions.

Bridging FWAs and Inclusiveness

FWAs uniquely benefit diverse populations by fostering inclusive work environments for underrepresented groups including aging populations, caregivers, and Black, Indigenous, and people of color (BIPOC). From an employee perspective, there is an increased demand for more flexibility in the workplace, such as flexible schedules and modified job duties, from Americans with disabilities as well as millennials and generation Z.[11] As an inclusion strategy, FWAs promote meaningful and sustainable career development over a lifespan.[12] Librarianship is a majority older workforce; FWAs can help promote active aging at work or "the process of optimizing opportunities for health, participation, and security in order to enhance quality of life as people age."[13]

Multiple studies conclude flexible work options benefit employers, employees, and society at large. Flextime and flexplace can help mothers maintain working hours after childbirth and increase satisfaction with work-life balance adaptations for family demands.[14] In their study, Jammaers and Williams found FWAs, such as working part-time, requesting flexible hours, and telework, helped workers with disabilities manage disability alongside a job.[15] In recent years, EID initiatives have targeted hiring and recruitment processes to provide increased opportunities for underrepresented candidates. Finally, FWAs are a novel strategy for improving the experiences of BIPOC employees because remote work, for example, minimizes emotional labor, opportunities for microaggressions, and commuting expenses, and increases equality in online communication.[16]

Flexible Work Arrangements in Academic Libraries

An early survey of FWAs in academic libraries was conducted by the Association of Research Libraries in 1992 in which member libraries completed questionnaires about alternative work arrangements, workplace climate, and the factors impacting their implementation.[17] Examples of FWAs cited were hybrid work, telecommuting, remote work, condensed workweeks, leave, part-time work, phased retirements, and flextime. Since the issuance of this report, few research writings have addressed embedding FWAs in academic libraries. Importantly, Reiter and Zabel's chapter called out the lack of transparency surrounding discussions of flexibility in academic libraries and encouraged more research attention to it.[18] In a 2021 survey of academic library employees on post-pandemic futures, respondents reported that they expect to work remotely at least some of the time during the next three to four years.[19] Despite the historical presence of FWAs, some have argued that options such as flextime and flexplace pose disadvantages for institutions. Germano contended that FWAs in libraries "represent loss of control as well as a reduction in accountability that could result in rampant abuse" of those FWAs.[20]

Diversifying through Inclusion in Academic Libraries

The library profession has diversified the workforce by launching several national programs and initiatives aimed at increasing representation from marginalized and underrepresented groups.[21] Leading library professional organizations have produced professional EID guidelines and evaluative tools for academic libraries.[22] In 2021, ALA's Committee on Diversity published a *Diversity, Equity, and Inclusion (DEI) Scorecard for Library and Information Organizations* "that centers accountability and transparency in determining organizational effectiveness in diversity, equity, and inclusion in the recruitment, hiring, retention, and promotion of people of color."[23] On a national level, academic libraries across the United States and Canada offer targeted recruitment efforts to diversify through internships, residency programs, mentorships, and professional development opportunities. The Association of College and Research Libraries developed the Diversity Alliance program, a paid membership for organizations with access to metrics and support, to aid academic libraries in increasing hiring and retention of BIPOC.[24] However, even with these emergent initiatives, the number of "visible minorities entering librarianship or advancing in their careers" is not significantly increasing.[25] According to Alabi, most academic library employees remain a traditional homogenous workforce.[26] In a compelling argument, Hathcock suggests that diversity programs in the profession do not adequately address this issue because "they are themselves coded to promote whiteness as the norm in the profession and unduly burden those individuals they are most intended to help."[27]

Library professional organizations have acknowledged that diversity alone does not cultivate inclusivity. Inclusion is a critical component of EID, yet it receives less overall emphasis in library literature and benchmarks that set inclusion standards. To expand the impact of EID efforts, in 2017 the ALA Council adopted the word *inclusion* in its Office for Diversity, Literacy and Outreach Services glossary of terms. To build inclusivity, the Association of Research Libraries offers the Leadership and Career Development Program, a fellowship that partners mid-career librarians from underrepresented groups with career coaches[28] and mandates cultural competency and diversity trainings for "learning LGBTQ+ terminology, autism spectrum disorder awareness, ways of successfully working with veterans, or those living with different mental health issues."[29]

A strong thread weaves together strategies to create equitable opportunities in the workplace. However, the ties that bind FWAs, EID, and inclusivity have not yet been fully explored. Inclusivity in the workplace for academic librarians has been examined through a multitude of lenses including organizational structures and accessibility. Disparities between professional ranks, such as faculty librarians and professional staff, can create insular divisions of marginalization, hierarchies, separation, and difference. Petropoulos and colleagues' research explored the unintentional inward exclusion of library employees through language that groups "librarians" and "library staff" as separate. They found that library websites often associate librarian positions with their areas of expertise, whereas staff are listed with less specific titles that fail to recognize the employee's uniqueness.[30] From an accessibility perspective, Betz's research argued that the hiring process can be adapted to better accommodate academic librarians with disabilities; recommendations were to offer predetermined breaks and to encourage candidates to ask for accessible adjustments during campus tours.[31] Through conducting interviews with academic librarians about how libraries meet EID commitments, Bresnahan found that EID committees with institutional support, such as investment in dedicated positions and a budget, were more successful.[32]

Discussion

In the past thirty years, libraries have made strides to emphasize EID in human resource management, but they have not centered FWAs in these dialogues. This discussion advocates integration of EID for hiring and retention. It identifies inclusive workplace elements, describes how they are experienced, points out subjective perceptions in hiring and retention, and suggests how managers might develop a FWA program with an eye toward increasing diversity.

Inclusive Workplace Elements

Incorporating inclusive work practices in human resource activities is imperative and should take into account the needs of librarians at all career stages. A 2020 report issued by McKinsey and Company found that "even where companies are more diverse, many appear as yet unable to cultivate work environments which effectively promote inclusive leadership and accountability among managers, equality and fairness of opportunity, and openness and freedom from bias and discrimination."[33] To change this narrative, academic libraries can reevaluate the employment life cycle through an EID lens. A framework for sustainable hiring and retention should be guided by the organization's articulated strategic priorities, mission, and values. The practical stages of this cycle include attracting and recruiting; onboarding; development; retention and engagement; offboarding and separation; and advocacy.[34] Elements of inclusiveness can be embedded in each phase.

An initial, actionable step in organizational planning is to collectively select terms that represent inclusiveness in local library contexts. Figure 16.1 depicts a sample word cloud yielded from an ideation activity to compile terms. The word cloud visualizes connections between the aspirational ideals for inclusive workplace elements.[35] The interconnected library organizational values, traits, and practicalities named in this exercise are listed here: authenticity, belonging, communication, fairness, identity, meaningful work, opportunities, policy, relationships, and transparency.

Figure 16.1. Inclusive workplace elements in hiring and retention.

Subjective Perceptions in Hiring and Retention

Subjectivity is ingrained in hiring and retention practices. Diverse attitudes, emotions, and feelings in the workplace can affect the employment life cycle. Understanding how to leverage these differences and why they occur is key to building inclusive workplaces. Mapping workplace elements to their manifestations is a way to conceptualize connections between inclusiveness and flexible work. Table 16.1 represents an exercise in cross-walking aspirational inclusive elements to subjective perceptions in the employment life cycle. This ideation activity is a technique to bridge personal and interpersonal dynamics. The interpersonal terms reflect the convergence of encounters and communications between librarian and administrator personas.

Table 16.1. Map of inclusive workplace elements to subjective perceptions in hiring and retention.

Inclusive Workplace Element	Librarian→	Interpersonal	←Administrator
Authenticity	True	Trustworthy	Credible
Belonging	Accepted	Respectful	Valued
Communication	Open	Collegial	Transparent
Fairness	Honesty	Principled	Equitable
Identity	Character	Virtuous	Integrity
Meaningful	Worthwhile	Purposeful	Impactful
Opportunities	Possibilities	Aspirational	Actions
Policy	Guidance	Directional	Leadership
Relationships	Rapport	Connected	Facilitator
Transparency	Candid	Understood	Clear

Inclusive FWA Framework Design

Thirty years of library reports and literature document the desire among librarians for flexible work and the ways this type of work arrangement positively contributes to inclusive workplace cultures. Taking several factors into consideration is important when designing an inclusive FWA framework. Long-term sustainment of FWAs is predicated on administrators, middle managers, and staff having mutual understandings of the benefits accrued from transforming the workplace through flexibility. At the institutional level, inclusivity commitments should be articulated in formal mission and value statements. Administrators need to be transparent and equitable in their policies for granting FWAs. Note that managers may be reluctant to grant flexible work, as it can place undue pressures in understaffed and under-resourced departments. Therefore, library administrators have to be accountable for finding solutions to endemic problems and expand access to flexibility across ranks and departments.

Hiring managers in academic libraries should codify and market a spectrum of FWAs focused on the employee life cycle to demonstrate the prioritization of EID. These options might include compressed workweeks, flextime, hybrid work, job sharing, part-time work, remote work, research leaves, staggered schedules, and telecommuting. Libraries will be more equipped to make strides toward inclusive cultures through organization-level tactics, such as devising a values statement within an EID framework, implementing EID assessment through stay and exit surveys, and publishing a public policy detailing FWA options. During the recruitment phase, a FWA statement can be appended to job postings, search committees could receive training in EID and FWAs, and interview formats could have both in-person and virtual options. Decentering physical requirements within academic librarian job searches, which traditionally include an all-day, in-person interview, would be especially inclusive for persons with disabilities. Finally, retention strategies should target accountability, such as by creating benchmarks to measure inclusiveness. Career growth can be prioritized by offering FWA as a means to support tenure activities, promotions, reskilling, and training. FWAs can also lead to more inclusive professional positions by defraying cost of living expenses and supporting a work-life balance.

This framework demonstrates the potential of FWAs to enhance inclusivity; however, the authors want to emphasize that EID initiatives are not a checklist. Shared understandings of FWAs between librarians, administrators, and the organization serve to improve interpersonal dynamics between the employer and employee. Reluctance to use FWAs or unfamiliarity with the practice can be addressed through training. Concerns about productivity can be ameliorated by annual reviews that assess job performances. For organizations, FWAs convey willingness to adapt to individual schedules, increase efficiencies, and incentivize retention. For staff, work-life balance is more attainable. Through FWAs, libraries can demonstrate their receptiveness to change and responsiveness to diversifying the workplace. These practical measures affirm commitment to EID while boosting the recruitment and retention of highly qualified and diverse library workers.

Conclusion

FWAs are not a trend; they are here to stay. When organizations are inflexible, employees can experience low morale, diminished engagement, and higher rates of attrition.[36] By making FWAs the norm, libraries will be better positioned to recruit and retain a diverse and multigenerational librarian workforce.[37] These three points summarize the key takeaways based on the survey of literature and review of the library profession's historical use of FWAs:

- FWAs align library human resources with core values of librarianship. They extend inclusiveness in organizational climate and culture by expanding the spectrum of workplace diversity.

- FWAs are a proven tool to increase EID in librarian recruitment and retention and should be appended to professional guidance and benchmarking tools.
- Meaningful progress toward sustainable inclusivity practices demands accountability, investment, and a culture of continuous assessment.

FWAs can produce positive outcomes for the enterprise and the individual. More than remotely possible, FWAs are key to transforming organizational culture and structure through inclusive recruitment and retention of academic librarians.

Notes

1. Society for Human Resource Management, "Introduction to the Human Resources Discipline of Diversity, Equity and Inclusion," September 11, 2019, https://www.shrm.org/resourcesandtools/tools-and-samples/toolkits/pages/introdiversity.aspx (requires login).
2. Claire-Lise Bénaud, Elizabeth N. Steinhagen and Sharon A. Moynahan, "Flexibility in the Management of Cataloging," *Cataloging and Classification Quarterly* 30, no. 2–3 (2000): 281–98, https://doi.org/10.1300/J104v30n02_08; Anna R. Craft, "Remote Work in Technical Services: What Have We Learned? Where Are We Going?" *Serials Review* 48, no. 3–4 (2022): 243–47, https://doi.org/10.1080/00987913.2022.2132106; Association of Research Libraries, Office of Management Services, *Flexible Work Arrangements in ARL Libraries, SPEC Kit #180* (Washington, DC: Association of Research Libraries, 1992).
3. Association of Research Libraries, Office of Management Services, *Flexible Work Arrangements*.
4. Cooperative Extension, "Diversity, Equity, and Inclusion," accessed November 13, 2022, https://publications.extension.org/view/1049966584/.
5. American Library Association, "ODLOS Glossary of Terms," accessed November 15, 2022, https://www.ala.org/aboutala/odlos-glossary-terms.
6. AFL-CIO Department for Professional Employees, "Library Professionals: Facts & Figures 2021," accessed November 21, 2022, https://www.dpeaflcio.org/factsheets/library-professionals-facts-and-figures (page content changed).
7. Mihoko Hosoi, Lauren Reiter, and Diane Zabel, "Reshaping Perspectives on Flexible Work: The Impact of COVID-19 on Academic Library Management," *portal: Libraries and the Academy* 21, no. 4 (2021): 695–713, https://doi.org/10.1353/pla.2021.0038; P. Matthijs Bal and Luc Dorenbosch, "Age-Related Differences in the Relations between Individualised HRM and Organisational Performance: A Large-Scale Employer Survey," *Human Resource Management Journal* 25, no. 1 (2015): 41–61, https://doi.org/10.1111/1748-8583.12058; Carolyn Timms et al., "Flexible Work Arrangements, Work Engagement, Turnover Intentions and Psychological Health," *Asia Pacific Journal of Human Resources* 53, no. 1 (January 2015): 83–103, https://doi.org/10.1111/1744-7941.12030.
8. Office of Disability Employment Policy, US Department of Labor, "Flexible Work Arrangements," accessed November 18, 2022, https://www.dol.gov/agencies/odep/program-areas/employment-supports/flexible-work-arrangements.
9. David Rock, Heidi Grant, and Jacqui Grey, "Diverse Teams Feel Less Comfortable—and That's Why They Perform Better," *Harvard Business Review*, September 22, 2016, https://hbr.org/2016/09/diverse-teams-feel-less-comfortable-and-thats-why-they-perform-better.
10. Lauren Reiter and Diane Zabel, "New Ways of Working: Flexible Work Arrangements in Academic Libraries," in *Leading in the New Academic Library*, ed. Becky Albitz, Christine Avery, and Diane Zabel (Santa Barbara, CA: Libraries Unlimited, 2017), 85.
11. Vidya Sundar et al., "Striving to Work and Overcoming Barriers: Employment Strategies and Successes of People with Disabilities," *Journal of Vocational Rehabilitation* 48, no. 1 (2018): 93-109, https://doi.org/10.3233/JVR-170918; Marcie Zaharee et al., "Recruitment and Retention of Early-Career Technical Talent," *Research-Technology Management* 61, no. 5 (2018): 51–61, https://doi.org/10.1080/08956308.2018.1495966.
12. Noemi Nagy, Ariane Froidevaux, and Andreas Hirschi, "Lifespan Perspectives on Careers and Career Development," in *Work across the Lifespan*, ed. Boris B. Baltes, Cort W. Rudolph, and Hannes Zacher (London: Academic Press, 2019), 235–59.
13. Dorien Hannes Zacher, T. A. M. Kooij, and Margaret E. Beier, *Active Aging at Work*, white paper (Alliance for Organizational Psychology, 2019), 2, http://eawop.org/ckeditor_assets/attachments/1264/active_aging_whitepaper.pdf.
14. Heejung Chung and Tanja Van der Lippe, "Flexible Working, Work–Life Balance, and Gender Equality: Introduction," *Social Indicators Research* 151, no. 2 (2020): 365–81.

15. Eline Jammaers and Jannine Williams, "Care for the Self, Overcompensation and Bodily Crafting: The Work–Life Balance of Disabled People," *Gender, Work and Organization* 28, no. 1 (January 2021): 119–37, https://doi.org/10.1111/gwao.12531.
16. Eliot Bush, "Why Hybrid, Remote and Flexible Work Appeals Even More to BIPOC Employees," *Great Place to Work* (blog), February 8, 2022, https://www.greatplacetowork.com/resources/blog/how-racial-inequities-make-hybrid-remote-flexible-work-even-more-appealing.
17. Association of Research Libraries, Office of Management Services, *Flexible Work Arrangements*.; ViewSonic, "8 Types of Flexible Work Arrangements Explained," June 1, 2021, https://www.viewsonic.com/library/business/8-types-of-flexible-work-arrangements-explained.
18. Reiter and Zabel, "New Ways of Working."
19. Ashlea Green, "Post Covid-19: Expectations for Academic Library Collections, Remote Work, and Resource Description and Discovery Staffing," *Journal of Academic Librarianship* 48, no. 4 (July 2022): article 102564, https://doi.org/10.1016/j.acalib.2022.102564.
20. Michael A. Germano, "Does Workplace Inflexibility Cost Libraries," *Library Worklife* 7, no. 3 (March 2010), https://ala-apa.org/newsletter/2010/03/28/does-workplace-inflexibility-cost-libraries/.
21. Hui-Fen Chang, "Ethnic and Racial Diversity in Academic Research Libraries: Past, Present, and Future," in *Proceedings of the 2013 ACRL Conference, Indianapolis, Indiana, April 10–13, 2013*, 183–93, https://www.ala.org/acrl/sites/ala.org.acrl/files/content/conferences/confsandpreconfs/2013/papers/Chang_Ethnic.pdf.
22. American Library Association, "Diversity in the Workplace," accessed November 15, 2022, https://www.ala.org/advocacy/diversity/workplace.
23. ALA Committee on Diversity, *Diversity, Equity, and Inclusion (DEI) Scorecard for Library and Information Organizations*. (Chicago: American Library Association, 2021), 1, https://www.ala.org/aboutala/sites/ala.org.aboutala/files/content/2021%20EQUITY%20SCORECARD%20FOR%20LIBRARY%20AND%20INFORMATION%20ORGANIZATIONS.pdf.
24. Association of College and Research Libraries, "ACRL Diversity Alliance," accessed November 15, 2022, https://www.ala.org/acrl/issues/diversityalliance.
25. Janice Y. Kung, K-Lee Fraser, and Dee Winn, "Diversity Initiatives to Recruit and Retain Academic Librarians: A Systematic Review," *College and Research Libraries* 81, no. 1 (2020): 104, https://doi.org/10.5860/crl.81.1.96.
26. Jaena Alabi, "From Hostile to Inclusive: Strategies for Improving the Racial Climate of Academic Libraries," *Library Trends* 67, no. 1 (Summer 2018): 131–46, https://doi.org/10.1353/lib.2018.0029.
27. April Hathcock, "White Librarianship in Blackface: Diversity Initiatives in LIS," *In the Library with the Lead Pipe*, October 7, 2015, http://www.inthelibrarywiththeleadpipe.org/2015/lis-diversity/.
28. Association of Research Libraries, "Leadership and Career Development Program," November 17, 2022, https://www.arl.org/category/our-priorities/diversity-equity-inclusion/leadership-and-career-development-program/.
29. Lindsey M. Harper, "Recruitment and Retention Strategies of LIS Students and Professionals from Underrepresented Groups in the United States," *Library Management* 41, no. 2–3 (2020): 73, https://doi.org/10.1108/LM-07-2019-0044.
30. Jo-Anne Petropoulos et al., "Contextualizing Inclusivity in Terms of Language: Distinguishing Librarians from 'Library Staff,'" *Journal of Library Administration* 62, no. 4 (2022): 535–56, https://doi.org/10.1080/01930826.2022.2057131.
31. Gail Betz, "Navigating the Academic Hiring Process with Disabilities," *In the Library with the Lead Pipe*, April 6, 2022, https://www.inthelibrarywiththeleadpipe.org/2022/hiring-with-disabilities/.
32. Megan Bresnahan, "Library Diversity and Inclusion Statements in Action," *Journal of Library Administration* 62, no. 4 (2022): 419–37, https://doi.org/10.1080/01930826.2022.2057125.
33. Sundiatu Dixon-Fyle et al., *Diversity Wins* (Summit, NJ: McKinsey & Company, 2020), 6, https://www.mckinsey.com/featured-insights/diversity-and-inclusion/diversity-wins-how-inclusion-matters.
34. Paychex, "The Employee Life Cycle and Why It's Important," January 20, 2023, https://www.paychex.com/articles/human-resources/what-is-employee-lifecycle.
35. Dana Reijerkerk and Kristen J. Nyitray, *Inclusive Workplace Elements*, November 23, 2022, distributed by Voyant Tools, https://voyant-tools.org/?corpus=13c0472882d611689863fceeaf6eb7b5.
36. Kaetrena Davis Kendrick, "The Low Morale Experience of Academic Librarians: A Phenomenological Study," *Journal of Library Administration* 57, no. 8 (2017): 846–78, https://doi.org/10.1080/01930826.2017.1368325; Kaetrena Davis Kendrick and Ione T. Damasco, "Low Morale in Ethnic and Racial Minority Academic Librarians: An Experiential Study," *Library Trends* 68, no. 2 (2019): 174–212, https://doi.org/10.1353/lib.2019.0036.
37. Andrea Falcone and Lyda Fontes McCartin, "Strategies for Retaining and Sustaining the Academic Librarian Workforce in Times of Crises," *Journal of Library Administration* 62, no. 4 (2022): 557–63, https://doi.org/10.1080/01930826.2022.2057132.

Bibliography

AFL-CIO Department for Professional Employees. "Library Professionals: Facts & Figures 2021." Accessed November 21, 2022. https://www.dpeaflcio.org/factsheets/library-professionals-facts-and-figures (page content changed).

Alabi, Jaena. "From Hostile to Inclusive: Strategies for Improving the Racial Climate of Academic Libraries." *Library Trends* 67, no.1 (Summer 2018): 131–46. https://doi.org/10.1353/lib.2018.0029.

ALA Committee on Diversity. *Diversity, Equity, and Inclusion (DEI) Scorecard for Library and Information Organizations*. Chicago: American Library Association, 2021. https://www.ala.org/aboutala/sites/ala.org.aboutala/files/content/2021%20EQUITY%20SCORECARD%20FOR%20LIBRARY%20AND%20INFORMATION%20ORGANIZATIONS.pdf.

American Library Association. "Diversity in the Workplace." Accessed November 15, 2022. https://www.ala.org/advocacy/diversity/workplace.

———. "ODLOS Glossary of Terms." Accessed November 15, 2022. https://www.ala.org/aboutala/odlos-glossary-terms.

Association of College and Research Libraries. "ACRL Diversity Alliance." Accessed November 15, 2022. https://www.ala.org/acrl/issues/diversityalliance.

Association of Research Libraries. "Leadership and Career Development Program." Accessed November 17, 2022. https://www.arl.org/category/our-priorities/diversity-equity-inclusion/leadership-and-career-development-program/.

Association of Research Libraries, Office of Management Services. *Flexible Work Arrangements in ARL Libraries, SPEC Kit #180*. Washington, DC: Association of Research Libraries, 1992.

Bal, P. Matthijs, and Luc Dorenbosch. "Age-Related Differences in the Relations between Individualised HRM and Organisational Performance: A Large-Scale Employer Survey." *Human Resource Management Journal* 25, no. 1 (2015): 41–61. https://doi.org/10.1111/1748-8583.12058.

Bénaud, Claire-Lise, Elizabeth N. Steinhagen and Sharon A. Moynahan. "Flexibility in the Management of Cataloging." *Cataloging and Classification Quarterly* 30, no. 2–3 (2000): 281–98. https://doi.org/10.1300/J104v30n02_08.

Betz, Gail. "Navigating the Academic Hiring Process with Disabilities." *In the Library with the Lead Pipe*, April 6, 2022. https://www.inthelibrarywiththeleadpipe.org/2022/hiring-with-disabilities/.

Bresnahan, Megan. "Library Diversity and Inclusion Statements in Action." *Journal of Library Administration* 62, no. 4 (2022): 419–37. https://doi.org/10.1080/01930826.2022.2057125.

Bush, Eliot. "Why Hybrid, Remote and Flexible Work Appeals Even More to BIPOC Employees." *Great Place to Work* (blog), February 8, 2022. https://www.greatplacetowork.com/resources/how-racial-inequities-make-hybrid-remote-flexible-work-even-more-appealing.

Chang, Hui-Fen. "Ethnic and Racial Diversity in Academic Research Libraries: Past, Present, and Future." In *Proceedings of the 2013 ACRL Conference, Indianapolis, Indiana, April 10–13, 2013*, 182–93. Chicago: Association of College and Research Libraries, 2013. https://www.ala.org/acrl/sites/ala.org.acrl/files/content/conferences/confsandpreconfs/2013/papers/Chang_Ethnic.pdf.

Chung, Heejung, and Tanja Van der Lippe. "Flexible Working, Work–Life Balance, and Gender Equality: Introduction." *Social Indicators Research* 151, no. 2 (2020): 365–81.

Cooperative Extension. "Diversity, Equity, and Inclusion." Accessed November 13, 2022. https://publications.extension.org/view/1049966584/.

Craft, Anna R. "Remote Work in Technical Services: What Have We Learned? Where Are We Going?" *Serials Review* 48, no. 3–4 (2022): 243–47. https://doi.org/10.1080/00987913.2022.2132106.

Davis Kendrick, Kaetrena. "The Low Morale Experience of Academic Librarians: A Phenomenological Study." *Journal of Library Administration* 57, no. 8 (2017): 846–78. https://doi.org/10.1080/01930826.2017.1368325.

Davis Kendrick, Kaetrena, and Ione T. Damasco. "Low Morale in Ethnic and Racial Minority Academic Librarians: An Experiential Study." *Library Trends* 68, no. 2 (2019): 174–212. https://doi.org/10.1353/lib.2019.0036.

Dixon-Fyle, Sundiatu, Kevin Dolan, Dame Vivian Hunt, and Sara Prince. *Diversity Wins: How Inclusion Matters*. Summit, NJ: McKinsey & Co., 2020. https://www.mckinsey.com/featured-insights/diversity-and-inclusion/diversity-wins-how-inclusion-matters.

Falcone, Andrea, and Lyda Fontes McCartin. "Strategies for Retaining and Sustaining the Academic Librarian Workforce in Times of Crises." *Journal of Library Administration* 62, no. 4 (2022): 557–63. https://doi.org/10.1080/01930826.2022.2057132.

Germano, Michael A. "Does Workplace Inflexibility Cost Libraries?" *Library Worklife* 7, no. 3 (March 2010). https://ala-apa.org/newsletter/2010/03/28/does-workplace-inflexibility-cost-libraries/.

Green, Ashlea. "Post Covid-19: Expectations for Academic Library Collections, Remote Work, and Resource Description and Discovery Staffing." *Journal of Academic Librarianship* 48, no. 4 (July 2022): article 102564. https://doi.org/10.1016/j.acalib.2022.102564.

Harper, Lindsey M. "Recruitment and Retention Strategies of LIS Students and Professionals from Underrepresented Groups in the United States." *Library Management* 41, no. 2–3 (2020): 67–77. https://doi.org/10.1108/LM-07-2019-0044.

Hathcock, April. "White Librarianship in Blackface: Diversity Initiatives in LIS." *In the Library with the Lead Pipe*, October 7, 2015. http://www.inthelibrarywiththeleadpipe.org/2015/lis-diversity/.

Hosoi, Mihoko, Lauren Reiter, and Diane Zabel. "Reshaping Perspectives on Flexible Work: The Impact of COVID-19 on Academic Library Management." *portal: Libraries and the Academy* 21, no. 4 (2021): 695–713. https://doi.org/10.1353/pla.2021.0038.

Jammaers, Eline, and Jannine Williams. "Care for the Self, Overcompensation and Bodily Crafting: The Work–Life Balance of Disabled People." *Gender, Work and Organization* 28, no. 1 (January 2021): 119–37. https://doi.org/10.1111/gwao.12531.

Kung, Janice Y., K-Lee Fraser, and Dee Winn. "Diversity Initiatives to Recruit and Retain Academic Librarians: A Systematic Review." *College and Research Libraries* 81, no. 1 (2020): 96–108. https://doi.org/10.5860/crl.81.1.96.

Nagy, Noemi, Ariane Froidevaux, and Andreas Hirschi. "Lifespan Perspectives on Careers and Career Development." In *Work across the Lifespan*, edited by Boris B. Baltes, Cort W. Rudolph, and Hannes Zacher, 235–59. London: Academic Press, 2019.

Office of Disability Employment Policy, US Department of Labor. "Flexible Work Arrangements." Accessed November 18, 2022. https://www.dol.gov/agencies/odep/program-areas/employment-supports/flexible-work-arrangements.

Paychex. "The Employee Life Cycle and Why It's Important." January 20, 2023. https://www.paychex.com/articles/human-resources/what-is-employee-lifecycle.

Petropoulos, Jo-Anne, Laura Banfield, Elizabeth Obermeyer, and Jennifer McKinnell. "Contextualizing Inclusivity in Terms of Language: Distinguishing Librarians from 'Library Staff.'" *Journal of Library Administration* 62, no. 4 (2022): 535–56. https://doi.org/10.1080/01930826.2022.2057131.

Reijerkerk, Dana, and Kristen J. Nyitray. *Inclusive Workplace Elements*. November 23, 2022. Distributed by Voyant Tools. https://voyant-tools.org/?corpus=13c0472882d611689863fceeaf6eb7b5.

Reiter, Lauren, and Diane Zabel. "New Ways of Working: Flexible Work Arrangements in Academic Libraries." In *Leading in the New Academic Library*, edited by Becky Albitz, Christine Avery, and Diane Zabel, 83–92. Santa Barbara, CA: Libraries Unlimited, 2017.

Rock, David, Heidi Grant, and Jacqui Grey. "Diverse Teams Feel Less Comfortable—and That's Why They Perform Better." *Harvard Business Review*, September 22, 2016. https://hbr.org/2016/09/diverse-teams-feel-less-comfortable-and-thats-why-they-perform-better.

Shroyer, Aaron, and Veronica Gaitán. "Four Reasons Why Employers Should Care about Housing." Housing Matters, September 11, 2019. https://housingmatters.urban.org/articles/four-reasons-why-employers-should-care-about-housing.

Society for Human Resource Management. "Introduction to the Human Resources Discipline of Diversity, Equity and Inclusion." Accessed April 17, 2023. https://www.shrm.org/resourcesandtools/tools-and-samples/toolkits/pages/introdiversity.aspx (requires login).

Sundar, Vidya, John O'Neill, Andrew J. Houtenville, Kimberly G. Phillips, Tracy Keirns, Andrew Smith, and Elaine E. Katz. "Striving to Work and Overcoming Barriers: Employment Strategies and Successes of People with Disabilities." *Journal of Vocational Rehabilitation* 48, no. 1 (2018): 93–109. https://doi.org/10.3233/JVR-170918.

Timms, Carolyn, Paula Brouch, Michael O'Driscoll, Thomas Kalliath, Oi Ling Siu, Cindy Sit, and Danny Lo. "Flexible Work Arrangements, Work Engagement, Turnover Intentions and Psychological Health." *Asia Pacific Journal of Human Resources* 53, no. 1 (January 2015): 83–103. https://doi.org/10.1111/1744-7941.12030.

ViewSonic. "8 Types of Flexible Work Arrangements Explained." July 11, 2021. https://www.viewsonic.com/library/business/8-types-of-flexible-work-arrangements-explained.

Zacher, Hannes, Dorien T. A. M. Kooij, and Margaret E. Beier. *Active Aging at Work*. White paper. Alliance for Organizational Psychology, 2019. http://eawop.org/ckeditor_assets/attachments/1264/active_aging_whitepaper.pdf.

Zaharee, Marcie, Tristan Lipkie, Steward K. Mehlman, and Susan K. Neylon. "Recruitment and Retention of Early-Career Technical Talent." *Research-Technology Management* 61, no. 5 (2018): 51–61. https://doi.org/10.1080/08956308.2018.1495966.

Strategic Planning and Reorganizing

CHAPTER 17

Empowering Employees through Strategic Initiatives

Jessica J. Boyer

Once a new five-year strategic plan has been written, figuring out how to achieve that plan can be daunting. Accomplishing strategic goals means bringing change to the library, and change is never easy. Strategic planning implementation is often a comprehensive activity that stretches to all organizational areas and all employees in the library. Implementing these changes in a way that allows for smooth library operations and buy-in from all employees can be challenging, and it can be particularly difficult to continue that process annually for the full five-year time frame of a strategic plan.

The Hugh J. Phillips Library at Mount St. Mary's University has found one way to address this challenge. We have developed a successful strategic planning implementation process for our library. Each year, the library staff select strategic objectives from our current plan to be the focus of the upcoming academic year. Each employee then serves as the project lead for at least one of these objectives. This process has empowered employees to take on leadership roles within the department and departs from traditional library norms where leadership falls to a library administration or a librarian. As a result, this practice has been particularly impactful to professional, nonlibrarian employees. With many strategic objectives related to collaboration with other campus areas, this process has also increased the visibility of many library employees across campus and has allowed them to be seen as leaders in their areas. As a result of all employees leading in their respective strategic objective projects, the library is growing in the ways outlined in our strategic plan while also allowing for the professional growth of each employee. As we enter the final year of our five-year strategic plan, the library is on track to achieve its outlined goals and objectives, but of equal importance is the personal professional growth that each employee has achieved along the way.

Problem Definition

This chapter will address the challenges of providing supportive leadership opportunities to all library employees and successfully implementing the library's strategic plan. This issue will be explored through a case study of successful strategic planning implementation at Mount St. Mary's University, a liberal arts university in central Maryland. This issue is significant because it is common to all academic libraries, which face questions such as these: How do we address the daunting challenge of carrying out our five-year strategic plan? How do we get buy-in from employees to participate in the process and complete the work? How do we support and empower our employees to accomplish this additional work? This chapter will explore a successful methodology one academic library employed to answer these questions.

Literature Review

Employee engagement and academic library strategic plans are often related. A recent study found that 73 percent of the academic library strategic plans included objectives related to library staff.[1] While most academic libraries include employee engagement in their written strategic plans, including it in the implementation of their strategic plans has led to more mixed results. An engaged library staff is critical to the success of a strategic plan, as "the implementation of strategic plan goals ultimately rests on the staff who work the day-to-day operation of the library. It can provide buy-in from staff and enable them to work *with* the leadership."[2] In one case study on successful strategic plan implementation, the library director explains that

> each of the [library's] strategic plans has precipitated innovation and appears to have motivated employees to *own* particular goals and objectives, thus they work hard to realize the vision articulated in the plan. Since the entire staff collaborated on the development of each plan, buy-in has been strong.... Because everyone in the library has a voice in determining the future direction of the organization, they are motivated to advance new ideas and work hard to make that improved vision of their library a reality.[3]

The literature demonstrates that employee engagement is critical for success throughout strategic planning implementation.

Although the literature shows the importance of engagement of all employees in strategic planning implementation, that reality can be challenging to achieve due to the diversity of employee types found in academic libraries.[4] As scholar Dennis R. Defa explains,

> while the academic library is not the only administrative unit on a campus with this mix of faculty, exempt, nonexempt, part-time, permanent, temporary, student, and nonstudent employees, it is one of the only places where all these employees interact in a number of ways, and in none of these other offices is the mix of employees such that patrons can mistake one for the other.[5]

In relation to strategic planning implementation, these differences can create internal tensions, such as librarians versus staff, or those with faculty status versus those without faculty status. Libraries are then challenged with how to engage all of these different employees in strategic planning implementation so that all employees have a voice in the process and are valued. This challenge is reflected in a 2011 study of strategic planning in college libraries. When asked "Who is responsible for the implementation of the strategic plan?" only 12.7 percent of respondents indicated "all library employees."[6] This statistic demonstrates that much work is needed to successfully involve a greater number of library employees in strategic planning implementation.

Shared leadership provides a theoretical framework to approach this challenge. Scholar Laura Krier champions shared leadership as a successful tool for strategic planning in academic libraries.[7] She explains:

> A foundation of shared leadership is critical for effective strategic planning. Shared leadership builds capacity for strategic thinking throughout the library, enabling people at every level to see beyond their position's or department's needs to what is best for the library as a whole. A practice of shared leadership develops the problem-solving and consensus-building skills that are necessary for meaningful participation in the planning processes. And perhaps most importantly, it is only through a framework of shared leadership that shared vision can emerge. Without shared vision, there is no possibility of establishing priorities and creating plans to which everyone will feel committed and work to achieve.[8]

This framework of shared leadership allows all library employees to actively participate in strategic planning and provides individual ownership of the future success of the library. This framework provides a cohesive vision of leadership that can empower library employees.

Overall, the literature demonstrates the importance of engaging all employees in strategic planning implementation but also notes the challenges presented by the diverse types of employees found in libraries. Utilizing a theoretical framework of shared leadership, this chapter seeks to bridge that gap by presenting a case study of a successful strategic planning implementation that actively involved and empowered all library employees.

Discussion

In 2018, the Phillips Library at Mount St. Mary's University developed a strategic plan to guide the library for the next five years, which aligned with the university's strategic plan period. Simultaneous with the adoption of the 2018 strategic plan, the library developed an implementation plan that would lead to both the achievement of the library's strategic goals and the engagement and empowerment of all library employees. Through this process, the library has grown in the strategic directions outlined in the plan while library employees have continued to grow professionally. The library's implementation process involves four key steps: (1) identifying annual objectives and project leads, (2) developing a project proposal, (3) executing the project, and (4) final reporting.

Identifying Objectives and Project Leads

At the start of each academic year, the library director identifies and proposes seven to eight strategic objectives for the upcoming year, as well as proposed project leads who will be responsible for oversight and project management of the objective. Given the collaborative nature of library work, the project lead often works with other members of the team to produce tangible results of the objective. Depending on the nature of the project and objective, project coleads are sometimes used. After the library director identifies proposed strategic objectives and project leads for the year, the proposal is brought to the full library team for discussion, feedback, and revision as needed. Each year, the team has easily reached a consensus regarding both the planned objectives and project leads for the upcoming year.

Every member of the library staff serves as project lead for at least one objective each year. It is important to our team that all members have the opportunity to serve as project leads, not just librarians or those who have explicit leadership roles. As the literature demonstrates, having all members of the library staff actively participate in strategic planning is key to successful implementation.[9] Additionally, this approach levels the playing field among employees by recognizing that all employees have the potential to lead the library in their area of expertise.

With the limited hours they work each week, student workers do not serve as project leads but often have an assistive role in carrying out the strategic objectives. We place importance on making sure that our student workers feel that they are an integral part of our team and are involved in the strategic direction of the library. Our student workers are particularly invaluable when it comes to objectives that rely on student feedback. An example of one such objective would be a reconfiguration of the furniture on the library's main floor in order to maximize study spaces. Our student workers were very helpful in both providing their own feedback and soliciting feedback from other students.

As the library team discusses the proposed objectives and project leads for the year, we reflect on both opportunities to showcase an individual employee's strengths and opportunities for personal and professional growth. Allowing all members of the library staff to serve as project leads can provide them with opportunities to showcase the strengths that they bring to the library. Some strengths may be obvious: for example, it was logical for our interlibrary loan specialist to serve as project lead on an objective related to improving resource sharing. Other employees may bring personal strengths to a particular strategic objective that is outside the position's traditional scope of work.

For example, the role of acquisitions manager does not traditionally involve marketing. However, our current acquisitions manager has a background in graphic design and was willing to share his expertise and serve as project lead for one of our strategic objectives related to elevating the library's brand and marketing materials. He was able to develop a series of marketing templates that were on brand for both the library and the university, as well as helpful tutorial instructions. His outstanding work and detailed instructions have created a meaningful resource that all members of the library staff have been able to utilize and build upon. While this project did not relate to purchasing, this objective allowed our acquisitions manager to utilize his strengths in graphic design and help the library progress in implementing its strategic plan.

Although in this case the acquisitions manager was willing to help with this objective, library leaders should exercise caution when proposing employees take on projects outside of their traditional job description. Some employees may have expertise in certain areas from previous experience; however, that does not mean that they wish to use their skills in their current position if those skills fall outside of their specific job description. Library leaders should discuss these objectives with the employee and provide space for them to decline the opportunity or provide conditions under which they would accept. Examples of such conditions could include a decreased workload in other areas to focus on this opportunity or increased compensation for additional hours worked to accommodate the project.

Others may serve as project leads to grow their professional skills in a related area of interest. For example, open education resources (OERs) are a focus of our strategic plan. Since the university and library have worked with OERs only in a limited capacity thus far, no one on our staff had meaningful experience with them. When it was time to focus on the OER strategic objectives, the director needed to have a conversation with the proposed project lead to discuss his level of interest in the project and desire for professional growth in this area. The librarian had previously discussed OERs with several faculty members and was eager to pursue additional professional development. As the project lead, he was able to fulfill a personal professional development goal, while also supporting the library's strategic direction. The role of the director is always to provide the project lead with the resources to be successful. However, that role is especially significant when the lead has limited experience in the focus area of the strategic objective. The main resource that the director should provide is adequate resources and time to pursue professional development opportunities. At the end of this objective, the project lead grew confident in his own skills and his ability to guide the library in supporting OERs on campus.

Project Proposal

After designating the project lead, the next step is for each project lead to draft a proposal. This proposal includes a work plan with the specific actions to be undertaken, a time line that highlights when key milestones will be achieved, and a means of assessment. The assessment component helps us to identify whether we successfully achieved the objective. Depending on the nature of the objective, the assessment may be a tangible outcome, such as a written report or plan; it may also be a plan for a measurement if an objective is to grow a particular service by 10 percent; or the assessment may take the form of a survey or focus group to gain feedback from patrons. The director then reviews the proposal and provides feedback to the project lead before the work plan is set into motion. This discussion allows the director to be aware of and provide the needed time and resources for the employee to be successful in completing the project. This discussion also includes how the director can support the employee's professional growth through this project, particularly since serving in a leadership role has pushed some employees outside of their comfort zone. The proposal time line provides the director and employee with helpful dates to touch base, review the status of the work plan, and revise as necessary.

This discussion during the project proposal stage is a critical step in encouraging employees not only to successfully achieve their objective but also to lead the library in an area of strategic growth. The director must recognize that since employees are being asked to take on the additional work of leading a strategic objective, they must be given the time, space, and resources to be successful. Practically, this process often manifests itself with the director taking an additional shift at the reference desk some weeks or jumping in to package up interlibrary loans other weeks so that the librarians and staff in those areas have additional hours to work on their objectives. This sharing of duties requires the director to understand the work of all employees so that the employees can ask the director to step in when needed. In order for this to work successfully, the director's calendar, choices, and budget need to accommodate and reflect the library's current strategic projects. These choices may include the director ensuring that their calendar is open when project leads have upcoming milestones in their work plan, in case they need to devote extra hours to their projects. The director also needs to craft a budget that allocates necessary funding to support the strategic objectives for that year. Examples of specific budget allocations may include professional development opportunities for project leads' development in certain areas or an increase in the supplies budget to support an objective related to outreach. Overall, the role of the director is one of support and ensuring all members of the team have what they need to be successful.

Many strategic objectives involve collaboration with faculty or other campus departments. Having employees other than library administration serve as project lead has increased the visibility of many library employees across campus, allowing them to act as leaders in their area. Our strategic plan has two goals related to increasing collaboration. One goal is related to faculty collaborations and supporting the curricula. The other goal is related to collaborations with other student-success-focused offices on campus, such as orientation, the writing center, and the learning services office. Library administration intentionally did not serve as project lead for these objectives. Allowing other members of the team to lead allowed the library staff to build cross-campus relationships with other departments and be viewed by the wider community as leaders in their areas.

Directors should provide the financial support for employees to be successful as project leads. This need for and level of support may greatly vary depending on the specific strategic objectives. Directors need to adjust their annual budgets in order to provide the resources that the project leads need to be successful. Libraries' budgets are notoriously strapped, and we cannot fund everything. Saying "yes" to funding a specific strategic objective one year will likely mean that several other objectives cannot be completed until later in the five-year cycle. When funding is stretched, financial support may also take the shape of providing the space and authority for project leads to write grant proposals to support their initiatives or work with development to cultivate donors for a particular project. Likely, the strategic plan already contains goals related to grants and development. Some of those objectives may need to be tackled early in the five-year time line to fund other objectives later on. Additionally, there may be objectives specifically related to budget allocations, such as devoting increased funding to a specific area of collection development or to more professional development for the team. Directors may take on those objectives as a project lead themselves.

Executing the Project

In an ideal world, executing the project would happen seamlessly as outlined in the project proposal. However, that is not the typical reality of how our libraries and institutions operate. Frequently, there may be disruptions to our libraries that call for a change of plan. These disruptions may include a new campus-wide initiative that causes the library to reprioritize, the departure of a staff member, or an unexpected budget cut. When these disruptions occur, it is imperative that the director meet with project leads to revisit the project proposal and revise the plans to meet the current situation. If a staff member departed midyear, the director may need to pause the implementation of an objective that they were leading. Similarly, new campus-wide initiatives should be compared to the library's strategic plan. Certain objectives may be prioritized over others due to their timeliness relating to the campus-wide initiative. In this way, the project proposal can serve as guidelines for strategic planning initiatives rather than plans set in stone. Disruptions to well-laid plans are never easy, and directors should be flexible in helping project leads adjust their plans to meet changing circumstances with which they may be presented.

Final Reporting

The last step in our annual strategic planning implementation process is assessment and reporting. Each project lead submits a one-to-two-page executive summary of their strategic objectives that outlines the work completed and how the proposed objective was met. A template is used for executive summaries, which are then compiled into an annual strategic planning report for the library. This report is shared with academic affairs administration, as well as the university's effectiveness and assessment office. The report is also used internally within the library to document the strategic planning implementation work completed and to inform multiyear departmental assessment. In compiling this report, the accomplishments of each staff member are clearly noted in each of their executive summaries. The tough job of implementing a strategic plan is done through the excellent work of each library employee, who should be properly recognized and given credit for their time and efforts. Employee performance reviews can also be a good opportunity to recognize and document employee contributions to strategic planning implementation. Now, at the conclusion of our five-year strategic plan, rereading our annual reports is very rewarding. It is exciting not only to see everything the library has been able to accomplish, but also to read the final reports of each employee and see how they have grown.

Conclusion

Strategic planning is an important aspect of innovation and growth in our libraries. We spend much time crafting a thoughtful plan only to later be challenged in determining how to implement the plan. This challenge requires a large-scale effort that takes the active participation of the full library staff. This case study from Mount St. Mary's University provides one example of how to successfully implement a strategic plan while also empowering employees to take ownership and a leadership role in the implementation of that plan each year.

There are several steps directors can take to lay the groundwork for successful strategic planning implementation:

- All employees should have equal opportunity to lead during strategic planning implementation regardless of status or department. Each employee has the potential to make meaningful contributions to the library's success and lead in a particular area.
- Directors should be conscious of the workload for employees and set them up to be successful in their projects. Directors should ask the project leads what

they require to be successful in achieving their objective, and then should actively work to provide the necessary space, time, and resources to ensure the project leads' success.
- Directors should strive to be flexible in response to changing needs and environment of the library and institution. As changes arise, work with project leads to adjust their project workplan accordingly.
- Directors should give credit where credit is due. Use this process to recognize employees for the meaningful contributions they are making to the library.

While this list is not exhaustive, these takeaways can provide a strong foundation for keeping the library's strategic plan out of a drawer and on the minds of all employees. Together, you can successfully achieve your strategic plan and bring positive change and innovation to your library.

Notes

1. Laura Saunders, "Academic Libraries' Strategic Plans: Top Trends and Under-recognized Areas," *Journal of Academic Librarianship* 41, no. 3 (May 2015): 288, https://doi.org/10.1016/j.acalib.2015.03.011.
2. Laura Newton Miller, "What Is Helpful (and Not) in the Strategic Planning Process? An Exploratory Survey and Literature Review," *Library Leadership and Management* 32, no. 3 (2018): 7, https://llm.corejournals.org/llm/article/view/7267.
3. Anne Marie Casey, "Grassroots Strategic Planning: Involving the Library Staff from the Beginning," *Journal of Library Administration* 55, no. 4 (2015): 339, https://doi.org/10.1080/01930826.2015.1038935.
4. Joy M. Perrin, "Strategic Planning from the Bottom Up: A Unit Strategic Plan That Pushes Change," *Journal of Library Administration* 57, no. 6 (2017): 719, https://doi.org/10.1080/01930826.2017.1340771.
5. Dennis R. Defa, "Human Resource Administration in the Academic Library," *Library Leadership and Management* 22 no. 3 (2008): 149, https://llm.corejournals.org/llm/article/view/1729.
6. Eleonora Dubicki, *Strategic Planning in College Libraries* Clip Note#43 (Chicago: Association of College and Research Libraries, 2011), 19.
7. Laura Krier, "A Framework for Shared Leadership: A Perspective on Strategic Planning for Academic Libraries," *Journal of Academic Librarianship* 48, no. 6 (November 2022): article 102503, p. 1, https://doi.org/10.1016/j.acalib.2022.102503.
8. Krier, "Framework for Shared Leadership," 1.
9. Miller, "What Is Helpful," 7; Casey, "Grassroots Strategic Planning," 339.

Bibliography

Casey, Anne Marie. "Grassroots Strategic Planning: Involving the Library Staff from the Beginning." *Journal of Library Administration* 55, no. 4 (2015): 329–40. https://doi.org/10.1080/01930826.2015.1038935.
Defa, Dennis R. "Human Resource Administration in the Academic Library." *Library Leadership and Management* 22, no. 3 (2008): 138–41. https://llm.corejournals.org/llm/article/view/1729.
Dubicki, Eleonora. *Strategic Planning in College Libraries*. Clip Note #43. Chicago: Association of College and Research Libraries, 2011.
Krier, Laura. "A Framework for Shared Leadership: A Perspective on Strategic Planning for Academic Libraries." *Journal of Academic Librarianship* 48, no. 6 (November 2022): article 102503. https://doi.org/10.1016/j.acalib.2022.102503.
Miller, Laura Newton. "What Is Helpful (and Not) in the Strategic Planning Process? An Exploratory Survey and Literature Review." *Library Leadership and Management* 32, no. 3 (2018): 1–27. https://llm.corejournals.org/llm/article/view/7267.
Perrin, Joy M. "Strategic Planning from the Bottom Up: A Unit Strategic Plan That Pushes Change." *Journal of Library Administration* 57, no. 6 (2017): 712–22. https://doi.org/10.1080/01930826.2017.1340771.

Saunders, Laura. "Academic Libraries' Strategic Plans: Top Trends and Under-recognized Areas." *Journal of Academic Librarianship* 41, no. 3 (May 2015): 285–91. https://doi.org/10.1016/j.acalib.2015.03.011.

CHAPTER 18

Breaking Down Structures to Build Up Staff
Organizational Change in an Academic Library

Isaac Gilman

Librarianship in Western, non-Indigenous contexts is built on hierarchical classification; this is reflected not only in the way information is organized and granted authority, but also in the way that library workers are organized and granted authority. The long-standing distinction between professional and paraprofessional library work, usually demarcated by a requirement for a master's degree, has consistently been used to structure responsibilities within libraries and to signal which work is most highly valued and respected. This is especially true of academic libraries, which function within the larger hierarchical system of higher education institutions and often inherit the faculty and staff structures and dynamics of those institutions.[1] These structures within libraries can create significant inequities in power and privilege between library workers in different positions, which can in turn have negative impacts on engagement, morale, and retention—especially for employees in positions classified as staff or nonlibrarian, but professional.

Problem Definition

Within academic libraries, any potential rationale for structural determinants—such as compensation, representation in decision-making, or individual agency—to define which workers hold the most authority and responsibility has eroded over time (assuming it was ever necessary), as individuals in all positions now frequently have similar education and ability to contribute to the library's work. In order to improve morale, reduce turnover, and create more equitable organizations, there is instead an increasing push to acknowledge—in concrete, structural ways—the value and interdependence of "all of the labor performed in the [academic] library,"[2] with a particular emphasis on providing more equitable recognition of the contributions across both faculty librarian and staff roles.* This requires going beyond efforts to encourage individual, interpersonal respect and acknowledgment between different groups of library workers (though this is also necessary) and moving to deconstruct arbitrary classifications that divide the groups in the first place. Although it can be especially challenging for academic libraries to break away from the library profession's norms and from those inherited from their larger institutions (i.e., faculty/staff hierarchies), such change is necessary to create more healthy, inclusive work environments.

Using the case of a library at a small, private university, this chapter explores the equity, morale, and retention issues created through historically defined distinctions between faculty librarian and staff positions. The chapter then discusses the process of implementing a new organizational model that challenges those long-standing ideas about the ways positions are structured and compensated, and the ways varying types of work are valued. In doing so, the goal is to illustrate the power of breaking down arbitrary divisions between faculty librarian and staff responsibilities—in service of an ultimate vision of creating a library whose structures communicate the message that all labor is valuable and all workers are valued.

Literature Review

Factors in library employee low morale have received increasing attention in the last five years.[3] This focus has sharpened as library leaders try to address the ways in which preexisting issues related to workload and employee burnout have become more pronounced with the added stressors of the COVID-19 pandemic.[4] While the literature on library employee morale (and the associated outcome of turnover) considers interpersonal factors important, there is consistent recognition of a critical need to address organizational factors (e.g., culture, structure, salary) that create work environments in which harmful

---

* In this chapter, *librarian* is used to denote roles that require a MLIS or equivalent degree/experience, and which are engaged in a level of work that necessitates largely autonomous management or decision-making with regard to library operations/services.

power dynamics between employees can flourish;[5] and, conversely, the possibility of shaping organizational culture and structures in ways that can improve library employee morale, motivation, and engagement.[6]

In describing the general role of organizational culture in employee satisfaction and turnover, Ehrhart and Kuenzi identify the "deepest level of culture" as the "taken-for-granted assumptions that guide day-to-day life in organizations."[7] Within libraries (and especially academic libraries, with their inherited distinctions in power and privilege between faculty and staff roles), one of the most persistent assumptions is that there is a different value for different forms of library work, and implicitly a higher value for the work of librarians or faculty librarians (in relation to library staff). The impacts of this assumption—disparities in power, agency, and compensation between library position types—are identified as one of the core structural issues underlying library employee morale issues. In examining factors in academic librarian turnover, Heady and colleagues found this issue even *within* librarian roles—with varying levels of satisfaction and morale depending on whether librarians had faculty appointments or staff status.[8]

Bowman and Samsky have observed that a preponderance of the literature that considers library structural issues is based on librarians' perspectives (such as Heady and colleagues).[9] However, Glusker and colleagues have recently provided one of the first comprehensive examinations of library employee morale from a staff perspective, in which they note the challenge of growing numbers of MLIS-credentialed staff who are underemployed in their current roles.[10] This context exacerbates real and perceived disparities when such staff members are not treated as equally valuable within their organizations, despite being equally as qualified as their peers who are in librarian positions. As Glusker and colleagues explore this, and propose a framework for understanding "morale impact avenues in librarian organizational structures," they recognize the intersection of multiple factors that contribute to low morale for library workers in staff roles, and specifically call out "the powerful impact of the librarian/staff divide."[11] Within that, they report experiences of library staff "being treated as 'less than' [and] being consistently disrespected through microaggressions aimed at them by librarians, whether intentionally or not."[12] Glusker and colleagues found that these negative interpersonal dynamics occurred alongside enabling structural and cultural issues that were "contributing directly to low morale experiences among library staff." For example, staff were "allowed less control over their job content and schedules"[13] than librarians, received fewer professional development opportunities than librarians, and were excluded from communications and decision-making in which librarians were engaged.

Although there are recommendations in the literature regarding how best to mitigate the interpersonal and structural issues leading to low morale for library employees (especially staff),[14] there are few published examples of organizations that have implemented broad structural changes to address these issues. The following case represents an effort to do just that, with implications for several aspects of library human resources, including recruitment, professional development, and compensation.

Discussion

Beginning in the late 1990s, librarian positions in the Pacific University Libraries (PUL) held faculty status and the librarians served as the PUL leadership group, both in support of the library director and, briefly, as part of a collective Library Management Team. Although the number of staff (non-librarian) positions within PUL continued to grow gradually and the level of responsibility within staff positions also expanded, this model of librarian leadership continued through 2010. For example, the faculty librarians met regularly with the library director as a Librarians' Council to assist with strategic planning and service design. While this group evolved over the next decade to include staff members, both in ex officio functional roles and as at-large staff representatives, the PUL legacy structure created a culture in which faculty librarians' voices and contributions were privileged both implicitly and explicitly in collaborative work, decision-making, autonomy, and compensation. Anecdotally, the negative impacts of this environment manifested in three primary ways: low morale among staff who felt their knowledge or roles were not appropriately compensated by PUL or recognized by colleagues; staff being reluctant to contribute in groups with librarians; and, finally, some librarians and staff feeling unwelcome with members of the other group. It is important to note that these issues were not universal—not all staff or faculty librarians reported these experiences, and many individual staff-librarian relationships were healthy and productive. However, similar issues occurred over time and across employee turnover, suggesting entrenched structural issues that had an ongoing impact on employees' sense of being valued; on the ability of individual employees to work together effectively; and on some employees' decisions to leave the library for other opportunities.

As both a prior staff member and, more recently, a faculty librarian within PUL, I brought firsthand experience in both roles to my new position as, first, library director and then dean. In those roles, both staff and faculty librarian colleagues shared directly with me about their experiences of feeling devalued either by the organization or by other individuals. My first attempts at addressing this issue were, in retrospect, largely aimed at treating symptoms of the actual structural issue. More specifically, my efforts consisted of

- eliminating both the Librarians' Council and all-staff meetings, both of which I perceived as contributing to siloing between position types;
- increasing staff representation on the newly named Library Steering Team, and focusing on making this team a shared faculty librarian and staff space to assist in planning and decision-making;
- bringing in facilitators to work with PUL as a whole on communication styles and strategies;

- shifting PUL professional development funding from primarily supporting librarian professional development to promoting use of those funds (and flexibility in scheduling to do so) by both librarians and staff;
- creating new cross-departmental standing committees to promote collaborative work, ensuring there was shared staff and librarian representation in committee memberships, and encouraging staff leadership of committees; and
- consistently communicating the equal weight and value that I was placing on both librarian and staff input in PUL service planning and delivery.

While these measures improved staff representation and leadership in PUL activities, it was clear that both perceived and real power differentials remained between faculty librarian and staff roles. For example, while project and leadership teams had broader representation, not everyone felt comfortable participating in those groups, or believed that their voices were equally valued in those settings.

Because most of the measures implemented to that point had been based on anecdotal accounts and my own observations, before considering any more substantial changes, I conducted an all PUL climate and culture survey,[15] followed by individual meetings with each employee to get their perspective on themes reported in the survey. The survey results, along with the follow-up conversations, affirmed my existing assumptions: that PUL structures—organizationally, as well as in terms of compensation and real and perceived power in shared work and decision-making—were set up to present staff roles as lesser in terms of their contributions to PUL. Those structural attributes had a negative impact on staff morale, engagement, and retention, and contributed to interpersonal challenges for employees, regardless of role.

With the data collected from the survey and individual meetings to guide me, I began addressing the interwoven structural and interpersonal issues that had been reported with the goals of (1) creating clear expectations that communication should reflect shared respect and value for colleagues as the foundation for our collective work; (2) removing artificial organizational structures that explicitly or implicitly created hierarchies of value across employee types; and, (3) removing, to the extent practical, artificial barriers between faculty librarian and staff work that had historically reinforced those hierarchies of value. The ultimate intended outcomes of this work were to create a workplace where all employees, regardless of employee type or role, experience their contributions as valued by the organization and their colleagues—in the ways they are treated, recognized for their knowledge, and compensated.

To work toward the first goal around shared respect and value, I retained an external facilitator to help develop a community agreement focused on communication. This participatory process was valuable not only for its ultimate outcome, a written agreement to which we could hold one another accountable, but also because it reinforced the need for the planned structural work. Issues raised during the community agreement process pointed to the negative impact of the faculty librarian/staff hierarchy and its relationship to siloing and communication issues. Our structural divisions resulted in a lack of connection and communication, which contributed to assumptions about others and other groups—an environment that worked against the success of even the best-intentioned employees.

Although the community agreement and its resulting expectations were important, without addressing the second goal of removing explicitly or implicitly created hierarchies of value through organizational changes, it was clear that the existing structural issues would continue to work against any improvements in relationships. From my perspective, these issues could be addressed only by transforming our compensation, recognition, and hierarchical structures. In order to better recognize the value that staff roles bring to PUL—including the degree to which staff roles, and not just faculty librarians, are now responsible for the practice of professional librarianship—I began implementing the following changes (with the expectation that salary changes in particular would take multiple years to calibrate based on available funding).

Extending "librarian" status beyond faculty positions. The title of *librarian* has historically been connected to faculty positions within PUL. However, due to PUL's growth and the responsibilities in staff roles expanding, we had several exempt staff positions that required a master's degree or equivalent (primarily in librarianship) and were performing professional library work—but these positions were not being recognized as librarians. To allow the education and knowledge of MLIS degree holders who are performing professional-level work to be recognized, I expanded use of the librarian title to include both faculty positions and exempt staff positions that require a master's degree in librarianship. This immediately increased the number of librarians from seven to twelve, and more appropriately recognized the level of work being performed in several staff roles. While this potentially introduced a new point of conflict between librarians who have faculty status and those who do not (an issue noted by Heady and colleagues[16]), my goal was to reduce structural distinctions between those two groups and emphasize the faculty status is not related to organizational value but to specific types of job responsibilities—much in the same way that library faculty have very different job responsibilities but all feel equally valued. One significant step in that direction was to address compensation differences between the two groups of librarians, as noted below.

Establishing similar starting salaries for all roles engaged in professional librarianship. Starting salaries for faculty librarian positions in PUL have consistently been between 15 to 20 percent higher than exempt staff positions, even as those staff positions have increasingly performed higher-level duties and required similar levels of education. Over time, the arbitrariness of this disparity has become more obvious as the level and amount of work in faculty and exempt staff roles has—while remaining different in *kind*, based on the functional role of the position (e.g., collection development versus systems management work)—converged with regard to the complexity and autonomy required and level of importance to the organization. To address this disparity, I began a plan to increase (gradually, as funding allowed) the minimum starting salary for all exempt staff positions in PUL that require graduate education or equivalent so that all positions engaged in professional librarianship (whether classified as faculty or exempt staff) would have the same baseline for starting salary.*

Providing staff with education and experience in library instruction. At Pacific, instruction has historically been an area of work reserved for faculty librarians, even though frontline staff regularly provide informal instruction and outreach and play an integral role in students' gaining knowledge and comfort with using the library. This has meant that staff—even staff with professional education and in professional roles—who are interested in gaining instruction experience have not had the opportunity to do so.† As a result, lack of training and experience in instruction has become a barrier to staff either advancing into Pacific faculty librarian positions or librarian positions at other libraries. To address this, I asked our Center for Educational Technology and Curricular Innovation (part of PUL) to develop a formal Library Instruction Institute open to all employees that would provide similar training as early-career faculty receive at Pacific, within the context of our usual one-shot library instruction. To complement the formality of the institute with the opportunity to gain experience, I also opened a portion of PUL's undergraduate instruction program to participation by all staff and faculty within PUL. More specifically, I invited participation in PUL's presence in the undergraduate first-year seminar. While any interested staff could be included, I anticipated it would primarily be staff in Access Services involved in redesigning the curriculum and delivering the sessions in these programs. With its public-facing role, Access Services is a critical point of connection for our students and already regularly engages in outreach activities, so extending this to an instructional role seemed natural.

Focusing committee membership on functional roles. Even as I developed new standing committees for PUL with the goal of creating collaborative spaces for staff and faculty librarians to work together, I unconsciously contributed to furthering divisions in the way I initially structured the committee memberships. Similar to committee structures within the university, for most committees I created at-large positions for both faculty librarian and staff representatives. While the goal was ensuring shared representation, this was (rightly) received by some as further emphasizing that faculty librarians and staff both needed to be represented *as groups* because they each brought different perspectives and value to PUL. In response to this feedback, I changed all standing committee membership to focus only on representation from relevant functional areas, as well as having general at-large positions that anyone may hold—regardless of position type.

These combined changes were intended to address local needs that have also been identified in the library literature: to better recognize and compensate the knowledge of

---

* I also began to increase the minimum starting salary for all staff positions within PUL so that they are more appropriately compensated and don't suffer from further salary compression when other staff salaries are increased.

† Several faculty librarians recently started an informal instruction roundtable within PUL open to all faculty and staff interested in discussing instruction, which was very well-received, but due to capacity issues, wasn't sustained.

responsibilities in staff positions; to eliminate inequities that have evolved in compensation between faculty librarian and staff positions; to provide increased opportunities for professional development for all staff; and to create collaborative connections between the work of library staff and faculty that emphasize their roles as peers. The ultimate goal was to improve morale, job satisfaction, both faculty and staff work experiences, and staff retention. Although it is too early to tell if this goal will be met since some of these initiatives are only partially implemented, there have been positive signs—gleaned mostly through informal feedback—that the acknowledgment of long-standing concerns and opportunities to be better recognized for expertise and potential contributions, has generated hopefulness for the promise of a more equitable organization.

Conclusions

As reported in the library literature, many library employee morale issues are related not to job satisfaction, but rather to the environment and culture in which a job is performed;[17] in other words, how employees experience themselves as valued and respected by their libraries and their colleagues. While individual interactions and interpersonal dynamics are clearly one factor in creating a library work culture—good or bad—they are, at a certain level, only manifestations or symptoms of the structures within which that culture is created. In my experience as a leader, it has become clear that efforts to address these symptoms—specifically, focusing on personal practice or responsibility or on increasing representation in leadership or decision-making—are not sufficient to create lasting change in morale, especially for library staff. Libraries must also consider the ways in which our positions are structured and compensated, and in which our different types of work are implicitly valued or given priority. As we do this, we should begin to name and reframe the assumptions that guide those decisions so that all work is appropriately acknowledged and valued and we have an equitable starting point for communication and collaboration.

While there is no one-size-fits-all approach for libraries exploring this type of structural transformation (much depends on the current mix of position types within each library, and the ways in which they interact), the following questions gleaned through my experience (and, admittedly, my personal missteps) may be useful for other academic library leaders to consider.

Where have you created representation without addressing underlying power imbalances? When beginning to address concerns about lack of voice in planning or decision-making (an issue that can contribute to low morale, especially for staff or any positions lower within a structural or compensation hierarchy), a first step is creating representation—providing a seat at the table. However, if there are real or perceived power differentials between the positions or people within a group, those with less perceived agency may not feel empowered to participate or may fear their voice will not matter in decision-making.

Representation is important, but is not enough if any individual positions or groups that are represented do not experience themselves as equally valued.

What systems or structures from outside the library have a direct or indirect impact on the way positions and work are organized and compensated within the library? The most common example of this is the designation of some library employees as faculty, and the way in which those faculty positions are required to align with and interact with faculty and university governance systems outside of the library. The degree to which these structures and systems need to be inherited or replicated within the library is worth consideration.

For libraries with faculty positions, what is the explicit or implicit place of those library faculty within university structures and hierarchies, and how does that impact library faculty's sense of value? Even if the primary goal of restructuring is to address issues with staff positions, it is important to be aware of how changes within the library may intersect with the experiences of librarians within the larger institution. Glusker and colleagues call out the ways in which "the stresses and uncertainties of librarians' own experiences of striving to belong and feeling less-than,"[18] and the need to reinforce their value within the larger institution, can unintentionally influence the way roles inside the library are viewed and valued. Considering how best to support and uplift library faculty in this larger context while not devaluing staff colleagues within the library is critical when planning structural changes.

How, if at all, is the explicit or implicit value of certain position types constructed in relationship to other position types within the library? Understanding the ways in which certain positions may be implicitly assumed or understood to do *more* work or *more valuable* work (in relationship to other positions) is critical for being able to address disparities in compensation, benefits, or other forms of recognition across position types that may be performing different types of work. Without this understanding, leaders' attempts to rectify persistent undervaluing of some positions or position types (whether through compensation or other means) can result in others feeling devalued as a result. It is important to be able to clearly communicate that differences in the *nature* of different forms of library work do not necessarily imply differences in the amount or value of that work and that shifts that flatten hierarchies of compensation, recognition, or agency are intentionally recognizing this.

How would you structure, or restructure, the library's positions if there were no one in them right now? As abstract as they may seem, questions of structural change in positions can never fully be divorced from the people who are in the positions now. Leaders must be able to balance simultaneously stepping back from this reality and acknowledging it. *Stepping back*, in that planning for structural change has to be done with the overall health and future of the library in mind, regardless of who currently holds positions; and *acknowledgment*, in that any discussions about changes in positions will be almost impossible for people to consider without overlaying their perceptions, whether positive or negative, of current position-holders. Maintaining focus on the overall structural rationale may be useful in addressing questions about why there are changes for specific individuals within the library.

Even if the answers to these questions are clear, there are often external constraints on our ability to enact systemic change to address the answers. Those constraints may be financial, may be related to larger institutional staffing structures or contracts, or may even be related to our employees' collective capacity for change at a given point in time (for example, after a global pandemic). However, while there can be temporary barriers to implementing larger changes, gathering data and input to inform potential changes, and engaging employees in thinking about what positive change could look like, should in itself be a constructive step toward improving morale. From there, implementing incremental steps as possible—and continually communicating what has been done and what still remains to be done—can instill confidence that progress is being made toward creating a library where all employees, regardless of role, feel valued and recognized for their contributions to our shared work.

Notes

1. Ann Glusker et al., "'Viewed as Equals': The Impacts of Library Organizational Cultures and Management on Library Staff Morale," *Journal of Library Administration* 62, no. 2 (2022): 153–89, https://doi.org/10.1080/01930826.2022.2026119.
2. Maura Seale and Rafia Mirza, "Empty Presence: Library Labor, Prestige, and the MLS," *Library Trends* 68, no. 2 (2019): 263, https://doi.org/10.1353/lib.2019.0038.
3. For example: Max Bowman and Monica Samsky, "Access Services: Not Waving, But Drowning" in *Deconstructing Service in Libraries: Intersections of Identities and Expectations*, ed. Veronica Arellano Douglas and Joanna Gadsby (Sacramento, CA: Litwin Books, 2020), 79–94, https://digitalcommons.colby.edu/faculty_scholarship/75; Kaetrena Davis Kendrick, "The Low Morale Experience of Academic Librarians: A Phenomenological Study," *Journal of Library Administration* 57, no. 8 (2017): 846–78, https://doi.org/10.1080/01930826.2017.1368325; Kaetrena Davis Kendrick and Ione T. Damasco, "Low Morale in Ethnic and Racial Minority Academic Librarians: An Experiential Study," *Library Trends* 68, no. 2 (2019): 174–212, https://doi.org/10.1353/lib.2019.0036; Emily C. Weyant, Rick L. Wallace, and Nakia J. Woodward, "Contributions to Low Morale, Part 1: Review of Existing Literature on Librarian and Library Staff Morale," *Journal of Library Administration* 61, no. 7 (2021): 854–68, https://doi.org/10.1080/01930826.2021.1972732; Emily C. Weyant, Rick L. Wallace, and Nakia J. Woodward, "Suggestions for Improving Morale, Part 2: Review of Existing Literature on Librarian and Library Staff Morale," *Journal of Library Administration* 61, no. 8 (2021): 996–1007, https://doi.org/10.1080/01930826.2021.1984142.
4. Edward M. Corrado, "Low Morale and Burnout in Libraries," *Technical Services Quarterly* 39, no. 1 (2022): 37–48, https://doi.org/10.1080/07317131.2021.2011149.
5. Glusker et al., "Viewed as Equals."
6. Giyeong Kim et al., "What Makes a 'Happy' Workplace for Librarians? Exploring the Organizational Functions of Academic Libraries in South Korea," *Journal of Academic Librarianship* 48, no. 6 (2022): article 102594, pp. 1–11, https://doi.org/10.1016/j.acalib.2022.102594.
7. Mark G. Ehrhart and Maribeth Kuenzi, "The Impact of Organizational Climate and Culture on Employee Turnover," in *The Wiley Blackwell Handbook of the Psychology of Recruitment, Selection and Employee Retention*, ed. Harold W. Goldstein, Elaine D. Pulakos, Jonathan Passmore and Carla Semedo (Malden, MA: John Wiley, 2017), 495, https://doi.org/10.1002/9781118972472.ch23.
8. Christina Heady et al., "Contributory Factors to Academic Librarian Turnover: A Mixed-Methods Study," *Journal of Library Administration* 60, no. 6 (2020): 579–99, https://doi.org/10.1080/01930826.2020.1748425.
9. Bowman and Samsky, "Access Services."
10. Glusker et al., "Viewed as Equals."
11. Glusker et al., "Viewed as Equals," 164.
12. Glusker et al., "Viewed as Equals," 167.

13. Glusker et al., "Viewed as Equals," 167.
14. For example: Glusker et al., "Viewed as Equals;" Heady et al., "Contributory Factors;" Weyant et al., "Suggestions."
15. The survey instrument and scoring were adapted from the Organizational Climate Questionnaire [Adrian Furnham and Leonard D. Goodstein,. "The Organizational Climate Questionnaire (OCQ)," in *The 1997 Annual: Volume 2, Consulting* (San Francisco: Pfeiffer, 1997)], resulting in identifying areas to "Celebrate," "Fix" (immediate attention needed), or "Consider" (attention needed next) across the following domains: Mission, Vision, and Organizational Focus; Work Environment; Work Conditions; Working with Colleagues; People Management; Communication and Decision-Making; Opportunities; and Rewards and Recognition.
16. Heady et al., "Contributory Factors."
17. Heady et al., "Contributory Factors."
18. Glusker et al., "Viewed as Equals," 181.

Bibliography

Bowman, Max, and Monica Samsky. "Access Services: Not Waving, But Drowning." In *Deconstructing Service in Libraries: Intersections of Identities and Expectations*, edited by Veronica Arellano Douglas and Joanna Gadsby, 79–94. Sacramento, CA: Litwin Books, 2020. https://digitalcommons.colby.edu/faculty_scholarship/75.

Corrado, Edward M. "Low Morale and Burnout in Libraries." *Technical Services Quarterly* 39, no. 1 (2022): 37–48. https://doi.org/10.1080/07317131.2021.2011149.

Ehrhart, Mark G., and Maribeth Kuenzi. "The Impact of Organizational Climate and Culture on Employee Turnover." In *The Wiley Blackwell Handbook of the Psychology of Recruitment, Selection and Employee Retention*, edited by Harold W. Goldstein, Elaine D. Pulakos, Jonathan Passmore, and Carla Semedo, 494–512. Malden, MA: John Wiley, 2017. https://doi.org/10.1002/9781118972472.ch23.

Furnham, Adrian, and Leonard D. Goodstein. "The Organizational Climate Questionnaire (OCQ)." In *The 1997 Annual: Volume 2, Consulting*. San Francisco: Pfeiffer, 1997.

Glusker, Ann, Celia Emmelhainz, Natalia Estrada, and Bonita Dyess. "'Viewed as Equals': The Impacts of Library Organizational Cultures and Management on Library Staff Morale." *Journal of Library Administration* 62, no. 2 (2022): 153–89. https://doi.org/10.1080/01930826.2022.2026119.

Heady, Christina, Amy F. Fyn, Amanda Foster Kaufman, Allison Hosier, and Millicent Weber. "Contributory Factors to Academic Librarian Turnover: A Mixed-Methods Study." *Journal of Library Administration* 60, no. 6 (2020): 579–99. https://doi.org/10.1080/01930826.2020.1748425.

Kendrick, Kaetrena Davis. "The Low Morale Experience of Academic Librarians: A Phenomenological Study." *Journal of Library Administration* 57, no. 8 (2017): 846–78. https://doi.org/10.1080/01930826.2017.1368325.

Kendrick, Kaetrena Davis, and Ione T. Damasco. "Low Morale in Ethnic and Racial Minority Academic Librarians: An Experiential Study." *Library Trends* 68, no. 2 (2019): 174–212. https://doi.org/10.1353/lib.2019.0036.

Kim, Giyeong, Chohae Kim, Go Eun Lee, Jieun Yeon, and Jee Yeon Lee. "What Makes a 'Happy' Workplace for Librarians? Exploring the Organizational Functions of Academic Libraries in South Korea." *Journal of Academic Librarianship* 48, no. 6 (2022): article 102594. https://doi.org/10.1016/j.acalib.2022.102594.

Seale, Maura, and Rafia Mirza. "Empty Presence: Library Labor, Prestige, and the MLS." *Library Trends* 68, no. 2 (2019): 252–68. https://doi.org/10.1353/lib.2019.0038.

Weyant, Emily C., Rick L. Wallace, and Nakia J. Woodward. "Contributions to Low Morale, Part 1: Review of Existing Literature on Librarian and Library Staff Morale." *Journal of Library Administration* 61, no. 7 (2021): 854–68. https://doi.org/10.1080/01930826.2021.1972732.

———. "Suggestions for Improving Morale, Part 2: Review of Existing Literature on Librarian and Library Staff Morale." *Journal of Library Administration* 61, no. 8 (2021): 996–1007. https://doi.org/10.1080/01930826.2021.1984142.

CHAPTER 19

Envision, Revision, and Balance

A Case Study of a Participation-Based, Employee-Focused Academic Library Unit Restructuring

Vickie Albrecht, Kristy McKeown, Coralee Leroux, and Geoff Sinclair

Human resources restructuring is rarely received warmly by employees. Often viewed as a euphemism for downsizing or layoffs, the practice of restructuring has been demonstrated to have a negative effect on employee well-being.[1] However, human resources restructuring in libraries may be necessary to adapt to rapid shifts in technology, student and faculty needs, physical space, institutional growth, and more. Is it possible to successfully reorganize a library unit in a way that balances organizational needs and goals, while maintaining an approach that recognizes the dignity of unit staff, reduces the negative impacts on affected employees, and involves them in the process? This chapter will provide an overview of a project initiated in fall 2020 to restructure the Library Services unit at Trent University Library and Archives while attempting to include staff participation and reduce staff anxiety and fear. Ultimately our shared unit goals were to create a clear and logical organizational chart and robust job descriptions for the entire team—an ambitious undertaking for a project team without any previous restructuring experience. The intention of the chapter is not to describe the results of the project; rather, we aim to detail the processes we used in our attempt to balance organizational goals and staff well-being throughout the project, as well as to share our lessons learned.

Literature Review

Change has been a long-standing challenge in libraries, requiring flexibility from staff members and their willingness to perform a variety of tasks.[2] When shifts in technology, workflows, or mission result in procedural gaps or outdated job descriptions, substantial transformation is advisable. Restructuring refers to a significant organizational change, which may include closure, outsourcing, merging, expansion, or other complex reorganization of one or more units.[3] The process of significantly modifying workplace organization can be a source of considerable stress for employees and can negatively impact employee well-being,[4] an outcome our project team was cognizant of and eager to avoid. Without understanding the concerns of staff, management risks losing their cooperation, making reorganization efforts likely to fail.[5]

The literature suggests that few managers use a defined model for library restructuring.[6] In our case, we wanted to be purposeful in how we conducted the project after noting that an intentional, active leadership approach to organizational restructuring correlates to increased job satisfaction and reduced work-related burnout.[7] While there is evidence of the effectiveness of principles found in a variety of models, application still requires some experimentation and local adaptation on the part of managers,[8] something that resonated with our experience of trying to develop a restructuring model that would best address the unique situation in our library.

While restructuring refers to a substantial organizational change that often affects current employees, job design is the process of determining the contents, methods, and relationships of jobs to meet organizational requirements for productivity, efficiency, and quality while satisfying the personal needs of the jobholder.[9] This differs from a static job description in that it is a continuous process based on environmental, organizational, and individual factors.[10] While job design can take place during reorganization, it is not limited to that situation. The process can be formal or informal, enforced by a manager or influenced by the employee.[11] Involving workers in both job design and job restructuring allows the organization to gain insight from those best positioned to suggest improvements and improves worker morale,[12] while also resulting in greater harmony between employees and the organization.[13] These factors influenced the project, which we envisioned would allow staff to participate in both processes.

Job enrichment is commonly a goal of job design, and both can play a role in enhancing job quality. Enriched jobs are those that give "discretion, variety, and high levels of responsibility,"[14] and which aim to improve employee interest by boosting the challenge of work while also increasing the employee's control over how they carry out the work.[15] Researchers have positively linked enhanced positions to individual employee and organizational performance.[16] Job enrichment differs from job enlargement, which is the practice of adding more tasks of a similar level, rather than increasing responsibility, control, and decision-making.[17] Also referred to as horizontal job loading, job enlargement is unlikely to increase employee motivation.[18] The project team discussed and agreed that the reorganization of Library Services should result in positions with increased variety, autonomy, and complexity. This resulted in a decision early on that each position would support multiple functional areas (job enlargement) but also have an area of specialization, in which the incumbent could build expertise, have increased authority, and become the go-to person in the unit (job enrichment).

When redesigning positions within an academic library, to balance support staff job enrichment against librarian de-professionalization, it is useful to see what peer institutions are doing. For example, while original cataloguing may have traditionally been performed by librarians, how is this work organized at other institutions? Do support staff, librarians, or both groups perform original cataloguing? There are useful surveys of support staff tasks performed in cataloging units, electronic resources units, and research units,[19] which challenge our long-standing librarian versus support staff dividing lines, often revealing that tasks were seldom performed exclusively by one group or the other. This research helped to build our case for support staff job enrichment. Examining surveys of this sort may point to new types of collaborations that already exist elsewhere between librarians and support staff.[20] A particularly instructive case study offered perspectives of the support staff in a small university's electronic resources management unit. They shared firsthand accounts of the challenges of moving from primarily print-based workflows to ERM workflows, revealing challenges in communication and reinforcing the need for a more hands-on, collaborative managerial style when enriching jobs.[21]

Remember that language matters when crafting positions, and updating job descriptions provides an opportunity to remove objectionable terms, even when language is not intentionally meant to be demeaning.[22] When existing job descriptions in our library included responsibilities with qualitative adjectives, we learned that staff often interpreted this language as didactic rather than descriptive. For example, the phrase "responds in a professional manner" was seen by some staff members as condescending or as a backhanded criticism of staff behaviour. It was also clear that some language helped to reinforce silos between librarians and support staff, as well as barriers between functional areas in our library. It was our intention, therefore, to use wording that promoted staff empowerment, the significant value of staff contributions, and fluidity between functional areas.

Discussion

Project Background

Trent University Library and Archives is a small Canadian academic library which employs thirty-four people and serves a student population of approximately 11,000 full-time equivalents across two campuses in Ontario—the primary Symons campus in Peterborough, and the smaller Durham campus in Oshawa—a figure that has grown by 36 percent in the past five years. The two libraries that make up the Library and Archives are the Bata Library—Trent's four-story flagship library in Peterborough, which at the time of the project employed eight librarians, two managers, and fifteen support staff —and the Trent Durham Campus Library and Learning Centre in Oshawa, a single-room library staffed by one manager and two library technicians.

Over the past five years, both libraries have undergone tremendous change. An extensive renovation of the Bata Library that finished in 2018 resulted in a significant move away from print materials as space for the collection was drastically reduced, requiring a new focus on electronic resources and interlibrary loans. In the spring of 2019, the Client Service unit and Technical Services units at Bata Library were merged into a single Library Services unit, resulting in a change in responsibilities for the ten paraprofessional staff that made up these teams. At the same time, one of the Library Services staff positions was not replaced after a retirement, the former head of Technical Services went on sabbatical, and a new librarian and a new manager were hired, both having responsibilities for different aspects of Library Services functions. These fast-paced changes left the ten staff members in the Bata Library Services unit with dated job descriptions; gaps in knowledge, skills, and competencies; and an unclear reporting structure. At the time, staff and management alike acknowledged that change was needed, and yet there was no intentional plan in place for training or redeploying staff.

The strained staff situation was further impacted by the implementation of a new library services platform (Alma/Primo VE) in late 2019. While the new system promised to simplify unit workflows, it would require significant retraining and changes to long-standing practices. Preparations for the new software also surfaced multiple discrepancies in client support and technical services practices between the two libraries. Additionally, the new library services platform implementation was a consortial initiative, necessitating another shift in focus and requiring that our workflows and services be realigned with the consortium's mission and time lines. To move forward at the set pace, it was clear that the current staffing model was not sustainable and that Library Services was not staffed in a way that allowed for growth, innovation, or meeting the library's goals. Change was needed.

Project Design and Approach

To address this situation, in the fall of 2020, the Trent University Library and Archives began a project to restructure the new Library Services unit. A project team was formed, consisting of one manager and three librarians. By November 2020, we had developed a project charter with the following goals:

- Realign Library Services staffing with the library's current systems, services, and workflows and with the library's goals for the next five years.
- Assess and document required skills, knowledge, and expertise, and identify gaps that need to be filled.
- Provide a plan to address gaps in skills, knowledge, and expertise as well as upcoming retirements.
- Address outdated job descriptions.
- Provide concrete justification for salary budget and staffing requirements.

While the Library Services unit initially consisted of the merged Bata client support and technical services teams, we decided the two staff positions at the Durham Library and Learning Centre would be included in the project. Not only did they have very similar responsibilities to the Bata Library Services team, but we hoped that by addressing staffing at both libraries and expanding Library Services to include both campuses, the existing silos between the teams could be removed. This meant that twelve job descriptions needed to be rewritten.

While it was not documented in the charter, the project team agreed that in addition to the above, we wanted the project to be conducted in a way that recognized the impact these changes would have on staff members. We chose to use a participation-based and consultative approach, not only as a strategic measure to gain buy-in from staff, but also to ensure that the project resulted in shared unit goals; robust, high-quality positions for the entire team; and a reduction in staff anxiety associated with the evolution of their job roles and responsibilities.

During the planning process, the following high-level deliverables were identified:[*]

1. Identify and document functional areas of responsibility within Library Services.
2. Analyze the current state of each functional area.
3. Determine future needs to meet functional goals.
4. Identify internal and external factors that could impact the new staffing model.
5. Develop new job descriptions and reporting structure.

---

[*] The project methodology was informed by an article by the Society for Human Resource Management (SHRM) on staffing plan development, which at the time was freely available on its website: https://www.shrm.org. However, the article has since been moved behind a paywall, requiring a paid membership to view.

The project team agreed to share drafts of all deliverables with each other, provide opportunities for questions and feedback, survey staff about existing and future positions, and conduct open sessions for staff to express concerns or raise questions. This included sharing the project charter and plan for input, as well as distributing an initial survey to all affected staff with questions about the responsibilities missing from their job description and other inaccuracies, areas of interest, and opportunities for their positions; which core duties needed more support; and ideas for improving staffing. We indicated to the team that while we could not promise any specific outcomes, we would try our best to accommodate interests where possible. The team chose to use Confluence, an online collaborative team software that was already in use by library personnel, to share project documents, track project progress, and solicit feedback from Library Services staff and the rest of the library team.

Identifying and Documenting Functional Areas of Responsibility within Library Services

For the first deliverable, the project team brainstormed and then drafted a list of responsibilities for Library Services staff grouped by functional area. In addition, we drafted a set of high-level goals for each area, using the following questions as prompts:

- What are the library's major strategic and tactical goals for the next five years?
- How will Library Services support those goals?
- What goals need to be set for each function to ensure they are aligned with the library's goals?
- What support do other departments expect from Library Services in the next five years?
- What internal goals would each functional area like to achieve over the next five years?

The results of the initial draft were then shared with the Library Services team for feedback and validation, including the question prompts. To accommodate different comfort levels, staff were invited to provide feedback through multiple channels, including adding comments, edits, and questions to a shared document using the track changes feature; e-mailing feedback to their manager; or speaking directly to a member of the project team. Once the responses were collected, revisions were made and confirmed with staff before moving to the next deliverable.

Several goals were repeated under multiple functional areas, and these were eventually pulled out as overall goals that applied to all areas, including reducing silos, mapping processes and documenting workflows, building workflows to allow for robust and accurate statistics reporting, development of staff specializations to allow for greater depth of knowledge in particular areas, and cross-training on essential processes.

Analyzing the Current State of Each Functional Area

During the second phase, the project team determined the current staffing full-time equivalents (FTEs) for each functional area. At Trent a full-time staff position, or 1.0 FTE, is equal to a person working thirty-five hours per week. To ensure that numbers were accurate and reflected the experience of those working in each area, Library Services staff were given a list of the functional areas and asked to estimate the percentage of their time spent on each area, with their percentages adding up to 100 percent. The team then reviewed responses, asked questions about results that were unexpected, and revised numbers through discussions with staff. Although the FTEs may seem abstract when discussing staffing, it was helpful to have a measure for time spent on each functional area and to be able to compare staffing levels between each function. It was also useful to understand that the twelve staff members provided us with eleven FTEs due to a combination of part-time positions, recurring positions where staff members work eight months of the year, and positions where a staff member's time is divided with another unit.

The other portion of this deliverable was identifying current competencies and challenges for each functional area. The language used during this step was purposeful, and terms such as *weaknesses* or *shortcomings* were not used when referring to staff and staff skills to avoid value judgments. The aim was to reflect the existing state of staffing for each function, not to create a document that adjudicated how successful individual team members were in their roles.

The following question prompts were used:

- What expertise, competencies, and skills do staff bring to their roles?
- What skills are available within the team that perhaps are not being used?
- Is help from other employees outside of the unit regularly required to achieve the goals of the functional area?
- Do vendors, contractors, or others outside the library regularly contribute to achieving team goals?
- What other resources are available? For example, student employees.
- What data is available to help analyze the current state of each function?

The resulting document provided the current FTEs, competencies, and challenges for each functional area, as well as a notes section where additional impacts could be recorded. The draft was then shared with staff for questions and feedback, a step that proved vital as it allowed us to include more details that reflected our colleagues' daily experiences working in the library. For example, a staff member suggested adding emergency situations as an additional challenge to the Space and Facilities Management functional area; because campus security and university emergency responders are not always available to act quickly during a crisis, staff felt that they must try to manage these situations on

Determining Future Needs to Meet Functional Goals

The project team's next step was to outline a Library Services staffing model that would meet the unit's newly defined goals. Goals were mapped to the staffing competencies needed to achieve them, with ideas generated using professional resources, such as the Canadian Federation of Library Associations' *Guidelines for the Education of Library Technicians* and the American Library Association Library Competencies statements, as well as other libraries' job postings. Once the desired competencies were drafted, they were compared to the list of existing staff competencies developed in the previous step. This was then used to generate a list of competency gaps. The desired competencies and five-year goals were then compared to existing FTEs and used to create a desired FTE for each functional area (table 19.1). The results indicated that the unit would need an additional 2.25 FTE to achieve the goals we had outlined, which was not surprising given the changes the library had experienced and the university's growth.

Table 19.1. Comparison of current and required staffing FTEs by function.

Functional Area	Current Staffing FTE	Required Staffing FTE	FTE Gap
Acquisitions	0.70	1.00	0.30
Electronic Resources	0.60	1.00	0.40
Metadata Management	0.35	0.75	0.40
Physical Processing	0.60	0.50	−0.10
Course Reading Support	0.50	1.00	0.50
Accessibility	0.00	0.25	0.25
Copyright	0.45	1.00	0.55
Fulfillment	1.40	1.00	−0.40
Information Services	1.20	1.50	0.30
Resource Sharing	1.60	1.25	−0.35
Physical Collections	1.00	1.25	0.25
Patron User Group Management	0.10	0.00	−0.10
Space & Facilities Management	0.60	0.75	0.15
Student Employee Management	1.40	1.25	−0.15
Marketing & Outreach	0.50	0.75	0.25
TOTAL	11.00	13.25	2.25

While areas such as fulfillment, resource sharing, and physical processing called for a reduction in FTEs, it was determined that metadata management, copyright, and course reading support required significant increases in staffing. These changing needs could be partially addressed through rebalancing assigned functional areas in each position. To achieve an overall increase in FTEs, a case would need to be made for a new position, or for partial increases to existing positions by requesting funds to transform part-time or recurring positions into full-time positions.

Once again, this deliverable was shared with staff members. Having articulated the desired competencies, staff were eager to provide further input regarding competencies they believed they already had or that they were interested in building. The new vision aligned with the goals we had collectively generated early in the project, which created some excitement as staff began to see the possibilities for growth in the new positions. At the same time, questions arose about how we would meet the desired FTE levels, given that we would need budget approval from university administration for new or expanded positions.

At this point in the project, the team conducted a series of staff listening sessions where all Library Services staff members were invited to participate in an open discussion about the project. The sessions were well attended, with questions focusing on the structure and content of the new positions. Some staff asked about the process of the restructuring itself, such as whether they would need to apply for the new positions or if they would simply be assigned a new job. Additionally, staff were very interested in how the job banding process works, which is the process by which positions are evaluated to determine the appropriate salary. While we could not answer all questions, as we were still awaiting clarification from the human resources department about university and union requirements, we tried to be as transparent as possible and share what we could.

These sessions also allowed us to discuss the principles the project team would be applying to the design of the new positions. These included the following:

- Positions must reflect the organizational needs and goals defined during the project.
- Each position makes sense on its own and as part of the whole.
- There will be no multi-incumbent positions, but there will be redundancies in some duties to ensure key processes can continue if someone is away.
- Each position will have an area of specialization.
- Low-level duties will be reassigned to student employees so that staff positions can be enriched with more complex work. For this reason, we shared that we did not anticipate any salary bands to decrease.

Staff communicated that they appreciated our transparency, but it was evident that they wanted more clarity about the future of their positions and salary, something that we could not yet provide.

Identifying Internal and External Factors That May Impact the New Staffing Plan

The final step before creating the new staffing model was to consider potential internal and external impacts on the restructuring that were outside of our control. This step was informed by the following guiding questions:

- What trends are we seeing at the institutional level to which we will have to adapt?
- What societal changes or challenges will impact us?
- What trends are affecting skill development and talent availability?
- What technological changes are outside of our control?
- Will economic or financial factors affect our staffing plans?
- Do we need to account for constraints or impacts from facilities or infrastructure?

A list of impacts was then drafted, which included considerations such as library budget (possible budget reductions, rejection of requests for new positions, changes to provincial funding for postsecondary education); university changes (changes in enrollment, growth and expansion of the Trent Durham campus, shifting university administration priorities); societal and environmental effects (the continuing effects of the COVID-19 pandemic); existing and emerging technology (changes in software and hardware dictated by the university, implementation of new software and features decided by our consortium); and library personnel changes (timing of retirements and leaves, the job market, and recruitment challenges).

Discussing this deliverable with staff provided the opportunity for additional impacts to be considered; but more importantly, the project team and staff now shared an awareness of how the new staffing model could be challenged: we knew that staff were aware of how we may need to shift to take into account unavoidable changes, and staff knew that we were aware of and had considered potential risks and fluctuations.

Developing New Job Descriptions and Reporting Structures

After obtaining the current job description template from human resources, two documents were created in tandem: a document for new job descriptions and a spreadsheet to capture desired staffing by functional area as distributed across the new positions.

To begin developing the job descriptions, a team member drafted a single position description for the rest of the team to review. When the team was satisfied with the structure of the position, the other Library Services positions were completed. The language in the existing job descriptions was reviewed but not always repurposed, and often other libraries' job postings were used to generate ideas for language that captured the responsibilities and qualifications that reflected desired competencies. Language was used to increase and clarify the level of responsibility and autonomy within the position, to align with our desire for enhanced positions. At the head of the document, we mapped out teams for the functional areas and identified the positions that would be part of each team (table 19.2).

Table 19.2. An example of how we defined and documented functional teams, which included defining the scope, roles, membership, and reporting structure.

Acquisitions Team	
Scope	Acquisitions tasks for all material types (electronic, print, media, microform, atlas, database, special collections) from all suppliers (consortia, agents, publishers, individuals, OER), whether one-time (firm) or continuous (serials, monographic series). Includes budgets, reporting, and financial transactions related to acquisitions.
Lead	Acquisitions Specialist
Members	Acquisitions & Finance Associate, Library Services & Fulfillment Coordinator, Electronic Resources & Licensing Associate
Reports to	Scholarly Resources Librarian

The second document was a spreadsheet of the functional teams, which allowed the team to verify that responsibilities divided among the functional areas would add up to the desired FTEs. At the same time, this process was valuable to ensure that no staff member would be assigned too many or too few duties. It was our intention to develop positions that had variety but that also allowed staff to build an area of specialization, while avoiding creating positions with so many responsibilities that they would lead to staff burnout. The spreadsheet allowed us to visualize that equilibrium.

Once the preliminary mapping was complete, the project team used a shared Microsoft Word document to review the job descriptions and solicit feedback and further clarification from subject matter experts. We attempted to match language when functional areas and key responsibilities were shared by more than one job description. For example, circulation desk workflows were mostly identical, while acquisitions tasks were still split between specialized and supporting work.

With the positions drafted, the results were discussed at a high level with staff, but the document itself was not shared. Although the project team had always intended to share the draft job descriptions with staff for feedback, the human resources department mandated that job descriptions were to be presented to staff in their final form at an in-person meeting. The human resources department had encountered opposition to revised job descriptions in previous university restructuring situations, and its instruction not to provide drafts to staff was informed by those experiences. It also indicated that going back and forth with draft job descriptions would lengthen the time required to get employees into their new jobs. As our project had already taken longer than anticipated, we did not want to create further delays. However, this meant that our original goal of including staff in the job design process was not achieved.

With the functional part of the job descriptions complete, the next phase was to add job evaluation factors, which would be used to assign salary bands to positions. Trent University has a Joint Job Evaluation Committee (JJEC) comprised of unionized staff and human resources staff. JJEC analyzes job descriptions to determine their complexity and compares them to other job descriptions in the organization, resulting in the appropriate compensation for the same level of work. Once it has gone through JJEC, a job description will receive a score that corresponds to a salary range. Several factors are considered by JJEC in reviewing job descriptions, such as independence of decision-making, complexity of analytical reasoning, required expertise and education, and the extent of supervisory duties. A librarian on the staffing team who had previous experience in this process took the lead on completing the job evaluation submission for each position. The goal was to clearly define the level of skill needed in these positions prior to presenting to JJEC.

Job descriptions were submitted to human resources and presented to JJEC in spring 2022. Managers of Library Services staff met with JJEC twice to provide more information about the job descriptions and answer any questions about the positions. Once clarifications were made, JJEC provided the job description bandings and asked that these be reviewed prior to finalizing the job descriptions.

Roadblocks

Despite a clear project plan, staff willing to participate, and a management team committed to the successful completion of the restructuring project, several challenges hindered progress and at times resulted in the need to revisit our best-laid plans. Looming over the entire project was the COVID-19 pandemic. In March 2020, the library had shifted to an online service model, and by June, some staff returned to campus to implement a curbside pickup service, while most others continued working from home. By September 2020, some in-person service had returned, while online services were still being maintained. This led to a shift in priorities as the team scrambled to adapt to rapidly changing government and institutional mandates while maintaining multiple service models. In-person services were closed several times as the province of Ontario adapted to the developments of the global pandemic. Changes in service models to accommodate building closures and evolving regulations required substantial resources, and staff required considerable support to adjust to each change. With resources and priorities focused on navigating each new scenario, the staffing project was deprioritized.

While the global pandemic triggered a delay in the progress of the project, this delay was compounded when two librarians, initially on the project team, retired.[*] This left gaps

---

[*] The authors would like to acknowledge the contributions of two librarians emeriti: Jean Luyben, learning and liaison librarian, and Marisa Scigliano, scholarly resources librarian. Both made a significant contribution to the restructuring as members of the project team until their retirements in December 2021.

in the team, both in numbers and in institutional knowledge, while the remaining team members shuffled their roles and responsibilities and new members were appointed to the vacancies, including two new managers overseeing Library Services staff at each campus. This meant additional time for onboarding new members to the project and reconsidering aspects of the project through new perspectives.

Other challenges cropped up when the intention of the project team did not align with instructions received from the human resources department. That department, too, had staff turnover, and our point of contact changed. In the experience of human resources, restructuring often results in loss of jobs, and its policies are written to manage such negative impacts in a unionized environment. In contrast to the experience shared by human resources, it was clear from the beginning that our project would not result in job loss, and we expected changes to be favorably received by most, if not all, staff members. Instead of continuing to share information, we followed the requirement that we not share the job descriptions, even though this did not fit with the intention of our project. The new jobs were presented to each staff member by a manager and a panel of representatives from the union and human resources, and their job band, which would impact whether there would be any change in their salary, was also revealed during this meeting. This presentation format and the forced silence after so much ongoing communication notably increased feelings of uncertainty and anxiety for staff members. It would leave a lasting impression on both the project team and Library Services staff members when reviewing the outcomes of the project.

Conclusions
Project Results

The project was officially completed in August 2022, with all Library Services staff receiving their new job descriptions. Cross-functional teams were confirmed, and reporting lines clarified in an updated organizational chart.

Staff Feedback

In early 2023, approximately six months after the new positions and structure were implemented, a short, open-ended, anonymous survey was distributed to Library Services staff asking about their experience with the restructuring. Overall, respondents indicated they had ample opportunity to participate and provide feedback throughout the project and described their appreciation for being able to track the project and each deliverable in Confluence. One respondent noted that while initially their input seemed to be going into a black box, in hindsight they felt that they had been heard and that their new job description reflected that. Another expressed disappointment that they were not permitted to provide input on the job descriptions before they were finalized, due to HR's requirement that we not share the positions prior to their being assigned to staff.

The responses were mixed when it came to the level of anxiety experienced by staff due to restructuring, with some staff members indicating there was no anxiety associated with the project and others noting moderate to significant stress. This was primarily attributed to the length of the project and gaps in communications: "I did feel a bit anxious when it seemed there was no action or no progress on the restructuring process. The longer it took, the more I wondered what strange and nefarious [things were] happening within and to the restructuring process." The long time frame and delays in the process were noted by almost all respondents, with ideas such as having a larger project team, hiring outside consultants, and not rewriting all job descriptions at the same time provided as potential future solutions.

Other recommendations to improve the process included clearer communication, more clarity on human resources' involvement including the job evaluation and banding process, and more transparency in discussions after the new positions were assigned in order to stave off the whispering and gossip that occurred afterward.

Another high anxiety point was the human resources meetings where staff were each assigned a new job that they were not permitted to review before arriving at the meeting. It was clear that this was in stark contrast to the rest of the project, where there had been considerably more transparency and opportunity to engage. Although the process was explained to Library Services employees, and managers provided some high-level position overviews in advance, it was no less daunting as staff could not prepare for what would be assigned to them in the meeting or how their salary might be impacted. Appreciation for the participation-based structure of the rest of the project was a common thread in the responses: "I was very appreciative of the fact that we were asked what aspects of our current job we liked and which parts we did not. I have never been asked that before and I DID feel that my input was taken seriously." This clarity around the importance of staff engagement in the project and the stress caused when that participation was not possible was a valuable takeaway for the project team.

Lessons Learned

Gain buy-in for participation-based restructuring from human resources. Several challenges were faced when our team's approach did not align with practices mandated by the human resources department. That department had not supported managers through a participation-based restructuring before and required that jobs not be shared with incumbents before the formal start date. While staff were informed of the process along the way, this shift in information sharing did not sit well with the team. While human resources were supportive of the plan in theory, it would have been beneficial to have more consultations where the project team's intent was conveyed more clearly. Regular consultation between the project team and human resources throughout the process would have been a benefit and moved the interaction between the two groups to look at the entire plan, rather than a "what next" approach.

Expect the unexpected. Delays outside of the team's control also had an impact on the length of the project, which had been planned to take eight months, but in the end took almost two years. Project team members retired or moved into new positions, and such turnover impacted project momentum. Interruptions caused by the COVID-19 pandemic lasted longer than anticipated. Learning that JJEC takes a hiatus for two months each year was another setback. Certainly, delays and unanticipated challenges in a project of this scope are inevitable, but some might have been mitigated by increased communication with external departments and stakeholders.

Consistency in communication to staff is key. Delays also impacted the staff waiting for their new job descriptions. Staff had questions about the delays and were anxious that the regular status updates they had grown accustomed to slowed down or stopped entirely while the project team waited for information from other departments. Following the project, the team learned that those breaks in communication led to some anxiety in staff members. Communicating consistently and intentionally, even when an update was simply to say nothing had changed, would have reduced anxiety and increased transparency. The response to the project was best when staff were getting regular project updates and could track progress on Confluence. The use of a collaborative tool was also useful for the project team in keeping organized.

Keep job descriptions up to date. Designing fourteen new positions consecutively because the existing descriptions are no longer accurate or relevant was extremely challenging and time-consuming. Even when restructuring leads to significant change, being able to refer to existing positions that capture current duties is helpful. Job descriptions should be reviewed every one to two years and updated accordingly. These incremental changes will not only ensure that descriptions remain relevant and useful but will also save you a lot of time in the long run.

Notes

1. Tanja de Jong et al., "The Impact of Restructuring on Employee Well-being: A Systematic Review of Longitudinal Studies," *Work and Stress* 30, no. 1 (2016): 91–92, https://doi.org/10.1080/02678373.2015.1136710; Gro Ellen Mathisen et al., "Identifying and Managing Psychosocial Risks during Organizational Restructuring: It's *What* You Do and *How* You Do It," *Safety Science* 100, Part A (2017): 21, https://doi.org/10.1016/j.ssci.2016.12.007.
2. Cheryl Martin, "The Organization of the Cataloguing Function at McMaster University," *Cataloging and Classification Quarterly* 30, no. 1 (2000): 114, https://doi.org/10.1300/J104v30n01_07.
3. de Jong et al., "Impact of Restructuring," 93.
4. Mathisen et al., "Identifying and Managing," 20.
5. Gechinti Bede Onyeneke and Tomokazu Abe, "The Effect of Change Leadership on Employee Attitudinal Support for Planned Organizational Change," *Journal of Organizational Change Management* 34, no. 2 (2021): 404, https://doi.org/10.1108/JOCM-08-2020-0244.
6. John Novak and Annette Day, "'The Libraries They Are A-Changin': How Libraries Reorganize," *College and Undergraduate Libraries* 22, no. 3–4 (2015): 359, https://doi.org/10.1080/10691316.2015.1067663.

7. Robert Lundmark, Anne Richter, and Susanne Tafvelin, "Consequences of Managers' Laissez-Faire Leadership during Organizational Restructuring," *Journal of Change Management* 22, no. 1 (2022): 50, https://doi.org/10.1080/14697017.2021.1951811.
8. Jeroen Stouten, Denise M. Rousseau, and David De Cremer, "Successful Organizational Change: Integrating the Management Practice and Scholarly Literatures," *Academy of Management Annals* 12, no. 2 (2018): 779, https://doi.org/10.5465/annals.2016.0095.
9. Michael Armstrong, "Job Design," *Armstrong's Handbook of Human Resource Management Practice*, (London: KoganPage, 2020), 225.
10. Thomas W. Shaughnessy, "Redesigning Library Jobs," *Journal of the American Society for Information Science* 29, no. 4 (July 1978): 187, https://doi.org/10.1002/asi.4630290406.
11. Armstrong, "Job Design," 225.
12. Trevor Owens, "A Good Jobs Strategy for Libraries," *Library Leadership and Management* 35, no. 3 (2021): 1–14, https://llm.corejournals.org/llm/article/view/7486.
13. Klaus Musmann, "Socio-technical Theory and Job Design in Libraries," *College and Research Libraries* 39, no. 1 (1978): 27, https://doi.org/10.5860/crl_39_01_20.
14. Stephen Wood et al., "Enriched Job Design, High Involvement Management and Organizational Performance: The Mediating Roles of Job Satisfaction and Well-Being," *Human Relations* 65, no. 4 (2012): 419, https://doi.org/10.1177/0018726711432476.
15. Armstrong, "Job Design," 227.
16. Wood et al., "Enriched Job Design," 432; M. Venith Vijay, and R. Indradevi, "A Study on Job Enrichment and Individual Performance among Faculties with Special Reference to a Private University," *Mediterranean Journal of Social Sciences* 6, no. 1 (2015): 259, https://doi.org/10.5901/mjss.2015.v6n1p252.
17. Shaughnessy, "Redesigning Library Jobs," 189.
18. Susan Nnadozie Umeozor, "Motivation and Human Resources in Libraries," *International Journal of Knowledge Content Development and Technology* 8, no. 3 (2018): 36, https://doi.org/10.5865/IJKCT.2018.8.3.029.
19. Liz Woolcott and Jeremy Myntti, "Cataloging Tasks," Organization of Cataloging Units in Academic Libraries, 2016, https://catalogingunitorg.wordpress.com/category/cataloging-tasks/; Rachel Erb and Brian Erb, "The Use of Paraprofessionals in Electronic Resources Management: Results of a Survey," *Journal of Academic Librarianship* 41, no. 4 (July 2015): 399–400, https://doi.org/10.1016/j.acalib.2015.05.006; Glyneva Bradley-Ridout and Alissa Epworth, "Library Technicians Collaborating with Librarians on Knowledge Syntheses: A Survey of Current Perspectives," *Journal of the Canadian Health Libraries Association* 42, no. 3 (2020): 91, https://doi.org/10.29173/jchla29459.
20. Bradley-Ridout and Epworth, "Library Technicians Collaborating," 95.
21. Randall A. Lowe, Nancy A. Frost, and Emily A. Zumbrun, "The Evolution of E-Resources Management in a Small Academic Library—Paraprofessional Staff and Librarian Perspectives," *Journal of Electronic Resources Librarianship* 32, no. 3 (2020): 221–28, https://doi.org/10.1080/1941126X.2020.1791439.
22. Hannah Schilperoort, Alvaro Quezada, and Frances Lezcano, "Words Matter: Interpretations and Implications of 'Para' in Paraprofessional," *Journal of the Medical Library Association* 109, no. 1 (2021): 13–22, https://doi.org/10.5195/jmla.2021.933.

Bibliography

Armstrong, Michael. "Job Design." In *Armstrong's Handbook of Human Resource Management Practice*, 223–231. London: KoganPage, 2020.
Bradley-Ridout, Glyneva, and Alissa Epworth. "Library Technicians Collaborating with Librarians on Knowledge Syntheses: A Survey of Current Perspectives." *Journal of the Canadian Health Libraries Association* 42, no. 3 (2020): 88–103. https://doi.org/10.29173/jchla29459.
de Jong, Tanja, Noortje Wiezer, Marjolein de Weerd, Karina Nielsen, Pauliina Mattila-Holappa, and Zosia Mockałło. "The Impact of Restructuring on Employee Well-Being: A Systematic Review of Longitudinal Studies." *Work and Stress* 30, no. 1 (2016): 91–114. https://doi.org/10.1080/02678373.2015.1136710.
Erb, Rachel, and Brian Erb. "The Use of Paraprofessionals in Electronic Resources Management: Results of a Survey." *Journal of Academic Librarianship* 41, no. 4 (July 2015): 394–415. https://doi.org/10.1016/j.acalib.2015.05.006.
Lowe, Randall A., Nancy A. Frost, and Emily A. Zumbrun. "The Evolution of E-Resources Management in a Small Academic Library—Paraprofessional Staff and Librarian Perspectives." *Journal of Electronic Resources Librarianship* 32, no. 3 (2020): 221–28. https://doi.org/10.1080/1941126X.2020.1791439.
Lundmark, Robert, Anne Richter, and Susanne Tafvelin. "Consequences of Managers' Laissez-Faire Leadership during Organizational Restructuring." *Journal of Change Management* 22, no. 1 (2022): 40–58. https://doi.org/10.1080/14697017.2021.1951811.

Martin, Cheryl. "The Organization of the Cataloguing Function at McMaster University." *Cataloging and Classification Quarterly* 30, no. 1 (2000): 111–21. https://doi.org/10.1300/J104v30n01_07.

Mathisen, Gro Ellen, Kolbjørn Brønnick, Knut Jørgen Arntzen, and Linn Iren Vestly Bergh. "Identifying and Managing Psychosocial Risks during Organizational Restructuring: It's *What* You Do and *How* You Do It." *Safety Science* 100, Part A (2017): 20–29. https://doi.org/10.1016/j.ssci.2016.12.007.

Musmann, Klaus. "Socio-technical Theory and Job Design in Libraries." *College and Research Libraries* 39, no. 1 (1978): 20–28. https://doi.org/10.5860/crl_39_01_20.

Novak, John, and Annette Day. "The Libraries They Are A-Changin': How Libraries Reorganize." *College and Undergraduate Libraries* 22, no. 3–4 (2015): 358–73. https://doi.org/10.1080/10691316.2015.1067663.

Onyeneke, Gechinti Bede, and Tomokazu Abe. "The Effect of Change Leadership on Employee Attitudinal Support for Planned Organizational Change." *Journal of Organizational Change Management* 34, no. 2 (2021): 403–15. https://doi.org/10.1108/JOCM-08-2020-0244.

Owens, Trevor. "A Good Jobs Strategy for Libraries." *Library Leadership and Management* 35, no. 3 (2021): 1–14. https://llm.corejournals.org/llm/article/view/7486.

Schilperoort, Hannah, Alvaro Quezada, and Frances Lezcano. "Words Matter: Interpretations and Implications of 'Para' in Paraprofessional." *Journal of the Medical Library Association* 109, no. 1 (2021): 13–22. https://doi.org/10.5195/jmla.2021.933.

Shaughnessy, Thomas W. "Redesigning Library Jobs." *Journal of the American Society for Information Science* 29, no. 4 (July 1978): 187–90. https://doi.org/10.1002/asi.4630290406.

Stouten, Jeroen, Denise M. Rousseau, and David De Cremer. "Successful Organizational Change: Integrating the Management Practice and Scholarly Literatures." *Academy of Management Annals* 12, no. 2 (2018): 752–88. https://doi.org/10.5465/annals.2016.0095.

Umeozor, Susan Nnadozie. "Motivation and Human Resources in Libraries." *International Journal of Knowledge Content Development and Technology* 8, no. 3 (2018): 29–40. https://doi.org/10.5865/IJKCT.2018.8.3.029.

Vijay, M. Venith, and R. Indradevi. "A Study on Job Enrichment and Individual Performance among Faculties with Special Reference to a Private University." *Mediterranean Journal of Social Sciences* 6, no. 1 (2015): 252–60. https://doi.org/10.5901/mjss.2015.v6n1p252.

Wood, Stephen, Marc Van Veldhoven, Marcel Croon, and Lilian M. de Menezes. "Enriched Job Design, High Involvement Management and Organizational Performance: The Mediating Roles of Job Satisfaction and Well-Being." *Human Relations* 65, no. 4 (2012): 419–45. https://doi.org/10.1177/0018726711432476.

Woolcott, Liz, and Jeremy Myntti. "Cataloging Tasks." Organization of Cataloging Units in Academic Libraries, 2016. https://catalogingunitorg.wordpress.com/category/cataloging-tasks/.

CHAPTER 20

Rebuilding the Structure at a Medium-Sized Research Library

A Case Study

Kimberly Burke Sweetman

The University of New Hampshire (UNH), the flagship research campus of the University System of New Hampshire, provides over 900,000 print titles and 1.6 million electronic titles to a student community of approximately 13,000 students (2,000 graduate and 11,000 undergraduate) and almost 1,000 faculty members.[1] On July 1, 2021, the UNH Library moved from a traditional hierarchical structure to what we call a programmatic organizational structure—a structure defined by each employee serving on multiple groups or programs. Motivated by campus-driven cost cutting, the loss of ten library employees—20 percent of our colleagues—through a campus retirement incentive package, a comprehensive review of the strengths and weaknesses of our hierarchical structure, and a desire to be more future-focused, the programmatic structure was selected through a well-planned process.

Organizational structure is "a system that outlines how certain activities are directed in order to achieve the goals of the organization. These activities include rules, roles and responsibilities. Organizational structure also determines how information flows… within a company."[2] The UNH Library took this broad approach and implemented an organizational structure that is much broader than simply departments and reporting lines but addresses all of the ways in which we accomplish our mission.

The UNH Library had restructured only five years before, in 2016, in a similar response to organizational turnover. At that time, in addition to providing reference and instruction service to university departments and programs through each librarian maintaining a subject specialty, we reorganized library work from twelve units into six divisions, each led by a faculty librarian: Resource Acquisition and Discovery, encompassing cataloging, acquisitions, discovery, interlibrary loan and collections; Academic and Community Engagement, encompassing circulation, course reserves, branch libraries, and outreach; Research and Learning Services encompassing reference, information, and instructional services; Special Collections and Archives, encompassing university archives and distinctive collections; and, Technology, Scholarship and Publishing, encompassing library information technology, data services, scholarly communication, and locally created digital collections. Divisions were led for a term of three years by faculty members selected through a competitive process, who were compensated to provide division leadership for up to 20 percent of their time. The idea was that the workload of leadership would be shared through temporary terms.

As the library organized into divisions, the purpose of an organizational structure was identified as a means to provide strategic alignment between the organization's operations and institutional needs; reflect and operationalize the mission, vision, values, and culture; create strong ties between the organization and those external to the organization; and provide all employees with a logical home base of manageable size, facilitating communication, collaboration, decision-making, and workflow. The library endeavored to group like functions together while avoiding silos and to foster a balance between stability of operations and agility and responsiveness to a changing environment. It was important to keep the structure relatively flat and add leadership and coordination in the middle where we observed it was needed.

Under the division structure, the UNH Library experienced improved coordination and collaboration since division heads met regularly to work on projects like activating our "Vision for a Healthy Work Environment" document, identifying organizational and service gaps, and prioritizing new positions. Divisions also met regularly to organize their work and form workplace identity. However, the division structure offered some significant limitations. The assumption that division leaders would spend only 20 percent of their time on leadership activities proved an unrealistic time estimate, and the workload to lead a division was cumbersome. One division struggled with the fact that they lacked faculty members with direct work responsibility related to their scope, while conversely, the leader of a division made up entirely of faculty members struggled with peer leadership. The library faculty as a group, which is an essential planning body, was not well integrated into the structure. Additionally, the anticipated loss of ten library employees through a university retirement incentive meant their positions would be eliminated by

July 1, 2021. In the fall of 2020, a review of the division structure was conducted to determine the best path forward for the UNH Library.

Problem Definition

Given the anticipated reduction of staff, the shortcomings of the division structure, the ways in which library work had changed, and the uneven staffing created by years of attrition without much planning, the challenge was determining how to structure a medium-sized research library to meet the needs of our campus within our current resources, as well as the appropriate process to identify a new structure in our highly collaborative organizational culture.

The structure review followed closely UNH being designated a top-tier research institution with very high research activity by the Carnegie Classification of Institutions of Higher Education and coincided with the considerable upheaval caused by the start of the largest public health crisis in recent history (COVID-19), as well as the national racial reckoning sparked by the murder of George Floyd. As a result, we knew from the start of this investigation that our colleagues potentially had limited bandwidth to process change and were already processing considerable stress due to important national and international events. As part of the review of the division structure, a survey of UNH Library employees was conducted in October 2020, and a focus group was conducted with UNH Library division heads at the end of that month. Restructuring planning was conducted by the dean and associate dean of the University Library, and one of their main concerns was colleagues' tolerance for change given the societal stress everyone was experiencing. This all coincided with the deadline for the campus retirement incentive, and ten colleagues had indicated their intention to retire on or before June 2021. By mid-November, the dean of the UNH Library had accumulated considerable information on which to base a decision about the structure. Given the considerable societal upheaval and resultant stress, it was clear that restructuring was something to consider very carefully and with input from all library colleagues.

While the division structure successfully addressed leadership of divisions, it was less effective in shaping how the divisions were structured internally. In many divisions there had not been changes in roles or organization beyond attrition, and the result was that staffing and assignments were misaligned with current need, and imbalances existed between supervisors and staff (for example, one division had six managers and five staff members). While staff positions had been repurposed and, in some cases, cut through attrition due to the evolution of library work, there was less turnover in managerial roles. Survey results indicated that issues such as the rotating nature of the division head term concerned some employees who desired more stability. The estimated time commitment of the division head role seemed unrealistic to those in the role. The division head role was designed as a visionary role, but in practice the need for operational leadership was so great that in large part the role defaulted to this. The workload implications of management meant that the need for a strong middle layer of leadership still existed in our organization. There were concerns with workload—particularly tension between increased workload of divisions heads and how promotion and tenure responsibilities could be accomplished by those division heads who were not yet tenured. There was room for improvement around communication between divisions and, despite our best intentions, our work had become siloed. There were also concerns about possible conflict between certain aspects of the division structure and how faculty governance functions at the UNH Library as well as overwhelming support for the library faculty as a group being better represented within the structure.

In addition to uncovering opinions about the organizational structure, the structure review survey also illustrated that the organization had too many supervisors. Nearly half (48 percent) of our employees identified as supervisors. In an organization of our size (at the time slightly fewer than fifty employees), ten to twelve managers would be appropriate, not twenty-three. Many of these individuals focused on supervising people rather than developing or improving functions or services, which directed our scarce resources internally rather than toward serving our campus community. This inward focus resulted in a de facto prioritization of personnel management over user focus, which made it difficult to accomplish our mission of serving the research needs of the UNH community. The need to move away from roles that were purely human resources management positions in favor of positions that take a leadership role for service improvements while leading colleagues was clear. Perhaps due to the library's size, each employee had a unique position description and most performed a wide array of tasks, through both their divisions and several library committees. Therefore, a team-based or matrix structure clearly emerged as something to consider early in the investigations.

Regardless of whatever organizational structure was chosen, the survey results uncovered multiple opportunities for creating a shared understanding of roles, work processes, and language. Some of the areas that needed to be addressed included these:

- disagreement about the definition of the term *operational*
- tension between a desire for communication and a frustration with having to explain everything
- a misunderstanding that the same role should not be responsible for vision and operations and that only titular leaders needed to be visionary
- a need to clarify the purpose and nature of structure, and a misunderstanding that structure of any type is the enemy of innovation
- an assumption that collaboration across divisions was not allowed without division head approval
- misunderstandings about the faculty librarian role on the part of nonlibrarian library employees
- a need to clarify foundational processes such as our defined decision-making process

- a misunderstanding that leaders need to have engaged in every aspect of the work to effectively lead it, and an assumption that one person holding multiple roles is problematic or undesirable when the complexity of organizations often necessitates this

While the original focus was to create a better organizational structure in terms of our organizational chart and reporting lines, it became clear that these types of structural improvements would be successful only with improved understanding of our organizational identity related to these misunderstandings.

Structure review input was considered alongside an analysis of the gaps in our organization that the division heads conducted, a review of the library's strategic plan, and a review of our committee structure.

Literature Review

A review of the literature published on library restructuring indicates few articles published in the last twenty-five years that describe the design or implementation process of a full library restructuring, as articles published on restructuring tend to focus on the restructuring of specific departments or library membership organizations.

Perhaps one of the best-known library restructurings is the University of Arizona's move to a team-based structure in the 1990s.[3] This approach, which retains something of a traditional library structure while adopting a team-based management approach, was the inspiration for the reorganization at Teton County Library in Jackson Hole, Wyoming.[4]

The literature suggests several reasons for embarking on a structural change. The reason cited most often is the changing nature of the work, particularly changes caused by the adoption and evolution of technology, as referenced in Higa, Yoose and Knight, and Nelson[5]. Crumpton also notes budget and finance as a reason for restructuring.[6]

Ithaka S+R's 2016 report, *Organizing the Work of the Research Library*, published the results of interviews with eighteen library leaders on the ways in which their libraries are organized and general trends in library structure.[7] Yoose and Knight, Crumpton, and Burns and Brannon all discuss the relationship between organizational structure and organizational culture.[8]

The matrix organizational structure is characterized by having multiple lines of reporting managers.[9] Award-winning authors and experts in global management Christopher Bartlett and Sumantra Ghoshal, in their article about the shift toward matrix management as companies globalized in the 1980s, write about the importance of attending to culture while structuring an organization:

> For those companies that adopted matrix structures, the problem was not in the way they defined the goal. They correctly recognized the need for a multi-dimensional organization to respond to growing external

complexity. The problem was that they defined their organizational objectives in purely structural terms. Yet the term *formal structure* describes only the organization's basic anatomy. Companies must also concern themselves with organizational physiology—the systems and relationships that allow the lifeblood of information to flow through the organization. They also need to develop a healthy organizational psychology—the shared norms, values and beliefs that shape the way individual managers think and act.[10]

This quote, which outlines Bartlett and Ghoshal's concept that organizational structure includes all the documented ways that an organization achieves its mission, became a guidepost for the UNH Library's restructuring work.

Discussion

Process

The initial process for determining possible structure options included learning about organizational structure generally, as well as critically evaluating the current structure to identify known and anticipated gaps in the organization. The UNH Library did this by conducting the survey previously described, holding focus group conversations with key groups, and consulting broader university stakeholders like human resources. The library's dean and associate dean looked at the structures of peer libraries, reviewed known gaps in the organization, and regularly consulted with the library's leadership team (made up of the dean and associate dean, who led the structure redesign, as well as the assistant dean and faculty chair). Clear goals for a new structure were developed from the results of the structure review survey. These results and how they informed the choices we made were shared transparently to ensure that all colleagues understood that the goals for the new structure were directly related to the input they provided about what was needed in the new structure. This was an important approach for all employees to understand that their concerns were integral to the structure development process, and it was well received. The detailed list of what was shared is in table 20.1.

Using all this information, the dean and associate dean devised and presented three possible structure options:

- A traditional, hierarchical model with two associate deans, one leading collections and discovery and the other leading public services.
- A modified version of the current division structure, which would reduce our current divisions from six to three, addressing resource acquisition and discovery, access services, and distinctive and digital collections, with each division being led by a partnership of a faculty member and a nonlibrarian professional.

Table 20.1. A representation of the concerns voiced through the structure survey and our thoughts about how to address them.

We heard the current structure...	So we decided the new structure should...
Was designed for a larger library.	Work well for our size and be scalable to allow us to grow as a research library.
Does not sufficiently focus on or foster the work of our strategic plan.	Address as many known structural gaps as possible while addressing traditional and emerging areas of librarianship.
Involves too much hierarchy/bureaucracy, which impedes the ability of everyone to contribute fully.	Support individual agency and accountability. Recognize our reliance on collaboration over typical lines of authority.
Relies on faculty division heads who are challenged to devote adequate time to the leadership role; the focus on vision over operational responsibility for division heads does not provide adequate operational direction.	Recognize and address the need for leadership around both vision/planning and execution of those plans. Facilitate operations and encourage the evolution of operational practices.
Was intended to break down existing silos, but the term division is problematic.	Recognize the systemic nature of libraries and facilitate the interdependence and connectedness of everything we do. Stress unity and encourage a unified approach to our work.
Does not always strike the right balance between providing each person clarity about their role and recognizing the multiple roles that any individual might play.	Provide clear roles and the support and authority everyone needs to be successful. Recognize the multivariate nature of our work and the multiple hats each library team member wears.
Does not represent well the various components of faculty work.	Integrate the collective work as a faculty body into the structure, including the role of the chair.
Relies too much on librarian experts to provide direct supervision.	Carefully consider the skills and abilities of potential leaders and managers.
(and a few additional goals...)	Provide a degree of change our organization is willing to accept and able to tolerate.
	Encourage a broader library focus while maintaining the cohesiveness of a base.
	Enable an outward service focus to our work rather than getting tripped up by internal workings.
	Work well for the foreseeable future.

- A structure consisting of eleven programs, defining *program* as a service we provide, thereby putting the emphasis on the user. As employees would serve on multiple programs, each employee also needed a single administrative leader to compile annual coaching and keep their time and attendance records.

Almost immediately these options were narrowed to two, eliminating the two associate dean model, since resources for a second associate dean seemed unlikely. After presenting these options to all library employees, feedback was considered, and options were weighed in the context of how well each one filled organizational gaps and addressed the goals identified for a new structure. Since each employee would be a member of more than one program, essentially reporting to multiple supervisors, administrative functions of management like annual reviews and timekeeping were assigned to a different role: the administrative lead. Pros and cons of each option were explored, and options were presented with their strengths and weaknesses at a meeting of library employees. All employees had an opportunity to attend several open office hours sessions to get their questions answers, learn more about the options through discussion, and provide input. All colleagues were asked to reply to a brief survey about their preferences.

As indicated in Bartlett and Ghoshal's article, changes in organizational structure are not the cure-all for an organization's challenges. Bartlett and Ghoshal liken an organizational structure to an organization's anatomy and note that the physiology (interpersonal relationships, decision processes, and other systems that allow the lifeblood of information to flow through the organization) and psychology (shared norms, values, and beliefs that shape the way managers think and act) must also be considered.[11] This resonated with the UNH Library's dean and associate dean as they considered structure options, particularly since the responses to the original structure review survey had uncovered some fundamental tensions in shared organizational understanding.

That same survey indicated that library employees were looking for a significant change, but it was clear that the specific things that were cited as needing change were not all going to be addressed by a change in reporting lines. A conscious decision was made to use the structure adjustment process not only to develop a common understanding of various fundamental organizational concepts, but also to highlight our organization's agreed-upon processes, values, and ways of working as a means of shoring up whatever organizational structure we chose, including the following:

- clearly articulating and regularly revisiting our organizational vision, core services, strategic plan and initiatives, and library learning outcomes
- refamiliarizing ourselves with our foundational documents, including "Vision for a Healthy Work Environment," decision process, and policies
- aligning department, division, and personal goals with strategic goals
- meeting regularly at appropriate intervals with notes and action items recorded and revisited

- clarifying our common language and asking for clarification or specificity when communication is vague
- articulating a commitment to collaborating across structural groupings
- working toward greater role clarity (that everyone is responsible for executing a vision, that everyone is responsible for improvement and innovation, that a manager keeps the work organized and does not need to be an expert in all aspects of the work, and that faculty librarians as a group are responsible for the vision, direction, and development of library policy and services to provide research support, instruction, collections, and information access to our community)
- articulating the need to be present- and future-focused

Implementation

Input was carefully considered, and the dean of the UNH Library made the decision to implement a hybrid of the two structures that remained under consideration: a program structure that used the modified division structure, at least temporarily, as the administrative side of the structure, with employees in sections designed to provide each with a supportive home base and led by a section lead (figure 20.1). Faculty members in sections were identified as faculty affiliates, and each employee had an administrative lead to manage their time, attendance, and annual coaching.

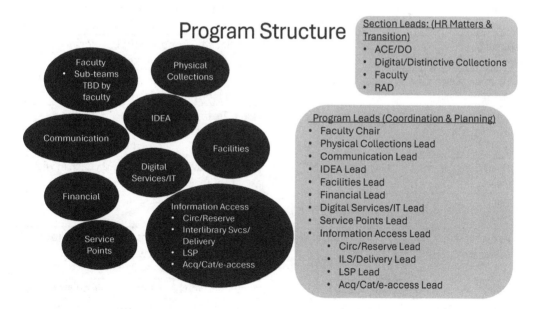

Figure 20.1. The organizational chart we originally used when introducing the program structure to library employees.

As noted, the twin public health crises of COVID-19 and racial injustice caused considerable disruption and stress. Library leadership knew they needed to carefully consider colleagues' tolerance for such a major workplace change in an already stressful social environment. Given the broader social and political landscape and the stress it has caused, the library followed a careful process to support all employees through the implementation of the new structure. This work began months before the dean decided on a new structure. In October, the dean shared the library's challenging budget situation, including the fact that several colleagues had applied for the early retirement incentive, and a process for reenvisioning the UNH Library. This signaled the need to identify our core services, keep a user focus, identify what we might streamline or stop doing, and the fact that a more involved restructuring than originally planned may come out of the structure review survey. This reenvisioning was framed as an exploration of what the institution and users would need from a research library in five years. By December 2020, library leaders developed a process for determining a new structure that was also broadly shared (table 20.2). Monthly library meetings throughout that year highlighted topics such as defining our essential services and rightsizing our recently identified strategic initiatives given budget and staffing constraints.

Table 20.2. A rough outline of the process steps taken to introduce our new structure.

Who	When	What
Divisions	November 2020	Divisions begin to assess the impact of the COVID retirement incentives (CERPs) and how those could be addressed (adjusting workflows, workflow/service cessation, temporary hires, new positions).
Faculty	November 2020	The library faculty propose a process for identifying, by March 1, our core services.
Structure Review Task Force	December 2020	Structure Review Task Force submits recommendations to the dean.
Leadership Team	April 7, 2021	Leadership Team announces three potential organization structures under consideration for the UNH library, soliciting internal input.
Dean & Assistant Dean	April 15–17, 2021	Check in with provost for input, and check in with HR partner for initial input.
Dean	April 15–19, 2021	Structure decision is made and announced internally.
Assistant and Associate Deans	April 20, 2021	Analyze position descriptions and draft where individuals would fit in a new organizational structure.
Dean	May 4, 2021	Special meeting to share more details on structure.
Leadership Team	May 2021	LT devises a strategy and approach for externally communicating structural changes.

Table 20.2. A rough outline of the process steps taken to introduce our new structure.

Who	When	What
Associate and Assistant Deans	May 19, 2021	Design and post survey call for participation—Based on your PD, what groups do you think you should lead? What groups do you anticipate being on? Results due by 5/21.
Leadership Team	May 26, 2021	Identify and finalize leaders of programs & section leadership.
Assistant and Associate Deans	June 3, 2021	Write leader role descriptions.
Associate Dean	June 3, 2021	Update sections document.
Assistant and Associate Deans	June 2–8, 2021	Meet individually with potential program/section leaders, share draft role description.
Assistant and Associate Deans	Beginning June 9, 2021	Meet individually with all library employees about section and program assignments.
Dean	June 14, 2021	Share assignments library-wide (program lead and section leads).
Associate and Assistant Deans	June 15, 2021	Outline all processes and substructures that need to be consistent across programs and sections; communicate these.
Associate Dean	June 16, 2021	Provide update at library-wide meeting.
Associate Dean	June 20, 2021	Convene first meetings of program; determine their frequency.
Assistant Dean	June 20, 2021	Convene first meeting of section leads—ground rules, charge, determine meeting frequency, etc.
Dean	July 1, 2021	Announce official start of the new structure.
Dean and Assistant and Associate Deans	July 1, 2021	Create a high-level structure picture for post-transition and a new formal organizational chart; seek input; finalize and put on the website.
Assistant Associate Deans	July/August 2021	Begin to work with HR partner and supervisors on potential adjustments to PDs and any that need classification review. As changes are likely to be incremental, classification review will be requested once the position changes warrant it.
Section and Program Leads	July 2021	Determine a file/records taxonomy and structure that works for the new structure.
Dean's Office Assistant	July 2021	Set up files for new structure.
Assistant and Associate Deans		Work with DHs and supervisors on position description adjustments.

Table 20.2. A rough outline of the process steps taken to introduce our new structure.

Who	When	What
Assistant and Associate Deans		Meet with individuals about position changes.
Dean and others TBD	July 2021	Library communicates structural changes externally.
New Section Leadership	June 2021	Start regularly meeting to identify training, meeting topics, etc. to ensure a smooth transition.
New Programmatic Leadership	June 2021	Start meeting regularly to begin planning work.
Assistant Dean? Associate Dean? Dean's Office Staff?	July 2021	Review foundational documents for needed updates related to references to old structure..
Leadership Team	June–August 2021	Evolve a plan to align structure with planning processes, other organizational mechanisms (e.g., hiring, goal setting, merit, coaching, etc.), foundational documents, etc.
Assistant and Associate Deans, HR Partner	August 1?	Determine if additional compensation needs to be requested. If so, make recommendation to dean.
Associate Dean	August 2021	Document the changes made for the annual report.
Assistant Dean	July 31, 2021	Determine how we handle student labor in the first year of the new structure.
Assistant and Associate Deans	November 2021	Brainstorm/identify several line reporting mechanisms for a more permanent implementation in our new structure. This may involve suggestions and input from current section leads, our HR partner, colleagues from PSU, etc.
Assistant and Associate Deans	November 2021	Develop a process for changing, adding, or retiring a program.
Assistant Dean	December 2021	Determine how we handle student labor moving forward.
Library Employees	Moving forward	Programs (and sections?) and individuals all commit to having at least one goal in support of a strategic initiative. Division heads, group leaders, and individuals will develop these goals in partnership with the appropriate strategic initiative relevant leader and work with the relevant leader on goal progress.

In early May 2021, an overview of the new structure was presented to all library employees, followed the next week by detailed program descriptions, defined roles and responsibilities, and a call for individual input on the programs each employee felt were appropriate to their position. The UNH Library's leadership team made decisions on program leadership based on existing position descriptions and shared those decisions with new leaders. Program membership was determined by position descriptions and employee input and was shared directly with each employee in a private meeting. By the end of May, program membership was announced broadly.

Throughout the process of presenting structure options and explaining our new structure, library leadership was careful to be clear about what change in how we are organized would and would not do and to attend to those organizational aspects that were uncovered as needing attention. The associate dean and assistant dean wrote and shared definitions of program language to ensure everyone had a common understanding of our new structure. They also compiled a lengthy list of processes that would need updating as the library began to work in new ways. From August 2021 to January 2022, the library held several staff meetings on topics such as the library's decision-making process, our "Vision for a Healthy Work Environment" statement, and giving and receiving feedback. A concurrent conversation about library subject specialty was also occurring among the library faculty. The ultimate outcome of this discussion was a full realization of a subject-specialist model that placed at least one dedicated subject-specialist librarian whose primary professional responsibility is service to each college at UNH beginning in the fall of 2021. This led to a change in position description for two librarians—the information literacy librarian and the government documents librarian—to serve as the librarians for the College of Liberal Arts, serving Arts and Humanities and Social Sciences respectively.

Shortly after launching the new structure, the UNH Library implemented Microsoft Teams as a communication tool. The library was set up as a single team, with each program having a channel. This allows anyone in the library to read about the work going on in any program, creating greater transparency and less siloing.

In the program structure, each employee is a member of at least one program, with most employees serving on three or four. The structure also temporarily organized individual employees into four sections intended to provide a strong home base as we transitioned. This is an innovative approach for libraries, as it moves away from a traditional hierarchy and emphasizes work direction over supervision while giving employees at all levels considerable autonomy in their work. Program leadership included professional colleagues from both faculty and nonfaculty classifications, thereby offering a more diverse leadership perspective.

On July 1, 2021, the UNH Library officially began the program structure, understanding it would take the better part of a year to adjust and realize the structure's benefits. While Bartlett and Ghoshal assert that the matrix structure "proved all but unmanageable,"[12] the UNH Library put in place a manageable version of a traditional matrix, which is often described as, "the most confusing and least used" organizational structure.[13] Bartlett and Ghoshal write that dual reporting led to conflict and confusion.[14] The UNH Library addressed potential conflict and confusion by putting the worker in charge of their workload, with clear position descriptions that state the percentage of time each employee dedicates to each program and a commitment from all program leads to consult with one another regularly. The library has no committees; instead, the library built a library-wide team to discourage turf battles. Work direction comes from program leads, and employees are empowered to complete their work. The structure takes the emphasis off top-level managers, which is a more sensible approach now, in the age of social networks and personal relationships, than it was in the 1980s when matrix management first gained favor.

In October 2021, the UNH Library launched a multifaceted evaluation to review the programmatic structure and determine necessary adjustments. Adjustments could take the form of additional programs, adjustments to sections, clarifications in the scope of programs, adjustments to position descriptions, or other tweaks; but it was too soon to evaluate the impact of the structure. Rather, the library set out to determine what minor changes could improve the structure relative to the work that we do and the goals that we had when designing a new structure. An efficacy review of the structure is a planned future phase.

The evaluation of the new structure was conducted by the associate dean and assistant dean, and included the following goals:

- Position descriptions accurately describe responsibilities of role.
- Program leadership is appropriate to meet our goals.
- Program membership is appropriate to meet our goals.
- Program-level strategy is aligned with library and university strategic initiatives.
- Roles of faculty affiliate, administrative lead, and section lead are clarified; a decision is made about their need to continue; and a determination is made about the need for sections.

To achieve these evaluation goals, the associate dean and assistant dean examined the definitions, visions, and goals of each program, and program leads negotiated any identified overlap. Library administration met with library faculty about the structure and noted aspects faculty felt were needed. The dean and associate dean revisited the goals set for the new structure, exploring the degree to which those were met. The associate dean audited the library's former groups and committees to ensure that all work previously captured was covered by the new structure. Program leads reviewed program membership to determine if changes were necessary. Administrative partners worked with employees to review position descriptions to ensure they accurately reflected the work.

Since the assistant dean is responsible for library human resources, she and the associate dean reviewed all the information gathered to determine if any broader changes were needed. As a result of this evaluation, they made several recommendations, including retiring the section side of the structure in favor of launching a human resources (HR) program. This HR program would address workplace coaching and goal setting, as well as the optimization the library's student employment program and other human resources needs. The HR program includes administrative leads (renamed administrative partners to mirror language used more broadly at the university) and also any additional employees who supervise non-benefitted, adjunct labor (such as students, interns, and part-time workers). This program provides support for them. Rather than some administrative leads serving seven or more employees and others serving one employee, this change also allowed the library to make a more equitable distribution of the administrative partner role, which compiles annual coaching and approves time and leave for an employee. The first configuration of this role had not been equitably distributed throughout the organization. At this point the library not only reassigned three or four employees to each administrative partner, but also ensured the role served either exempt or nonexempt staff because both coaching and time and leave recording are different for different classifications of employees. The nonsupervisory nature of the role was also highlighted and clarified since only program leads provide work direction in the structure.

The library also developed a new Leadership and Planning program that collects and directs the strategic work of the library that was not originally well captured in the structure. The Leadership and Planning program is responsible for faculty hiring, library-wide celebrations and events, library fundraising and development, administrative aspects of promotion and tenure, accreditation and library assessment, and support of the dean's work. Led by the dean of the UNH Library, the Leadership and Planning program membership includes the faculty chair, assistant dean, associate dean, library senior administrative assistant, senior library manager, and the library's development officer (figure 20.2).

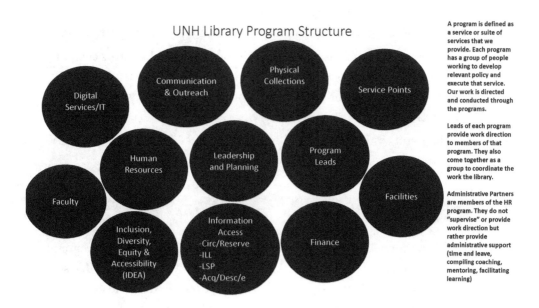

Figure 20.2. The revised organizational chart we use after improving the program structure based on our evaluation.

The library refined program membership, moving away from the broad, inclusive approach to membership originally taken. Given the transparency of information available on Microsoft Teams, no one needs to serve on a program simply to get information. Other roles were identified as needing more involvement than originally anticipated. As a result, five adjustments to program membership were made.

Finally, the library resolved to consider affinities among programs. Since programs are working together in new ways, continued evolution of the programs was recommended. Two questions arose from the review of goals for the new structure, and the library is giving these aspects of the current structure one more year to consider:

- the future of the internal structure of the Information Access program
- ways to expand involvement in work that is managed through the faculty program

For the first question about the structural arrangement of circulation, course reserves, interlibrary loan, cataloging, acquisitions, e-resources, and the library services platform being grouped together under the information access umbrella, it remains unclear if these programs share closer ties to each other than any of the other four programs. The somewhat hierarchical arrangement grouping these programs into an umbrella information access program will remain for further evaluation by those leading programs within it.

For the second question about expanding involvement in work that is managed through the faculty program, this is likely to happen as a natural and appropriate evolution of the structure. As faculty conceptualize work that is squarely in their domain, aspects of that work may spin off to different programs. Examples of this are already evident, for example in the FY2023 faculty program goals:

- Collaborate with the Service Points program on research support initiatives.
- Build library faculty skills to support the ability for faculty across campus to identify diverse scholars and their work for inclusion in course syllabi, which integrates the work of the Inclusion, Diversity, Equity and Accessibility program.

The faculty chair and associate dean will monitor progress on this question as the year progresses.

Conclusions

The UNH Library's move from a division-based hierarchical structure to a programmatic structure has been successful overall but has not been without its challenges. The structure has allowed the library the flexibility needed to improve our services and operations. The change also allowed the library to restart previously stalled talks about consolidating the circulation and research desks into a unified information desk, which was successfully launched during the first year of the programmatic structure.

The structure further allowed the library to use our limited human resources in more efficient ways. By unifying materials description, acquisitions, and e-access into one program, the library was able to consolidate and streamline these workflows. Description and acquisitions work that was previously done by seven full-time staff members is now accomplished by five full-time staff members, many of whom also serve on other programs. Unifying the research desk with the circulation desk allowed us to repurpose the circulation desk manager role to focus on circulation service improvements as program lead for circulation and library programming, two gaps that had existed in the organization. The senior manager for circulation also had a change in duties and now focuses on library-wide management issues, primarily human resources.

After working within the structure for more than a year, the importance of articulating that program membership is comprised of individuals in different job roles and classifications who therefore contribute to program work in different ways was clear. As an organization, it is important for the library to acknowledge these differences and allow them to inform our work. Additionally, it is now expected that each employee will review their position description and program assignments as part of the annual coaching process, since positions naturally evolve.

One of the most important things the leadership of the UNH Library learned was the need to attend to our organization through clear goals, strategy, and communication. Structure alone does not make a healthy organization; rather, the common understandings of how members of the organization contribute to the health and well-being of an organization do achieve organizational health. For the UNH Library, this meant developing clear definitions and visions for all programs; sharing each program's goals and updates on progress toward those goals; and reaffirming several of our organization's foundational documents, such as our strategic plan, "Vision for a Healthy Work Environment," and decision-making process. The library developed new meeting norms and documented important policies and procedures.

Some things remain a challenge—programs have a variety of organizational maturity levels, and individual employees have embraced the structure to different degrees. Some of our colleagues have found a nonhierarchical approach difficult to get used to. In fact, two of our colleagues found employment elsewhere in the early days of the new structure, at least in part because of discomfort with the new way of working. Overall, the library has observed a positive impact on our culture, with more openness, communication, and collaboration, which is not a result of the structure change alone. For the structure to be successful, it was necessary to look at our organizational processes and agreed-upon ways of working—the physiology of the organization, as described by Bartlett and Ghoshal.[15] The shared understanding, foundational documents, and organizational processes are a vital part of the library's success. The UNH Library is persisting with a programmatic structure and will continue to adjust and make tweaks as needed. For example, the library has recently begun to think about guidelines for the ideal number of programs in which an employee can participate.

In the future, a more comprehensive evaluation of the structure will be needed, perhaps by using the Organizational Culture Assessment Instrument and the Competing Values Framework, as Yoose and Knight demonstrated.[16] At the time of this writing, the program structure is still quite new, and the UNH Library does not know if it will stand the test of time. So far, changing the structure has allowed the library to address not only some structural gaps, but also some of the ways of working that were not beneficial to our organization. A team-based structure in which employees are members of several teams better addresses the work of a mid-sized, leanly staffed research library than the division structure.

Lessons Learned

Through the process of updating our organizational structure, the leadership of the UNH Library was reminded of four important lessons that will not only inform structural changes going forward, but will also be helpful as we approach any major change:

1. *Take the broad view*. We learned that structure is so much more than reporting lines. It includes all documentation confirming how we work together as an organization. When embarking on a major change, this becomes an important touchstone to remind colleagues of what is staying the same.
2. *Keep to process*. It's important to map out a process going into any major change. Knowing the steps to investigate and implement a change helps leaders stay on course and colleagues know what is happening.
3. *Communicate*. Checking in regularly and often with stakeholders before, during, and after a change keeps everyone attuned to the change and can help prevent resistance and backsliding.
4. *Listen*. It's important to be open to feedback and use that feedback to make iterative improvements on a change.

Notes

1. University of New Hampshire, "Enrollment," accessed June 28, 2022, https://www.unh.edu/institutional-research/data-reports/student-data/enrollment; Institute for Educational Sciences, National Center for Education Statistics, "Staff by Employment Status and Occupational Category," accessed June 28, 2022, https://nces.ed.gov/ipeds/data-center/instituionprofile.aspx?unitId=183044 (page discontinued).
2. Will Kenton, "Organizational Structure for Companies with Examples and Benefits," *Investopedia*, March 16, 2023, https://www.investopedia.com/terms/o/organizational-structure.asp.
3. Shelley A. Phipps, "The System Design Approach to Organizational Development: The University of Arizona Model," *Library Trends* 53, no. 1 (Summer 2004): 68–111.
4. Betsy A. Bernfeld, "Developing a Team Management Structure in a Public Library, " *Library Trends* 53, no. 1 (Summer 2004): 112–28.
5. Mori Lou Higa et al., "Redesigning a Library's Organizational Structure," *College and Research Libraries* 66, no. 1 (January 2005): 41–58, https://doi.org/10.5860/crl.66.1.41; Becky Yoose and Cecilia Knight, "Clusters: A Study of

a Non-traditional Academic Library Organizational Model," *Library Leadership and Management* 30, no. 3 (2016), https://llm.corejournals.org/llm/article/view/7131; Jeremy Nelson, "Organizing Libraries," in *Becoming a Lean Library: Lessons from the World of Technology Start-ups* (Waltham. MA: Chandos, 2016), ProQuest Ebook Central, https://doi.org/10.1016/B978-1-84334-779-8.00002-1.
6. Michael A. Crumpton, "Organizational Structures in Academic Libraries," in *Strategic Human Resources Planning for Academic Libraries: Information, Technology and Organization* (Waltham, MA: Chandos, 2015), ProQuest Ebook Central, https://doi.org/10.1016/B978-1-84334-764-4.00004-6.
7. Roger C. Schonfeld, *Organizing the Work of the Research Library* (New York: Ithaka S+R, August 18, 2016), https://doi.org/10.18665/sr.283717.
8. Yoose and Knight, "Clusters"; Crumpton, "Organizational Structures"; Douglas Burns and Sian Brannon, "Getting Started with Organizational Design at Your Library, " *Library Leadership and Management* 33, no. 1 (2018): 1–9, https://llm.corejournals.org/llm/article/view/7311.
9. *Economic Times*, "What Is 'Matrix Organization,'" https://economictimes.indiatimes.com/definition/matrix-organization.
10. Christopher A. Bartlett and Sumantra Ghoshal, "Matrix Management: Not a Structure, a Frame of Mind," *Harvard Business Review*, July–August 1990, 148-156, https://hbr.org/1990/07/matrix-management-not-a-structure-a-frame-of-mind.
11. Bartlett and Ghoshal, "Matrix Management."
12. Bartlett and Ghoshal, "Matrix Management," 148-156.
13. Kenton, "Organizational Structure for Companies."
14. Bartlett and Ghoshal, "Matrix Management."
15. Bartlett and Ghoshal, "Matrix Management."
16. Yoose and Knight, "Clusters."

Bibliography

Bartlett, Christopher A., and Sumantra Ghoshal. "Matrix Management: Not a Structure, a Frame of Mind." *Harvard Business Review* 68, no. 4 (1990): 138–45.
Bernfeld, Betsy A. "Developing a Team Management Structure in a Public Library: Organizational Development and Leadership." *Library Trends* 53, no. 1 (Summer 2004): 112–28.
Burns, Douglas, and Sian Brannon. "Getting Started with Organizational Design at Your Library." *Library Leadership and Management* 33, no. 1 (2018): 1–9. https://llm.corejournals.org/llm/article/view/7311.
Crumpton, Michael A. "Organizational Structures in Academic Libraries." In *Strategic Human Resource Planning for Academic Libraries: Information, Technology and Organization*, 31–43. Waltham, MA: Chandos, 2015. ProQuest Ebook Central. https://doi.org/10.1016/B978-1-84334-764-4.00004-6.
Economic Times. "What Is 'Matrix Organization.'" https://economictimes.indiatimes.com/definition/matrix-organization.
Higa, Mori Lou, Brian Bunnett, Bill Maina, Jeff Perkins, Therona Ramos, Laurie Thompson, and Richard Wayne. "Redesigning a Library's Organizational Structure." *College and Research Libraries* 66, no. 1 (January 2005): 41–58. https://doi.org/10.5860/crl.66.1.41.
Institute for Educational Sciences, National Center for Education Statistics. "Staff by Employment Status and Occupational Category." Accessed June 28, 2022. https://nces.ed.gov/ipeds/datacenter/instituionprofile.aspx?unitId=183044 (page discontinued).
Kenton, Will. "Organizational Structure for Companies with Examples and Benefits." *Investopedia*, March 16, 2023. https://www.investopedia.com/terms/o/organizational-structure.asp.
Nelson, Jeremy. "Organizing Libraries." In *Becoming a Lean Library: Lessons from the World of Technology Start-ups*, 15–27. Waltham, MA: Chandos, 2016. ProQuest Ebook Central. https://doi.org/10.1016/B978-1-84334-779-8.00002-1.
Phipps, Shelley A. "The System Design Approach to Organizational Development: The University of Arizona Model." *Library Trends* 53, no. 1 (Summer 2004): 68–111.
Schonfeld, Roger C. *Organizing the Work of the Research Library.* New York: Ithaka S+R, August 18, 2016. https://doi.org/10.18665/sr.283717.
University of New Hampshire. "Enrollment." Accessed June 28, 2022. https://www.unh.edu/institutional-research/data-reports/student-data/enrollment.
Yoose, Becky, and Cecilia Knight. "Clusters: A Study of a Non-traditional Academic Library Organizational Model." *Library Leadership and Management* 30, no. 3 (2016). https://llm.corejournals.org/llm/article/view/7131.

CHAPTER 21

Rightsizing Technical Services
Practical Adaptations for Rapidly Evolving Libraries

Kathaleen McCormick, Kristy White, and Tracie Ballock

After years of downsizing physical collections and upsizing electronic collections, the traditional technical services areas at Duquesne University's Gumberg Library reinvented and streamlined workflows and job responsibilities. As traditional technical services functions changed or faded away, duties in support of access and management of both electronic resources and unique special collections continued to grow and change at a rapid pace. Duties that supported physical collections had to be transitioned to the access and management of electronic resources and unique digitized content. To make these electronic collections accessible, new systems and other emerging technologies were investigated, mastered, and integrated with existing systems, such as EBSCO Discovery Service (EDS); Sierra, the integrated library system (ILS); ArchivesSpace, the open-source archives information management application; CONTENTdm, the digital assess management software; and LibInsight, the library analytics tool, to mention a few. Unlike the physical collections, we found that the electronic resource life cycle required continuous monitoring. Additionally, turnover that occurred during COVID-19 increased opportunities to reevaluate positions and responsibilities. Throughout this process, we discovered that our technical services department was not dissolving but evolving.

The metamorphosis of the department from maintaining a mostly physical collection to managing a primarily electronic collection provided new opportunities. For example, we were able to make unique archival collections searchable in our discovery layer by creating catalog records with links to ArchivesSpace finding aids. This also provided an opportunity for our department to create initiatives in support of the campus community. Traditionally, technical services departments were supportive in nature, but behind the scenes. Today, we have emerged as a more visible, front-facing service provider. Services in support of students and faculty were developed that revolutionized the role of technical services within our library. The current services are focused on linking faculty syllabi to library content and open education resources (OERs).

Gumberg Library's Technical Services department endured many years of downsizing and cost containment, reduction of physical items, increase in electronic collections, and significant changes in workflows. All of these changes united two separate technical services areas into one rightsized, newly organized Collections and Metadata Services department positioned to meet future challenges and opportunities.

Problem Definition

Libraries play a critical role in providing access to information and resources for their communities. Over the years, the role of libraries has evolved, and the transformation of collection development has played a significant part in this evolution. The COVID-19 pandemic accelerated this evolution by emphasizing the need for access to electronic resources. In this chapter, we will describe how Gumberg Library optimized library staff and workflows to keep up with rapid changes in collections, staffing, and budgets.

Literature Review

We will examine the transformation of collection development, staffing, workflows, budgets, and the impact of the COVID-19 pandemic on libraries. Collections are shifting from print to electronic resources, budgets and staffing are being reduced, and libraries are adjusting workflows in response.

Collection development is a crucial aspect of library services, and it has undergone significant transformations over the years. According to a study in *Technical Services Quarterly*, the shift toward digital resources has had a profound impact on collection development, with libraries placing a greater emphasis on acquiring digital resources and online databases.[1] In response to these changes, libraries have had to reevaluate their collection development strategies to meet the needs of users. For example, a study by De Groote and Scoulas found that libraries have increased their investments in digital resources, including e-books and online databases, to support remote access to information.[2] The ongoing debate over the relative merits of print versus electronic resources has also affected library technical services. While many libraries have shifted their focus to electronic resources, print materials remain an important part of many collections. This has resulted in new challenges related to managing hybrid collections and integrating print and electronic resources into discovery systems.[3] Additionally, the shift to electronic resources has led to concerns about access, preservation, and the long-term sustainability of the scholarly record.[4]

These changes have had an impact on staffing in technical services. Many libraries have reduced or restructured staffing levels, particularly in areas related to print materials. According to McAllister, this has resulted in a greater reliance on part-time and temporary staff, as well as the outsourcing of certain technical services functions.[5] Davis also states that the rise of electronic resources has created new opportunities for staff members to develop specialized skills in areas such as metadata management, licensing, and vendor relations.[6]

Budget constraints have also been a major driver of the transformation of library technical services in recent years. The shift to electronic resources has allowed libraries to reduce their spending on physical materials but has increased costs related to licensing, access, and infrastructure. The ongoing pandemic has further constrained library budgets, leading many libraries to adopt conservative collection development strategies and to explore new models for acquiring new resources and making them available to patrons.[7]

While all of these changes have presented new challenges, they have also created new opportunities for libraries to better serve their communities and to develop specialized skills and expertise in technical services. As the field continues to evolve, libraries will need to remain flexible and adaptable in order to meet the needs of their users and to provide high-quality technical services.

Discussion
Collection Transformation

Gumberg Library's collection transformation began with the introduction of electronic journals and databases, as well as the creation of our first electronic access librarian position. Additionally, between 1990 and 1994, Duquesne University opened two new schools: the John G. Rangos Sr. School of Health Sciences and the Bayer School of Natural and Environmental Sciences. The new schools' increased demand for costly electronic resources kept pace with their increasing availability, especially in the area of science. These electronic resources were priced differently and cost more than print journal subscriptions. Moreover, our integrated library system could not create access points for electronic formats, and some faculty felt the image quality in the electronic resources was inadequate for their research needs. Gumberg spent the early 2000s addressing these issues.

The first big collection transformation project was a print reference collection review, conducted from 2004 to 2006. The goal of this endeavor was to create student study space on the fourth floor of the library. By withdrawing outdated ready reference materials, replacing needed reference works with electronic equivalents, and shifting remaining volumes into the general collection, floor space formerly filled with stacks of books was transformed into study carrels and tables. As the demand for additional student study space grew, Gumberg searched for other ways to create space by downsizing physical collections. The mammoth fifth floor had the potential to provide such space since it was filled with stacks of underutilized print journals; large collections of LP records, VHS tapes, DVDs, and CDs; and rows of heavy microfilm cabinets (figure 21.1). If this material could be replaced with electronic versions, the fifth floor could be opened up. We started by investigating how to acquire electronic replacements for at least some of our print journals. By 2006, we recognized that JSTOR was a stable platform dedicated to the preservation of scholarly journal archives, and as early adopters of the platform, we were given an affordable option for replacing print with electronic. Additionally, its collections encompassed full runs of hundreds of scholarly titles owned by Gumberg. This launched the beginning of many print journal review projects at our library, which continue today. Over the years, we have replaced print and microfilm journals with current electronic journal subscriptions and extensive electronic journal back files. We have also provided access to numerous aggregated database collections. In 2008, the library installed a large section of compact shelving on the ground floor. The goal was to assess, downsize, and methodically move all print journals off of the fifth floor. By 2020, our fifth floor was totally renovated: all remaining print journals and all AV materials were moved off of the floor (figure 21.2).

Figure 21.1. Gumberg Library fifth floor—before.

Figure 21.2. Gumberg Library fifth floor—after

Gumberg Library continues to focus on collection assessment, deselection, and digitization projects throughout the library for all material types. Whenever possible, we continue to replace large print journal holdings with their electronic counterparts. The removal of the print runs creates space in the compact shelving, making room to house other print collections. This in turn frees up additional space for student study.

On top of the adjustments that almost every library has faced in the past twenty years with changing formats, shifting patron service demands, and the need for new and improved spaces, in the fall semester of 2019 Gumberg received the unexpected and shocking news that an entire floor of the library was to be repurposed. Half of this massive space would house a library for the new College of Osteopathic Medicine, and the other half would accommodate the creation of a University Wellness Center. The initial deadline for the floor to be cleared of approximately 267,000 books—which accounted for more than 40 percent of our entire collection—was July 2021, though the pandemic caused the project deadline to be pushed back by six months. Luckily, before the nationwide March 2020 pandemic lockdown, the Greenglass collection analysis was completed, an assessment plan with criteria was developed, an informational web page was created to keep the campus updated,[8] and meetings between library administrators and unhappy stakeholders from across campus were conducted to explain the project's goals. Throughout the next five months, librarians reviewed hundreds of thousands of titles using extensive information, such as circulation statistics, the number of OCLC holdings, HathiTrust public access information, and number of copies in the collection in order to make decisions on what to keep and what to discard.

In July 2020, library staff were permitted back into the building with staggered schedules, and there was limited patron access to the building. The silver lining to these pandemic restrictions was that they provided a unique opportunity for staff from all departments to assist with identifying and removing books from the stacks, as well as packing up the pallet-sized Gaylord containers of discarded books being shipped to Better World Books. In December 2021, the third-floor project was completed. When the last Gaylord containers left the building, all remaining books were relocated to the second floor, and all shelving was removed from the third floor. A library project celebration event was scheduled for January 2022 to thank all library staff and campus partners for helping make this project a success. In the end, roughly 392,000 general collection titles were reviewed and 260,389 volumes—two-thirds of the general collection—were removed, resulting in 299 Gaylord containers of discarded books being sent to Better World Books (figure 21.3). The herculean effort exerted to successfully complete this project in a timely manner—and during a global pandemic—resulted in the library receiving the university's Teamwork Award at the 2022 staff awards ceremony.

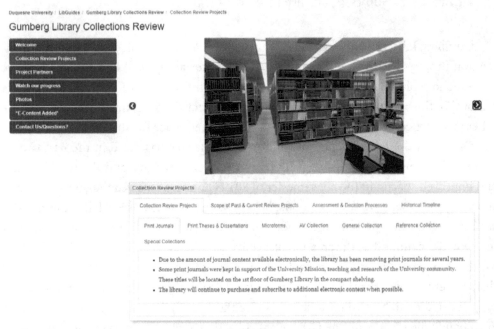

Figure 21.3. Collection project website

Since the completion of the third-floor project, we have continued to assess and downsize other areas of the collection. For instance, by comparing our holdings and usage of physical items against our e-resources, we have greatly reduced our CD, DVD, and microform collections and increased our electronic holdings. Going forward, when purchasing new resources, Gumberg Library has moved to an e-preferred collection development model. This does not mean that we no longer purchase any physical items.

Format decisions are now made based on subject area, the requestor's needs, demand for the item, and availability.

Each of these projects, from the ready reference collection to the general collection reassessment, has allowed us to successfully reach our goals of creating new and exciting spaces for our students, as well as providing space for the addition of a new medical library and University Wellness Center. This has also made our physical resources easier to find and has created the shelf space needed to acquire new and relevant print resources.

Technology Changes and Updates

In addition to the transformation of the library physical spaces, the shift toward electronic resources has led to changes in library resource management and access technologies, which, in turn, has had a profound impact on library staffing and the way librarians think about their roles. New systems are constantly being researched and evaluated by our library staff and committees. Once decisions are made, it takes considerable time and effort to learn and master these new products. One of the first of these technologies we implemented was the online ILS. Gumberg Library made the switch from a card catalog to Data Research Associates' (DRA) Online Public Access Catalogue (OPAC), called DRA Classic, in 1994. After the Sirsi Corporation acquired DRA in 2001, the DRA Classic OPAC was no longer supported. As a result, our ILS changed to Sirsi Symphony. In 2014, for the very first time, the Law Library (which supports the School of Law) and Gumberg Library (which supports approximately 8,000 enrolled students) coordinated efforts by migrating together to Innovative's Sierra ILS. Each ILS migration has provided an opportunity to adopt new, more efficient workflows. In June 2023, we migrated to FOLIO hosted by EBSCO,[9] which provided more opportunities for improved efficiency and flexibility.

Prior to 2014, Gumberg was using the SFX link resolver and our OPAC to locate and access our electronic resources. When this no longer served our students' and researchers' needs, discovery systems were investigated. In 2014, we adopted Encore, the discovery layer bundled with Sierra that employs an EDS backend. When it did not meet expectations, the library chose to drop Encore and adopt EDS for discovery in 2019. Our researchers' interactions with the discovery layer improved even further when we moved from Sierra to FOLIO, since it is more compatible with EDS.

Another suite of products that has helped transform technical services workflows is Springshare, which provides several products that our library uses in a number of ways. One of those products, LibGuides, is used to create research guides to supplement or highlight resources for specific classes, making our collections more accessible. We also use LibGuides for special collections such as our Curriculum Collection, Music Resources, Phenomenology Center, University Archives, and Library of Things. Our A–Z database list is also updated and maintained through LibGuides. Springshare's LibInsight, a powerful analytics tool for reporting and comparing COUNTER-compliant usage statistics for a large portion of our e-resources, was implemented for gathering electronic resource usage statistics in 2017. Since 2018, LibAnswers, a multichannel communication platform, has been used to track access problems. Prior to using LibAnswers, access problems were sent to the electronic resources and discovery librarian via e-mail. LibAnswers keeps records of problems and resolutions in a single, accessible location.

To improve online access to the University Archives collections, ArchivesSpace was acquired in 2017. Although there were collection-level records for archival material in the ILS that could be retrieved via the discovery layer, the finding aids for archival collections were either Microsoft Word documents or printed documents with no clear organization or common access point. Transferring this information into ArchivesSpace resulted in web access from universal search engines, such as Google, to all of the University Archives finding aid information.

To manage our expanding digital collections—which includes curated collections as well as theses, dissertations, and other scholarship produced or associated with Duquesne University—we transitioned to Bepress, a digital repository, in 2017. Our cataloging and metadata librarian assists in the creation of metadata for digitized collections using this platform, making them more accessible and easier to find.

With this shift toward electronic resources, the roles of library staff have transformed, requiring them to develop new skills, adapt to changing technologies, and adopt a more user-centric approach. Librarians now play pivotal roles in managing, curating, and providing access to digital content while supporting patrons in navigating the digital landscape effectively.

Staffing Adjustments

Gumberg Library never had a traditional technical services department, but instead had two separate departments: Acquisitions, and Cataloging and Processing. This began to change around 1990, when a new position, head of collection development, was created and acquisitions was moved to this new department.

During the 2011–2012 fiscal year the university began cost containment measures, which included drastic budget cuts, including a 5 percent cut in Gumberg's materials budget and a faculty and staff retirement buyout. By 2012, there was a marked reduction in physical items being added to the library collections, resulting in less cataloging and a shift in workload from physical to e-resource management (figure 21.4). Therefore, when the junior cataloger accepted the first retirement buyout offer in 2011, the cataloging department could not justify hiring a replacement cataloger. As the university's controlled spending efforts continued, all remaining faculty and staff job responsibilities were reevaluated and, as others retired or resigned, their positions were rewritten. Justifications for filling vacant positions had to be submitted to the university administration for approval. We used these staffing departures as opportunities to streamline processes, cross-train, teach long-time staff new skills, and eliminate unnecessary tasks. For example, when the acquisitions accounting specialist retired, we were able to move another

Figure 21.4. Technical Services organizational chart 2012

support staff member from the cataloging department into this position, merging the remaining necessary duties into one position. Likewise, the retirement of a full-time staff member from the cataloging department in 2017 provided the opportunity to merge this position with the part-time cataloging librarian to create a new, full-time cataloging and metadata librarian position, which encompassed all of the cataloging duties of the part-time position, in addition to gathering ER usage data, metadata, instruction, and service responsibilities.

Finally, in 2018 all technical services functions were merged to create one new department called Collections and Metadata Services (CMS). This newly formed department was responsible for collection needs assessment and analysis, establishment of collections policies and procedures, budgeting, selection and deselection of resources, acquisitions of library resources in all formats, cataloging and processing of all collection materials in all formats, management and access of all electronic resources, and oversight of gift materials. When the pandemic started in 2020, the department was comprised of five full-time faculty members: the assistant university librarian for collections and metadata services, the acquisitions librarian, the access and discovery librarian, the head of cataloging, and the cataloging and metadata librarian, as well as four full-time support staff: the acquisitions accounting assistant, the acquisitions ordering assistant, the cataloging and processing assistant, and the collection management assistant.

The ongoing pandemic, with its constant disruptions, exerted an extreme financial drain on the university, and university administration offered a volunteer retirement program for tenured faculty. The head of the cataloging department, the last tenured librarian, accepted a three-year retirement plan and began working 17.5 hours a week. This position no longer supervises staff and will be eliminated in July 2024. A cost containment plan implemented in March 2021 eliminated one of the two clerical positions in the CMS department. The department lost two additional positions, one full-time clerical and one full-time faculty librarian. Both found positions outside of the university. Due to additional cost containment, neither position was replaced, and once more, the CMS department had to cross-train staff and streamline processes. Recently, a new part-time position was created to assist with the processing of physical items, a collection labeling project, and organizing e-resource usage.

As difficult as some of these situations and changes were, Gumberg CMS staff worked together to come up with solutions that have made the department work smarter, allowing for the creation of new forward-thinking processes and services. Figure 21.5 is the current CMS department's organizational chart.

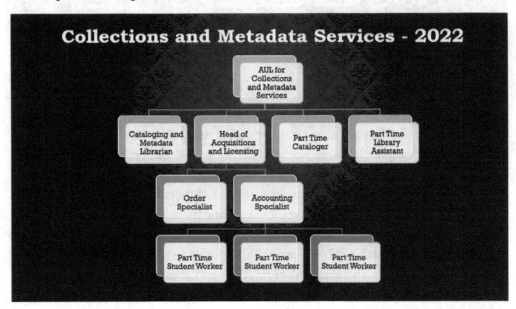

Figure 21.5. Collections and Metadata Services organizational chart 2022

Workflow Evolution

As collections and staffing have changed, so have workflows. The cataloging and processing of physical items at Gumberg Library have been impacted by a decline in the number of items being added to the collection, a reduction in repairs, and the adoption of a new ILS. In 2012, almost 8,000 physical items were cataloged and processed by the cataloging department. By 2022, that number had been reduced to under 2,000 items. In addition to processing new items, historically, a large part of the processing workload included repairs. Most repairs were done in-house to add shelf life to items, not for preservation. Usage and relevancy of all damaged items are now reviewed to determine if the items are still needed in the collection. Retained items may be replaced with electronic editions or sent to the bindery, leaving very few items to be repaired in-house.

The cataloging process was streamlined when the library migrated to Sierra in 2014, a system that allowed catalogers to upload item records together with bib records directly into the ILS. Previously, items records were added individually into the ILS by staff. Spine labels, which had to be typed separately, could now be printed in batches, making the process more efficient and accurate. As a result of new systems and streamlined processes, the cataloging and processing of physical items can now be completed with half the staff needed ten years ago.

The evolution of library acquisitions has also resulted in a significant transformation over the past few decades. The move from print to electronic resources has brought about significant changes in the way that libraries acquire, manage, and make their resources available to patrons. According to Pilgrim and Dolabaille, a key change associated with the shift to electronic resources is the need to adopt new licensing models.[10] As many of our electronic resources are now licensed rather than purchased, acquisitions must negotiate and manage agreements with publishers and other content providers—a complex and time-consuming process. We must balance the need to provide patrons with access to necessary resources, while also managing costs and ensuring that resource users are adhering to the terms of the licensing agreements. In an effort to better represent the complicated responsibilities tied to electronic resources, our acquisitions librarian's title was recently changed to head of licensing and acquisitions.

As the life cycle of electronic resources has become more complex, the workflow for e-resources management has undergone significant changes. Previously, the serials and electronic resources librarian spent a considerable amount of time managing print and microfilm serials. When the position was evaluated after a retirement in 2014, the responsibilities changed to focus on management of only e-journals and other e-resources and was renamed electronic resources and discovery librarian. The small amount of work needed to maintain the print and microfilm serials was absorbed by the cataloging department. When the electronic resources and discovery librarian left in 2017, the job description was reevaluated. It was retitled access and discovery librarian to underscore the primary duty of providing access to e-resources and maintaining the discovery layer. This position was not replaced after the incumbent left in 2022. The head of acquisitions and licensing librarian assumed responsibility for turning on access when new orders are made and turning off access when titles are cancelled, streamlining that process. The cataloging and metadata librarian assumed responsibility for e-resource usage collection and reporting. Using LibInsight, vendors that are COUNTER-compliant can have their usage harvested automatically at regular intervals, and usage gathered can be analyzed easily, in order to make data-driven collection decisions. The chart in figure 21.6 shows an example of the kind of analysis that can be done in LibInsight.

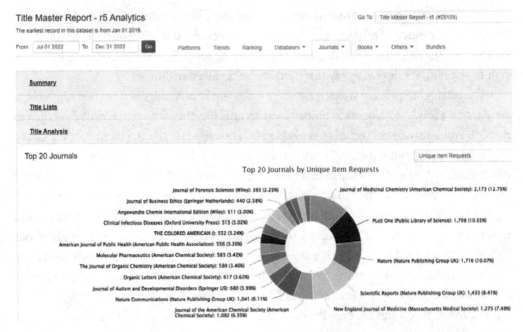

Figure 21.6. LibInsight screenshot

Vendors that are not COUNTER-compliant still need to have their usage gathered. This is done by contacting each vendor individually, using unique logins and passwords. This vendor information, which is needed by several people in the department, has been moved from a shared spreadsheet to a password manager. This streamlined the process, making the information easier to access and keeping it up to date. Implementing a group e-mail for the department and updating vendor logins to use the group e-mail was a simple, but very effective, improvement. Usage no longer gets bottlenecked waiting for a single personal e-mail to respond to a vendor request or security question. These improvements have led to a more accurate and comprehensive gathering of usage statistics, which can be analyzed in a variety of ways to improve decision-making.

Another change that has come with the shift to electronic resources is the need for libraries to develop new skills and expertise to manage these resources. For example, CMS staff must be familiar with the technical infrastructure required to access and use electronic resources, as well as the metadata standards and workflows necessary to effectively catalog and manage these resources.

In the past, most academic libraries operated under a just-in-case model, where they purchased resources, regardless of their current usage or demand.[11] During several of our collection assessment projects, we found many books purchased in this way were never used. With the current economic climate, academic libraries are facing limited budgets and reduced funding, making the just-in-case model unsustainable. For this reason, the budgeting strategy for our library has shifted from a just-in-case model to more of a just-in-time model, where materials are purchased at the time of need. This model allows us to provide relevant and up-to-date resources and materials to our patrons by focusing on acquiring resources based on current needs and demand. This enables us to reduce costs, provide better services, and more directly support our academic community. The goal of Gumberg's collection development model is to find the right balance of both models.

There are several misconceptions surrounding the management of library resources, particularly when it comes to electronic versus print in academic libraries. One of the most common misconceptions is that electronic resources are easier to manage than print resources; managing electronic resources can be more complex and laborious due to frequent updates and changes.[12] In addition, negotiating license agreements for electronic resources can be a time-consuming process due to the complexity of the agreements and multiple stakeholders involved. Whenever possible, we take advantage of the strategies developed to streamline the negotiation process, such as using standard licensing agreements and consortial or group purchasing.

Another misconception is that electronic resources are less expensive than print resources. The truth is that ongoing costs associated with maintaining and updating electronic resources can make them more expensive. Inflationary cost and subscriptions have been a major concern for libraries, as the cost of academic journals has increased by over 300 percent in the last thirty years.[13] Gumberg utilizes various strategies to manage our budget, such as negotiating with publishers and entering multiyear agreements to reduce costs, consortial purchasing, and one-time purchases of large packages of content.

Even though print resources can be costlier, they are highly valued by many patrons in academic libraries due to their availability, reliability, and ease of use without relying on technology or internet connectivity.[14] For this reason, it is crucial for academic libraries to consider the unique needs and preferences of their patrons when managing both electronic and print resources.

Future Opportunities

In the past, library technical services departments, including our own, were often viewed as a behind-the-scenes operations, focused only on acquiring, cataloging, and processing library materials. However, in recent years, the role of technical services has evolved, and we are increasingly becoming service providers to library patrons. According to McAllister, future library technical services will play a more prominent role in providing direct service to patrons.[15] This shift is driven by the changing needs and expectations of patrons, as well as the increasing complexity of library resources, particularly electronic resources. For instance, our acquisitions unit implemented a process where faculty send us their syllabi, and our staff determine what materials we have and what materials we can purchase, adding links to the syllabi whenever possible. Another example is our OER project with the university bookstore, in which the library is able to provide online access to e-books used for university core courses. These types of projects help alleviate some financial stresses for students. As faculty and students become more reliant on digital resources, we hope to develop more services like these.

We have found that the growth of open access publishing and digital repository initiatives has increased the importance of library technical services. Our cataloging and metadata librarian will be helping to create metadata for some digitized collections, as these initiatives require expertise to ensure that the content is accessible and discoverable to patrons. In addition, the increasing focus on user-centered services, CMS staff will continue to play a critical role in developing and implementing effective discovery tools and services, as well as in providing training and support in using these tools.

Conclusion

Technical services at Gumberg Library, including collection development, workflows, and staffing, have undergone a significant transformation. We now recognize these changes were necessary for us to keep pace with the evolving needs of our users. The impact of COVID-19 accelerated this evolution, as we had to suddenly adapt to new ways of serving all users remotely. However, we quickly realized that due to our vast electronic collection and processes for handling e-resources, we were better positioned to deal with this situation than we first thought.

Lessons Learned

- Change is constant. New technologies, patron expectations, and workflows have to be anticipated and addressed.
- Start small. Test runs with smaller assessment projects allowed us to fine-tune processes so that when we were hit with a huge, unexpected plan we were ready for it.
- Work together and be flexible. Having employees who are always willing to pitch in and learn something new was critical to our success.

Takeaways for Other Libraries

- Be proactive by reviewing and updating workflows, staffing, and best practices regularly.
- Invest in staff development and training. This will ensure that staff will have the necessary skills and knowledge to keep up with emerging trends and technologies.

- Create a culture of change. Staff should not just be comfortable with change, but should expect it, and even initiate it themselves.
- Be willing to experiment with new approaches or ideas.

Notes

1. Mary S. Laskowski and Jennifer A. Maddox Abbot, "The Evolution of Technical Services: Learning from the Past and Embracing the Future," *Technical Services Quarterly* 31, no. 1 (2014): 13–30.
2. S. De Groote and J. M. Scoulas, "Impact of COVID-19 on the Use of the Academic Library," *Reference Services Review* 49, no. 3/4, (2021): 281–301, https://doi.org/10.1108/RSR-07-2021-0043.
3. Laskowski and Maddox, " Evolution of Technical Services"
4. Martaza Ashiq, Farhat Jabeen, and Khalid Mahmood, "Transformation of Libraries during Covid-19 Pandemic: A Systematic Review," *Journal of Academic Librarianship* 48, no. 4 (July 2022): article 102534.
5. Courtney McAllister, "Out from the Shadows: Transforming Technical Services during an Academic Library's Reorganization," in *Library Technical Services: Adapting to a Changing Environment*, ed. Stacey Marien (West Lafayette, IN: Purdue University Press, 2020): 309–22.
6. Jeehyun Yun Davis, "Transforming Technical Services: Evolving Functions in Large Research University Libraries," *Library Resources and Technical Services* 60, no. 1 (2016): 52–65, https://repositories.lib.utexas.edu/bitstream/handle/2152/41233/final_lrts.pdf?sequence=3.
7. Ashiq, Jabeen, and Mahmood, "Transformation of Libraries."
8. Kristy White and Tracie Ballock, "Gumberg Library Collections Review," LibGuide, Duquesne University, last modified January 20, 2023, https://guides.library.duq.edu/collectionsprojects.
9. Peter Murray, "Welcome to the FOLIO Wiki," FOLIO Project, last modified April 21, 2023, https://wiki.folio.org/.
10. Mariella Pilgrim and Arlene Dolabaille, "Our Journey from Print to Electronic Resources: An Acquisitions Perspective at a Caribbean Academic Library," *Serials Librarian* 61, no. 1 (2011): 90–104.
11. Doralyn Rossmann and Kenning Arlitsch, "From Acquisitions to Access: The Changing Nature of Library Budgeting," *Journal of Library Administration* 55, no. 5 (2015): 394–404.
12. Jiebei Luo, "A Statistical Analysis of Patrons' In-Library Information Consumption Behaviors of Print Materials," *College and Research Libraries* 82, no. 6 (2021): 863.
13. Heather Morrison, "Economics of Scholarly Communication in Transition," *First Monday* 18, no. 6 (2013), https://doi.org/10.5210/fm.v18i6.4370.
14. Luo, " Statistical Analysis of Patrons," 863.
15. McAllister. "Out from the Shadows," 309–22.

Bibliography

Ashiq, Murtaza, Farhat Jabeen, and Khalid Mahmood. "Transformation of Libraries during Covid-19 Pandemic: A Systematic Review," *Journal of Academic Librarianship* 48, no. 4 (July 2022): article 102534. https://www.sciencedirect.com/science/article/pii/S0099133322000507.

Davis, Jeehyun Yun. "Transforming Technical Services: Evolving Functions in Large Research University Libraries." *Library Resources and Technical Services* 60, no. 1 (2016): 52–65. https://repositories.lib.utexas.edu/bitstream/handle/2152/41233/final_lrts.pdf?sequence=3.

De Groote, S., and J. M. Scoulas, "Impact of COVID-19 on the Use of the Academic Library." *Reference Services Review* 49, no. 3/4 (2021): 281–301. https://doi.org/10.1108/RSR-07-2021-0043.

Laskowski, Mary S., and Jennifer A. Maddox Abbot. "The Evolution of Technical Services: Learning from the Past and Embracing the Future." *Technical Services Quarterly* 31, no. 1 (2014): 13–30.

Luo, Jiebei. "A Statistical Analysis of Patrons' In-Library Information Consumption Behaviors of Print Materials." *College and Research Libraries* 82, no. 6 (2021): 863–75.

McAllister, Courtney. "Out from the Shadows: Transforming Technical Services during an Academic Library's Reorganization." In *Library Technical Services: Adapting to a Changing Environment*, edited by Stacey Marien, 309–22. West Lafayette, IN: Purdue University Press, 2020.

Morrison, Heather. "Economics of Scholarly Communication in Transition." *First Monday* 18, no. 6 (2013). https://doi.org/10.5210/fm.v18i6.4370.

Murray, Peter. "Welcome to the FOLIO Wiki." FOLIO Project. Last modified April 21, 2023. https://wiki.folio.org/.

Pilgrim, Mariella, and Arlene Dolabaille. "Our Journey from Print to Electronic Resources: An Acquisitions Perspective at a Caribbean Academic Library." *Serials Librarian* 61, no. 1 (2011): 90–104.

Rossmann, Doralyn, and Kenning Arlitsch. "From Acquisitions to Access: The Changing Nature of Library Budgeting." *Journal of Library Administration* 55, no. 5 (2015): 394–404.

White, Kristy, and Tracie Ballock. "Gumberg Library Collections Review." LibGuide, Duquesne University. Last modified January 20, 2023. https://guides.library.duq.edu/collectionsprojects.

CHAPTER 22

Calming the Chaos of Library Technology

Todd R. Digby and Laurie N. Taylor

Library technology departments are a vital component of academic and research libraries, serving as the primary entity for supporting the daily computing and information technology (IT) needs of staff throughout a library organization. The library technology department has an additional role in system and software development activities, which is responding to the unique needs of today's academic and research libraries. In order to fill positions that require a high level of technical skill, academic library technology departments are often forced to hire someone with an IT background but little or no library experience or credentials. Managing a technology department within a library can present a unique challenge, both leading and integrating the IT staff into the broader library culture.

This case study will examine how these staffing challenges were navigated within the Library Technology Services (LTS) department at the University of Florida (UF), George A. Smathers Libraries (UF Libraries). The UF, with a student enrollment of over 55,000 students and 5,400 full-time faculty members, is a public land-grant research university located in Gainesville, Florida. As with many large universities and colleges, there is a centralized IT department (UF-IT), serving the broad technology and infrastructure needs of campus, as well as smaller IT departments or units that are located at the school or college level that serve the unique needs of a given college or division. Within UF, the LTS department fulfills the role of the library-situated IT department. The LTS department has eighteen staff members who provide an array of technology services and support for the 250 full-time library staff who are located across ten locations.

Problem Definition

A library-wide ClimateQUAL: Organizational Climate and Diversity Assessment, developed by the Association of Research Libraries, was administered by the libraries in 2014 to assess the organizational climate.[1] During this initial ClimateQUAL evaluation, it was revealed that the LTS department had scores that were significantly lower than other departments, indicating that staff in the department were not feeling positive about their work environment and their place within the library organization. Given these results, library and LTS leadership endeavored to actively engage in efforts to address the workplace issues and stressors being experienced within the department. This chapter will focus on innovative structural and socio-technical practices that have been successfully implemented by UF Libraries' LTS department during the past seven years.

There are a wide range of different ways that technology departments are structured in academic and research libraries. The makeup of the library technology department at UF has evolved during the past seven years to adapt to the changing needs of the library, as well as shifts in how the library interacts with UF-IT. Currently, the LTS department consists of four units: Digital Development, Software, Web, and Enterprise Support. The Digital Development unit consists of a unit manager, programmers, and developers who all focus on the development and maintenance of our digital library systems, including front-end interfaces, backend and production tools used to carry out the day-to-day digitization efforts, and digital preservation systems. The Software unit consists of programmers and database experts who are responsible for developing and maintaining library-specific technologies, such as various databases, internal operational systems (e.g., for tracking and processing travel funds), and library-specific database tools (e.g., for interacting with the catalog, patron data, etc.). The Web unit maintains the library's public-facing websites and related tools, such as WordPress sites, LibGuides, and Domain of One's Own systems. Finally, the Enterprise Support unit focuses primarily on library staff computing and hardware needs.

In addition to these LTS units, department leadership has partnered with a variety of UF entities to ensure that technology needs that are not supported by LTS staff are covered. For example, the department partners with UF-IT to maintain public-facing computing across the many library locations to ensure a common student experience across campus. Previous iterations of the LTS department (previously named the Library IT department), included only two units and a disconnected separate library technology unit that was located at the Health Science Center Library. Most of the staff members within the LTS department have IT-related educational backgrounds and work histories, with some having developed their technology skill sets through on-the-job learning and training. In fact, out of eighteen people in the LTS department, only the department chair and one other person have library degrees.

Before examining the efforts that were undertaken, it is important to look at the research literature to understand if the LTS department was unique in the job satisfaction levels reported or if this is something that is more broadly encountered within the IT sectors.

Literature Review

Academic libraries continue to evolve and change to meet the needs of our user communities and institutions. With these changes, there has been a recognition of emerging trends, including changes to resources, technology, and service models.[2] Highlighted in the literature are trends related "directly to staffing and the need to strategically approach hiring, training, or repurposing staff for a new environment, which focuses on new technologies, enhanced user expectations, and new challenges to curating scholarly works."[3] The importance of technology and the technology professionals who help support these institutions necessitates understanding how to improve the job satisfaction and morale of the technology department within an academic library.

Within the academic fields of management and human resource development, there is considerable research conducted on job satisfaction and workplace morale. With the focus of this chapter being specifically on an IT department, the question that arises is this: Are there unique factors that influence technology workers when it comes to their job satisfaction and workplace morale?

Recent studies point out that job dissatisfaction is commonplace within the IT industry.[4] When examining what may be the reasons for this job dissatisfaction, the literature points to multiple ways that this question may be investigated. One way is to look at the impacts of job satisfaction. Another perspective is to look at what factors motivate employees. Studies indicated that if approached from the lens of motivating factors for IT workers, there is evidence that they are motivated by effective leadership, sound workplace relationships, challenging work, feeling respected, and a balanced work life;[5] whereas, if approached from the viewpoint of the facets that influence job satisfaction, findings indicated that these include role clarity, absence of conflict, a supervisor's behavior, job design, compensation, and training and development.[6]

Issues such as role ambiguity, role conflict, and leadership effectiveness were identified by LTS staff and therefore were important to understand. Role ambiguity, for instance, causes confusion due to "a lack of information and clarity concerning an employee's job functions, which can be translated into a stressful experience, while role conflict involves conflicting or opposing expectations from coworkers that influence role performance."[7] The issues that the LTS department was exhibiting and that were measured by the ClimateQUAL study directly aligned with specific factors noted in the research on job satisfaction and job motivations.

Supervisor role, in part determined by the individual's leadership style, directly impacts job satisfaction, in that satisfaction is increased when employees feel supported in their work efforts by their supervisor. Effective managers and supervisors are characterized by positive behaviors and skills such as being adept at listening, interviewing, questioning, observing, analyzing, communicating, and motivating.[8]

Discussion

In 2014, library leadership undertook an effort to better understand the workplace climate of library staff across the libraries by administering the ClimateQUAL survey.[9] ClimateQUAL was identified as an appropriate tool by UF Library leadership in their effort "to better understand the dynamics of our working environment, identify areas for growth and improvement, and assess progress towards improving diversity, equity, and inclusion throughout the [UF] Libraries."[10] The survey explored multiple dimensions that are categorized into two principal areas: Climate Dimensions and Attitude Dimensions. These results were then grouped by the individual library departments and branches. The LTS department scored significantly lower across the board than other library departments, but our focus here will examine the Job Satisfaction and Leader-Membership Relationship Quality results. For the Job Satisfaction category in 2014, the LTS department had a combined score of only 2.27, compared to the library-wide average of 5.19, making it the lowest scoring department within the library by a wide margin. Likewise, in the category of Leadership-Membership Relationship Quality, the LTS department scored a combined 3.43 versus a score of 5.81 as the library-wide average.

After reviewing the results of this ClimateQUAL survey, library leadership perceived a clear need to address workplace issues and low morale within the LTS department. An important first step to understanding the LTS department's overall discontent is to understand what makes the department different from other library departments. Unlike many of the other functional departments or units across the library, the LTS department's role is primarily concentrated on responding to library staff needs, unlike other departments, which support library users or library collections. Further discussions with LTS department staff helped build the case that they felt disconnected from the mission of the library as a whole and from other library departments. In an effort to address the workplace issues, a number of steps were undertaken.

The first major change came a year or so after the 2014 ClimateQUAL survey, when the dean of libraries decided to hire a dedicated chair for the department. Until 2016 the LTS department had a department head with a technology background who reported to an associate dean of libraries who had no expertise in library technologies. To compensate for this gap in knowledge, a hierarchical structure was utilized to allow the associate dean to use a single reporting line for technology-related issues. In contrast, the newly appointed department chair position would be a library faculty member with a background in leading people and managing library technology. This library-centered technology leadership position was created to function as a more effective conduit between the LTS department and the library as a whole. Ideally, the new department chair would serve as a champion for the LTS department staff. Issues within the LTS department were communicated to the position candidates, as well as the expectation that the successful candidate would have the skills necessary to improve morale and efficiency and to elevate the department's perceived role across the library.

The new department chair was hired in 2016, arriving with years of experience working in the field of library technology in a variety of academic library environments. After extensive engagement with staff both within the LTS department and across the library, the department chair initiated several changes with the intention of bringing about positive changes.

The department chair's initial step was to understand the rationale behind and evaluate the efficacy of the existing organization of the LTS department. The departmental structure had remnants of a previous effort to align two separate library technology units together, when the UF Health Science Center Library (HSCL) came under the administrative umbrella of the main UF Libraries system. The interim LTS organizational structure put into place before the hiring of the department chair merged the responsibilities of the existing LTS staff with the UF HSCL technology staff. This structure inadvertently caused issues in the newly formed LTS department's ability to act as a single unified entity and resulted in department staff feeling that, given their siloed responsibilities at different library locations (HSCL versus other branches), they were not necessarily part of the larger department. In making additional changes to reporting lines and responsibilities, the intention was to promote the perception that the responsibilities of each technology staff member was not confined to a single location so that they would feel like a member of a library-wide technology department.

Adding a department chair with a background in both libraries and technology also presented an opportunity for more attention to be placed on the individual work areas of the department and accommodated a flattening of the organizational structure. This resulted in the creation of four distinct work units within the department that had a direct communication line to the department chair, facilitating recognition and responsiveness for their work efforts and any issues they experienced. Additionally, the department chair's ability to lead and work with the LTS units on a daily basis resulted in better planning and prioritization of technology projects and provided for a better communication pathway from the LTS department to other library leaders about the work of the department. Leveraging extensive combined library and technology experience, the LTS department chair served as a translator between library leadership and the LTS department staff regarding complex technical issues.

As we investigated the issues identified by the LTS department through the responses to the ClimateQUAL survey, there was a prevailing feeling from department staff that they belonged to their individual units, but the department itself did not feel like a single entity. One of the main reasons expressed within individual, unit, and department-wide meetings by LTS staff for not feeling part of the department was that their offices were spread over five different locations in four different libraries. The staff of the Enterprise Support unit, for instance, were located at three different libraries. This separation led to limited interactions between department members, seeing other departmental staff only at monthly LTS department-wide staff meetings.

To address these issues, we prioritized bringing members of the LTS department together and reducing the number of different locations at which staff were stationed. This turned into a multiyear process that took advantage of space as it opened across the libraries. After initially reducing the locations from five to four, we ultimately succeeded in having LTS staff at only two different library locations to enable staff teammates within a single LTS unit to be colocated. This brought all the computer service technicians together, where previously they were scattered across the libraries. All the programmers and developers were brought together as well. The attention to the physical location of the various LTS units ultimately resulted in the creation of a dedicated LTS workshop, storage, and office area for the entire Enterprise Support unit, leading to improved staff interaction and better team building between LTS staff within units.

One of the initial changes was to focus on the overall name of the department. Although we have used the LTS department name throughout this chapter for consistency, until 2018 it was known as the Library IT department. As mentioned earlier, at UF there is both a centralized campus IT department, or UF-IT, and the LTS department. With some responsibilities overlapping, there was confusion by the library staff regarding what issues to report to UF-IT versus those that needed to be reported to LTS. For example, e-mail configurations, username issues, and password resets—which are the responsibility of the UF-IT department—were often mistakenly reported to the LTS department. Additionally, when staff raised issues or concerns about interactions or support by IT, it was difficult to determine if these were concerns with UF-IT or library IT. With this uncertainty, library staff's negative views of UF-IT support led to feelings of demoralization among LTS department staff. There was an overall feeling by LTS staff that they were unnecessarily being blamed for issues that were caused by UF-IT. With these issues identified, it was decided to rebrand the Library IT department as Library Technology Services department, or LTS. This change would result in the removal of the IT acronym from the department name and would emphasize the LTS department's role as providing services. Using the new acronym LTS would also reduce the existing name confusions that were taking place and the resulting division of responsibilities for problem reporting.

As these changes were implemented within the department, a follow-up Climate-QUAL survey was conducted in 2019. This follow-up study resulted in a significant increase in scores within the LTS department, which brought them closer to alignment with other departments across the libraries. For example, the Job Satisfaction category scored a 4.92 in 2019, where it scored only a 2.27 in 2019. Likewise, in 2019, the category of Leadership-Membership Relationship Quality, the LTS department scored a 5.03, increasing from a 3.43 in 2014 (see more in tables 22.1 and 22.2).

Table 22.1. ClimateQUAL Job Satisfaction results for 2014 and 2019

Year	Dept Avg	UF Avg	National Avg
2014	2.27	5.19	5.14
2019	4.92	5.34	5.17

Table 22.2. ClimateQUAL Leader-Membership Relationship Quality results for 2014 and 2019

Year	Dept Avg	UF Avg	National Avg
2014	3.43	5.81	5.67
2019	5.03	5.72	5.70

Although significant improvements within the department were demonstrated with the 2019 ClimateQUAL results, we continued to look for opportunities to improve the work environment for LTS department staff, given the continued growth and changing library technology environment needs. There was a need for additional staffing at the leadership level to provide support for the increased library technology projects the LTS department was engaged in. This resulted in the creation of a senior director position that would oversee the LTS department and the library's Digital Partnership and Strategies department. Additional library technology leadership staffing was instrumental in helping manage and guide the successful implementation of several highly visible implementation and migration projects that were simultaneously taking place within the libraries. These projects included an upgrade to the library's integrated library system, a full migration of the library web pages and related web management system, and the development and implementation of a newly redesigned and locally developed digital library system. The addition of the senior director position brought about additional ways of working, including deep collaboration with the LTS department chair to seek further ways to increase employee morale and build a more cohesive and positively focused department where staff felt connected to their unit teams, the department, and to the UF Libraries as a whole.

Working as a leadership team, the senior director and LTS department chair engaged staff in developing a guiding framework for the work we do within the department. Unlike developing a department-level mission or vision statement, the goal was to develop a working model that represented how we approached the daily work and projects that we were engaged with. This took place at about the same time we were confronted with the beginning of the COVID-19 pandemic. The pandemic forced the department to shift its own working conditions to being largely remote, while at the same time responding to the technology support needs of the entire library staff, who were now working remotely.

With the shifts in working environments and increased stressors caused by the pandemic, we developed a framework that focused on the emotional side of our engagement with those we serve. Ultimately, we ended up with a compassionate computing approach to our work. Our guiding statement is shared on our website:

> LTS practices compassionate computing, which means we operate with compassion for our users, our systems, and ourselves. To support this, we use product management (and project management) methods and strategies, utilize compassionate communication practices, and work to ensure maintainable systems and practices, for working at a sustainable pace.[11]

We used the framework of compassionate computing to develop a work environment where, through a structured approach, we could lower stress and anxiety and improve the morale and success of the department, while also improving how our users throughout the libraries view and interact with us.[12]

To implement the broader concepts within our definition of compassionate computing, we made adjustments to our work that included fostering an environment of open communication, clear documentation, and realistic expectation setting. The components of this framework were especially important in supporting the impacts to library staff that resulted from multiple major system migrations and the stressful technology impacts that resulted from moving to fully remote work during the pandemic and to an ongoing hybrid work environment.

We realized that unstructured project planning and documentation led to stress and lack of productivity, and there was a need to implement a more structured approach to project management within the LTS department. Working with those outside of LTS, using a more defined project planning and requirement gathering process, we were able to build a better understanding of the project deliverables and the sign-off process for completed deliverables. Prior to using this planning process, many projects were initiated without clearly articulated goals or end points, which led to constant scope creep, or projects that seem to keep expanding and without a definite completion point.

We developed a standardized initial project briefing template to scope projects and allow us to communicate the scope, need, and impact of project requests to library leadership. Bringing projects forward in a clear and digestible format using the project briefing template, leadership could provide meaningful input and help guide and prioritize the work, given the limited number of developers available for any one project. The structure within project management allowed for increased flexibility and success within the department. The implementation of defined operational frameworks allowed those working on projects (both LTS staff and library staff) to understand the progress being made toward the mutually agreed-upon goals. Bringing a more structured approach to initiate projects was an important step toward aligning our principles outlined in our definition of compassionate computing.

An additional aspect of the compassionate computing approach is the idea of framing our work in ways that ensures maintainable systems and practices, while at the same time working at a sustainable pace. The Digital Development unit was tasked with modernizing our aging UF Digital Collections digital library system and concurrently maintaining the existing system. These dual priorities resulted in the constant need to shift work to fixing issues on the old system, which significantly impacted our capacity for developing our next-generation digital library system. Using the tenets set out in our compassionate computing framework, we implemented a more structured, agile system development methodology and a better error reporting and vetting system. This resulted in being able to more accurately plan the developers' work and protect their time for the upcoming time period without requiring a response to ongoing interruptions caused by issues reported by stakeholders. With the move to an agile development methodology, the team introduced daily standup meetings, held virtually, which included the LTS departmental leadership. The benefit of this approach was the development team being able to communicate directly with LTS leadership to answer development questions as they happened. Easy access to decision-makers helped to quickly address outstanding issues and move the development process forward. These regular daily meetings among the unit and department leadership also presented an opportunity to build a much closer team within the unit.

These types of changes were not always easy, since we had also to work to defend these decisions with our stakeholders, who in the past experienced immediate responses for their problems and now were being asked to wait until there was a time in the development cycle for issues to be addressed. With this approach, the new digital library system saw progress, and it became more apparent to stakeholders that the new process was resulting in positive change that was beneficial to them as well.

Each of the work area units of the LTS department has unique responsibilities and different processes. With disparate workflows and project development needs, LTS department leadership worked with each of these units to better align and actualize their processes to fit within the broad goals outlined in the compassionate computing framework. In addition to focusing on the individual units and their workflows, LTS department leadership also strove to increase the feeling of belonging within the department. We had always had monthly departmental meetings where we shared information and work activities, but these did little to help build a more cohesive sense of belonging to the department and the library. To facilitate a connection to the broader library, we concentrated on increasing a sense of ownership for technology projects that LTS staff were participating in.

To further the sense of belonging at the department level, we added annual strategic planning events for the department in addition to the monthly departmental meetings. We promoted LTS department staff engagement throughout the year by enhancing those meetings with training, support guest speakers, and scaffolded activities, including opportunities to share stories of their work with the rest of the LTS department staff.

Employee morale and job satisfaction are important to keep a healthy and positive workplace for staff. Not only is it important to recognize when there are issues with employee job satisfaction and low morale, it is also as important to attempt to address these issues. The LTS department has witnessed significant improvements through the structural and cultural changes that have been implemented to date. As technologies continue to shift and affect academic libraries, the stress that comes along with these shifts will continue to be felt by the technology staff and other departments and units within our institutions. Examining the root causes of employee low morale or stress can better position us to implement adjustments to work processes or organizational structure that mediate these stressors. Implementing adjustments in project planning with a focus on better clarity is vital toward building realistic expectations about project outcomes. Using working principles and frameworks, such as the compassionate computing framework, is an important step toward building a more open, transparent, and healthier culture within our organizations.

Takeaways

- Seek to determine what underlying issues, both internal and external, may be impeding just satisfaction and motivation, resulting in low morale among staff.
- Examine work processes to see where additional structure and transparency can be added to more clearly set expectations.
- Implement a guiding framework built on principles that help address any identified stressors.
- Clearly communicate these guiding principles to ensure structural and procedural changes are accepted.

Notes

1. Martha Kyrillidou and M. Sue Baughman, "ClimateQUAL: Organizational Climate and Diversity Assessment," *College and Research Libraries News* 70, no. 3 (2009): 154–57, https://doi.org/10.5860/crln.70.3.8145.
2. Michael A. Crumpton, "Emerging Trends in Academic Libraries," chapter 5 in *Strategic Human Resource Planning for Academic Libraries* (Oxford, UK: Chandos, 2015), 45–57, https://doi.org/10.1016/B978-1-84334-764-4.00005-8.
3. Crumpton, "Emerging Trends in Academic Libraries," 46.
4. Sérgio Moro, Ricardo F. Ramos, and Paulo Rita, "What Drives Job Satisfaction in IT Companies?" *International Journal of Productivity and Performance Management* 70, no. 2 (2021): 391–407, https://doi.org/10.1108/IJPPM-03-2019-0124.
5. Francesca E. Abii, David C. N. Ogula, and Jonathan M. Rose, "Effects of Individual and Organizational Factors on the Turnover Intentions of Information Technology Professionals," *International Journal of Management* 30, no. 2 (June 2013), 740–56. ProQuest.
6. Moro, Ramos, and Rita, "What Drives Job Satisfaction in IT Companies?"
7. Moro, Ramos, and Rita, "What Drives Job Satisfaction in IT Companies?" 393.

8. Andrea D. Ellinger, "Supportive Supervisors and Managerial Coaching: Exploring Their Intersections," *Journal of Occupational and Organizational Psychology* 86, no. 3 (2013): 310–16, https://doi.org/10.1111/joop.12021.
9. Charles B. Lowry, ed. *ClimateQUAL* (Lanham, MD: Rowman & Littlefield, 2017).
10. University of Florida, Library Human Resources, "ClimateQUAL," 2023, https://hr.uflib.ufl.edu/current-employees/climatequal/.
11. Library Technology Services, "Compassionate Computing Resources," LibGuide, University of Florida, last modified January 26, 2023, https://guides.uflib.ufl.edu/lts/compassionatecomputing.
12. Laurie N. Taylor and Todd Digby, "Compassionate Computing: Reframing Technology Work for Cultural Change and Optimal Work Performance," *Trends and Issues in Library Technology*, IFLA IT Section Newsletter, May/June 2021, 2–4, https://repository.ifla.org/bitstream/123456789/1733/1/tilt_newsletter_june_2021.pdf.

Bibliography

Abii, Francesca E., David C. N. Ogula, and Jonathan M. Rose. "Effects of Individual and Organizational Factors on the Turnover Intentions of Information Technology Professionals." *International Journal of Management* 30, no. 2 (June 2013): 740–56. ProQuest.

Crumpton, Michael A. "Emerging Trends in Academic Libraries." Chapter 5 in *Strategic Human Resource Planning for Academic Libraries: Information, Technology and Organization*, 45–57. Oxford: Chandos, 2015. https://doi.org/10.1016/B978-1-84334-764-4.00005-8.

Ellinger, Andrea D. "Supportive Supervisors and Managerial Coaching: Exploring Their Intersections." *Journal of Occupational and Organizational Psychology* 86, no. 3 (2013): 310–16. https://doi.org/10.1111/joop.12021.

Kyrillidou, Martha, and M. Sue Baughman. "ClimateQUAL: Organizational Climate and Diversity Assessment." *College and Research Libraries News* 70, no. 3 (March 2009): 154–57. https://doi.org/10.5860/crln.70.3.8145.

Library Technology Services. "Compassionate Computing Resources." LibGuide. University of Florida. Last modified January 26, 2023. https://guides.uflib.ufl.edu/lts/compassionatecomputing.

Lowry, Charles B., ed. *ClimateQUAL: Advancing Organizational Health, Leadership, and Diversity in the Service of Libraries*. Lanham, MD: Rowman & Littlefield, 2017.

Moro, Sérgio, Ricardo F. Ramos, and Paulo Rita. "What Drives Job Satisfaction in IT Companies?" *International Journal of Productivity and Performance Management* 70, no. 2 (2021): 391–407. https://doi.org/10.1108/IJPPM-03-2019-0124.

Taylor, Laurie N., and Todd Digby. "Compassionate Computing: Reframing Technology Work for Cultural Change and Optimal Work Performance." *Trends and Issues in Library Technology*, IFLA IT Section Newsletter, May/June 2021, 2–4. https://repository.ifla.org/bitstream/123456789/1733/1/tilt_newsletter_june_2021.pdf.

University of Florida, Library Human Resources. "ClimateQUAL." 2023. https://hr.uflib.ufl.edu/current-employees/climatequal/

About the Editors and Authors

Vickie Albrecht is the manager for the Durham Campus Library and Learning Centre at Trent University's Durham GTA Campus. Vickie has been working in academic libraries for more than ten years. She loves learning and is currently working on a postgraduate certificate in human resources from Trent University.

Xan Arch is dean of the library at Portland State University. In this and previous roles, Arch has focused on the development of library initiatives that support student success and sense of belonging within the library and the university. Arch has researched and published on first-generation student experiences in libraries, as well as academic library hiring practices; her coauthored book *Academic Library Services for First-Generation Students* was published in 2020 by Libraries Unlimited.

Tracie Ballock is the assistant university librarian for collections and metadata services at Gumberg Library, Duquesne University, and has worked in technical services for thirty years. Her primary interests are leadership and strategic visioning for developing library collections, spaces, and services for the future. https://orcid.org/0000-0002-6157-0192

Jennifer Batson has a master of humanities from Tiffin University and a master of library science from Texas Woman's University. She is the cataloger and an information literacy instructor for a variety of liaison areas at the University of Mary Hardin-Baylor. Jennifer is interested in best practices in instruction and in creating positive, user-friendly library environments.

Annie Bélanger (she/her) is the dean of university libraries at Grand Valley State University. Being an accessibility and inclusion advocate as well as her experiences in academic, corporate, and public libraries and government settings define her career. Her research now focuses on leadership and skills development, inclusive hiring and culture development, human-centered change leadership, and strengths-based empathetic workforce development. Annie is Québécoise and disabled. She received her master's in library and information sciences from Western University, Canada. She is an ARL Leadership Fellow.

Melinda "Mindy" H. Berg, MLIS, AHIP, cataloging and metadata librarian, University of South Florida Health Libraries. Her research interests include the development of early career librarians, workplace wellness, and art and design in health.

Jessica J. Boyer has more than a decade of experience in libraries and has served as the director of the library at Mount St. Mary's University since 2017. She holds an MSLS from Pennsylvania Western University and a PhD in higher education leadership from Concordia University Chicago. Her research focuses on library administration and the intersection of library leadership and higher education leadership.

Lea J. Briggs is manager of administration and operations in the College of University Libraries and Learning Sciences at the University of New Mexico. Briggs has held librarian positions at Northern State University and the University of New Mexico and has served as director of libraries at Presentation College and Northwest Missouri State University. She is involved in state and national library association work. Briggs earned an MLS at Emporia State University and a doctor of education at the University of South Dakota. Her research interests center on process improvement in libraries, project management, strategic planning, and library space

Janet Chan, MLIS, AHIP, RN, research and education librarian, University of South Florida Health Libraries. In addition to being a librarian, she has ten years of experience as an RN, which fuels her research interest in health and wellness. Her research areas include digital health, graphic medicine, wellness, and bibliotherapy.

Kim Clarke, BA, LLB, MLIS, is the director of staff engagement and the law librarian for Libraries and Cultural Resources at the University of Calgary. Kim was in library administration for more than twenty-five years, previously serving as a branch library director and as the associate vice-provost of research services for Libraries and Cultural Resources. Prior to this, she worked as the acquisitions and collection development librarian at The Ohio State University's Moritz Law Library and as the assistant dean for library and research services at the University of the Pacific's McGeorge School of Law.

Ann Coppola, MLIS, associate director, Pasco-Hernando State College, Porter Campus Library. Prior to transitioning to academia, she was a public librarian for several years. Ann's research interests include accessibility in the workplace and leadership development as it relates to improving the library employee experience.

Jennifer E. M. Cotton (she/her) has been working in the University of Maryland, College Park Libraries since 2014, where she is currently the course reserves coordinator. She holds an MLS with a specialization in information and diverse populations from the University of Maryland, College Park. Her professional interests include supporting equity, accessibility, and affordable learning efforts, as well as developing data-informed decision-making practices.

Margaret Dawson has a master of arts in English and a master of library science from Texas Woman's University. From 2014 to 2021, she worked at Texas A&M University-Central Texas in Killeen, Texas, as an outreach and instruction librarian and has developed programs for university students, their children, and the general public. She is currently the co-head of public services and outreach at A&M-Central Texas. She has presented and published on the topics of instruction and outreach.

Sandra Yvette Desjardins has an MS in counseling psychology, an MA in English, and an MLS, and she will complete her PhD in community psychology in 2024. At the library, she enjoys engaging with her patrons through one-on-one consultations or when hosting classroom instruction and orientation sessions. She also enjoys helping her fellow librarians and LIS students as the cochair of the South Central Chapter of the Medical Library Association's Early Career Librarian Initiative. Currently, Sandra is a liaison librarian at the Houston Academy of Medicine—Texas Medical Center Library. Her research interests include health, wellness, and outreach programs.

Todd R. Digby is the chair of the Library Technology Services department at the University of Florida Libraries. He leads a department that researches, develops, optimizes, and supports advanced library information systems and technology for the University of Florida Libraries, including the University of Florida Digital Collections, Digital Library of the Caribbean, and Florida Digital Newspaper Library. He has previously held library and academic technology leadership positions at the Minnesota State Colleges and Universities system and the University of Wisconsin-River Falls. Todd holds an EdD and a master of library and information studies.

Joyce Garczynski is the assistant university librarian for communication and digital scholarship at Towson University's Albert S. Cook Library in Maryland. In this role she manages the Communication, Outreach, and Digital Scholarship department, teaches communication students about the research process, and manages her library's marketing. She obtained her master's in library science from the University of Maryland, College Park, and has a master's in communication from the Annenberg School at the University of Pennsylvania. She also received the 2019 Distinguished Education and Behavioral Sciences Librarian Award from the Association of College and Research Libraries for her excellence in teaching and service to the profession.

About the Editors and Authors

Isaac Gilman, PhD, MLIS is executive director of the Orbis Cascade Alliance, a regional academic library consortium. Prior to joining Orbis Cascade, he was dean of university libraries at Pacific University for eight years, where he previously was a member of the library faculty and a staff member in access services. His research and work focus on exploring inequitable structures and systems within libraries, higher education, and scholarly communication.

Dawn M. Harris serves as the collection development coordinator at Texas A&M University-Central Texas and holds the rank of associate librarian. Her duties entail overseeing collection development, acquisitions, interlibrary loan, and cataloging. Prior to serving at A&M-Central Texas, she was the assistant director of library services at Killeen Public Library in Killeen, Texas. She has published on the topics of institutional program review, evolving library liaison duties, and creating an education resource center.

Lisa Kallman Hopkins is an associate librarian at Texas A&M University-Central Texas in Killeen near Fort Cavazos. She is the head of Technical Services and assistant dean of the University Library and Archives. In her role as head of Technical Services, she is directly responsible for systems and e-resources and manages cataloging and acquisitions, interlibrary loan, e-reserves, and textbook reserves. She is the university copyright specialist and copyeditor. She has submitted chapters to *Transforming Acquisitions and Collection Services: Perspectives on Collaboration within and across Libraries* and *Technical Services: Adapting to the Changing Environment*; has coauthored a chapter in *Universal Design for Learning in Academic Libraries: Theory into Practice*; and has coedited this book.

Rebecca L. Hopkins is a graduate student at Texas A&M University-Central Texas, where she is working toward a specialist degree in school psychology. She has a master of science in educational psychology and was a Montessori guide for several years. Her research interests include inclusive education, teacher attitudes, and neurodiverse learning.

Cinthya Ippoliti has been a librarian for over twenty years and has held roles at a wide variety of academic institutions. Most recently, as director of the Auraria Library, Cinthya provides direct administrative leadership for library services, spaces, partnerships, and programming on the tri-institutional Auraria Campus, which includes the University of Colorado, Denver; Metropolitan State University of Denver; and Community College of Denver, and serves approximately 35,000 highly diverse students in an urban setting. In collaboration with the library's administrative team, she sets a strategic vision to develop new services, foster creativity and collaboration, and provide professional development and mentorship opportunities for all library employees. Prior to joining the Auraria Library she was the associate dean for research and learning services at Oklahoma State University and head of teaching and learning at the University of Maryland Libraries.

Her research interests include psychology of leadership, organizational development, and managing change.

Shawna Kennedy-Witthar is the director of information and library resources at Cornette Library, West Texas A&M University, where she has led the library since 2010. She has an MA and MLS from Indiana University and has been a certified archivist. She enjoys building relationships with patrons, as well as encouraging the growth of new academic librarians, thus ensuring the future of Cornette Library.

Carla Lee is currently the deputy university librarian at the University of Virginia Library, where she oversees administration, strategic planning, project management, and facilities. She began working as a science and technology librarian in 1990, where she served as a library associate at the Natural Sciences Library of the University of Michigan. In 1992, she moved to the Science Library at Loyola University Chicago, where she served in several roles, including reference coordinator and head of the Science Library. In 2005, she began work at the University of Virginia. Through the course of her career at UVa, Carla has held multiple positions, including digital collections librarian, collections strategist, senior director for collections, access and discovery, and interim head of special collections.

Coralee Leroux is the scholarly resources librarian at Trent University Library and Archives, where she has also held roles as manager of library services and interim university librarian. Previously she worked for an academic library consortium for seven years, where she honed skills in electronic resources management, service design and review, and project management.

Rodney Lippard is currently the director of Torreyson Library at the University of Central Arkansas (UCA). He earned his MLIS from the University of North Carolina Greensboro and an EdD from Bay Path University in Massachusetts. Lippard held directorships at Barton College, Rowan-Cabarrus Community College, and the University of South Carolina Aiken before UCA. His interests are library management, library marketing and promotion, innovative library services, student success, and serving students.

Sheila García Mazari (she/her) is the online learning librarian at the University of California, Santa Cruz. She received her MLIS from Wayne State University. Sheila has a decade of experience in public and academic libraries and is both a 2016 American Library Association Spectrum Scholar and a 2019 ALA Emerging Leader. Sheila's research interests intersect critical information literacy, critical management studies, and theories of relationality rooted in cultural values.

Bridgit McCafferty is the dean of the University Library and Archives at Texas A&M University-Central Texas and has led the library for eleven years. Prior to this, she was in charge of reference and instruction services. She has taken on major administrative projects for her university, including recently chairing the SACSCOC Accreditation Reaffirmation Compliance Committee. She is the author of *Library Management: A Practical Guide for Librarians* and the coauthor of *British Postmodernism: Strategies and Sources*.

Kathaleen McCormick is the collections and metadata librarian at Gumberg Library, Duquesne University. She has over twenty-five years of experience in cataloging and metadata creation in both public and academic libraries. https://orcid.org/0000-0003-2188-3431

Kristy McKeown is the manager of library services at Trent University Library and Archives in Peterborough. She is highly experienced in several access services roles within the library profession. Her passion is leading a high-performance team that's founded on employee enthusiasm, engagement, and participation.

Bruna Ngassa (she/her) is a senior at Grand Valley State University and part of the Honors College. She is graduating in April 2023 with a BA in writing and a minor in advertising and public relations. She works at the GVSU Library in Allendale as the dean's office assistant and was a part of the Diversity and Inclusion committee in 2021, which aimed to modify student hiring practices to be more inclusive. She comes from a multicultural background, which has influenced her interest in inclusive hiring and research into diversity in education. She hopes to work in Chicago as a book editor in the future, lending support to authors of color by uplifting their voices.

Brynne Norton (she/her) is the head of resource sharing and reserves at the University of Maryland College Park. She is in charge of a unit that includes nine FTE employees as well as student workers. She has a master of library and information science from the University of Pittsburgh and a master's in liberal arts from McDaniel College. Brynne has been supervising employees in various ways for over thirteen years. Her research interest is around career paths and career development in access services.

Kristen J. Nyitray is faculty and director of Special Collections and University Archives, and university archivist at Stony Brook University, USA. Her research focuses on U.S. social and cultural history, memory, archives and libraries, and public history. She is a Certified Archivist (CA) accredited through the Academy of Certified Archivists.

Johnnie Porter was an assistant librarian at Texas A&M University-Central Texas. As the e-resources librarian she was responsible for the life cycle of the library's electronic resources, which included content management and licensing of electronic resources. Her role also included ensuring discovery of the library's electronic serials and databases, as well as coordinating the e-reserve program. She was the chair of the Health and Wellness Committee, a committee that she had been on for nine years.

Dana Reijerkerk is an independent researcher and data freelancer situated in the USA whose work explores sociotechnical issues in data with emphasis on the intersections and borders between technology and social power structures. She has published on emotional intelligence, UX Design, and decolonizing Indian federal recognition laws. She has shipped several game jam and commercial video games on PC and Android as part of her indie game studio, Batbrained Games.

Janet Schalk is a librarian at Pasco-Hernando State College, Porter Campus. She holds an MA in History and an MLIS, both from the University of South Florida. Her research focuses on scholarly communication and critical librarianship. Other research interests include digital humanities, web design, archives, and Tampa Bay history.

Andria F. Schwegler has a PhD in experimental psychology and thirty years of experience teaching students from prekindergarten to graduate school with over ten years of experience in blended and online courses. She is an associate professor of psychology at Texas A&M University-Central Texas and is the program coordinator for the master of science in applied psychology. She is chair of the Counseling and Psychology department, working fully online as a remote employee who lives 800 miles from the university. She is dedicated to questioning assumptions and removing barriers that hamper access to higher education.

Geoff Sinclair has been the discovery and systems librarian at Trent University since 2019. He has worked within the Ontario college and university library systems and has managed library staff for more than fifteen years. In his free time, he is the orchestra personnel manager for the North Bay Symphony Orchestra.

Kimberly Burke Sweetman is the associate dean of the University of New Hampshire Library. As a member of the library leadership team, Kimberly coordinates library services, collections, and technology initiatives and translates library vision and goals into daily processes and operations for the UNH Library. Prior to her time at UNH, Kimberly managed a large public services department at New York University, one of the largest research libraries in North America, and most recently worked as an executive coach and consultant, helping libraries improve productivity and develop superior service through exceptional leadership.

Laurie N. Taylor is the associate university librarian for collections and discovery at the University of Connecticut Library. She leads Acquisitions and Discovery, Archives and Special Collections, Collections Strategies, Digital Imaging and Conservation, the Digital Preservation Repository Program (Connecticut Digital Archive), Digital Solutions, and Library Technology. Laurie joined UConn after serving at the University of Florida as senior director for library technology and digital strategies, chair of the Digital

Partnerships and Strategies department, the editor-in-chief of the LibraryPress@UF, and the operational lead and digital scholarship director of the Digital Library of the Caribbean. Laurie holds a PhD in English/media studies and digital humanities and a master of arts. She has published extensively and has been the principal investigator, co-PI, and investigator on many grants. In 2018, Laurie was awarded the Caribbean Information Professional of the Year by the Association of Caribbean University, Research and Institutional Libraries.

Donna Tolson is the associate dean for administration at the University of Virginia Library where she oversees budget and finance, assessment, and events and works collaboratively with UVA HR on staffing, recruitment, and employee development. In previous roles at the UVA Library, she incubated new strategic initiatives, oversaw assessment and data-gathering efforts, managed the undergraduate library, and led data services in the Scholars' Lab and Geostat Center. Before joining the University Library in 2002, she worked for many years as a demographic research analyst for the Weldon Cooper Center for Public Service at UVA.

Mira Waller is the associate university librarian for research and learning services and the associate dean for academic affairs at the University of Virginia Library. She oversees the subject liaison program, the teaching and learning program, faculty programs, information services and public spaces, and specialized user services including those for digital scholarship, multimedia production and use, and data management and analysis. Previously, Waller was the department head of research engagement in the North Carolina State University (NCSU) Libraries. Before joining the NCSU Libraries, Waller was director of publishing services for Project Euclid, an online community and platform for mathematics and statistics scholarship, managed jointly by Cornell University Library and Duke University Press. In a previous life Waller was also an archivist.

Gail White is the senior UVA HR business partner for the library. As a strategic advisor, collaborator, and proactive consultant to leadership, Gail works with leaders to provide innovative HR solutions to meet their business goals, including advising on competitive compensation strategies. Gail has supported the University of Virginia Library since 2018. Prior to that, she worked with the Virginia Department of Transportation in workforce development and training and Piedmont Virginia Community College in workforce development and as adjunct faculty for first-year student success courses. She holds an MS in education from Indiana University, Bloomington, and is an SHRM Senior Certified Professional and an HRCI Senior Professional in Human Resources.

Kristy White is the head of licensing and acquisitions at Gumberg Library, Duquesne University. Her primary research interests include organizational and management theories in libraries, workflow management, contract negotiations and data privacy and analysis. ORCID ID: https://orcid.org/0000-0003-4827-0563

Kelly Williams has a master of science in educational psychology from Texas A&M University-Central Texas and a master of science in library science from the University of North Texas. She's spent most of her library career working in the technical services departments of academic libraries but recently made a change to reference and instruction. She is currently a reference and instruction librarian at Texas A&M University-Central Texas. Her research interests include universal design, instruction, reference services, and creating inclusive library environments.